THE GREATEST DIRECT MAIL SALES LETTERS OF ALL TIME

WHY THEY SUCCEED

HOW THEY'RE CREATED

HOW YOU CAN CREATE GREAT SALES LETTERS, TOO!

By Richard S. Hodgson

Cover Illustration: Michael Klein

DARTNELL is a publisher serving the world of business with business books, business manuals, business newsletters and bulletins, training materials for business executives, managers, supervisors, salespeople, financial officials, personnel executives and office employees. In addition, Dartnell produces management and sales training films and cassettes, publishes many useful business forms, conducts scores of management seminars for business men and women and has many of its materials and films available in languages other than English. Dartnell, established in 1917, serves the world's whole business community. For details, catalogs, and product information, write: THE DARTNELL CORPORATION, 4660 Ravenswood Avenue, Chicago, Illinois 60640-4595 USA, or phone (312) 561-4000.

This publication is designed to provide accurate and authoritative information in regard to the subject matter covered. It is sold with the understanding that the publisher is not engaged in rendering legal, accounting, or other professional service. If legal advice or other expert assistance is required, the services of a competent professional should be sought.

From a Declaration of Principles jointly adopted by a Committee of the American Bar Association and a Committee of Publishers.

Published by the Dartnell Corporation
4660 N Ravenswood Ave, Chicago, IL 60640-4595

Copyright © 1995, The Dartnell Corporation
Printed in the U.S.A. by Dartnell Press
ISBN 85013-238-X

Library of Congress Number: 95-068836

CONTENTS

INTRODUCTION

What makes a great direct mail letter? The most obvious answer is one that produces maximum response. But lots of less-than-great letters produce excellent response thanks to superior lists, a great product, an outstanding offer, or other factors over which the writer has little or no control.

Some letters win contests; however, inferior letters have won contests just because the competition was weak. Other letters win the praise of the copywriter's peers — often just because they are clever.

To be truly great, however, a sales letter must have more than one dimension. Of course, it must achieve its objectives. Most often it will have won some contest and likely will have won special applause from peers. It must also stand the test of time and be the kind of letter others will turn to time and again to get inspiration and think, "Gee, I wish I had written that."

This is a book of such letters. Leading direct marketers from all over America provided samples of what they considered to be the all-time top direct mail letters and passed along the names of today's best direct response copywriters. Interestingly, I received a relatively small handful of names that were repeated time and again as today's top direct mail copywriters. Almost all are leading free-lance writers who have created the "control." Most of these "top names" responded to my request for letter samples; you'll find many of their letters throughout this book. And when they were asked to name those whom they considered today's best direct mail sales letter writers, the same names were repeated once again.

All the copywriters were invited to submit samples of their favorite letters — not just those they had written, but also letters written by others they considered truly great. To these were added some selected letters from my personal files. I've been saving samples of direct mail — the good and the bad — since I became involved in the field over 50 years ago and have one of the largest private collections of representative direct mail in the world. Interestingly, however, nearly every letter I culled from my files turned up on the lists of letters recommended by others.

When the collection of letters was assembled, there were more than 2,000 examples from which to select "The Greatest Direct Mail Sales Letters of All Time." That created the most difficult task in creating this book. All were excellent letters and each contained some element that could prove useful at that all too present moment when a letter has to be written and the right words remain elusive. But all 2,000 letters, of course, couldn't be included. So I read and reread each of the letters to select the very best. In the end, the selection was strictly personal. The real test was when I caught myself thinking, "Gee, I wish I had written that."

At this point, a unique problem presented itself. A high percentage of the truly great direct mail letters turned out to be from just two fields. The first was publishing. This could have been anticipated since a lot of the leading writers naturally gravitate to the publishing field because publishers tend to pay top dollar for a winning letter.

The second field was fund-raising. Although the dollars to be earned for copywriting don't come close to those offered by publishers (and quite often the letter copy is a personal contribution of the copywriter to a cause in which he or she is deeply involved), the satisfaction comes in other ways.

But to create a volume of nothing but publishers' and fund-raisers' letters would only have duplicated many excellent books already available devoted entirely to these two fields. So once the extra special "great" letters had been selected, I tried to find representative samples of other types of direct mail letters in the interest of providing everyone involved in direct mail with a comprehensive reference file to which they could turn for ideas and inspiration when they faced their specific letter writing situations. In many cases, I'm sure, there are dozens of equally good or, perhaps, even better examples that might have been included. But if I had continued to search for the "perfect" letter to fit every situation, this book would still be in the preliminary stages.

I'm convinced, in fact, the "perfect" sales letter has yet to be written — at least in modern times. If you want a wonderful collection of the greatest sales letters of all time, I recommend the collected works of Paul the Apostle and his coworkers, which you will find in the New Testament. Now, those were the all-time great letter writers!

ABOUT THE AUTHOR

Dick Hodgson got an early start in the direct marketing field when he began operating his own lettershop, The Gateway Advertising Agency, at age 14. Since that time he has worked as a printer, linotype operator, salesman, photographer, radio announcer and producer, reporter, editor, college instructor, public relations director, president of a publishing company, advertising agency account executive, advertising and sales promotion director, creative director, corporation executive, and consultant.

Today Hodgson is president of Sargeant House, a Westtown, Pennsylvania, company that provides direct marketing consulting and catalog development services to companies throughout the world. He is a member of the board of directors of Foster & Gallagher, Inc., a leading U. S. direct marketing firm, and was a charter member of the board of directors of QVC Network, Inc.

Before establishing his consulting business in 1975, Hodgson was vice president of The Franklin Mint, which he joined as creative director in 1972. Before joining The Franklin Mint, he was division director of the Creative Graphics Division, R. R. Donnelley & Sons Company. He originally joined Donnelley in 1962 as advertising and sales promotion manager. Previously he was president of American Marketing Services, a Boston publishing company. Prior to moving to Boston, he was executive editor of *Advertising Requirements* and *Industrial Marketing* magazines.

A 25-year veteran of both active and reserve service in the U.S. Marine Corps, Hodgson retired as a lieutenant colonel. He served as a Marine Corps combat correspondent in North China, and provided on-the-spot radio and press coverage of four atomic bomb tests, including the famed Operation Crossroads tests at Bikini in 1946. He later served as radio-TV chief for the Marine Corps; shows that he produced for network presentation were honored with the Peabody Award.

Between periods of Marine Corps active duty, Hodgson taught journalism and advertising at North Dakota State School of Science and magazine editing and magazine design at the University of Chicago. Today he is a frequent visiting lecturer at colleges and universities throughout the United States, and more than 100 schools and many catalog companies utilize the "Basics of Direct Marketing" multimedia teaching program and other videotapes he produced and donated to the Direct Marketing Educational Foundation.

Hodgson is a prolific author on direct marketing subjects. His "Direct Mail & Mail Order Handbook," published by Dartnell, is the most widely circulated book in the field, and he has written more than a dozen other books, including "Complete Guide to Catalog Marketing," "Successful Catalog Marketing," "The Greatest Direct Mail Sales Letters of All Time," "Direct Mail in the Political Process," "Direct Mail Showmanship," "How to Work With Mailing Lists," "How to Promote Meeting Attendance," and "Encyclopedia of Direct Mail." He has also written hundreds of magazine articles on direct marketing.

Hodgson has received numerous honors, including the prestigious Ed Mayer Award in recognition of his outstanding contribution to direct marketing education; the Jesse H. Neale Editorial Achievement Award; the Dartnell Gold Medal for excellence in business letter writing; Direct Marketer of the Year, presented by the Philadelphia Direct Marketing Association; Sales Promotion Man of the Year, and International Marketing Communicator of the Year. His direct mail campaigns and catalogs have won numerous awards, including the Direct Marketing Association's Gold Mailbox.

Long active in organizations serving advertising and marketing fields, Hodgson helped found the Chicago Association of Direct Marketing and served as one of its early presidents. He also served as international president of the Sales Promotion Executives Association and served four terms on the board of directors of the Direct Marketing Association and two terms on the board of directors of the Direct Marketing Educational Foundation. An active Rotarian, he is a past president of the Rotary Club of Westtown-Goshen.

A native of Breckenridge, Minnesota, Hodgson is a graduate of the North Dakota State School of Science and has attended Gustavus Adolphus College, Western Michigan College, and Northwestern University. He and his wife, Lois, live in Chester County, Pennsylvania, and he commutes daily to his office "across the driveway."

SPECIAL THANKS

Wherever possible, I've tried to include credit to the skilled writers who created the great letters featured in this book. Unfortunately, in many cases the identity of the writers were unknown, or my requests for this information went unanswered. I would welcome hearing from or about any of the writers who failed to get the credit they deserved so I can add this information to future editions.

It would take pages to thank everyone who assisted in providing material for this book. I am particularly indebted to the many experts whose guidelines for better direct mail letters have been included on these pages.

I'd like to pay special credit to Maxwell Ross, who passed away while this edition was being prepared. Max was a very special friend for many years and was often a source of guidance and inspiration. Many of yesterday's and today's finest letter writers learned their craft from Max. His extremely helpful checklists (many of which are included in this book) have guided writers for the past half century. And I'm sure his words of wisdom will continue to be of value to writers and editors into the 21st century.

Dick Hodgson
1433 Johnny's Way
Westtown, Pennsylvania 19395

HOW TO USE THIS BOOK

If you're like me, you'll find many of the letters in this book great reading. But that's not the primary purpose of the book. Although I'd never recommend simply adapting any of the letters in the book to serve your sales letter needs, I'm reminded of a comment that I usually attribute to Oliver Wendell Holmes:

■ To take someone else's idea and claim it for your own is stealing. But to take ideas from two or more sources and combine them — that's creativity.

Whatever direct mail assignment you face, you'll find examples of how today's leading writers tackled the task of writing letters for a similar assignment. Although you won't duplicate their exact words, a study of their approach should provide a strong starting point and help stir up your own creative juices.

This book, then, is best used as an idea source that shows how leading writers handled difficult writing assignments. Undoubtedly you'll find words and phrases that you can integrate into your own writing. Beware of trying to fit others' words and phrases into your sentences unless they truly fit. Good copy has a cohesive flow that can be interrupted by ill-fitting words and phrases no matter how great they may have been in their original environment.

SECTION I

CREATING DIRECT MAIL LETTERS

THE DIRECT MAIL LETTER

Of all the formats used in direct mail, none has more power to generate action than the letter. A basic rule followed by direct mail advertisers is that any package containing a letter will generally pull greater response than a package without a letter. Extensive testing has proved this to be true in most cases.

Perhaps the most important advantage of using letters to communicate through the mail is that everyone knows how to read a letter. A letter is instantly understood as a message from one person to another. And since direct mail is the *personal* medium of advertising, a person-to-person form of communication is highly desirable.

Other formats almost automatically wave a flag that says "this is a promotional message." And that flag has a tendency to put the reader on guard. But the "personal look" of a letter somehow reduces this guard. There's a friendly quality to a letter that is difficult to duplicate in other formats. Most everyone has grown up with a desire to receive more letters. They remember those days at summer camp, at college, in the service, or other times when they were separated from close friends and loved ones. The arrival of a letter from home was an event to be celebrated.

A letter is easy to read. No question of where to start, where to go next, or where it will end. This is not to say that direct mail letters automatically get attention and readership. However, the odds of achieving those ends are greatly enhanced with letters — especially well written letters that have a genuine person-to-person feel.

THE DIRECT MAIL PACKAGE

The best way to visualize the role of each of the elements in a direct mail package is to compare the mailing with a salesperson making a sales call.

THE ENVELOPE

This is the clothing the salesperson wears. Since it is the first thing a prospect sees, a judgment will likely be made before a word is spoken. Is this someone I can trust? Should I be on my guard against being pushed into doing something I don't want to do? Am I going to have to listen to a high-pressure pitch? Does this look like "someone" who is worthy of my time?

Very little selling is done by the envelope itself, but it can condition the audience to be in the right mood to receive your message. Too often, advertisers worry about getting their envelopes opened because they've often heard people claim, "I throw all of my junk mail away unopened." But research studies have clearly shown few mailings actually go into the wastebasket before the envelope is opened. As a general rule, nobody throws away an envelope until two questions are answered:

- *Who is it from?*

- *What is it about?*

Most people are too curious to throw anything away without first knowing its contents. But an envelope can serve as something other than a carrier of the contents: It can play the role of the warm-up person who introduces the main performer. It can set the mood. It can stimulate curiosity.

THE LETTER

The letter represents the words the salesperson speaks. This is the primary opportunity to deliver a message on a person-to-person basis. Just as a good salesperson doesn't deliver the same canned sales pitch to everyone, the ideal letter should be tailored to each audience it addresses. It should, in effect, say: "And this, Mrs. Jones, is why you should be interested in what my company has to offer."

Because the letter is the person-to-person part of the direct mail package, it presents the optimum opportunity to address each segment of your audience on a person-to-person — rather than a company-to-audience — basis. Of course, if computer personalization is available for your letter, each letter can deal with individuals rather than segments of the mailing list.

THE ENCLOSURES

All the printed enclosures in the direct mail package represent the sales tools a good salesperson uses: catalog sheets, samples, demonstration devices, flip charts, and so on. Just as such sales tools are generally created on a company-to-audience basis, the folders, broadsides, brochures, and other enclosures in a direct mail package are most often in a company-to-audience mode.

There are times, of course, when a major sale is imminent and the salesperson tailors his or her sales tools to the individual prospect for maximum impact. Likewise, mailing enclosures can be personalized for increased impact.

THE ORDER FORM

This is the salesperson's "close." Here the offer is summarized and the customer is asked to agree to the offer. It's where the name goes on the dotted line. Ideally, the order form will summarize the offer, clearly define the terms, and make clear the obligations of both the buyer and the seller.

From this comparison, it should be easy to visualize why the letter carries so much weight in a direct mail package. It's the primary element that develops the person-to-person approach, which distinguishes direct mail as the *personal* medium.

GUIDELINES FOR GOOD LETTERS

While it's generally agreed that any mailing with a letter will do better than a mailing without a letter, this should be further qualified: Enclosing a letter that looks and reads like a person-to-person letter will increase response. Too often, direct mail letters only are company-to-audience messages in semi-letter format and lose their advantage of communicating on a person-to-person basis.

One of the best guidelines for producing direct mail letters is to make them look and read like letters that would be dictated to a secretary and then transcribed in business letter format. For example, only a typewriter type should be used — not a printer's font that resembles typewriter type. Many of today's secretaries, of course, use word processors and may choose to create business letters using one of the proportionally spaced typefaces that resemble printer's type. But to give a direct mail letter a personal feeling, it is best to use a traditional typewriter monospaced type, such as Courier.

Ideally, the letter will have a salutation, or something that resembles a salutation. While business correspondence is normally dated, the absence of a date is only a minor step away from the appearance of a secretary-prepared letter and seldom seriously affects direct mail response. (The exception is when a "deadline date" is an important part of the offer. In such cases, it generally helps to include a date on the letter.) Margins and paragraphing should be much the same as would be used by a secretary. And, of course, the letter should be signed by an individual. Chances are, you'll also want to add a postscript.

While few people will believe the letter has been prepared for their eyes only, there's something about a secretary-prepared look that creates a person-to-person feeling.

THE FINE ART OF SQUIGGLING

Questions are often raised about what I refer to as "The Fine Art of Squiggling" — the use of bold face, all capital letters, underlines, indentations, marginal notes, and other "extras" that are often added to a letter.

My personal rule (and one followed by successful direct mail copywriters) is to use such devices only where you would add them to a business letter that had been transcribed from your dictation. In other words, go easy! Too much emphasis can quickly transform a letter from a person-to-person message into just another company-to-audience "advertising" message.

I recall the advice M. P. Brown, one of direct mail's pioneers, gave to someone who asked about the use of squiggles. "Son," he replied, "if you're really concerned about things like that, you've got a business built on sand." There are too many other important things: the letter copy, the offer, the mailing list, the timing, and so on that should receive primary attention. Common sense should be your guide. If the devices help to communicate and don't destroy the person-to-person feeling of the letter, go ahead and use them. But don't expect them to make major differences in response. There are those who have a writing style that makes squiggling natural. If you observe direct mail, you'll likely notice that these techniques are most often used when something is being presented as a "bargain" and when major emphasis is on price. Squiggles are used less frequently when copy concentrates primarily on quality and value.

HOW LONG SHOULD A LETTER BE?

One of the most frequently asked questions at basic direct mail seminars is, "How long should a letter be?" I have a standard answer: "There's no such thing as a letter that is too long — just one that is too boring." Successful direct mail letters have been six, eight, 10, and even 20 pages long. The role of a sales letter is to answer all the prospect's questions before he or she is willing to take the action requested. If you can answer all those questions in one paragraph, stop there; if it takes multiple pages, the letter should keep rolling until the last question has been answered.

This doesn't mean everyone is going to read your prose from start to finish. That's not important. Expect recipients to stop reading as soon as their questions have been answered. But you can keep going until you've answered questions others might have.

Reading Patterns

It's important to understand *how* people read letters. There's no question about the importance of the opening paragraph(s). They are, in effect, a screening device, giving readers an opportunity to decide whether or not the message will be of interest to them. Testing has shown that creating a good lead paragraph can make a major difference in response. Paul Bringe, the late copywriting expert, once created six different leads for a sales letter. Each, in his opinion, was equally good. But when a test mailing was made, one of those leads produced 300% more response than the other five.

Once the opening has done its job, however, you end up with only readers who, for one reason or another, want to know more about your proposition. Chances are you've sold them on *wanting* what you have to offer, but they haven't yet reached a point of decision and need some questions answered.

People like to buy, and want to be convinced they should say "yes" to a proposition. So the lead of a letter is critical. It quickly screens out those with little or no interest; and those who read on are in a positive frame of mind to go along with what you are proposing. One of the biggest mistakes direct mail letter writers can make is to continue trying to convince people they should be interested in the proposition. This fails to recognize that the only people who are still reading after the first paragraphs are those who have already decided they have an interest in your proposition.

Once the lead has been completed, the role of a letter is to answer unanswered questions — things a prospect needs to know before he or she can agree to say "yes" to your proposal. Most people tend to skim a letter, looking for answers to their questions. This suggests that the letter's body should be organized for easy location of these answers. As a result, the inside pages of a longer letter often feature indexing devices such as special headings, crosslines, paragraph notations, underlined words, and the like. Keep in mind that the first page of a letter should go easy on emphasis devices so as not to lose the person-to-person feeling.

The Johnson Box

A common opening device in many direct mail letters is the "Johnson Box" — a summary of an offer, usually in an indented paragraph and sometimes boxed, positioned at the top of the letter, and ahead of the salutation. The "Johnson Box" got its name from Frank Johnson, who successfully used the device in the letters he wrote for *American Heritage*. Actually, Johnson doesn't claim credit for the device he popularized: He just knew a good thing when he saw it, and put it to use to help sell subscriptions.

Although the "Johnson Box" is one step removed from a secretary-prepared letter, it quickly enables readers to decide whether or not they are interested. So once you get to the body of the letter, your entire audience is composed of people who want to be sold.

Signatures

A company doesn't write letters — people do. So a letter needs a personal signature. Who should sign it? A basic rule is to have the highest-ranking person in the organization (who would normally write such a letter) sign his or her name. Recipients generally respect a voice of authority;

a letter signed by a company's president, vice president, general manager, department head, publisher, editor, or director can command respect.

The late Ed Mayer, the man many consider the "dean" of direct mail, once suggested every letter should be signed by a vice president. "I don't mean you should print their signature. Make them sign each letter personally. It will give them something to do," he said. Even though he said this facetiously, the point is valid. The "cute" letter from the secretary, mailboy, shipping clerk, or the president's wife is seldom as effective as a straightforward letter from the top executive. There are times when a letter may be more believable when someone down the line is identified as the writer. Most of these letters, however, tend to be lighthearted and humorous — their odds of succeeding are far less than conventional letters. A few titles should be avoided in most cases: sales and marketing titles. A letter signed by a sales manager develops the same kind of resistance that occurs when an insurance salesman shows up at your door unannounced.

The signature should be readable and in a color that resembles a pen-and-ink signature. The majority of mail order letterheads are blue and black so the letter can have black body copy and a common blue ink signature when only two-color printing is used. I've heard people claim that an unusual color signature is more effective than ordinary blue. But in the long run, you won't find consistency when you test one color against another. The best idea is to do whatever is required to make the signature look "real." It's unlikely you'll find a substitute for normal blue ink signatures of any special value.

There's no evidence that one letter closing is better than another. "Sincerely yours" is probably as good as any. A correspondence school once tested 20 different complimentary closes, and the winner was "God bless you." ("Sincerely yours" was used anyhow.)

Salutation

Little evidence suggests one form of salutation works better than another. Common sense will usually lead to the right one. "Dear Friend:" and "Dear Customer:" are probably best unless you can be more specific. Regardless of the words used, it is wise to use some form of salutation that will help your letter seem more like a letter and less like an advertising message.

The Postscript

If you've studied direct mail letters, you've probably noticed a high percentage include a postscript at the end of the letter. This is the result of a continuing series of studies on how people read letters. These studies have been conducted for many years and consistently show most people read letters in the same manner.

Readers first look at the letterhead to see who the letter is from, then at the salutation to see to whom the letter is addressed, and then they look down the page to see who signed the letter. They want to know who they will be "listening to" as they read the letter. Even if the signature is at the bottom of page six, most readers search it out before continuing. However, if there is a postscript below the signature, it will most often be read *before* the reader returns to the beginning of the letter. Thus, the postscript is often the first copy to be read.

I like to use a postscript as a teaser (i.e., "Don't forget the special bonus you'll receive if you respond before July 1"). Now you've got a curious reader who will search the rest of the copy to see what this special offer is all about.

WHEN PEOPLE READ LETTERS

Nick Samstag, the long-time genius behind promotional mailings for Time, Inc., once reported on a series of tests that were conducted to determine *when* people read advertising in *Time* and *Life* magazines. It was discovered people only read ad copy when they were in the market for what was advertised. For example, people look only at the pictures of cars in a new automobile ad. The only time they read the copy is when they are in the market to buy a new car.

There's a lesson in these test results for direct mail letter writers. Emphasis should be on benefits — not features of a product or service. More people will be interested in a benefit rather than a feature. Remember, the lead of a letter is a screening device. If you lead off with a strong benefit, there's a greater chance that readers will want what is being offered, read more of the copy, and search for answers to their questions before they can make a "yes" or "no" decision.

Unfortunately, the world is full of copywriters whose main goal is composing copy that will win the applause of their peers. So they try to get cute, create peer-applauding prose, and tell wonderful little stories that exhibit their skill as wordsmiths. However, they get only polite applause from the audience for which the letter is intended — the kind which brings down the curtain and leaves the rest of the letter unread. This is because such copywriters only provide momentary interest. When the last period in the introductory story is found, readers have been entertained but are not convinced they should place an order.

Puns are particularly dangerous in a direct mail letter. "A pun," says Eleanor Bishop, "serves only the copywriter's ego unless it states a benefit or leads into one."

HUMOR IN COPY

Humor is one of the most difficult things to use successfully in direct mail copy. If done well, it can be both entertaining and entice the audience into wanting to know more about the product or service being promoted. But what is funny to the writer may easily lay an egg with the majority of readers. It takes a special skill — seldom found even among professional direct mail copywriters — to write humorous direct mail copy that sells.

Some writers can be consistently funny and keep their copy moving to the selling point. But not many. Just because your staff laughs at the copy you've written, don't be deceived: They're being paid to laugh at your jokes. It's best to test humorous copy on a wide variety of readers to make sure it appeals to all of them before putting it into print.

If you're Bill Jayme, you can get away with a teaser like, "Do you close the bathroom door, even when you're the only one home?" His copy is so great, unusual lines like this one he created for *Psychology Today* are often winners. For most of us, however, it's safer if we stick to straight copy rather than trying to be too clever. The late, great M. H. Habernickel, Jr., regularly wrote light-touch letters for Haband. Thousands of Haband customers eagerly awaited the arrival of his next sales letter. But when he died, no one could come close to his delicate touch in handling humor, even though two generations of his family keep trying and occasionally produce a gem. But his deft touch was lost. He was one in a million.

What is particularly difficult to create is whimsy. Few authors and even fewer direct mail copywriters have been able to handle the subtleties of this difficult form of writing. When done well — as in some of the great letters created by John Yeck — it can almost hypnotize an audience. But when even a step away from great, it usually falls flat on its face and does little to enhance the direct mail communications process.

WHY PEOPLE BUY

Many years ago, Paul Bringe offered this advice, which is just as true today as it was when he wrote it:

> ■ A good copywriter isn't in love with words, he is in love with people. All kinds of people, everywhere and anywhere. He is intensely interested in people, watches them closely, listens when they talk, lives their bad moments with them, and rejoices in their victories. He is so interested in other people he forgets all about himself, his own needs and wants, and after a time he knows why they think as they do. And he recognizes himself in them and knows what they do he is capable of doing whether it is good or bad. The way to write believable copy is to love people. Know what every living person fears, hates, loves, and rejoices just as you do. Let everything you write say to your reader, "I understand you. I have been in your shoes, I can help you, please let me try."

An important starting point for writing letters is to understand the things that motivate people to buy. While there may be several motivations that lead your readers to acquire what you are offering, it is best to focus on a primary motivation and build your sales story around it. Then, once you've established that your product or service can help your reader fulfill this desire, you can work in additional benefits. Consider the 100 basic motivations shown in Table 1. Some may seem to be duplicates of others, which were expressed differently. But these minor differences may amount to major advantages when it comes to selecting the best way to make your sales points in a direct mail letter.

TABLE 1
100 MOTIVATIONS FOR PEOPLE TO BUY

To satisfy curiosity	To find new and uncommon things
To get a surprise	To win others' affection
To be successful	To be more beautiful
To be more comfortable	To attract the opposite sex
To make work easier	To satisfy sexual desires
To gain prestige	To bring back "The Good Old Days"
To be sociable	To be lucky
To be creative	To live longer
To be efficient	To feel important
To safeguard self and family	To gain knowledge
To protect family's future	To improve appearance
To be good parents	To gain praise from others
To be well liked and loved	To be recognized as an authority
To appear different from others	To enhance leisure
To gain popularity	To save money
To add to life's pleasures	To have security in old age
To express a personality	To overcome obstacles
To be in fashion	To do things well
To avoid embarrassment	To get a better job
To fulfill fantasies	To be your own boss
To be up-to-date	To gain social acceptance
To own attractive things	To "keep up with the Joneses"
To collect valuable possessions	To appreciate beauty
To protect or conserve possessions	To be proud of possessions
To satisfy ego	To resist domination by others
To be "first"	To emulate the admirable
To accumulate money	To relieve boredom
To preserve money already accumulated	To gain self-respect
To save time	To win acclaim
To protect reputation	To gain admiration
To satisfy appetite	To win advancement
To enjoy exotic tastes	To seek adventure
To live in a clean atmosphere	To satisfy ambition
To be strong and healthy	To be among the leaders
To renew vigor and energy	To gain confidence
To get rid of aches and pains	To escape drudgery

To gain freedom from worry	To avoid trouble
To get on the bandwagon	To emulate others
To get something for nothing	To "one-up" others
To gain self-assurance	To be in style
To escape shame	To increase enjoyment
To avoid effort	To have or hold beautiful possessions
To get more comfort	To replace the obsolete
To gain praise	To add fun or spice to life
To be popular	To work less
To have safety in buying something else	To look better
To take advantage of opportunities	To conserve natural resources
To protect reputation	To protect the environment
To be an individual	To avoid shortages
To avoid criticism	To relax

CREATING A PERSON-TO-PERSON DIRECT MAIL LETTER

One of the most difficult jobs I've had over the years is trying to teach writers from other fields how to write strong direct mail copy. A good direct mail letter — even though sent to an audience — must carry the feeling it is from one person to another person, not a message for an entire audience. Although the proper format helps, other things are also important: primarily the subtle feeling that the letter is from a specific person to a specific recipient.

To create strong personal copy, audience-oriented copywriters should prepare a list of eight to 10 people they know personally — people who are typical of the audience to whom the letter will be sent. Then, they should start out writing to just one of these people . . . "Dear Joe." When the letter is complete, the names of the other people on the list should be substituted with "Dear Mary" . . . "Dear Susan" . . . "Dear Steve" . . . and so on to see if the letter still "fits." If it doesn't, the letter should be started over, and written to one of the other names on their list. It's amazing how quickly a letter becomes "personal" to individual members of an audience, even though it was originally written to just one person. It's important, however, to write to one person at a time and not cover the entire list all at once. That's writing to an audience, and the letter quickly loses the personal touch.

Generally, a letter can't be successfully edited to build in a personal touch. A letter that doesn't "fit" multiple recipients should be started from scratch each time. Of course, many of the words are likely to be repeated again. But there's a certain flow to a good personal letter; this is often eliminated when too much editing is done. If your job is to edit letters written by others, you can apply this same technique. Create your own list of names and then insert them one at a time to decide if it's good person-to-person communication, or just a message for an audience.

BEFORE THE WRITING STARTS

Most experienced copywriters follow a set procedure when creating their direct mail copy. Their individual techniques may vary, but they generally study "white mail," review competitors' copy, review old copy, gather facts, write key paragraphs, and establish a starting point.

White Mail

Before beginning to write direct mail copy, the first step is to expose yourself to the so-called "white mail" received by the advertiser. White mail is any correspondence other than an order or a payment received from a customer. Here is where you'll learn the language used and most easily understood by your customers. When you use the customer's language — rather than your own language — the whole communication process is improved.

Every business has its own language — one that is probably understood by everyone in the seller's organization, but perhaps not so readily understood by the recipients of your mailings. For example, some years ago, I was involved in a research project for Ford Motor Company. A dispute had developed in Dearborn between the marketing and engineering people at Ford about what should be included in the owner's manual of each new car. We surveyed 5,000 owners of new Fords. We interviewed 100 owners in each of 50 different markets in the United States and asked them what they would have liked to have had in the owner's manual. Surprisingly, in each of the markets surveyed, the most asked-for thing was the same: "How much gas does the gas tank hold?" The answer was already in their manuals, but was labeled "Fuel Capacity." The owners hadn't thought to look for it under that title. They wanted to know about "gas," not "fuel."

That's the problem with "internal words." Unless we're careful, we can quickly lose our audience by using words that are unfamiliar to our readers. Reading direct mail letters should be an easy process, with no need to stop and think for even a moment about what the writer is trying to say. Whenever a reader comes to a stopping point, there's a good excuse to stop reading — something every good copywriter should avoid. That's why we try not to end any page of a letter with a period. It's ideal to have a hyphenated word or at least an incomplete sentence so the reader will move quickly to the next page and not take advantage of an easy place to stop reading.

White mail can provide us with words that won't give our reader cause to stop and ponder their meaning. Reading white mail is a great way to get to know your customers as well as the language they use. If you don't get much white mail, use the telephone. A couple of dozen conversations with customers can be quite enlightening and provide you with a good feel for the language they use. Be sure to make an exact transcription of your customers' conversations without trying to convert what they say into your own words.

Competitors' Copy

It's important to know the environment in which your mailing will be received before writing begins. To do this, thoroughly review your competitors' copy, including every mailing that will be competing with your copy.

Review Old Copy

Although it may hurt the creative egos of some copywriters, there is no need to rewrite copy that works. No one — at least no one in the audience you want to reach — cares if you repeatedly use old copy, as long as it fits into the flow of your letter.

When analyzing successful mailings of the past, try to get a feel for what works and what doesn't. Be sure to pay special attention to mailings that didn't work. See if you can spot what's really different between successful mailings and those that failed.

One of the problems with reusing old copy is having a boss who believes a copywriter is not earning his or her keep if every word isn't new. But smarter bosses recognize one of the qualities of a good copywriter is the willingness to utilize tried and proved copy regardless of who originally put the words together. David Ogilvy once said, "One of the greatest wastes in advertising is to do away with copy which is still working." And it's important to remember the often repeated truism that when you start getting bored with an advertising message, that's about when the audience starts to notice it.

GATHER THE FACTS

By putting together all of the information you need before you begin writing, studying it thoroughly, and fixing the key points in your mind, you can concentrate on the writing itself. Good direct mail copy has a flow, and this can be broken if you have to stop to seek out the facts you need. I've made it a regular practice to develop "copywriter's packets" that provide ready reference on all the products and services I've dealt with. You'll find an outline of the ideal contents of a copywriter's packet on pages 20–22.

KEY PARAGRAPHS

Once the copywriter is familiar with all the facts and has studied them thoroughly, it's best to write a series of paragraphs — one about each of the things that must be included in the promotional package. This should be done without any particular thought as to where the information will appear. Next, the paragraphs should be arranged in a logical story-telling sequence. This will quickly show what is missing, what is redundant, what needs special emphasis, and what must be illustrated.

These assembled paragraphs don't represent finished copy — they are just a starting point. The time spent writing them, however, is not wasted because this exercise helps the writer structure words in ways that communicate best. This same sequence of words can be used in the actual copywriting, giving the copywriter a chance to move ahead at a pace that maintains a good conversational flow.

PLAIN PAPER DUMMY

Most experienced direct mail copywriters also prepare a folded paper rough sketch, or dummy, of the format as they envision it. These dummies are not intended to be a professional design, only as a "road map" for effective copywriting. If the copywriter can visualize where things will appear, the end result will be better communication. Once the copy has been written, edited, and approved, this folded paper dummy will help the designer understand how the copywriter intended to have the copy used.

THE STARTING POINT

All this has been preliminary to actually writing the copy itself. But now it's time for action, and that always starts in just one place. If there's one absolute rule for direct mail copywriting, it is: *always write the order form first!* If the copywriter is not responsible for writing the order form, whoever has that responsibility must complete that assignment before work starts on the letter or other enclosures.

The order form is the copywriter's target. Writing copy without an order form as a target is like trying to be a sharpshooter by simply shooting bullets against a blank wall and then drawing circles around the places the bullets hit. No one ever won a rifle championship that way, and you can't expect championship direct mail copy unless there is an order form target. As Wendell Forbes once said, "That's like trying to play handball against a blanket . . . or like trying to nail Jello to the wall."

EDITING COPY

Copywriters have a natural tendency to jump up from the typewriter when the copy is completed and rush over and read it to a colleague. That's the worst way to evaluate a piece of direct mail copy. When we read aloud to someone, we put the pauses, emphasis, and gestures where we intend them to go. But you can't read aloud your copy to everyone on a direct mail list. And your colleagues know only too well the problems you've had in writing the copy and will tend to be overly sympathetic if your copy isn't effective. So you may not get an objective opinion from your coworkers.

THE HAT TRICK

The best way to have your copy evaluated is to use "The Hat Trick." Put on your hat, get out of the office, take the copy to someone who doesn't know a thing about what you've just gone through to create it, and have them read the copy back to you. Listen carefully to where this person puts the pauses and emphasis. Carefully listen to questions on what the letter is all about. If there *are* questions, the copywriting job isn't over.

THE CROSS-OUT/WRITE-IN TEST

Another good test of copy effectiveness is to cross out all references to your company and its product or service and write in the name of your competitor and their product or service. If the copy still fits, you've got a lot of rewriting to do. A good copywriter should be able to come up with copy points that no competitor could say about their products or services. That's what often identifies the true professional in direct mail copywriting: the ability to create unique copy that will encourage a prospect to want to buy from *you*.

THE OPENING PARAGRAPHS

One of the first editors I worked with told me that, generally, if the first one or two paragraphs of any promotional copy are crossed out, you can come up with a stronger selling approach. Knowing how hard every writer works on the first few paragraphs of a letter, I originally questioned this observation. But after editing thousands of first drafts (including my own copy), I am now convinced that this is true.

The toughest job for any writer is to *start* writing. You have an assignment and a blank piece of paper. But where to start? You come up with every excuse under the sun to delay getting started. Finally, the deadline approaches, and you just can't procrastinate any longer. So you start by telling a story with an ancedote or maybe a historical reference or a quotation — anything to get started. Then, at about the second or third paragraph, you begin to get into the process of communicating with your audience. Those first paragraphs are often a device to get the *writer* started, not the *reader.* And more often than not, their elimination leads to more powerful selling copy.

THE COMMITTEE

Someone once observed that a camel was a horse that had been created by a committee. All too often, copy that has been subjected to the blue pencils of a committee is about as graceful as a camel when the job called for a sleek racehorse. After a committee has done its damage, it's time to send the copy back to the copywriter for a rewrite. That doesn't mean the writer can ignore the committee's no-no's and must-must's. But the writer can start from the beginning again, interweaving the changes into a smooth-flowing letter.

COIK

Someone in government came up with the acronym COIK — a way to describe copy that is difficult to understand:

> *Clear Only If Known*

This is an acronym that should be pasted on every copywriter's wall.

Too often we write copy that is only fully understood if our audience knows as much about our subject as we do — and this is seldom the case. The old saying, "you should write for the 12-year-old mentality" is dangerous today. Twelve-year-olds know more than ever before. Instead, it's better to write for the college freshman — eventually the chairman of the board will be able to figure it out! Seriously, it is important to keep the knowledge level of your audience clearly in mind as you write. A good rule to follow is:

> *Don't overestimate the knowledge of your audience . . .*
> *. . . but don't underestimate their intelligence.*

In other words, don't write "down" to your readers; make a special effort to remember just how much knowledge they are likely to have about your subject.

THE FIVE "MUSTS" OF DIRECT MAIL WRITING

Throughout this book, you'll find a wide variety of checklists for writing better direct mail letters. Before you consider any other factors, however, it is crucial to keep in mind the five "musts" of good direct mail writing:

- *Is it clear?*
- *Is it believable?*
- *Is it interesting?*
- *Is it friendly?*
- *Is it concise?**

* When it comes to writing direct mail letters, concise doesn't necessarily mean short. A letter should be as long as it takes to answer all the questions readers may have. But it's important to stop when you've answered those questions.

In my direct mail seminars, I've suggested that participants post this short list of basic rules where they will see it every time they write or edit direct mail copy.

COPYWRITING FORMULAS

Probably no other form of writing has brought forth more formulas than direct mail. Every copywriter, it seems, has his or her own set of guidelines for writing. And yet, when the time comes to do the writing, the "formula" recedes into the subconscious rather than serving as a step-by-step outline. However, formulas can be helpful as an organizational tool and as a method to analyze whether or not a piece of copy covers all the bases.

By far the most popular — and probably the oldest — of all direct mail copy formulas is one of the most simple: AIDA.

A Attract the reader's attention.

I Arouse the reader's interest in the proposition.

D Stimulate the reader's desire to take action.

A Ask the reader to take the action requested.

There are several variations on the AIDA formula. The late Robert Collier insisted the proper order for sales letters was:

Attention

Interest

Description

Persuasion

Proof

Close

Earle A. Buckley had this variation:

Interest

Desire

Conviction

Action

Victor O. Schwab suggested this formula:

A Get **A**ttention

A Show people an **A**dvantage

P **P**rove it

P **P**ersuade people to grasp this advantage

A **A**sk for action

Henry Hoke, Sr., took a different approach:

Picture

Promise

Prove

Push

Many writers have found Jack Lacy's Five Points an excellent guideline for their sales letters:

1. What will you do for me if I listen to your story?

2. How are you going to do this?

3. Who is responsible for the promises you make?

4. Who have you done this for?

5. What will it cost me?

Frank Egner offered a more detailed, nine-point formula:

1. The headline (or first paragraph) to get attention and arouse desire.

2. The inspirational lead-in.

3. A clear definition of the product.

4. Tell a success story about product use.

5. Include testimonials and endorsements.

6. List special features.

7. A definite statement of value to the prospect.

8. Specific urgent action copy.

9. A postscript.

Of all the formulas, I have found Bob Stone's seven steps the most helpful:

1. Promise a benefit in your headline or first paragraph — *your most important benefit*.

2. Immediately enlarge your most important benefit.

3. Tell the reader *specifically* what he or she is going to get.

4. Back up your statements with *proof* and *endorsements*.

5. Tell the reader what might be lost if he or she doesn't act.

6. Rephrase your prominent benefits in your closing.

7. Incite action — *now*.

There's one more approach many writers have built into their direct mail copy. It was the basis for much of Cy Frailey's teaching about effective letter writing. He credits a Chicago consultant, Dr. Frank W. Dignan, for creating the Star-Chain-Hook approach:

Star   An opening that quickly captures the reader's attention.

Chain   A series of facts to change the reader's casual attention to a real and sustained interest.

Hook   Something to impel the desired action.

Many teachers of writing often add a mathematical formula to these approaches. Several of these mathematical formulas are based on the readability formula introduced by Dr. Rudolf Flesch.* The late Maxwell Ross, whose name is in everybody's book as one of the all-time great direct mail writers, boiled it all down to this:

■ For every 100 words you write, make sure that approximately 75% are words of five letters or less.

In the classes I teach, I try to make it even simpler: *Concentrate on short words and action words.* The reason for this is that most formula-oriented copywriters have a tendency to lean too heavily on their formula. As a result, there is a stiffness to their copy that destroys the natural flow. Frankly, I'm convinced that none of the top direct mail writers really use their formulas when writing. It's just that when asked to give a speech on copywriting, the easiest thing to do is talk about a formula. The formulas that flow from the platforms at direct mail meetings are promptly forgotten when a writing assignment comes along.

* The Art of Plain Talk, *Rudolf Flesch, Ph.D., Harper & Brothers, New York, 1946.*

This doesn't mean copywriting formulas are without merit. They deserve to be studied and entered into the subconscious and can be useful in analyzing what's wrong with copy that doesn't hit the mark. When it comes to editing copy, there are many more sets of helpful guidelines.

The late, great Edward N. Mayer, Jr., who created the first series of continuing education programs for the Direct Marketing Association, often suggested this list:

1. Make every letter sell.

2. Know your subject thoroughly.

3. Make your letters clear.

4. Make your letters concise, but tell the whole story.

5. Know what you want — and ask for it.

6. Use simple language and short words to tell your story.

7. Make your letters friendly.

8. Make your copy sincere.

9. Make your copy tactful.

10. Always put a hook in your copy.

Another great copywriter, John Yeck, offers these guidelines:

1. Put yourself in the other person's shoes.

2. Be friendly.

3. Shoot for the bullseye (to take the reader from where she is to where you want her to be).

4. Keep your letters clear and easy to read.

5. Make them interesting and keep them moving.

6. Be believable.

7. B.U. — be yourself.

8. Write, write, write — carefully.

If you love formulas for writing and editing, you'll find many more of them in Dartnell's *Direct Mail and Mail Order Handbook.** The most useful formula, however, is Maxwell C. Ross's 20-point checklist for better direct mail copy:

* Direct Mail & Mail Order Handbook, *Richard S. Hodgson, Dartnell Corporation, Chicago, Third Edition, 1980.*

1. **Does the lead sentence get in step with the reader at once?** Do this by talking in terms of things that interest your reader — not in vague generalities or of things *you* want. Put yourself in *his* place! I can't think of a better way to say it than this: Get in step with your reader.

2. **Is your lead sentence more than two lines long?** But if it takes three lines or four lines or even more to get in step with your reader, use them.

3. **Do your opening paragraphs promise a benefit to the reader?** Lead with your best foot forward — your most important benefit. If you have trouble with your opening paragraph, try writing your lead at least six different ways. Then when you get six down on paper, you are quite likely to have at least one pretty good lead somewhere among them.

4. **Have you fired your biggest gun first?** Sometimes it's easy to get confused in trying to pick out the most important sales point to feature in your lead. But here is one way to tell: Years ago Richard Manville developed a technique that has been of great help. When you are pondering over leads, ask yourself if the reader wants more x or y?

5. **Is there a big idea behind your letter?** You may wonder what the difference is between firing your biggest gun and this big idea. In one case, for example, the big gun may be the introductory offer on an insurance policy, but the big idea behind the letter is a company that makes insurance available to the senior citizens. The big idea is important. My guess is that the lack of a big idea is why letters fail.

6. **Are your thoughts arranged in a logical order?** In other words, have you got the cart before the horse? It is a fundamental copywriting truth that your reader anticipates what you are going to say. So it may help to think of your reader as a passenger in a motorcycle sidecar — and you are the driver. You can take him or her straight to the destination, surely and swiftly and smoothly. Or you can dawdle along the way, over side roads, bumps, and curves, sometimes making such short turns that he or she may shoot off down the road without you. Unless you follow a charted course and make the ride as pleasant as possible, too often your "passenger" will say, "I'm tired. Let me off." This is another good reason for having a checklist to follow.

7. **Is what you say believable?** Here is a chance to offer proof and testimony to back up what you have said in your letter. (Notice I didn't say "true" instead of "believable." What you say may be true, but not necessarily believable.)

8. **Is it clear how the reader is to order, and did you ask for the order?** You would be surprised how easy it is to write a letter without asking for the order.

9. **Does the copy tie in with the order form, and have you directed attention to the order form in the letter?**

10. **Does the letter have the "you" attitude all the way through?**

11. **Does the letter have a conversational tone?**

12. **Have you formed a "bucket brigade" through your copy?** If you study the works of master letter writers, you will notice that all these letters have swing and movement — a joining together of paragraphs through the use of connecting links. Some of these connecting

links are little sentences like, "But that is not all". . . "So that is why". . . "Now, here is the next step" . . . "But there is one thing more." You can find dozens of ways to join your thoughts like this — in short, to take your reader by the hand and lead him through your copy — and avoid what I call "island paragraphs" that stand alone and are usually as dull as they look to the reader.

13. **Does the letter score between 70 and 80 one-syllable words for every 100 words you write?**

14. **Are there any sentences that begin with an article (a, an, the) where you might have avoided it?**

15. **Are there any places where you have strung together too many prepositional phrases?**

16. **Have you kept out "wandering" verbs?** You can often make sentences easier to read by rearranging them so that verbs are closer to their subjects.

17. **Have you used action verbs instead of noun construction?** You gain interest when you do this. Instead of saying, "This letter is of vital concern to . . ." say, "This letter vitally concerns . . ."

18. **Are there any "thats" you don't need?** Using too many "thats" is another strength-robber. Eliminate as many as you can, but be careful. Read your copy aloud to make sure you haven't trimmed out so many that your copy will slow down the reader.

19. **How does the copy rate on such letter-craftsmanship points as (a) using active voice instead of passive, (b) periodic sentences instead of loose, (c) too many participles, (d) splitting infinitives, and (e) repeating your company name too many times?** Moderation in copy is a great virtue.

20. **Does your letter look the way you want it to?**

Finally, from the wisdom of Guy L. Yolton, an outstanding copywriter, come seven guidelines for editing direct mail copy:

1. **Edit for warm-up.** This is first because it occurs at the beginning of a letter. It's the general type of statement that is perfectly obvious to your reader. It's usually just the copy-writer's warm-up to her subject, explaining to herself what this is all about. Statements like, "As an American businesswoman, you know that managing people is a difficult job . . ." The reader already knows that. If there's a personal message for her, or some interesting ideas coming later, she won't wait around for them. She wants to know: "Why am I getting this letter on this subject?" Or, "What have you got to say to me that's new?"

2. **Edit for stoppers.** These often show up when you read your draft copy back to yourself, or when you read it to someone else. Stoppers are words and phrases that are awkward, contrived, and out of the ordinary. They hold up your reader and interrupt the rhythm of a piece that otherwise flows smoothly from one idea to another. Stoppers sometimes get into the copy because the writer didn't.

3. **Edit for author's pride.** The well-turned phrase is fine if it adds a unique and powerful twist to a sales point and keeps the copy moving. But if you've come up with a catchy

expression that stops your reader along the way while he admires your handiwork and forgets what you're working at, you may never get him back on track. Sometimes these phrases may not have much meaning. "This public speaking course can be your capstone to success." What in the heck is a "capstone"? The reader might know it's the finishing stone of a structure, but if he stops to figure out how that metaphor applies to him and the product being sold, he'll probably never make it to the order card. Distrust and question those dandy little word structures that please you. Strike them out, and let the reader move on to the action.

4. **Edit for order.** Does this follow that? There are natural sequences of ideas that are easier for people to follow. Small, big, bigger, biggest. If you are describing the advantages of your product, this could be the best way to build them. Then, now, later on, future. If your explanation is related to time, this is the logical order for development. In testing whether your copy is orderly, question "Should the idea appear where I have it, sooner, or later?" You could wind up turning the whole piece upside-down.

5. **Edit for "reason why."** Do advantages you attribute to your product just sit there in mid-air, supported only by the fact that they appear on paper? Why does it do what you say it will? How did it get that way? What proof can you offer? The reader needs a little more than *unsupported puffery* to decide to buy. A mailing from a business publication says, "The unusual resources which the editors draw upon are unparalleled in American publishing." Why the resources are unusual . . . why they are unparalleled is never made clear.

6. **Edit to stretch benefits.** This is another way to help your copy get away from unsupported puffery. A circular tells me that I'll get new techniques in thinking . . . payoff tables . . . the "decision tree." Those sound like benefits, but they don't go far enough. Is it possible that "pay-off tables" could be stretched to: "How pay-off tables tell you when your decision is on the right track"? The decision tree could become: "Unique in approach, the 'decision tree' helps you put the elements of the problem in logical order." This kind of editing is related to what Elmer Wheeler meant when he said, "Sell the sizzle, not the steak."

7. **Edit for market.** Is your prospect male or female, educated or uneducated? An outdoor person or desk-bound? A specialist or generalist? In looking through your draft copy, is your language, style, and tone something your prospect can be comfortable with on his own terms? Writing for *Field & Stream* is entirely different from writing for the *Harvard Business Review* prospect.

THE COPYWRITER'S PACKET

Research and copywriting are two separate tasks even though they may be performed by the same individual. However, regardless of who does the pre-writing research, it's a good idea to maintain a continuing file of background information that can be used over and over whenever promotion copy is needed for the same product or service — or even as a starter file for similar products or services. My personal preference for copy packets is to keep all of the information in indexed ring binders, with the latest material always added to the front of each section. Then, when it's time for the writing to begin, the reference material is ready and waiting.

The copywriter's packet should include: old copy, results from previous mailings, competitors' copy, vendors' data, specification sheet, editorial references, sales records, and customer comments.

OLD COPY

Every previous promotion package for the product or service — no matter how long ago it was used — should be included in the copywriter's packet. It's helpful to clearly identify which promotion packages were successful and those that failed.

RESULTS FROM PREVIOUS MAILINGS

This will help identify your target audience, particularly if results are broken down by list segments. In this way, you can see those approaches that hit home and those that missed their mark.

COMPETITORS' COPY

Be aware of what others say about the same product or service, or at least the same *type* of product or service. This is not a suggestion for you to copy what others have said. In fact, you'll generally obtain much better results if you find a way to make a point that is uniquely your own. But it is important to be fully aware of the competitive environment your copy will encounter.

VENDORS' DATA

Ask the vendor of the product or service to provide as much information as possible about the product. Don't expect the vendors to know all the benefits of their products, or even the key selling points. They're often too close to the forest to see the trees. But there's no reason to reinvent the wheel — anything you get from a vendor means less time spent on research. Another, often overlooked, source of good background material is the vendor's customer service department. These departments frequently have special letters and enclosures loaded with helpful reference material.

If the product's package has information printed on it, include a reproduction of that information in the packet. If there are printed inserts in the package, make sure these are included as well. The same applies to instruction sheets and how-to-assemble directions.

SPECIFICATION SHEET

A standard specification sheet for each type of product or service an organization promotes should be available. This includes information such as dimensions, weight, colors, type of packaging, materials when the product was first introduced, how it is packaged, any warranties that cover the product, and the like. This information should be provided by the buyer or the product manager.

A key part of the specification sheet should include answers to key questions:

- *How does this product or service differ from similar products or services?*

- *Why should a customer buy this product or service rather than something similar?*

In addition, the specification sheet should identify key benefits of the product or service and its unique selling proposition (USP). (I believe no product is worthy of promotion if it doesn't have an identifiable USP.)

Strong management will make it a policy to have every detail completed on this specification sheet before the copy packet is given to a copywriter.

EDITORIAL REFERENCES

All editorial mentions of the product or service should be clipped on a regular basis and added to the copy packet. This should include newspaper and magazine articles; radio and television scripts and other "published" material from outside sources; and anything produced internally within the vendor's or seller's organizations including engineering reports, customer service reports, transcripts of focus group sessions, public relations releases, and so on.

SALES RECORDS

The copy packet should contain all records of previous sales of the product or service. Too often, the writer is left out of discussions concerning sales results, yet they are essential to a full understanding of how best to create words that will help sell the product or service.

CUSTOMER COMMENTS

This is perhaps the copy packet's most important item. A copy of every letter and record of each customer service phone call concerning the product or service should be added to the copy packet as they are received.

SECTION II

CLASSIC DIRECT MAIL LETTERS

From the thousands of excellent letters collected for this book, there are a few that stand out as truly exceptional. Most were mailed to large audiences, and are often the toughest of all letters to write since large audiences are usually diverse. Creating a "personal" letter to the majority of recipients is difficult, but the letters included in this section accomplished this difficult task. Some letters are directed to highly-defined audiences. The writing may be easier than large-audience letters, but the ones included here are real gems.

All the letters in this section are equally great, and (although they don't appear here) there are hundreds of other excellent letters that didn't get noticed by enough direct marketers to win the applause they deserved. For example, the most successful direct mail letter of this century wasn't written by a professional copywriter. It was written by London's city engineer, and accompanied 2,000 brochures that were distributed to try to sell — of all things — the London Bridge! Christian Brann, one of England's premiere direct marketers, wrote about it:*

■ Harold King, the City Engineer and no great salesman, was given the unenviable task of conducting this unique selling operation.

He went to a little graphic design studio around the corner and told them to produce a brochure. It consisted of 24 pages of pictures and descriptions about the history of London and its bridges, all ending with the specification of [The London Bridge] and, like all good direct mail packages, it contained the conditions of the sale.

The Corporation of London would be responsible for the costs of numbering and taking down all granite and other materials available for sale and for transporting these to a store site. The purchaser, on the other hand, would be responsible for crating, loading and transporting the materials to his new site.

The Corporation would supply plans and photographs, in duplicate, illustrating the numbered stones and their position free of cost and a deposit of 10 percent would be payable on completion of a contract of sale. No price was mentioned in this direct mail package. Instead, the bridge was offered for sale by tender and here is what amounts to be the order form:

We, the undersigned, hereby offer to purchase and remove materials resulting from the demolition of London Bridge, etc.

In short order, London's historic bridge was sold to the McCulloch Corporation for $2,460,000. It was moved to the middle of the Arizona desert and became the distinctive landmark of Lake Havasu City. The mailing only pulled a response of 0.05 percent, but as all good direct marketers learn, it's the bottom line that is important. The mailing cost $1,230, and produced $2,460,000 in sales — or $2,000 per dollar of promotion. Quite a bottom line!

*Cost-Effective Direct Marketing, *Christian Brann, Collectors' Books Ltd., Cirencester, Glos. (England), 1984.*

In this section, more than 100 great direct mail letters are presented in their entirety because (1) they represent successful approaches to different kinds of selling situations and (2) they contain ideas that may help writers handle difficult copy problems. Wherever possible, credit has been given to the writer of each letter. In some cases, the letters represent the work of a staff of creative people rather than a single writer.

NEWSWEEK "IF THE LIST UPON WHICH I FOUND YOUR NAME" LETTER

Probably nothing in the annals of direct mail has been more widely copied than the lead paragraph of a letter used by *Newsweek* magazine for nearly 15 years:

> If the list upon which I found your name is any indication, this is not the first — nor will it be the last — subscription letter you receive. Quite frankly, your education and income set you apart from the general population and make you a highly-rated prospect for everything from magazines to mutual funds.

This was the first letter Ed McLean wrote for S. Arthur "Red" Dembner at *Newsweek* magazine in 1960. Ed describes the experience:

> ■ Red's senior copywriters thought the copy approach was infantile and amateurish. Red insisted upon testing the new approach — which he dubbed the "sincere" letter — and a five-way copy test that fall proved him right.
>
> I brought the opening paragraph and the five remaining paragraphs of page one to the copy test meeting — along with 17 other ideas and openings. The reaction from the other copywriters in the room — all the old-timers — was negative. But Red liked the approach and told me to develop it further.
>
> That turned out to be anything but easy. The personal approach of the opening might get me to look at the letter, I was sure. But what would get me to send away the order form?
>
> When I had sold pots and pans door-to-door in Brooklyn, I learned quickly that I sold more when I did not stray from two key subjects:
>
> 1. The prospect's needs and wants
>
> 2. The product's benefits
>
> I decided to focus most of the letter on the reader's self-interest and tell how he or she would benefit from a trial subscription to *Newsweek*.

This is called the "you" orientation of a letter. And this letter has it in spades. The words "you" and "your" appear 55 times in the copy — perhaps an all-time record. But they aren't just tossed in for effect: They fit logically into the flow of the copy. Through test after test, this "sincere" letter remained *Newsweek's* control for nearly 15 years: Nothing else could beat it. And even today, the idea expressed in the opening paragraph — and often the exact words themselves — is copied over and over in one way or another, making it the starting point for more direct mail letters than any approach ever developed. Ed McLean's comments are interesting:

> ■ I stopped collecting adaptations and outright swipes of the sincere letter opening years ago. It is interesting that few, if any, of these "take-offs" were successful. I am convinced, now, that the mailers who used the sincere opening should not have stopped there. They should have also swiped the "you'll get" litany of any goodies on pages two and three.

Newsweek

NEWSWEEK • 117 EAST THIRD STREET • DAYTON 2, OHIO

Dear Reader:

If the list upon which I found your name is any indication, this is not the first -- nor will it be the last -- subscription letter you receive. Quite frankly, your education and income set you apart from the general population and make you a highly-rated prospect for everything from magazines to mutual funds.

You've undoubtedly 'heard everything' by now in the way of promises and premiums. I won't try to top any of them.

Nor will I insult your intelligence.

If you subscribe to Newsweek, you won't get rich quick. You won't bowl over friends and business associates with clever remarks and sage comments after your first copy of Newsweek arrives. (Your conversation will benefit from a better understanding of the events and forces of our era, but that's all. Wit and wisdom are gifts no magazine can bestow.) And should you attain further professional or business success during the term of your subscription, you'll have your own native ability and good luck to thank for it -- not Newsweek.

What, then, can Newsweek do for you?

The answer depends upon what type of person you happen to be. If you are not curious about what's going on outside your own immediate daily range of concern...if you are quickly bored when the topic of conversation shifts from your house, your car, your ambitions...if you couldn't care less about what's happening in Washington or Wall Street, in London or Moscow...then forget Newsweek. It can't do a thing for you.

If, on the other hand, you are the kind of individual who

- 2 -

would like to keep up with national and international affairs, space and nuclear science, the arts -- but cannot spend hours at it...if you're genuinely interested in what's going on with <u>other</u> members of the human race...if you recognize the big stake you have in decisions made in Washington and Wall Street, in London and Moscow...

then <u>Newsweek may well be the smartest investment you could make in the vital weeks and months ahead</u>!

For little more than 1¢ a day, as a Newsweek subscriber, your interest in national and international affairs will be served by over 200 top-notch reporters here and around the world. Each week, you'll read the most significant facts taken from their daily dispatches by Newsweek's editors.

You'll get the <u>facts</u>. No bias. No slanting. Newsweek respects your right to form your own opinion.

In the eventful weeks to come, you'll read about

-election strategy (Who will run against JFK? Medicare, education, unemployment: how will they sway voters?)

-Administration moves (New civil-rights bill in the works? Taxes: what next?)

-G.O.P. plans (Stepped-up activity in Dixie? New faces for Congressional races?)

-Kremlin maneuverings (Will Cold War policies change? New clashes with Red China?)

-Europe's future (New leaders, new programs? How can America compete with the Common Market?)

You'll also keep on top of latest developments in the exciting fields of space and nuclear science. Whether the story describes a space-dog's trip to Venus or the opening of a new area in the peaceful use of atomic fission, you'll learn the key facts in Newsweek's Space & The Atom feature -- the first and only weekly department devoted to space and nuclear science in any newsweekly.

The fascinating world of art will be reviewed and interviewed for you in Newsweek. Whether you are interested in books or ballet, painting or plays, movies or music -- or all of them -- you will find it covered fully and <u>fairly</u> in Newsweek.

Subscribe now and you'll read about

international film awards...new art shows at the Louvre in Paris...the opening of the Metropolitan and La Scala opera seasons...glittering first nights on and off Broadway...<u>plus</u> revealing interviews with famed authors and prima donnas, actors and symphony conductors.

AND you'll be briefed on happenings in the worlds of Business and Labor (More wage demands now?)...Education and Religion (Reforms in teacher training? More church mergers?)...Science and Medicine (Cancer, arthritis cures on the way?)...Sports and TV-Radio (New world records? More educational TV, fewer MD shows?)

You read Newsweek at your own pace. Its handy Top of the Week index lets you scan the top news stories of the week in two minutes. When you have a lull in your busy schedule, you can return to the story itself for full details. In this way, you are assured of an understanding of the events and forces of our era.

<u>TRY</u> Newsweek.

Try it at our special introductory offer:

37 WEEKS OF NEWSWEEK FOR ONLY $2.97

That's about 8¢ a week -- little more than a penny a day. You would pay $9.25 at newsstands for the same number of copies; $4.98 at our regular yearly subscription rates.

<u>And</u> <u>try</u> <u>it</u> <u>with</u> <u>this</u> <u>guarantee</u>: if, after examining several issues in your own home, you do not agree that Newsweek satisfies your news interests, you will receive a prompt refund.

An order form is enclosed, along with a postage-paid return envelope. Do initial and return the order form <u>today</u>. We'll bill you later, if you wish.

Sincerely,

S. Arthur Dembner

S. Arthur Dembner
Circulation Director

SAD/jnb

PSYCHOLOGY TODAY "BATHROOM DOOR" LETTER

When we asked direct mail authorities to name today's great letter copywriters, the most frequently mentioned name was Bill Jayme. Over the years, Jayme and his design partner, Heikki Ratalahti, have produced many of the most memorable direct mail packages of all time, particularly for the publishing industry.

Creating letters to sell magazine subscriptions and books is often a special challenge for copywriters because publishers are constantly testing to find a new approach to pull better response than previous efforts. To have your letter become the "control" letter means you've probably done a better job than other top-notch copywriters. If your letter is the control for a long time, your copy has most likely been put to the ultimate test — winning over other versions time and time again.

Top copywriters consider the ultimate achievement as having one of their letters beat a Bill Jayme control package. More often than not, however, a new Bill Jayme letter is what it takes to beat the old Bill Jayme control.

Bill Jayme — in addition to being the one most often singled out by direct mail authorities for top honors — is most distinguished by a single question that appeared on the envelope of a mailing for *Psychology Today*:

> Do you close the bathroom door
> even when you're the only one home?

How could anyone fail to open that envelope? And when they got inside, they found a two-page letter and questionnaire. In this case, the questionnaire is a screening device. As it says on page 3 of the letter, "The more questions you answered with 'yes,' the more you'll like *Psychology Today*." Asking questions in a letter — questions that might be answered the wrong way — can be dangerous. In this case, however, the odds were stacked in the magazine's favor. They knew the kinds of people who would be logical subscribers would give a "yes" answer to the majority of questions, thus "proving" to themselves that they should seriously consider subscribing.

Typical of Bill Jayme letters, this one starts with an interesting story — one that sets the mood for the selling story to follow. And when you get done reading all of the copy, right down to the quotation from Shakespeare at the end, you feel you've been complimented for your intelligence and not just put up with a sales pitch.

psychology today

Portland Place, Boulder, Colorado 80302

Dear probationer:

It happened to a friend who's a teller in a bank on New York's lower East Side.

The woman in the black babushka approached his window, her smile radiating gold teeth, and presented a savings passbook only slightly less worn than her face. She wanted to withdraw twenty dollars.

Our friend counted out two tens, but the woman pushed the bills back. "Is not my money," she said. "My money is fi' dollar size."

Experienced at meeting all kinds, our friend grasped the situation immediately. He replaced the two tens with four fives, and the woman went happily on her way. To her, a bank is a place where they put your money in a drawer. When you want it, they give it back. Since she had always deposited fives, those tens belonged to somebody else ...

... and the point of our story is this. You never really know what's inside people's heads until you have occasion to dig around.

We publish Psychology Today, which is all about people's heads. And we'd like to send you a complimentary copy. But before we do, we'd like permission to dig around a bit in your head. To find out what sort of person you are. To get some idea of whether our magazine is a journal you'll really enjoy.

And so, on the next two pages, you'll find a short psychological quiz. On the last page, you'll get the interpretation. Got a moment now? Feel in the mood? Don't mind? Then take up the enclosed pencil ...

... and GO:

From the Editors of Psychology Today
A COMPATIBILITY TEST
to help determine whether you'll find
our magazine a bore or a boon

	Yes	No
1. When stopping to talk to someone on the street, do you remove your sunglasses?	☐	☐
2. Do you prefer to do your own gift-wrapping instead of using the store's?	☐	☐
3. Have you ever changed your style of handwriting?	☐	☐
4. Do you think nothing of throwing out wilted flowers, but hesitate to discard a plant past its prime?	☐	☐
5. After giving a party, do you mentally keep track of who phones to thank you and who doesn't?	☐	☐
6. Do you often have a desire to be alone, to pursue your own interest and thoughts?	☐	☐
7. When washing windows, do you do the outside first?	☐	☐
8. Are you careful to glue stamps on envelopes right side up?	☐	☐
9. Are you pleased when someone turns up at the party wearing the same thing as you?	☐	☐
10. Have you changed your affiliation from the religion of your childhood?	☐	☐
11. Do you ask other people's children to call you by your first name?	☐	☐
12. Male or female—have you ever changed your hair color?	☐	☐
13. Do you ever go to the movies alone?	☐	☐
14. After you've finished reading the paper, do you put it back together again?	☐	☐
15. Do you, when instructed, write your account number on your check when paying bills?	☐	☐
16. If or when you wear pajamas, do you tuck in the top?	☐	☐
17. Do you turn your dinner plate so the meat faces you?	☐	☐
18. Without looking, can you reel off your social security number?	☐	☐
19. Do you often tell jokes at parties?	☐	☐
20. Do you keep a list of people to whom you send Christmas cards?	☐	☐
21. Do you give your teeth a good scrubbing before you go to the dentist?	☐	☐
22. When the teller has already counted your money twice, do you forego counting it a third time yourself?	☐	☐
23. Do you habitually tip bartenders?	☐	☐

	Yes	No
24. Do you feel awkward talking on the telephone when you're naked?	☐	☐
25. When parking parallel, do you back in whenever possible?	☐	☐
26. Have you ever seriously considered changing your name?	☐	☐
27. When giving a party, do you have a drink before the guests arrive?	☐	☐
28. When the tableware is simply dumped down in front of you, do you place the knife, fork and spoon where they belong?	☐	☐
29. Must all closet doors and dresser drawers in your bedroom be closed before you go to sleep?	☐	☐
30. When using book matches, do you tear out each match in order?	☐	☐
31. When lunching or dining by yourself at home, do you bother to set a place?	☐	☐
32. Do you set out your clothes for the morning the night before?	☐	☐
33. Do you feel guilt when you go to the movies in the daytime?.....................	☐	☐
34. Can you remember what you were wearing the day before last?	☐	☐
35. At the end of a meal in a restaurant, do you re-fold your napkin?	☐	☐
36. Do you usually try to arrive at appointments ahead of time?.....................	☐	☐
37. If it's the last one on the plate, do you hesitate to take it?	☐	☐
38. When leaving a theatre, do you fold up your seat?	☐	☐
39. Are you a collector?	☐	☐
40. Is the fruit you take the one that's just about to go bad?	☐	☐
41. When filling out an application, do you try to answer all questions?	☐	☐
42. Do you close the bathroom door, even when you're the only one home?	☐	☐

```
End of quiz.  Now turn
the page to see what's
been learned about you.
```

<u>Interpretation</u>: Generally, the more questions you answered with "yes," the more you'll like Psychology Today. What we've learned is that you are somewhat adventuresome (changing hair color, religious affiliation). You're concerned about what others think (altering handwriting, doing your own gift-wrap, tipping bartenders.)

You're highly considerate of others (writing in your account number, folding up your theatre seat, arriving ahead of time, putting the newspaper back together.) You're practical (backing in, setting out tomorrow's clothes, eating the one that's about to go bad.)

In short, you're a person who's highly self-aware -- and that's good. Moreover, the fact that you allowed yourself to be tested shows that you're interested in learning more about yourself -- and that's what Psychology Today's all about, as you'll discover from leafing through the enclosed folder.

A monthly magazine that's written for laymen as well as professionals in psychology. A magazine that's a triumph of graphics. A magazine that's as fascinating to read as the palm of your hand. And a magazine that can tell you more about yourself than the conversation when you've just left the room.

Our test also shows that you have a commendable sense of thrift (wanting to save the plant.) And our offer is made to order. Just place the token in the slot on the enclosed order card, place in the envelope and mail -- you'll get back

A COMPLIMENTARY COPY OF THE CURRENT ISSUE

You'll also be reserving the option to buy in at

HALF PRICE

Psychology Today is a dollar a copy -- $12 a year when bought on newsstands or by regular subscription. We'll bill you for only $6. And if you don't like the first issue, just write "Cancel" across the bill, and we're even-steven. You don't owe us a penny, and the sample issue is yours to keep.

"Oh, that you could turn your eyes towards the napes of your necks, and make but an interior survey of your good selves," said Shakespear's Menenius circa 1607. Oh Menenius, that thou wert alive now that we might send you our complimentary copy. What insights! What sapience! What <u>soul</u>!

Cordially yours,

T George Harris
Editor

The Reader's Digest "Two Pennies" Letter

The idea for this classic direct mail package came from the imaginative Walter Weintz, and the unique mailing produced a lot of interesting stories, and was one of the most successful mailings ever used by *The Reader's Digest*. Its unique feature — two bright, shiny pennies showing through a front-of-the-envelope window — is an idea that has been used frequently over the years by the *Digest* and widely copied by hundreds of others.

The envelope, which carried part of a quotation from an ancient Persian poet, led into the letter (written by Frank Herbert). It began:

> An ancient Persian poet said: "If thou hast two pennies, spend one for bread. With the other, buy hyacinths for thy soul."
>
> To buy "hyacinths" for the soul — to nourish your mind and heart with good reading; to become informed, alert, interesting in what you say to others — is just as important as progress in your business or social life.
>
> And it needn't be a task! One compact little magazine — 12 times a year — will stave off mental stagnation, give you something worthwhile to think about and talk about, keep you from being bored — and boring! That magazine is *The Reader's Digest*.
>
> So here (with our compliments) are two pennies for you. We invite you to keep one as your change — and with the other penny, seal the bargain for the finest "hyacinths" you can find anywhere — the next 12 issues of *The Reader's Digest*!

Then came the clincher:

> Just slip one penny into the pocket in the enclosed card, and mail today.

This was one of the early uses of "tokens" to stimulate response — and it worked like a charm.

Most of the stories about the letter concern the pennies. To get the millions they needed, the *Digest* used special freight shipments from the Denver Mint. Walter Weintz was shocked to learn the pennies were going to be shipped to Pleasantville, New York, on open flatbed railroad cars. He envisioned his hoard of pennies quickly disappearing enroute. "But," a Mint official responded, "can you imagine the difficulty someone would have trying to make off with a significant quantity of pennies from a moving railroad train?"

Another frequently repeated story concerns the pennies that were returned to the *Digest*. Because it would cost considerably more than two cents to have undeliverable pieces returned, the *Digest* asked the Post Office to simply destroy the "nixies." But the Post Office said they couldn't legally destroy or dispose of the pennies — and many recipients were sending their pennies back. As a result, the *Digest* found themselves with a warehouse of penny mailings. The *Digest* knew it would cost at least four cents to open each returned envelope to salvage the two pennies inside. The solution to this problem came in the form of the Mt. Kisco Boys Club, which needed money to build a new clubhouse. The mailings were trucked to the Boys Club, and the boys spent many hours opening the mailings, extracting the 50 million pennies that had accumulated, and sorting them into two equal piles.

One pile of pennies was returned to the *Digest* to be reused in future mailings. The Boys Club happily kept the other pile — and soon had their new clubhouse.

The Reader's Digest Association
PLEASANTVILLE, N. Y.
Return Postage Guaranteed

If thou hast
two pennies...

YOURS FOR ONLY $2 - -
The Best in Reading Pleasure for the next Twelve Months!

Dear Reader:

An ancient Persian poet said: "If thou hast two pennies, spend one for bread. With the other, buy hyacinths for thy soul."

Poetry, perhaps; but hard sense as well!

To buy "hyacinths" for the soul -- to nourish your mind and heart with good reading; to become informed, alert, interesting in what you say to others -- is just as important as progress in your business or social life.

And it needn't be a task! One compact little magazine -- 12 times a year -- will stave off mental stagnation, give you something worthwhile to think about and talk about, keep you from being bored -- and boring! That magazine is The Reader's Digest.

So here (with our compliments) are two pennies for <u>you</u>. We invite you to keep one as your change -- and with the other penny, seal the bargain for the finest "hyacinths" you can find anywhere -- the next 12 issues of The Reader's Digest!

Just slip one penny into the pocket in the enclosed card, and mail today. We'll send you the next twelve issues of the Digest -- worth $4.00 -- but we'll send you a statement for only $2.01. Thus you get twelve issues for the price of six -- and you get your change in advance!

This invitation cannot be extended again for at least two years. Therefore we urge you to act at once. Only by taking advantage of this opportunity <u>now</u> can you receive the next TWELVE issues of Reader's Digest for TWO DOLLARS.

Sincerely,

Carolyn Davis

For the Association

CD/MIT

THE READER'S DIGEST ASSOCIATION • PLEASANTVILLE, N.Y.

ADMIRAL RICHARD E. BYRD POLAR CENTER SEVEN-PAGE INVITATION TO JOIN AN AROUND-THE-WORLD EXPEDITION

Nobody reads long letters, right? They do if they are logical prospects for one of the most unusual propositions ever offered through the mails — an around-the-world trip. It took a seven-page letter to provide answers to all the questions before a recipient might be willing to part with the price of the trip: $10,000.

This classic letter was written by Henry B. (Hank) Burnett, Jr. of Santa Barbara, California, and starts right off by mentioning the price — something that is usually kept "secret" until the last few paragraphs:

> As Chairman of the Admiral Richard E. Byrd Polar Center, it is my privilege to invite you to become a member of an expedition which is destined to make both news and history. It will cost you $10,000 and about 26 days of your time. Frankly, you will endure some discomfort and may even face some danger.
>
> On the other hand, you will have the rare privilege of taking part in a mission of great importance for the United States and the entire world. A mission, incidentally, which has never before been attempted by man.

Burnett suggests there may be only two cases where you should emphasize price up front: when your primary selling point is a bargain price and when the price is unusually high. "At some point," he says, "a high price not only establishes value or worth of a thing, but — more important — flatters the reader."

The Admiral Byrd letter is more than just a great letter. It is a classic example of how a great letter alone can do a selling job. The total marketing budget for this project was just $5,000, which ruled out use of the usual four-color brochure included in almost every travel mailing. So Burnett, and his associates, Dick Benson and Christopher Stagg, had little choice but to let the letter do the job. And, thanks to Burnett's challenging copy, this seven-page letter sold out all 60 available seats and raised $600,000 for the Admiral Richard E. Byrd Polar Center.

KIRKLAND 7 9800

EDWARD C. BURSK
SOLDIERS FIELD
BOSTON MASSACHUSETTS 02163

EDITOR
HARVARD BUSINESS REVIEW

Please reply to me in care of:
Transpolar Expedition
Admiral Richard E. Byrd Polar Center
18 Tremont Street
Boston, Massachusetts 02108

September 3, 1968

Mr. Richard N. Archer
121 Corlies Ave.
Pelham, N.Y. 10803

Dear Mr. Archer:

As Chairman of the Admiral Richard E. Byrd Polar Center, it is my privilege to invite you to become a member of an expedition which is destined to make both news and history.

It will cost you $10,000 and about 26 days of your time. Frankly, you will endure some discomfort, and may even face some danger.

On the other hand, you will have the rare privilege of taking part in a mission of great significance for the United States and the entire world. A mission, incidentally, which has never before been attempted by man.

You will personally have the chance to help enrich mankind's fund of knowledge about two of the last earthly frontiers, the polar regions.

I am inviting you to join a distinguished group of 50 people who will fly around the world longitudinally, over both poles, on an expedition which will commemorate Admiral Richard E. Byrd's first Antarctic flight in 1929.

Among the highlights of this transpolar flight - the first commercial flight ever to cross both poles and touch down on all continents - will be stopovers at the American military/scientific bases at Thule, Greenland, and McMurdo Sound, Antarctica.

Because this expedition has the interest and support of much of the Free World, you and your fellow members will be honored guests (in many cases, even celebrities) at state and diplomatic receptions throughout the itinerary. You will have the opportunity to meet and talk with some of the world's important national leaders and public figures, such as Pope Paul VI, the Emperor of Japan, General Carlos Romulo, and many others who are already a part of history.

By agreeing to join this expedition, you will, in a sense, establish yourself in history too. For you will become a Founding Trustee of the new Admiral Richard E. Byrd Polar Center, sponsor of the expedition.

Your biography will be recorded in the Center's archives, available to future historians. The log, photographs and memorabilia of the expedition will be permanently displayed in the Center. And your name will be inscribed, with those of the other expedition members, on a bronze memorial tablet.

-2-

Before I continue with the details of the expedition, let me tell you more about the Byrd Polar Center and the reasoning which led to its establishment this summer.

Located in Boston, home of the late Admiral and point of origin for each of his seven expeditions, this nonprofit institution will house, catalog and preserve the papers and records of both Admiral Byrd and other Arctic and Antarctic explorers.

But the Center will have a more dynamic function than merely to enshrine the past. It will be a vital, viable organization devoted to furthering peaceful development of the polar regions, particularly Antarctica.

It will become, in effect, this country's headquarters for investigation and research into the scientific and commercial development of the poles. The Center will sponsor, support, initiate and conduct studies and expeditions. It will furnish comprehensive data or technical assistance to the United States, or to any university, institution, foundation, business organization or private individual legitimately interested in polar development.

In other words, the Center has set for itself a course which the Admiral before his death endorsed wholeheartedly. He foresaw that mankind would one day benefit enormously from development of Antarctica's vast potential. And he perceived that Antarctica's unique and diverse advantages and resources might best be developed by private capital in a free enterprise context.

The Byrd Polar Center is dedicated to these objectives. And the essential purpose of this commemorative expedition is to dramatize the role that private enterprise - and private citizens - can play in the opening of these last frontiers.

At the same time, the expedition should help prove a few other important points. It should demonstrate the feasibility of shrinking the world through longitudinal navigation. It should also help blaze a trail for commercial air travel over the South Pole. Presently, to fly from Chile to Australia, you must go by way of Los Angeles, even though a straight line trans-Antarctic route would be far shorter.

There is another factor I should mention, one which I think lends a certain urgency to the work of the Center. Development of the polar regions enjoys a high official priority in the Soviet Union - higher, some believe, than in the United States.

The Center's activities can provide a tangible, effective complement to those of our own government, and over the long term, contribute meaningfully to preservation of the Arctic and Antarctic regions for peaceful purposes.

These objectives, I think you will agree, are entirely valid. And important, for the future of humanity. It is for this reason that the inaugural activity of the Byrd Polar Center will be an expedition of such scope and magnitude.

The expedition will be led by Commander Fred G. Dustin, veteran of six polar expeditions, advisor to Admiral Byrd and one of the intrepid group which

-3-

spent the winter of 1934 in Little America on Byrd's Antarctic Expedition II. Commander Dustin is a member of the U.S. Antarctica Committee and President of the Byrd Polar Center.

Considered the ranking American authority on the polar regions, Fred Dustin is probably better qualified to lead this expedition - and brief members on virtually every aspect of the polar regions - than any man on earth. The Center and the expedition are fortunate to have Commander Dustin, as you will discover should you decide to participate.

The flight will be made in a specially outfitted, four-engine commercial jet with lounge-chair-and-table cabin configuration. A full flight crew of six will be headed by Captain Hal Neff, former pilot of Air Force One, the Presidential plane. Special clothing and equipment, such as Arctic survival gear, will be provided by the expedition and carried aboard the plane.

The expedition members will meet in Boston on the evening of November 7, 1968, for briefing and a reception and send-off party with the Governor of Massachusetts, Mayor of Boston, local officials and directors of the Byrd Polar Center. Next day, we will take off, head due north from Boston's Logan International Airport and follow this itinerary (as I have not yet visited all these places myself, I have drawn on the descriptions submitted to me by Commander Dustin and the other experienced people who have planned the expedition):

Thule, Greenland

Far above the Arctic Circle, past the chill reaches of Baffin Bay, lies desolate Thule, the northernmost U.S. air base. Almost 400 miles further north than the northern tip of Alaska, Thule was originally surveyed as a possible military site by Admiral Byrd and Commander Dustin. Here, in the deepening Arctic winter, you will get your first taste of the rigors of polar existence. You will have the chance to inspect the installation and meet the men for whom Arctic survival is a way of life.

North Pole

According to those who have crossed the North Pole, you will completely lose your day-night orientation. Sunrise and sunset can occur within minutes of each other, a strange and unforgettable phenomenon. After Thule, you will cross the geographic North Pole, just as Admiral Byrd did in his pioneering trans-Arctic flight with Floyd Bennett in 1926. A memorial flag will be dropped.

Anchorage, Alaska

After crossing the pole, the plane will bank into a 90° left turn and head south, over the Arctic Ocean and Beaufort Sea, past Mt. McKinley, North America's highest peak, and on to Anchorage. There, you will meet the Governor and key officials.

Tokyo, Japan

The highlight of your stopover in Japan will be an opportunity to meet the Emperor and Premier. (Fishing; excursion to Hakone and Atami by bullet train; tea ceremony at private homes.)

-4-

Manila, Philippines

General Carlos Romulo, the legendary patriot and statesman, an old friend of Admiral Byrd, will give the expedition a warm welcome in Manila. (Folklore performance; hunting for duck, deer, wild boar and a special species of water buffalo; fishing for tuna and marlin.)

You will note that here and elsewhere we have prearranged a considerable amount of hunting, fishing, and so on. These activities are optional. (Members of the expedition will be asked to indicate their preferences 30 days before the flight.) For those who do not want to participate in any of these events, there will be sight-seeing, golf and many other things to do.

Darwin, Australia

Hard by the Timor Sea, tropical Darwin offers some of the world's most superb beaches. You will have time not only to sample the sand and water sports, but to see Australia's great outback. With its spectacular chasms, canyons and gorges, the rarely visited outback is a scenic match for our own West.

Sydney, Australia

You can look forward to an enthusiastic reception in Sydney by the Prime Minister and government officials. For one thing, Australia is on particularly good terms with the United States. For another, Australia has traditionally been in the vanguard of nations involved in Antarctic exploration and development. (Hunting for kangaroo, crocodile, buffalo, wild boar, duck, and geese; or off-shore fishing for rifle fish, salmon, and giant grouper.)

Christchurch, New Zealand

This is our staging point for the flight to Antarctica, and it couldn't be more appropriate. Most of the early expeditions departed from New Zealand, and Admiral Byrd is still considered a national hero there. New Zealand is Antarctic-conscious and its people take almost a proprietary interest in the frozen continent. You will be something of a celebrity in New Zealand, and can expect a thoroughly enjoyable visit while the expedition awaits favorable weather reports from McMurdo Sound. (Deer hunting - where deer are so plentiful that they pay a bounty; fishing for all of the great species of marlin - in an area known for the greatest marlin fishing in the world - also Mako shark.)

McMurdo Sound, Antarctica

I am told that only a total eclipse of the sun is comparable, in emotional impact, to the first sight of Antarctica. Once experienced, neither can be forgotten. If you prove to be like most who have seen Antarctica, you will need somehow, someday, to return. And when you do, the emotional impact will be just as profound. That is what the Antarctic veterans say.

For Antarctica exists well beyond the boundaries of the world you know. You will see there a sun you have never before seen, breathe air you have never before breathed. You will see menacing white mountains towering for thousands

-5-

of feet over a black ocean in which, with luck, you might survive for 45 seconds. You will see the awesome Ross Ice Shelf, as large as France, with its 50 to 200 foot ice cliffs cleaving the sea for 400 miles. You will see the active volcano, Mt. Erebus, 13,000 feet of fire and ice.

And you will see the huts, so well preserved they seem to have been inhabited only yesterday, which Shackleton used in 1908 and the ill-fated Scott in 1911. Antarctica, apparently, is not subject to the passage of time as we know it.

At McMurdo Base, you will meet the military men and scientists who inhabit this strange, alien territory. And you will inhabit it for a while too - long enough to feel its bone-chilling cold, to hear its timeless silence, to perceive, at the very edge of your composure, the terror of its mindless hostility to human beings.

While you are there, you will learn, as few men have ever had the opportunity to learn, about Antarctica. You will learn about survival, but more important, about what men must accomplish to truly open this formidable frontier.

South Pole

Admiral Byrd was the first man to fly over the South Pole. In all of history, probably fewer than 200 men have crossed the pole, by air or otherwise. As a member of this expedition, you will join that select group.

Punta Arenas, Chile

From the South Pole, you will fly to Punta Arenas, on the tortuous Strait of Magellan which separates continental South America from bleak Tierra del Fuego. The visit here will be brief, but you should get some idea of the flavor of this nearly forgotten outpost.

Rio de Janeiro, Brazil

This memorable stopover will include a diplomatic reception. You will also have a chance to relax and sample the sights and sounds of fabulous Rio. (Special plane to Belo Horizonte for hunting boar, duck, jaguar, panther, water buffalo, crocodile and deer.)

Dakar, Senegal

You may never have expected to see Dakar, but you will on this expedition. (Tribal dancing; safari.)

Rome, Italy

No trip would be complete without a stop in Rome, where we will be received enthusiastically. During our stay there we will have a private audience with the Pope.

-6-

London, England

From London, the expedition will fly back across the Atlantic and terminate with a debriefing, critique and farewell dinner in Boston, on December 3.

As mementos of the expedition, you will receive a leather-bound, personalized copy of the log book and a piece of the fabric from Admiral Byrd's original plane, mounted in crystal.

You will also be presented with a framed certificate from the Admiral Richard E. Byrd Polar Center, affirming your appointment as a Founding Trustee and expressing appreciation for your interest in, contributions to and efforts on behalf of the Center and its objectives. In the future, you will be kept fully advised of the plans and activities of the Center, and be invited to participate to whatever extent you wish. And of course, you will have life-long access to the Center's archives and services.

Most important, you will take back with you a once-in-a-lifetime experience. The day may come when journeys to and over the poles are commonplace. But today, the privilege is available to very few.

It is true, I think, that this privilege does carry responsibility with it. By the time you return, you will have received a comprehensive indoctrination course in the polar regions by the world's leading authorities. Your responsibility will be to make the most of the knowledge you will gain, to become an active advocate - perhaps even a disciple - of polar research and development.

It is a responsibility which, I trust, will weigh easily upon you. For once the polar air has been absorbed into your bloodstream, there is no cure. Like others who have been stricken, you will probably find yourself reading every word you can find on the North and South Poles. And, most likely, thinking about your next trip.

But first of all, you must decide about this trip. If you have a sense of adventure, a certain pioneering spirit, and if the prospect of taking part in a mission of worldwide significance and historical importance appeals to you, perhaps you should consider joining the expedition. It is doubtful that you will ever have another chance like this.

Obviously, you can't make a decision of this magnitude instantly. But a word of caution: reservations will be accepted in the order received - a total of only 60, including ten standbys. The departure date, remember, is November 8, 1968, so there is little time to waste.

The price of $10,000 includes food and beverages, all accommodations (the best available under all circumstances) transportation, special clothing, insurance, side excursions - virtually everything except your travel to and from Boston.

Money received will go into escrow at the United States Trust Company in Boston until the time of the flight. To the extent that revenues from the

-7-

trip will exceed costs, the activities of the Polar Center will be accelerated.

To reserve your place in the expedition, just drop me a note on your letterhead or personal stationery, with your deposit check for $2,500, made out to the United States Trust Company. Incidentally, if anything prevents your leaving as planned, you can send another in your place; otherwise, cancellations cannot be accepted later than 30 days before departure.

If you have further questions, please write to me in care of the Transpolar Expedition, Admiral Richard E. Byrd Polar Center, 18 Tremont Street, Boston, Massachusetts 02108.

I hope we may hear from you soon - and that we will welcome you to the expedition.

Sincerely yours,

Edward C. Bursk

Edward C. Bursk

P.S.: We have just made arrangements for a professional camera crew to accompany the flight, and as a result we will be able to provide you with a short film clip and sound tape of your experiences.

THE KIPLINGER WASHINGTON LETTER "BOOM & INFLATION" LETTER

Probably no direct mail letter was used — with only minor changes — longer than Kiplinger's "Boom & Inflation Ahead" masterpiece. It was Kiplinger's control letter for over 35 years, and during that time hundreds of other letters were tested against it — including those written by some of the nation's top copywriters.

This all-time great letter, which may be the most widely circulated direct mail letter ever created, was originally written by Fanny B. Lyle. Although it has been updated annually, Lyle's original concept remains basically unchanged.

In his great book, *Successful Direct Marketing Methods,** Bob Stone uses this letter as a classic example of how his "Seven Steps" formula for direct mail letter writing can be applied.

The underscored heading, "Will There be BOOM and More INFLATION Ahead?" is the first step, setting forth the most prominent benefit.

The next two paragraphs are the second step, enlarging upon the most prominent benefit.

The third indented paragraph is step number three — telling the reader specifically what he is going to get.

The fourth and fifth paragraphs are step number four — proving the value with past experience.

The fifth step — telling the prospect what he will lose if he doesn't act — comes in the sixth paragraph.

Next comes summarizing prominent benefits in the closing offer — step six. And the remainder of the letter is devoted to step number seven — inciting action now.

*Successful Direct Marketing Methods, *Bob Stone. Third Edition. Crain Books, Chicago. 1984.*

STANLEY R. MAYES *ASSISTANT TO THE PRESIDENT*

THE KIPLINGER WASHINGTON EDITORS, INC.
1729 H STREET, NORTHWEST, WASHINGTON, D. C. 20006   TELEPHONE: 298-6400

THE KIPLINGER WASHINGTON LETTER THE KIPLINGER TAX LETTER
THE KIPLINGER AGRICULTURAL LETTER THE KIPLINGER FLORIDA LETTER
THE KIPLINGER CALIFORNIA LETTER THE KIPLINGER EUROPEAN LETTER
CHANGING TIMES MAGAZINE

<u>Will There Be BOOM and More INFLATION Ahead?</u>

The next few years will see business climb to the highest level this country has ever known. And with it...inflation. Not a boom, but steady growth accompanied by rising prices.

Those who prepare NOW for the growth and inflation that lies ahead will reap big dividends for their foresight...and avoid the blunders others will make.

You'll get the information you need for this type of planning in the Kiplinger Washington Letter... and the enclosed form will bring you the next 26 issues of this helpful service on a "Try-out" basis. The fee: <u>Only $16 for the six months just ahead,</u> a savings of almost 24% over the regular rate.

During the depression, in 1935, Kiplinger warned of inflation and told what to do about it. Those who heeded his advice were ready when prices began to rise.

Again, in January of 1946, Kiplinger renounced the widely-held view that a severe post-war depression was inevitable. Instead he predicted shortages, rising wages and prices, a high level of business. And again, those who heeded his advice were able to avoid losses, to cash in on the surging economy of the late 40's, early 50's and mid-60's.

Now Kiplinger not only foresees expansion ahead, but also continuing inflation, and in his weekly Letter to clients he points out profit opportunities in the future...and also dangers.

The Kiplinger Letter not only keeps you informed of present trends and developments, but gives you advance notice of new government policies...political moves and their real meaning...money policy... foreign affairs...taxes...prices...union plans and tactics... employment...wages...anything that will have an effect on you, your job, your personal finances, your family.

To take advantage of this opportunity to try the Letter and benefit from its keen judgments and helpful advice during the fast-

(Over, please)

changing months ahead...fill in and return the enclosed form along with your $16 payment. And do it with this guarantee: That you may cancel the service and get a prompt refund of the unused part of your payment, any time you feel it is not worth far more to you than it costs.

I'll start your service as soon as I hear from you, and you'll have each weekly issue on your desk every Monday morning thereafter.

Sincerely,

Stanley Mayes
Assistant to the President

SAM:kbc

P.S.   Half of all new trial subscribers sign up for 12 months for only $32 -- a significant savings against the regular rate of $42 for 12 months. We'll send you FREE five important Kiplinger Special Reports when you take a 12-month subscription, too. Same money-back guarantee applies -- see details on the enclosed slip.

THE KIPLINGER WASHINGTON LETTER

1729 H Street, Northwest, Washington, D.C. 20006

WILL THERE BE
BOOM & MORE INFLATION
AHEAD?

D HODGSON
POB 46
WESTTOWN PA 19395

(SEE DETAILS INSIDE.)

Barron's "Widow & Orphans" Letter

Another direct mail letter that proved unbeatable in test after test for dozens of years is the "Widow and Orphans" letter used by *Barron's* financial weekly. Although the statistics needed to be changed from time to time, the storytelling opening is a classic:

> Back in 1925, Barron's published an article suggesting how $100,000 might be well invested in securities for a widow with two small children.
>
> The plan was based on a set of ten rules for investors, stated in the article.
>
> The securities (stock and bonds), all picked in accordance with the first seven of the ten rules, are today worth $379,002.
>
> The stocks are worth $330,364 — many times over their original value of $51,000.
>
> Average annual income, for the entire forty-nine years, has exceeded $11,200.
>
> Latest reported income was $21,556.
>
> So here you have to date how a list of securities, compiled in the third year of Calvin Coolidge's presidency, weathered the wild twenties, the woeful thirties, World War II, and the 1969–1971 market plunge — yet without benefit of the important interim supervision provided for in the last three of the original ten rules.

The letter goes on to offer a booklet reprinting the ten rules as an incentive to order a trial subscription. As a general rule, booklets aren't particularly powerful as a premium. But with such a powerful letter opening, hundreds of thousands of new subscribers have eagerly sought the *Barron's* booklet.

BARRON'S
National Business and Financial Weekly • 22 Cortlandt Street • New York, New York 10007

Dear Friend of Barron's:

Back in 1925, Barron's published an article suggesting how $100,000 might be well invested in securities for a widow with two small children.

The plan was based on a set of ten rules for investors, stated in the article.

The securities (stocks and bonds), all picked in accordance with the first seven of the ten rules, are today worth $379,002.

The stocks are worth $330,364 - many times over their original value of $51,000.

Average annual income, for the entire forty-nine years, has exceeded $11,200.

Latest reported income was $21,556.

So here you have to date how a list of securities, compiled in the third year of Calvin Coolidge's presidency, weathered the wild twenties, the woeful thirties, World War II, and the 1969-1971 market plunge - <u>yet without benefit of the important interim supervision provided for in the last three of the original ten rules.</u>

                    *   *   *

We have now reprinted these ten rules in a little Barron's booklet, with interpretative comment on each rule.

As a piece of printed matter, the booklet is slight; takes you but a few minutes to read.

But I believe you will agree, its every word is pure gold.

You'll not only welcome the ten rules for their immediate value. I venture to predict you'll also come back to them re-

                                        (inside, please)

BARRON'S

- 2 -

peatedly in the future -- for their help on your ever-present
problem of safeguarding what you have, and making it grow and
produce for you.

But you can't buy this booklet. It's not for sale.

I would like you to accept it in return for a little
favor I'd like to ask of you -- one that I think will interest you.

*   *   *

Barron's, as you probably know, is a national financial
weekly -- the only one published by Dow Jones, the world's largest,
fastest business news-gathering organization.

By virtue of this close connection -- this day-in, day-out
working contact with Dow Jones' reporters, analysts, editors --
Barron's is an amazingly well-informed publication, continually
surprising its readers with the intimacy and vital investment
significance of its summaries and forecasts of industrial changes,
corporate and government affairs.

Barron's own large staff of experts weighs, sifts,
interprets -- to bring you each week just the information you need
about business and market trends, corporation prospects, the intrinsic values of securities -- clear, concise reports based on
firsthand, intimate knowledge of what's going on.

So you can readily see why Barron's (established 1921)
has become the source and authority for many economists, stock-
market services, investment consultants, and statisticians.

Yet the information for which you pay them high fees is
just as basically available to you in Barron's weekly pages as it
is to them.

I think you'll agree with me we have a honey of a story:

1. A worthwhile saving on what you must pay for financial
    information.

2. Thoroughly reliable data every week -- to guide you in
    the continuous supervision of your investment list --
    in the decisions you make on investment acquisitions
    or sales.

- 3 -

3. Comprehensive weekly trend reports -- political, industrial, financial -- to help you plan your investment moves with greater understanding and foresight -- with fewer worries -- with added peace of mind.

But you know how "funny," how unpredictable, people are. You can never be sure of their reactions until after you have spent a great deal of money to find out. That is, unless you test first.

Which brings me to the favor I want to ask of you.

Before we sink a lot of money into mailing thousands of circular letters to the large key groups of prospective new readers we have in mind, we come to you as a representative prospect.

Will you do this:

Merely try Barron's -- and judge the information in it for scope, brevity, reader interest, and practical money value.

See what you get on stock market trends, bonds, mutual funds -- "growth" stocks -- situations to consider for income -- securities to stay out of or sell now, because of serious weakness.

Compare Barron's with any other financial-information service, or combination of services, costing from $50 to $150 a year, or more. (Barron's costs $25 a year.)

Under this special trial arrangement, you pay ONLY OUR SHORT-TERM INTRODUCTORY PRICE, $6.25 for 13 WEEKLY ISSUES (3 months). You'll save 35% from the newsstand cost.

If Barron's does not live up to your expectations, will you send us a brief note giving us your frank and honest opinion of it?

Whether you become a Barron's enthusiast or not, we shall genuinely appreciate your part in this test.

Of course, you understand, if your participation is to be of value to us in deciding our coming mailings to the key groups, your immediate response is necessary.

- 4 -

Will you, therefore, check the accuracy of your name and address on the enclosed card and return it to us today in the accompanying self-addressed envelope that requires no postage?

Thank you for your help.

Sincerely yours,

Brian Olson

for Barron's

BJO:br
Encs.

P.S. When Barron's arrives, be sure to examine "The Market Week". It's conveniently located in the middle of each issue. This unique ready reference covers prices, earnings and dividends of ALL stocks traded on New York and American Stock Exchanges -- with conspicuous symbols signalling all new dividend declarations or omissions and all new earnings. Weekly range and other statistics. Also quotations on all more active stocks on the major U.S. regional exchanges, the leading Canadian exchanges, and over 1,500 Over-the-Counter quotations -- all with earnings, dividends, year's high and low. No other service like it anywhere!

Today is history. Tomorrow is
BARRON'S

HIGHLIGHTS FOR CHILDREN "HAPPY FACES" LETTER

The annual Christmas gift subscription promotion package, developed by the late Chris Stagg for *Highlights for Children* magazine, is a third long-running classic direct mail letter. Actually, the entire mailing package is classic.

The original envelope had this teaser:

> FREE happy buttons enclosed with an enduring Christmas idea for
> your favorite youngster.

The back window of the envelope featured a sheet of 12 orange-and-black self-adhesive stickers — 11 of them with "happy faces," and the 12th marked "yes." The letter inside the package tied everything together and featured a classic beginning:

> Share the enclosed happy face buttons with a favorite young friend
> or two . . . compliments of *HIGHLIGHTS FOR CHILDREN*.
>
> But please send the one marked YES to us.
>
> Place it on the enclosed special Christmas gift form; fill in the names
> and addresses of your favorite youngsters — and you'll be giving
> them far more than a charming, enduring, year-round present.
>
> You'll be giving them a head start in life.

The folder inside the package tied in with the "Happy Face" theme. The cover was illustrated with one of the happy faces and the copy read:

> This Christmas, help your favorite youngsters smile all next year!

The order form had a marked space in which the recipient was asked to place the "Yes" sticker. Such action devices often substantially increase response to mailings.

There's something about a stamp or token that arouses curiosity. The first thing they know, the recipients have detached the action device and are holding it in their hand. Now, what do you do with it? As Walter Weintz says, it's like a "hot potato." You can't just hold it. You have to do something with it. Many do exactly what they've been instructed to do — place the stamp or token in a marked place on an order form or card.

I call such devices an easy first step. People take the suggested action without having decided to order what is being offered, but the action has begun and inertia is now in your favor. As Chris Stagg's letter said:

> Send the one marked YES to us.

A postscript at the end of the letter added a nice closing touch:

> P.S. The happy buttons enclosed symbolize our wish for you and
> yours this holiday season. There is, of course, no obligation on

your part. They're our gift to you, in the hope that you'll decide
to say YES and give *Highlights* to a young friend or two.

The mailing package remained relatively unchanged for many years, except for the addition of a second window on the face of the envelope where a second sheet of happy face stickers could show through.

Dear Reader:

Share the enclosed happy face buttons with a favorite young friend or two ... compliments of HIGHLIGHTS FOR CHILDREN.

But please send the one marked YES to us.

Place it on the enclosed special Christmas gift form; fill in the names and addresses of your favorite youngsters -- and you'll be giving them far more than a charming, enduring year-round present.

<u>You'll be giving them a head start in life.</u>

You'll help them develop reading habits and attitudes toward learning that will benefit them as long as they live -- and aid their steps toward intellectual maturity while providing fun along the way.

A miracle?

No. HIGHLIGHTS FOR CHILDREN -- a concept, a plan, a proved method that gives children fun with a purpose. Please let me explain:

All children <u>enjoy</u> learning, until some adult stops the fun. Children's minds question, examine, become curious about everything they do not know or understand. Even babies want to learn by touching everything. And you must say "NO!" to a hot stove, of course. With the pressures of today's fast-paced world, even some well-meaning adults say "NO!" to a child's curiosity.

"Why? " children ask. Perhaps over and over and over again.

But they really want to know. And Highlights can help.

Help you provide your favorite youngsters with active, constructive learning, prepared by deeply concerned and experienced teachers and child psychologists ....

Help you solve the annual Christmas problem, in a day of transitory values, by giving the fun-filled gift that lasts all year long ....

Help you prove -- even to preschoolers -- that reading is fun and worthwhile, too ....

Help you teach the values you yourself hold dear: self-confidence, manners, thoughtfulness ....

All of a sudden, children are grown.

And then what? Where have they gone, what's happened to the lost opportunities to help make minds more attuned to intellectual achievement and an awareness of lasting values? The direction children take is determined very early in life -- and you have the privilege of helping to forge mature, responsible citizens.

Perhaps it's best said in the words of Highlights' Chairman (a former school principal, by the way):

"Having done one thing well, children do all things better."

You know it's true, because you've probably lived through the experience yourself. The problem, often, is to get children to do a thing well, to appreciate that they have, and then to want to repeat the experience.

As the enclosed folder shows, fun-filled issues of Highlights can help -- regardless of a child's age, from two to twelve.

*   *   *

If you believe your favorite youngsters deserve Highlights' helping hand, the enclosed shopping list provides the answer.

Say "Yes" (by sticking the proper button into place) and you'll be activating a series of happy surprises:

1. A gift announcement that you can sign as you wish will be provided with each subscription you order -- if you order early. (We will send you an acknowledgment/invoice confirming your order.) If your order is not received early enough, we'll send an announcement to the children in your name.

2. The first issue of HIGHLIGHTS FOR CHILDREN will follow shortly, jammed with fun and learning for all children -- interesting, fun-to-know, useful information.

3. Then, throughout the whole year, your favorite children will be reminded of you as a fresh, new issue of Highlights arrives -- addressed to each child, given by you.

*   *   *

Some additional facts about the magazine may provide reasonable reassurance, and they're contained in the accompanying brochure. You may wish to look it over now.

But it's worth repeating that Highlights' pages are uninterrupted by advertising. Frankly, I don't believe we could have achieved more than 2,000,000 enthusiastic parent and teacher subscribers if they were. And, as far as I know, there's no better gift for the price.

You need not pay for your gift subscriptions until after the holiday season, if you prefer. Remember, too, that one gift of

Highlights takes care of a whole family of children. A bargain by any standard.

Think about it now, won't you? So many gifts are given to children in haste or last-minute desperation. So few last beyond the moment, much less the season.

You have the chance to do better. Just think about your favorite youngsters, then say YES to Highlights.

They ... and you ... will be glad you did.

Sincerely yours,

Garry C. Myers
President

GCM:jh

P.S. The happy buttons enclosed symbolize our wish for you and yours this holiday season. There is, of course, no obligation on your part. They're our gift to you, in the hope that you'll decide to say YES and give Highlights to a young friend or two.

The world's most honored children's magazine

SERVICE	BROTHERHOOD	SAFETY	PATRIOTISM	ALL-AMERICA
National Association for Gifted Children **Certificate of Merit**	National Conference of Christians and Jews **Certificate of Recognition Brotherhood Award**	National Safety Council **For Exceptional Service to Safety**	Freedoms Foundation at Valley Forge **For Promoting the American Way of Life**	Educational Press Association of America **All-American Award**

2300 West Fifth Avenue / P.O. Box 269 / Columbus, Ohio 43272-0002

PZL-L5

Mercedes-Benz of North America "Americans Won't Buy It" Letter

In the mid 1970s, it wasn't a problem convincing car buyers to consider a diesel automobile. But back in 1965, the problem seemed insurmountable. Mercedes-Benz of North America had imported nearly 3,000 190Ds, and with the selling season nearing an end, had sold only 1,237 of them. At that time, there were only 2,300 diesel fuel stations throughout the U.S. (compared to over 200,000 gasoline stations). The car was extremely noisy, had only four cylinders, and barely reached 78 miles per hour on the open road. It sold for $4,068 — just $800 less than a Cadillac.

Moreover, Mercedes-Benz would soon introduce the new Model 200 to replace the 190D, and it was going to sell at a lower price. The challenge of preparing a promotion to quickly move the 1,500 diesels was presented to Ogilvy, Benson & Mather's direct mail group.

Ed McLean, then head of OBM's direct mail group, remembers:

> Dealers in both American and foreign cars had entered the traditional clean-up period before new model introductions in the most overstocked condition in history. By the time the direct mail package was mailed, big discounting had already started. But to preserve the Mercedes-Benz image, we had to sell this $4,068 car at full list price.

Of course, in the tradition of automobile advertising, the first thing the agency did was create an impressive, full-color brochure. Right? Wrong! In what was perhaps one of the most courageous moves in direct mail history — particularly for an agency that had just taken on the prestigious Mercedes-Benz account — they simply mailed a five-page letter signed by Heinz C. Hoppe, CEO of Mercedes-Benz of North America. But it was far from an ordinary letter: It invited recipients to test-drive a 190D, and included a classic offer:

> I will pay for all fuel, all motor oil, all oil filters, and all lubrications on the new Mercedes-Benz 190 Diesel for the first 15,000 miles you drive it.

The letter then utilized this unique offer to emphasize a key selling point — the car's economy:

> No other manufacturer of a full-size 4-door sedan in the entire world could afford to make this offer.

> I can make it because the Mercedes-Benz 190 Diesel averages over 30 miles per gallon of diesel fuel — and diesel fuel costs 1/3 less than gasoline in many states.

> In fact, the 190 Diesel regularly saves its owners more than 50 percent on fuel costs alone.

Interestingly, the budget for the entire direct mail campaign, which had as its objective to sell over $6 million in cars, was just $100,000. The first mailing went out on July 12, and, before September 1, it sold out all the remaining 1,500 190Ds and produced a substantial increase in sales of other Mercedes models.

MERCEDES-BENZ OF NORTH AMERICA, INC.

CABLE: MERCEBENZ FORT LEE
TWX: FORT LEE 201 947-5922
OVERSEAS TELEX: 23 01 2351
DOMESTIC TELEX: 01 2351

158 LINWOOD PLAZA
P.O. BOX 318
FORT LEE, NEW JERSEY 07024

HEINZ C. HOPPE
CHIEF EXECUTIVE OFFICER

July 12, 1965

Dear Sir:

"Forget it, Heinz," the experts told me. "It just won't sell here."

They were talking about the Mercedes-Benz 190 Diesel -- a car that is owned and driven daily by over 500,000 people overseas.

"Americans won't buy it," said the experts. "Why pay $4,068 for a German car with a noisy engine when for $891.37 more they can get a Cadillac?"

I had reason to believe the experts were wrong.

Some Americans have paid $4,068 for this German car with the "noisy engine."

As a matter of fact, if it wasn't for the "noisy engine" many of these Americans wouldn't have found out about the car. While in Europe, they saw Mercedes-Benz Diesel cars and noticed the noise made by the engine. Fascinated, they asked questions.

And what they learned from European drivers up and down the high-speed Autobahns convinced them the Mercedes-Benz Diesel is a great car.

As for the noise, they found it does sound different from a gasoline engine. In fact, a few people may give the car a second look as you idle at a traffic light. But you won't be bothered by the sound above 25 miles per hour. Some 190D drivers report they actually enjoy the unique

- 2 -

sound of the Diesel. Many owners tell me, "If it didn't make a little noise, people wouldn't know it's a Diesel!"

Mr. John J. Gray of Albany, Oregon is one of these owners.

He travels all over the western U.S. for his firm, Kashfinder, Inc. In the past 7 years, he has driven his Mercedes-Benz Diesel car 652,000 miles.

"652,000 miles is a long ways to drive one car," writes Mr. Gray. "It has taken me 7 years -- during which my faithful Mercedes-Benz Diesel has run more efficiently and far more cheaply than any car I have ever owned. And the car still doesn't rattle..."

Recently, we asked other Mercedes-Benz Diesel car owners in America:

"If you had it to do all over again, would you buy another of these automobiles?"

Before I tell you their answers, I'd like to reveal what I learned from the U.S. Automobile Manufacturers Association. I asked them how many Americans buy the same make and model of car they owned previously. They told me that fewer than four out of ten do.

Yet, when we asked our Mercedes-Benz Diesel car owners in America if they would buy another Mercedes-Benz Diesel, better than nine out of ten said YES.

The experts were wrong about these Americans. But one question remains unanswered for me.

How many other Americans want a great motorcar?

I'll soon know the answer.

You -- and a small number of others -- have been selected to receive the most unusual offer ever made by a car manufacturer.

I will pay for all fuel, all motor oil, all oil filters, and all lubrications on the

- 3 -

new Mercedes-Benz 190 Diesel for the first 15,000 miles you drive it.

This offer is from Mercedes-Benz of North America. It is not from your Mercedes-Benz dealer. It will not affect your trade-in or terms in any way. I feel certain you will like this car and will help me spread the word about it.

That's why I can offer you all fuel free. All motor oil free. All oil filters free. All lubrications free. All are yours free for the first 15,000 miles you own and drive your new Mercedes-Benz 190 Diesel.

No other manufacturer of a full-size 4-door sedan in the entire world could afford to make this offer.

I can make it because the Mercedes-Benz 190 Diesel averages over 30 miles per gallon of diesel fuel -- and diesel fuel costs 1/3 less than gasoline in many states.

In fact, the 190 Diesel regularly saves its owners more than 50 per cent on fuel costs alone.

And, like all Mercedes-Benz cars, the 190 Diesel is so finely machined it uses scarcely any motor oil.

That's not all.

The 190 Diesel never needs a tune-up. It has no carburetor to adjust or replace. No spark plugs, no points, no condensers, no distributor.

Mechanics will tell you that many cars need a new set of rings after 75,000 miles.

John Gray -- the Diesel owner in Oregon -- reports his car didn't need a ring job until after it had gone 275,000 miles!

Even crack mechanics are surprised by that.

We build the Mercedes-Benz 190 Diesel so that, with normal care, it will last for hundreds of thousands of

- 4 -

miles -- long after most of today's cars are chopped up for scrap!

We give it 7 coats of paint, <u>inside</u> and out.

We install special safety locks on all doors -- the same locks used on the Grand Mercedes 600 that sells for $20,291.

We equip it with two separate braking systems. If something happens to one system, you can stop with the other.

Most new cars are not built for high-speed panic stops. The car's wheels will pull to one side or the other. The back end swerves.

<u>The disc brakes on the Mercedes-Benz 190 Diesel bring it to an emergency stop from 80 mph -- in a straight line. There's no swerve. No fade. You are in control every foot of the way.</u>

Other car makers bolt the body on. We weld it. Welding guarantees a tighter, firmer body structure -- with less chance of annoying rattles.

We also give the 190 Diesel the same suspension system with independent rear axles that we use on the famous Mercedes-Benz 230SL sports car. (The 230SL sells for $6,239.)

All in all, we spend hundreds of dollars extra to make the Mercedes-Benz 190 Diesel a great motorcar. That's why we must place a price tag of $4,068 on it.

I personally believe that when you try it, you will agree: it's well worth the price.

Why not let me put one at your disposal?

Drive it as you would your own car. Put it through the paces of city and highway traffic. Try it on hills. See how it takes curves. Test its disc brakes, its 4 forward speeds -- or the optional 4-speed automatic transmission. (The only one of its kind in the world.)

I'm so confident you will want one of these remarkable automobiles, I will pay you for <u>all</u> fuel, <u>all</u> motor oil,

- 5 -

all oil filters, and <u>all</u> lubrications for the first
15,000 miles you drive your new Mercedes-Benz 190
Diesel.

So please accept my invitation to drive a 190D and
reach your own personal, private judgment. Simply
return the enclosed card in the postage-free envelope.
I will also send you a special brochure called "The
Amazing 190D."

My offer expires Monday, August 16, 1965, and is limited
to the first 1,000 people who respond. I hope you take
advantage of it. Thank you.

Yours truly,

Heinz C. Hoppe
Chief Executive Officer

HCH/a

Old American Insurance Company "Empty Shoes" Letter

Although most leading direct mail letter writers don't accept the old Chinese proverb, "One picture is worth more than ten thousand words," there are times when a picture makes such a strong point it becomes the starting point for a letter.

This was the case with a classic letter that has been used for many years by Old American Insurance Company. It was the last letter Max Ross wrote before leaving the company to go into consulting work nearly 20 years ago, and is still used for certain applications today.

It showed a well-worn pair of shoes accompanied by an enlarged typewriter type heading:

> This is an ordinary pair of shoes. They could belong to anybody —
> but suppose they were yours?

The copy goes on to say,

> Empty shoes — you no longer here. Who would pay the bills that
> always arise when someone departs this world? Would those you
> leave behind have the money to do it? Or would they have to scrimp
> and save — and do without things they need — for months, perhaps
> even years, after you have gone, just to get these bills paid off?

Imagine how much less impact those words would have if there hadn't been that worn pair of shoes helping to make the point.

But the letter is classic for more reasons than just its unique illustration. Max Ross is considered by many to be the guru of effective direct mail letter writing. He is a strong believer in using what he calls "a bucket brigade" through the copy — joining together paragraphs through the use of connecting links. As you read the letter, note these connectors:

> "To help you do this . . ." "What you do next . . ." "Remember . . ."

> "Here is another thing that's important to you." "Of course . . ."

> "Now — here is an added feature. So — let me ask you . . ."

This is an ordinary pair of shoes.
They could belong to anybody-BUT...

...SUPPOSE THEY WERE YOURS?

...Empty shoes-you no longer here. Who would pay the bills that always arise when someone departs this world? Would those you leave behind have the money to do it? Or would they have to scrimp and save-and do without things they need-for months, perhaps even years, after you have gone, just to get these bills paid off?

Dear Friend of Old American:

I know that you have indicated in the past that you <u>are</u> interested in insurance. But now I want to ask you a pointed (and perhaps undiplomatic) question:

<u>"Are you satisfied with what you have done about it?"</u>

I'm sorry if that question seems blunt. However, you CAN take a positive step -- <u>and you can do it right now</u>:

You can apply for an OLD AMERICAN $1,000 life insurance policy -- and keep it in force after your application has been approved.

This will provide $1,000 for your family to help take care of funeral expenses and other bills there is just no way of stopping.

It can be mighty difficult for your family when you are gone. You have provided for them to the best of your ability all along the way. They have appreciated it. There is no reason why they shouldn't keep right on appreciating you when you are gone -- remembering that you at least gave them a chance to start out even with the board.

-- please turn page --

-2-

If you died tomorrow, there could be all kinds of bills:

    — Doctor bills for final sickness
    — Hospital bills for related expenses
    — Funeral services
    — Burial lot and monument
    — Unpaid taxes
    — Regular unpaid monthly accounts

— and the list doesn't stop there!

Wouldn't it be comforting to your family if you had made arrangements in advance to help take care of these expenses?

To help you do this, we here at Old American want you to have this introductory rate for our $1,000 life insurance policy:

THE FIRST MONTH'S COVERAGE FOR ONLY $1.00

What you do next is turn to the application and fill it out — and then mail it as soon as possible with your introductory payment of $1.00.

When your application is approved, you will be insured for $1,000 on the introductory term basis. Then, when your first regular premium is paid, your policy begins on the whole life plan and builds up cash values over the years.

You can use these cash values in a lot of different ways. If you have to borrow money, you can do so against your policy (at a reasonable rate of interest, too).

Or you could apply the cash value on a smaller paid-up life insurance policy.

Here is another thing that's important to you. You don't have to go see a doctor and take a medical examination. You do fill out a statement of health on the application — and since the company only issues policies to people in good health, it does reserve the right to check out the statement should a claim come up in the first two policy years (but the company has this right only during those first two years). Pre-existing conditions are not covered during the first two policy years, but are covered from then on. Like most other companies, we don't cover suicide within the first two years.

Now — here is an added feature.

-3--

In the case of common carrier accidental death (which is always sudden and unexpected), the policy will pay an extra $1,000 — a total of $2,000 altogether. Death need not occur immediately, but at any time within 60 days from the date of the accident.

Of course, defining this type of benefit is sometimes difficult, so that is why we would like to explain it here in language closely following the actual policy provisions.

The policy pays $2,000 instead of $1,000 if death is caused solely by accidental bodily injuries which are sustained while (as a fare-paying passenger) the insured is riding in, entering, or alighting from any conveyance engaged at that time as a licensed common carrier of passengers.

Of course, this additional benefits provision will not apply if such death is caused or contributed to by any mental or bodily sickness, disease, or infirmity; by war or any act incident to war; or while the policy is in force as paid-up or extended term insurance.

This is just one of the many features of your Old American policy that make it so valuable — that will 'help fill your shoes and pay the bills when you are gone.

There is our story.

If this letter has seemed like a lot to read, it's because there is a lot to say.

But with it is a way for you to spare your family some of the tears and heartaches and sorrow that your death would cause.

You do know the value of insurance. You are interested in your family's welfare.

So — let me ask you once again — are you satisfied that you have done enough?

Remember — there is no such thing as a second chance after you are gone. What you do for your family, you must do now — not tomorrow, not next week, not next year — BUT TODAY!

— please turn page —

-4-

That's why I hope you'll take the time to fill out your application and send it off today — while you have this handy form in front of you.

You will always be glad you did.

Sincerely,

Joseph J. McGee
President

JM:dp
Enc: L997

P. S.   Because we are from the "Show Me" state of Missouri, let us "Show You" that this policy is everything we say it is by making this money-back guarantee of your introductory term payment if you are not completely satisfied.

No doctor will have to examine you when you apply

One of the many reasons policyowners find it easy to do business with Old American is because they are not required to go to a doctor and take a medical examination.

You must be in good health, of course, when your policy is issued. Because the company, as is customary, does require that you be in good health at that time, it reserves the right to further verify this fact in the event of death within 24 months after the policy is issued. (Note that the company has this right only during the first two policy years.) We DO care about your state of health, but as a matter of convenience to you, we do not require you to have a medical examination.

OLD AMERICAN INSURANCE COMPANY

4900 OAK STREET • KANSAS CITY, MISSOURI 64141

Games Magazine "Connect the Dots" Letter

The major advantage of direct mail as an advertising medium is that it is "the personal medium." Yet far too few users have taken advantage of the opportunities to add a personal touch to their mailings. Experience has shown the use of personalization can substantially increase response by 100% or more. Appropriately used, personalization generally will increase response from customer lists by an average of 30–35% and 20–25% from prospect lists.

Many direct mail users, however, confuse "personalization" and "personal." The best personalized letters do not try to trick the recipient into thinking the letter has been created "just for him." Instead, the techniques of personalization are used to — in effect — say, "You were specially selected to receive this mailing."

The majority of users of personalization have simply inserted the recipients' names into letters. While, in some cases, this may be enough to produce increased response, it doesn't represent the most effective use of personalization.

Consider, for example, this classic personalized mailing from *Games* magazine. A large window at the top of the envelope had a series of dots with consecutive numbers. The teaser message said, "Connect the dots and discover a surprise from *Games* magazine! Gift pencil enclosed." Any real prospect for *Games* could hardly resist the connect-the-dots challenge. And when the envelope was opened, the dots were there at the top of the letter, which started:

> Go on . . . connect the dots . . . and share the fun we had designing this puzzle just for you.
>
> And that's what GAMES magazine is all about — to fascinate you, tease you; involve you in something entirely different . . . to help keep your wits sharp and your mind buzzing with fresh ideas . . . to entertain and delight you for hours on end.
>
> You see, Richard Hodgson, GAMES magazine isn't a magazine you just read. It's a magazine you play.

There was other personalization in the letter, but the thing that made this letter such a classic was that when you connected the dots with the enclosed pencil — they spelled out your name! The computer programmer who created the dot structure to spell out each recipient's name was Bob Chelius, and he gets my applause for one of the most effective personalization techniques I've yet seen.

GA475

Get out your pencil and connect the dots.

HODGSON

A COPY OF
GAMES
MAGAZINE
HAS BEEN RESERVED IN YOUR NAME

Richard S. Hodgson
P. O. Box 46
Westtown, PA   19395

Dear Richard Hodgson,

Go on ... connect the dots ... and share the fun we had designing this puzzle just for you.

And that's what GAMES magazine is all about -- to fascinate you, tease you, involve you in something entirely different ... to help keep your wits sharp and your mind buzzing with fresh ideas ... to entertain and delight you for hours on end.

You see, **Richard Hodgson**, GAMES magazine isn't a magazine you just read. It's a magazine you **play**.

OPEN THE COVER AND DIVE IN!

Start with some puzzles from our 16-page **Pencilwise** section. Page after page of word games, number games, puzzles, riddles, anagrams, ciphers and logic games.

Try our **Eyeball Benders** -- where you guess the object from a photograph or just a piece of it ... **Beguilers** -- optical illusions that push your powers of observation to their uppermost limits -- or **Mappit** -- where we take a familiar shape and disguise it. (For instance, you probably can envision the outline of **Pennsylvania** -- but could you if it was upside down and backwards?)

Or take a chance with a **Wild Card** -- a bewildering (and always challenging) collection of brainteasers designed to drive you bananas. Plus ...

CROSSWORDS ... CROSSWORDS ... CROSS
W
R
D
Some of our readers just can't seem to get enough good ones -- so we carry several in every issue. There are right-angle crosswords and double acrostics, Kreuzwortratsel (a delightfully illustrated German version) and The World's Most Ornery Crossword Puzzle that contains two sets of clues -- one hard, one easy.

CONTESTS WE WANT YOU TO ENTER -- AND WIN!

If your competitive juices flow every time you see a contest, you'll want to enter the two terrific ones we have in every issue -- some submitted by our readers themselves -- that **everyone** has an opportunity to win.

And if you are a winner, you'll receive a valuable prize like a pinball machine, videocassette recorder, moped or camera. Runners-up get GAMES T-shirts. And everybody has a good time, win or not.

NEW GAMES ... OLD GAMES ... AND GAMES YOU MAKE UP

You'd expect us to have a chess corner and a backgammon column (and of course we do) -- but have you played **Wari**, the oldest game in recorded history ... **Senet**, the favorite board game of young King Tut ... or **Surakarta**, found literally scratched in the dust on the East Indian island of Java? Every issue brings you the rules and board layout -- as well as the fascinating history and romance -- of a bygone game.

Or get up to date and -- play Pop Dice, where every roll of the dice is another note in an original melody you compose ... **The Jungle Game**, an oriental board game where the object is to eat (that's right, eat!) as many of your opponent's pieces as you can before he eats yours ... and **Eleusis**, a riotous card game that changes every time you play because you make up a new secret rule with each hand!

AND THE FUN'S NOT OVER YET!

What was the name of Tonto's horse ... who was the chief engineer of Star Trek's Enterprise? Try a trivia quiz and refresh your memory. Or do your own sleuthing from photo clues supplied in our popular **Photocrimes.**

In short become one of our 600,000 subscriber fanatics who can't wait for their next jam-packed issue to arrive. Like them, you'll soon be whipping out your copy on trains, busses and planes -- on coffeebreaks and lunch hours, doing something challenging, rewarding and enjoyable by yourself or matching wits with your friends or family.

DON'T BE LEFT OUT OF THE GAME -- SUBSCRIBE TODAY!

Just take your pencil and check off "YES" to the attractive offer we're making to new subscribers.

So, send for the current issue and see for yourself if GAMES isn't the most exciting new magazine you've seen in a long, long time. Then, if it's not everything you expect (and more!) just write "cancel" on your bill.

Simply detach and mail the personal Reservation Form on the front of this letter today. We'll send you your first issue of this very special magazine to **play with** and enjoy, risk free!

Cordially,

Chip Block

Connect the dots and discover a surprise from **GAMES** magazine!

gift pencil enclosed

Richard S. Hodgson
P. O. Box 46
Westtown, PA   19395

BULK RATE
U.S. POSTAGE
PAID
GAMES
MAGAZINE

THE NATURE CONSERVANCY "DEVIL" LETTER

Direct mail letters aren't written to pull fan mail. In most cases, they are designed to bring in orders, contributions, or inquiries. But one of the classic membership solicitation letters of all time — the so-called "Devil" letter of The Nature Conservancy — not only produced spectacular results for its intended purpose and new memberships for The Nature Conservancy, it also pulled hundreds of fan letters praising the great copy.

Interestingly, it almost didn't get mailed. Frank Johnson, who wrote the copy, tells the background:

■ The then president of the Conservancy thought the letter was entirely too frivolous and refused it. So Tom Beers, who was serving as the Conservancy's advisor, said he'd sign it and mail it, which he did, and nothing anybody — including me — tried for three years afterward could touch its pull.

The package had an intriguing message on the envelope:

Join us and
the devil
to buy some
soggy real estate.

The letter inside began:

Dear Investor,

The devil we'd like you to join in a realty deal with us is the she-devil in "Anna Christie," Eugene O'Neill's great old play. Poor Anna's father, seadog Christopher Christopherson, knew who had dashed their hopes: "Dat ole davil, sea, sooner, later, she swallow dem up." (Act II.)

Now. Here's how you join us and dat ole davil in a fantastic real estate deal: a string of 18 barrier islands protects the east shore of Virginia's Delmarva Peninsula, the finger of land that forms the outer edge of Chesapeake Bay. Lovely beaches, millions of birds, glorious scenery.

"Ah!" said our 19th century, entrepreneurial ancestors. "It's Beulah land!" So they built hunting lodges, then big resort hotels, even a town called Broadwater. Coney Island, Miami Beach — you name it — were on their way . . .

Enter the davil, swallowing. Broadwater is under the Atlantic. Hurricanes and waves splintered the hotels. The sea keeps patting up a sand spit here, gulping down a dune there, growing salt marshes, spawning fish. Perfect places to lay an egg, raise a fox kit, have a fawn. But the developers' hopes and prices sank.

So we bought 13 of these islands. They're now the Virginia Coast Reserve: owned, protected and managed for the sea and its rich progeny by The Nature Conservancy.

Share the deal with us, won't you?

The islands cost four and a half million. But you can buy a bit of them — and 2,812 other parcels of land, just as wild and splendid — for less than you'd spend on half a barrel of light crude, delivered direct to your tank or crankcase from OPEC. Just $10. Tax deductible. Doesn't that suggest it's time you knew us, if you don't already?

Nothing startling about these well-turned phrases. But aimed at the right audience, they were powerful. Frank Johnson observes:

■ Direct mail doesn't have to raise its voice to be persuasive, or be semi-literate to be friendly, or be solemn-serious to be believed.

The fan mail (and memberships) his letter pulled proved it.

Two enclosures with The Nature Conservancy's "Devil" letter are worthy of special notice. The first was announced by a typewritten note below the address window on the envelope:

(Do not fold. Bumper sticker enclosed.)

Enclosed, of course, was a self-adhesive bumper sticker. This relatively low-cost enclosure added a special dimension to the package and subtly conveyed this thought: of course the recipient would want to become a member of The Nature Conservancy. This is an idea that has been widely copied by others.

Also enclosed was a lift memo. It had a picture of an owl on the outside, with the heading: "If a deal with the devil doesn't appeal to you . . ."

Copy inside read:

It also happens we can make you another offer — one that the devil wouldn't have thought of on the best day he ever had.

Up for grabs are six hazy, lazy, legendary river valleys — with fish . . . black bears . . . eagles . . . some Florida panthers . . . alligators . . . towering first growth hardwood forests . . . and more kinds of birds and rare plants than you'd find in most national forests.

Right now the Conservancy has first crack at this marvelous opportunity . . . but we need your help if generations of Americans are to enjoy and benefit from it.

And there are other offers. The last mid-Atlantic maritime forest — Nag's Head Woods on North Carolina's outer banks. Seriously endangered rain forests and bird varieties in Hawaii. Grassland ecosystems that are unique to Texas and provide habitat for species that live nowhere else in the United States . . . perhaps nowhere else in the world.

Take your pick. Choose a favorite. But whatever you do, please help. We need your $10, and all that comes with it. Your interest, your concern, and your voice. Because we've noticed that when the many voices of the Conservancy speak up, people listen and good things happen.

We need that. We need you. Please join us today.

To give a "second voice" to the mailing, this lift memo was signed by William D. Blair, Jr., president of The Nature Conservancy.

 1800 North Kent Street, Arlington, Va. 22209

```
Join us and

the devil

to buy some

soggy real estate.
```

(Do not fold.   Bumper sticker enclosed.)

Membership Director
Nancy C. MacKinnon

The Nature Conservancy

1800 North Kent Street
Arlington, Virginia 22209

Dear Investor,

The devil we'd like you to join in a realty deal with us is the she-devil in "Anna Christie," Eugene O'Neill's great old play. Poor Anna's father, seadog Christopher Christopherson, knew who had dashed their hopes: "Dat ole davil, sea, sooner, later, she swallow dem up." (Act II.)

Now. Here's how you join us and dat ole davil in a fantastic real estate deal: a string of 18 barrier islands protects the east shore of Virginia's Delmarva Peninsula, the finger of land that forms an outer edge of Chesapeake Bay. Lovely beaches, millions of birds, glorious scenery.

"Ah!" said our 19th-century, entrepreneurial ancestors. "It's Beulah land!" So they built hunting lodges, then big resort hotels, even a town called Broadwater. Coney Island, Miami Beach -- you name it -- were on their way....

Enter the davil, swallowing. Broadwater is under the Atlantic. Hurricanes and waves splintered the hotels. The sea keeps patting up a sand spit here, gulping down a dune there, growing salt marshes, spawning fish. Perfect places to lay an egg, raise a fox kit, have a fawn. But the developers' hopes and prices sank.

So we bought 13 of these islands. They're now the Virginia Coast Reserve: owned, protected and managed for the sea and its rich progeny by The Nature Conservancy.

Share the deal with us, won't you?

The islands cost four and a half million. But you can buy a bit of them -- and 2,812 other parcels of land, just as wild and splendid -- for less than you'd spend on half a barrel of light crude, delivered direct to your tank or crankcase from OPEC. Just $10. Tax deductible. Doesn't that suggest it's time you knew us, if you don't already?

The Nature Conservancy is a non-profit conservation organization -- with a difference. Like most conservation groups, and I hope like you,

-2-

we feel it's urgent to preserve what we can of the world's natural balance before human kind wobbles it too far.

But we don't sue or picket or preach. We simply do our best to locate, scientifically, those spots on earth where something wild and rare and beautiful is thriving, or hanging on precariously.

Then we buy them.

We're good at it. In just over three decades we've acquired -- by purchase, gift, easement and various horse trades -- Rhode Island, twice over: some 1,800,000 acres, scattered over 2,800 spots, from Panama to every one of our 50 states to Canada and back to the Caribbean.

Our taste, like nature's, is catholic. Recently we've acquired and protected eleven islands in the Potomac River, and two off California: huge Santa Cruz, and little Castle Rock -- 14 acres that serve as airport and motel for 100,000 birds, as well as a hauling-out site for seals and sea lions. We got AMTRAK to agree not to tamper with 4 miles of right of way near Kalamazoo which contain 15 threatened or rare plants. Want a rare plant site? Yours, for $10.

We outbid several land developers at an outdoor auction to buy 145 lovely, wild acres just 55 miles southwest of Chicago. For a dollar a year, a big paper company agreed to protect a golden eagle nesting spot it owns in the Adirondacks. A utility, at our request, detoured a power line around a sanctuary in the Big Thicket area in Texas -- then gave us their right of way. We've bought a few Oregon acres to save a tiny butterfly; thousands of Texas marsh acres -- winter refuge for arctic peregrine falcons and whooping cranes. Save a crane. $10.

Do we keep all that property? No. We deed or lease or sell much of it to various government bodies and educational institutions which can promise (with appropriate legalities) to preserve it, as is, with public access, for all caring people. But we also administer much of it ourselves and maintain 720 natural area sanctuaries, with or without partners. You can be a stewardship partner. For $10.

We have some 300 expert employees, from canny lawyers to Ph.D. ecologists, with offices in San Francisco, Minneapolis, Boston and Arlington, Virginia. There are 35 active Nature Conservancy chapters in 29 states. Look in your phone book, or call me: (703) 841-5388. I'll tell you if you're near enough to drop in on a chapter for a warm welcome, or to visit one of our sanctuaries, for soul warming. Tell your friends it's yours, for $10.

I know you're near enough to several of our properties, wherever you live or vacation in the U.S.A., to get to them easily. Take the family,

-3-

a date, or a child if you have one handy. (The wild land will still be there when the child grows up.)

Look for such things as Henderson's fawn lily, black-crowned night herons, the beaked dodder, twig-rush, cinnamon teal, Table Rock (can't miss it; towers 700 feet over the Rogue River). Every one is rare or threatened. But it's safe under our wing.

That jaunt will heighten your interest in other Nature Conservancy programs. For example, we're well along on an enormous, on-going inventory of the "natural elements" in 29 states. These "State Natural Heritage Programs" help the states (and all conservationists) identify their unique or invaluable and rare plants, locales, animals, birds, bugs, whatever natural resources or wonders need help.

Another example:

We have to date raised $29,000,000 for the Land Preservation Fund. And because we can stretch a dollar like you wouldn't believe, we expect that revolving $29,000,000 to protect $200,000,000 worth of land in the next decade. Watch us stretch your $10.

But if we're wallowing in $29,000,000, why do we need you? Because you'll be one of about 134,000 of us, and that's a pile of tens. Because we urgently need your informed interest in our work. We need your curious ear and intelligent voice.

We'd like to hear your ideas, use your volunteer services when you have time, know that you're with us.

To keep in touch, we'll send you THE NATURE CONSERVANCY NEWS every other month. It's a compact (no ads, 32 pages), strikingly illustrated magazine. Every issue has several well informed articles on some aspect of the lands we're working to save: from the ecology of America's deserts to what goes on in a rain forest. (Lots.)

These issues describe our newest projects, invite you to join any of our well-led tours of the properties, keep you up-to-date on your fellow members. You'll also receive bulletins about our projects in your area, chapter meetings and so on. We won't send you a lot to read. We will give you many opportunities to have some adventures, meet some bright and friendly people -- and buy land, with us.

Please join us, right now. Like this:

Tick and initial the "Membership Application" form that's right in front of you. Remove, sign and pocket the attached Interim Membership card. Mail

-4-

the form with or without your $10 check (Glad to
bill you later, but be sure to write "Tax deductible" on your check stub).

That's it, you're in. Put the oak leaf sign on your bumper, boat,
bike, poolside. Quite a few people who count will recognize it and
smile benignly. Watch for your welcoming kit in a few weeks: your
permanent membership card, and a handsome decal. And shortly, your first
issue of THE NATURE CONSERVANCY NEWS. You're automatically a member of
a Nature Conservancy chapter in your state if we have one. (If we don't
yet -- there's an idea for you.)

Welcome, Dear Fellow Conservationist. You've just made a devilish
good bet that we may still save our ark.

Thank you.

Sincerely,

Nancy C. MacKinnon

Nancy C. MacKinnon
Membership Director

NCM/cv

**The
Nature
Conservancy**

1800 North Kent Street
Arlington, Virginia 22209

Dear Friend:

It also happens we can make you another offer -- one that the devil wouldn't have thought of on the best day he ever had.

Up for grabs are six hazy, lazy, legendary river valleys -- with fish ... black bears ... eagles ... some Florida panthers ... alligators ... towering first-growth hardwood forests ... and more kinds of birds and rare plants than you'd find in most national parks.

Right now the Conservancy has first crack at this marvelous opportunity ... but we need your help if generations of Americans are to enjoy and benefit from it.

And there are other offers. The last mid-Atlantic maritime forest -- Nag's Head Woods on North Carolina's outer banks. Seriously endangered rain forest and bird varieties in Hawaii. Grassland ecosystems that are unique to Texas and provide habitat for species that live nowhere else in the United States ... perhaps nowhere else in the world.

Take your pick. Choose a favorite. But whatever you do, please help. We need your $10, and all that comes with it. Your interest, your concern, and your voice. Because we've noticed that when the many voices of the Conservancy speak up, people listen and good things happen.

We need that. We need <u>you</u>. Please join us today.

Cordially,

William D Blair

William D. Blair, Jr.
President

AMBASSADOR LETTER-BROCHURE COMBINATION

Although a separate letter and brochure often works best in a direct mail package, there are times when the two can be combined for special impact. A classic example is a six-page letter-brochure combination, created by Robert Hanford, which worked exceptionally well for Ambassador in both the United States and Europe. The product is Ambassador's Super Organizer ladies' handbag, which is distinguished by a host of special built-in features. To try to explain the features of the handbag with words alone would have been difficult. But by combining illustrations that normally would have been used in a separate brochure with the words of the letter, the product's benefits came through loud and clear. Bob Hanford's letter begins:

> I hate a messy pocketbook. But I've always had to carry one. My handkerchief . . . my compact . . . credit cards . . . checkbook . . . all jumbled up in the bottom of my handbag, no matter how carefully I tried to keep them neat.
>
> But for the last few weeks I've been carrying an entirely new kind of purse. The SUPER ORGANIZER. I designed it myself, here at Ambassador's headquarters. And the difference is amazing. No more mess . . . no more fumbling for things . . . I'm sudddenly a well-organized woman again! And I love it.
>
> The secret? Very simple. The SUPER ORGANIZER gives you a place for everything you carry . . . so you can find anything in just three seconds. Your sunglasses . . . your department store charge cards . . . your keys . . . or the picture of your children. Anything!
>
> I'd like to send you one.

Then, step-by-step, the letter covers each of the many features of the Super Organizer with steadily flowing letter copy illustrated with inset photographs. One example of how a photograph helps supplement letter copy is a paragraph about the bag's special strap:

> . . . We know that the strap is the weak point on most bags. It's the strap that gives first.
>
> And so we've developed a "piggyback" strap. Here's what it looks like. Two straps sewn together. That gives super-strength. And it looks just great!

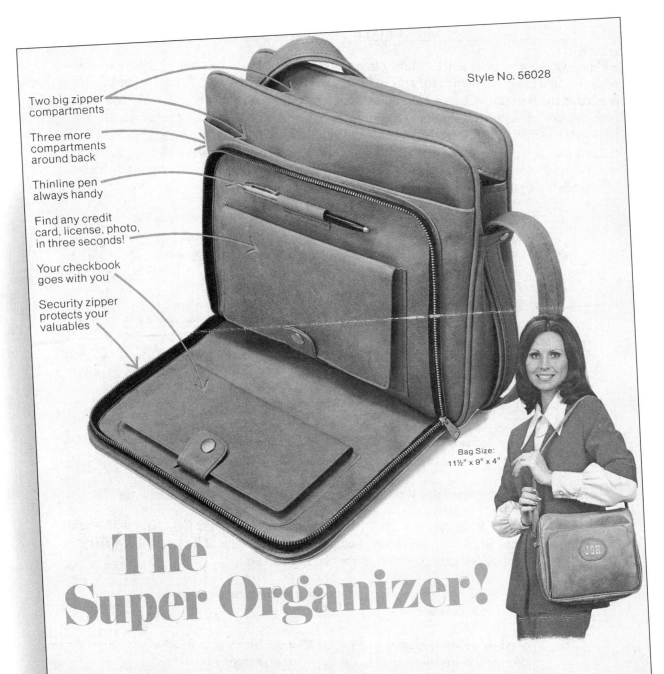

Style No. 56028

Two big zipper compartments

Three more compartments around back

Thinline pen always handy

Find any credit card, license, photo, in three seconds!

Your checkbook goes with you

Security zipper protects your valuables

Bag Size: 11½" x 9" x 4"

The Super Organizer!

Dear Friend,

I <u>hate</u> a messy pocketbook. But I've always had to carry one. My handkerchief...my compact...credit cards...checkbook...all jumbled up in the bottom of my handbag, no matter how carefully I tried to keep them neat.

But for the last few weeks I've been carrying an entirely new kind of purse. The SUPER ORGANIZER. I designed it myself, here at Ambassador's headquarters. And the difference is amazing. No more mess...no more fumbling for things... I'm suddenly a well-organized woman again! And I <u>love</u> it.

The secret? Very simple. <u>The SUPER ORGANIZER gives you a place</u>

<u>for everything you carry</u>...so you can find anything in just three seconds. Your sunglasses...your department store charge cards...your keys...or the picture of your children. Anything!

I'd like to send you one.

I'll send it to you on a 30-day no-risk trial, so you can see yourself just how lovely and useful it is.

But first let me show you everything that your SUPER ORGANIZER will do for you.

<u>We start off with a "security" compartment</u>

We call the first part of the bag the "security" compartment. It's the secret of how the SUPER ORGANIZER works. There's nothing like it in any other bag <u>ever</u> made. The front flap opens and -- presto -- there are your credit cards, your checkbook, and a pen all ready for you.

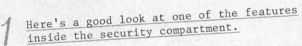

1 <u>Here's a good look at one of the features inside the security compartment.</u>

Just imagine a trim little magazine with "pages" made up of tough, transparent pockets. You slip 16 -- or more -- credit cards, photos, or licenses into the pockets...and there they are! Always available, always ready.

For me, this is a wonderful feature, because I carry so much. I have three gasoline cards... a library card...my Arizona driver's license... a bank card...credit cards from three department stores... and lots of pictures of my children. They are all on display in my organizer, and I can find anything I want in a second or two.

And the organizer section can be removed to make its own little wallet, complete with currency compartment and snap-fastener. Whenever I go out in the evening or want to switch handbags, I simply remove the organizer and pop it into the purse I want to carry.

Next, there's a checkbook holder.

I like to carry a checkbook when I go shopping. And so I designed a checkbook holder right in the SUPER ORGANIZER. The front flap of the security compartment opens down to make a little "desk" for you to write your check on.

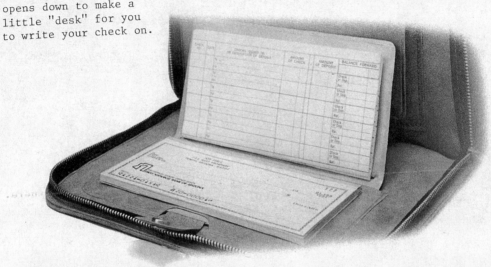

You can see this feature in the photo. You can see how it opens up, and how both the checkbook and the check register are right there together. That's important for me, because my husband gets upset when my checking account doesn't balance. With the register there, I never forget to record every check.

I designed the checkholder, by the way, to hold either the top-bound or side-bound checkbooks. Whichever you have, they'll fit. And, as you see here, the checkbook holder also can be removed for carrying in another purse.

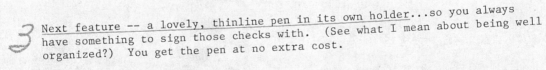 Next feature -- a lovely, thinline pen in its own holder...so you always have something to sign those checks with. (See what I mean about being well organized?) You get the pen at no extra cost.

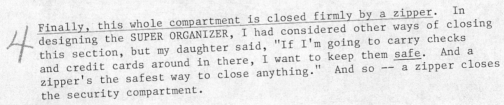 Finally, this whole compartment is closed firmly by a zipper. In designing the SUPER ORGANIZER, I had considered other ways of closing this section, but my daughter said, "If I'm going to carry checks and credit cards around in there, I want to keep them safe. And a zipper's the safest way to close anything." And so -- a zipper closes the security compartment.

Now...let's talk about the other compartments. I love a bag with lots of compartments, and so the SUPER ORGANIZER has plenty.

First off, there are two nice, big, roomy middle compartments. Each of them is closed with a zipper.

The first one carries my beauty aids. Make-up, comb and brush. Kleenex. Handkerchief. All stashed away nice and neat. The photographer put a scarf in it so you can see it at right.

The other compartment gets important papers, receipts, savings stamps, letters, and so on. (My daughter calls it "valuable junk.")

There's a side utility pocket built into this middle compartment. (The photographer can't figure out how to show it to you.) I keep my keycase there.

And that's important! I hate to stand out by my front door after an evening shopping trip, fumbling down somewhere in the bottom of my purse for my keys. Now I know exactly where they are.

Three more compartments around back

On the back of the SUPER ORGANIZER you'll find three more compartments -- open ones.

There's a big one that I designed so you could put a scarf and gloves into it. Another that's just right for cigarettes (if you smoke). And still another that I made to carry my glasses.

Straps are a problem...so I designed a special strap

We expect the SUPER ORGANIZER to be the most useful pocketbook you've ever owned. You'll carry it everywhere...and sometimes you'll load it as full as you can.

Well, we know that the strap is the weak point on most bags. It's the strap that gives first.

And so we've developed a "piggyback" strap. Here's what it looks like. Two straps sewn together. That gives super-strength. And it looks just great!

In addition, I made the strap adjustable, so you can use the SUPER ORGANIZER either as a shoulder bag or as a handbag, whichever you prefer.

(Please turn over...)

-4-

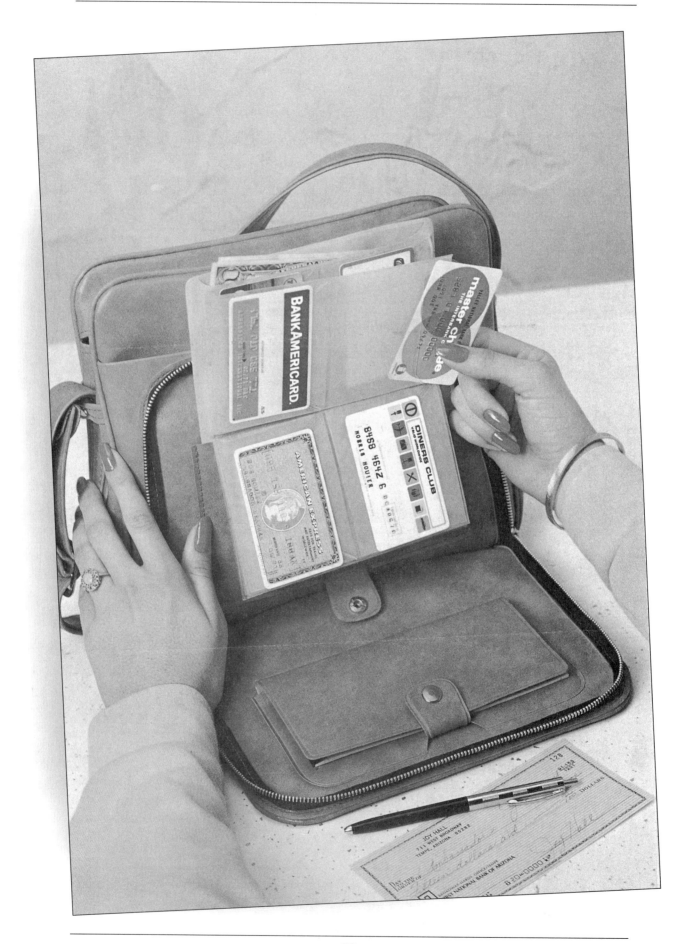

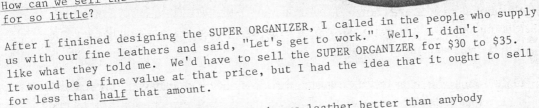

<u>As a final touch...your three initials</u>

There's something nice about initials on a
purse -- and so we supply yours at no cost
at all. Here you see them, full size.

<u>How can we sell the SUPER ORGANIZER
for so little?</u>

After I finished designing the SUPER ORGANIZER, I called in the people who supply
us with our fine leathers and said, "Let's get to work." Well, I didn't
like what they told me. We'd have to sell the SUPER ORGANIZER for $30 to $35.
It would be a fine value at that price, but I had the idea that it ought to sell
for less than <u>half</u> that amount.

So I turned to my husband, Murray. <u>He</u> knows leather better than anybody
I've ever seen.

"Leather?" said Murray. "I know a <u>vinyl</u> we ought to use. It's beautiful,
it's sturdy, and it's long-wearing, too. Won't scuff and scar like leather,
either. And it costs half what leather costs."

Well, that's what we did. Made the SUPER ORGANIZER up in a vinyl that's
absolutely terrific! Strong and beautiful on the outside, neat and easy to clean
on the inside, with a faille grain vinyl lining.

And the price? Just $12.98. (Plus a charge for shipping and handling.)
I want you to see the SUPER ORGANIZER, handle it, wear it and enjoy it for thirty
days. Then, if you like, send it back and I'll repay every cent.

But please -- as a favor to me -- get your order in right away. Our supply of
these wonderful purses is limited...and I'd hate to disappoint you. Best time
of all is right now, when you're thinking of it.

                    Cordially,

                    Joy Hall

                    Joy Hall

Desert Bone   British Tan   Cocoa Brown   Black

Ambassador

711 West Broadway/Tempe, Arizona 85282

75-5050

©Ambassador International 1975
Division of Amba Marketing Systems, Inc.

THE FIRST BAPTIST CHURCH "ORGAN" LETTER

An even shorter letter than the *Reader's Digest* "Two Pennies" letter is perhaps the greatest fund-raising letter of all time. It was written for The First Baptist Church of Dayton, Ohio, by a member of the Direct Marketing Hall of Fame, John Yeck. He tells this story about the letter:

■ I'm not a member of The First Baptist Church, though some of my friends are. One of these was cochairman of a committee to raise $80,000 for a new church organ.

He and the committee thought that would be easy enough. They first identified every substantial giver to the church. They broke down the $80,000, decided how much each member could be expected to give, divided the pledge cards among the committee members, and went calling.

Only trouble was, after they'd exhausted their lists, they had managed to raise a little less than $50,000. So they called and asked me to prepare a series of three letters to go out to the "rest" of the congregation.

The first of these letters was the classic "organ" letter. It brought in $40,000 — more than enough to finish paying for the organ, and eliminating the need for the two follow-up letters originally planned. It also won the cherished Gold Mailbox award from the Direct Marketing Association, and was circulated and reprinted all over the country. But this additional circulation hasn't pulled a single additional penny for The First Baptist Church's organ fund.

"There's nothing surprising about that," John Yeck says. "These admirers of the letter wouldn't have sent any money if they had received the letter when it was originally mailed. The correct mailing list for this letter was made up of members of The First Baptist Church, as no one else was likely to be affected. That's the way it is with mailing lists. You'd better have the right people on them."

Excellent advice for anyone using direct mail letters for any purpose.

THE FIRST BAPTIST CHURCH

DAYTON, OHIO 45402

Director of Music
DONALD L. LEHMAN

Organist
MADONNA WINE GOSS

Ministers
RICHARD B. HARDY
OTIS I. LANDIS
BRENTON C. DODGE

Nothing gives like a church organ.

It gives joy at weddings; strength at funerals; family greetings at baptism. It gives wings to worship; power to praise; humility to thanksgiving. It gives rest to the weary; welcome to strangers; binding ties to friends.

It gives to congregations of sons who follow fathers and then give way to sons and sons again.

It finally gives itself.

For over five generations the present church organ at First Baptist has given, freely, generously, bounteously without stint.

Think of an organ's gifts, as you have received them; as your children will in days to come.

Then give to a church organ, like a church organ, ... freely, generously, bounteously ...

without stint,

David E. Detrick
Chairman, Board of Trustees

Mrs. J. H. Hornbeck
Chairman, Organ Committee

MONUMENT AVENUE AT LUDLOW STREET, DAYTON, OHIO 45402   TELEPHONE (513) 222-4691

THE FRANKLIN MINT "100 GREATEST BOOKS" LETTERS

When the history of direct marketing in the twentieth century is written, chances are the greatest single success story will be the mailing used by The Franklin Mint to enter the book publishing field. With just a single mailing to two lists — The Franklin Mint's customer file and American Express's merchandise buyers list — this classic package sold $110,00,000 worth of product.

Few organizations have ever devoted so much time, talent, and energy into fine-tuning letter copy. At The Franklin Mint, it's a committee effort. Many of the country's top copywriters and marketing executives add collective input to make sure every word, every sentence, and every paragraph works to its maximum.

It's been said that a camel was a horse produced by a committee, and most committee-produced letters are about as sleek as a camel. But thanks to a great copy chief, Ed Trautman, and marketing staffs who understood the need for smooth-flowing copy, Franklin Mint letters always ended up in the hands of a skilled copywriter and copy editor for a final polishing that smoothed out the rough edges created by the multiple voices of the committee.

Because the typical Franklin Mint collectible was a highly visual product, an elegant full-color brochure nearly always was part of the mailing. Yet letters were considered so important that many mailings had not one, but two letters. Such was the case in introducing the highly successful "100 Greatest Books" collection.

The first letter, which The Franklin Mint called an "imprimatur letter," was used to introduce the basic selling letter. This is a valuable technique when the seller doesn't have established authority in a given field. Turning to someone with established authority and using an introductory letter to "transfer" authority to the seller permits the selling to get right into the sales story without a lengthy introduction to convince the reader the message is worthy of attention.

For this mailing, there were two imprimatur letters. The one to The Franklin Mint's customers was signed by Charles Andes, president of The Franklin Mint. It began:

> As an established Franklin Mint collector, you know how satisfying it is to collect things of beauty in precious metal.
>
> In the accompanying letter, you will learn about another form of collecting — one which can be equally rewarding. The collecting of fine books.

The other letter, used for the portion of the mailing going to American Express merchandise buyers, was signed by James A. Lancaster, an American Express vice president. It began:

> What I believe will be the finest collection of books published in a lifetime is described for you in the accompanying prospectus from The Franklin Library. The Franklin Library is the publishing division of the world-famous Franklin Mint.

> I am extremely pleased to tell you that arrangements have been concluded to make this unique collection available exclusively to American Express Cardmembers and established Franklin Mint collectors.

With these imprimatur letters laying the groundwork, the basic selling letter from The Franklin Library, signed by Robert Vincent O'Brien, publisher, was able to get right into the job of selling:

> Dear Collector:
>
> Soon a very limited number of people will begin to acquire a private library of the one hundred greatest books of all time — in the most beautiful edition ever published.
>
> The books in this extraordinary private library have been selected by a distinguished international board of scholars. And, as is appropriate to a collection of this importance, each volume will be produced with the utmost luxury — fully bound in genuine leather and ornamented in 24 karat gold.

When the mailing went out, several of my friends in the publishing field suggested we had embarked on perhaps the greatest folly in all of publishing. "Imagine," they laughed, "being so naive as to think you can get people to pay several thousands of dollars to buy a collection of 100 books . . . and you don't even tell them what the titles or who the authors will be."

But their laughter died quickly when this single mailing made The Franklin Mint one of the world's largest book publishers overnight. Thanks to the dedicated effort of a hard-working committee, it was determined that the kind of collector The Franklin Mint was serving would rather own a collection selected by "a distinguished international board of scholars" than build a collection on their own. If the 100 titles had been announced, many of the buyers would likely have concluded they already owned some of the titles so it would be impractical to add duplicates to their libraries.

Bob O'Brien's letter concluded:

> Because you have a collector's instinct and an appreciation of fine things, owning this private library has many rewards. There is, of course, the pleasure of great literature. Beyond that, the satisfaction of providing a cultural heirloom for your family — and the ownership of what may well become a most valuable and sought-after collection.

THE FRANKLIN LIBRARY

FRANKLIN CENTER PENNSYLVANIA 19063

Dear Collector:

Soon a very limited number of people will begin to acquire a private library of the one hundred greatest books of all time — in the most beautiful edition ever published.

The books in this extraordinary private library have been selected by a distinguished international board of scholars. And, as is appropriate to a collection of this importance, each volume will be produced with the utmost luxury — fully bound in genuine leather and ornamented in 24 karat gold.

Each book in the collection will be unique in itself. The color and grain of the leathers will vary. The pure gold cover designs will all be different. The paper, typography and illustration will be distinctive. Even the sizes of the books will vary throughout the collection.

Yet together, "The 100 Greatest Books of All Time" will comprise a complete and harmonious collection — the kind of library that would be difficult to assemble even if you were a rare book collector with unlimited time and resources.

Unlike ordinary volumes which are printed in many editions, the books in this collection will be published in <u>only one edition</u>. The limit of that edition will be determined by the exact number of subscribers to the collection, and the books will be custom-printed and bound <u>solely</u> for those who subscribe. The collection will not be available through book dealers, nor will the volumes be sold individually.

Furthermore, the only people being invited to acquire this collection are established collectors of The Franklin Mint and American Express Cardmembers. No one else will ever be invited to subscribe. And there will never be another edition of "The 100 Greatest Books of All Time."

There is no need to send any payment now. Your subscription will be acknowledged and you will be notified when you can expect to receive the first volume.

A subscriber may discontinue his subscription at any time upon thirty days' notice. May I point out, however, that once your subscription is discontinued it can never be reinstated — and your private library can therefore never be complete.

Because you have a collector's instinct and an appreciation of fine things, owning this private library has many rewards. There is, of course, the pleasure of great literature. Beyond that, the satisfaction of providing a cultural heirloom for your family — and the ownership of what may well become a most valuable and sought-after collection.

Please remember that your application for "The 100 Greatest Books of All Time" must be postmarked by March 31st.

Sincerely,

Robert Vincent O'Brien
Publisher

RVO: 1tb

THE FRANKLIN MINT

FRANKLIN CENTER PENNSYLVANIA 19091

Dear Collector:

As an established Franklin Mint collector, you know how satisfying it is to collect things of beauty in precious metal.

In the accompanying letter, you will learn about another form of collecting — one which can be equally rewarding. The collecting of fine books.

This letter is signed by the publisher of The Franklin Library, a new division of The Franklin Mint which we have established to revive the great tradition of publishing limited-edition collections of fine books in superb bindings.

The first such collection, "The 100 Greatest Books of All Time," is described in the enclosed prospectus. I bring it to your attention because I believe it may well be the most beautiful collection of books to be published in our lifetime.

"The 100 Greatest Books of All Time" is being offered by invitation only. Because you are a Franklin Mint collector, I think you may be particularly interested in collecting books of this quality and importance.

If you wish to become a subscriber, your application must be entered by March 31, 1974. I therefore suggest you give it your immediate attention.

Sincerely,

Charles Andes

Charles Andes
President

CA:1tr

AMERICAN EXPRESS COMPANY · BROADWAY, NEW YORK, N.Y. 10004

JAMES A. LANCASTER
VICE PRESIDENT

January 2, 1974

Dear American Express Cardmember:

What I believe will be the finest collection of books published in a lifetime is described for you in the accompanying prospectus from The Franklin Library. The Franklin Library is the publishing division of the world-famous Franklin Mint.

I am extremely pleased to tell you that arrangements have been concluded to make this unique collection available <u>exclusively</u> to American Express Cardmembers and established Franklin Mint collectors.

The collection, "The 100 Greatest Books of All Time," is being offered by invitation only. The books will be published and printed <u>solely</u> for those who become patrons. Therefore, it will be an exceptionally limited edition, a very rare acquisition and, in my opinion, the finest private library one could own.

If you wish to become a patron, your application must be entered by January 31, 1974. May I suggest that you give it your immediate attention.

Sincerely,

James A. Lancaster
Vice President, Card Division
American Express Company

JAL:laa

BRECK'S PERSONALIZED CATALOG WRAPS

One of the earliest users of computer personalization on catalogs was Foster & Gallagher, Inc. In the heyday of novelty merchandise catalogs, their Foster House and Hellen Gallagher catalogs regularly featured many unique forms of personalization. In the early days of personalization, primary emphasis was on inserting the name of the recipient in a piece over and over again. Today, however, the most effective personalization involves far more than simply repeating a recipient's name. Foster & Gallagher was one of the first to make maximum use of multiple elements of personalization.

Interestingly, most of the elements of personalization come directly from zip codes. With readily available programs, the zip code could trigger insertions of city, county, area, and state. One of the more difficult jobs was locating two pairs of well-known cities for each of the 50 states — one north-to-south, the other east-to-west. This alone would have been simple, but the space available for these state-by-state personalizations permitted a maximum of 20 characters for each pair.

Breck Holland, B.V.

Pastoorslaan Rood
Hillegom, The Netherlands   WILLEM H. DEE
MANAGING DIRECTEUR

Dear Mrs. Wyman:

I'd like to share with you a secret that has been bringing pleasure to Massachusetts families for many years.

Ever wonder how some of your neighbors in Elandford seem to do nothing special and yet have a garden just bursting with Spring Beauty...a floral display seemingly transplanted by magic from Holland's finest gardens?

Chances are many of these beautiful Spring displays do have a touch of Dutch Magic...and you'll find the secret of this magic in the enclosed Breck's Holland Bulb Book.

Last year 301 of your Springfield area neighbors received a similar catalog and decided to give their gardens a touch of Dutch Magic by ordering Holland Bulbs from Breck's. And throughout Massachusetts, 32,893 gardeners placed their trust in our "Selected for Beauty" bulbs.

The "magic" offered by Breck's is not really mysterious...particularly in Hampden County, where soil and weather conditions are generally ideal for growing our carefully selected top quality Dutch Bulbs.

In Massachusetts --
from Boston to Holyoke --
Breck's gardeners have long favored Breck's Colossal Daffodils.

From Lee to Gloucester --
our daffodils for naturalizing bring beauty to the countryside. (See pages 54-70 for big savings on all of our special daffodils.)

You'll also find savings of as much as 50% on Tulips, Hyacinths, Crocus, Iris and other prize Dutch Bulbs.

All of Breck's Bulbs come from the top 5% grown in Holland. Only 1 of every 20 bulbs meets Breck's tough standards. And each bulb is backed by our time-honored guarantee:

If, for any reason, you aren't completely satisfied, Breck's will give full refund, replacement or exchange anytime up to July 31, 1977!

You don't have to send a single cent now. We'll bill you when your bulbs arrive at proper Fall planting time in Massachusetts.

Willem H. Dee

Thompson Cigar Company "15 Rivers To Cross" Letter

Some years ago, story-telling direct mail letters were quite common. But in this "Age of Skepticism," they frequently fail to win in copy tests against straightforward selling letters. Perhaps prospects are suspicious of a proposition that is introduced with a long story, or, perhaps they prefer TV for stories and want printed copy to get to the point (or it may be that great storytellers are all writing for TV today).

Whatever the reason, lengthy stories in direct mail letters often lead to reduced sales. But not so for the Thompson Cigar Company. Among the great direct mail letters are several created by John Lyle Shimek for Thompson. Consider this classic letter that explains the reason for the story:

> I used to think that the only way to have a real adventure anymore was to be an astronaut or something. But that was before my recent trip to the Hidden Valley in Honduras, where the alluvial soil is six feet deep and everybody and his brother carries a six-shooter for bandit insurance.
>
> Maybe you thought I just sit around writing letters to my good customers and wrapping cigar boxes to take to the Post Office.
>
> Not so. You don't get the best tobacco settin' at home on your resources. And, believe me, you don't always find the comforts of home elsewhere.
>
> Sometimes I wonder why I'm in this business at all — and why I go all over Hell's half-acre to insure my supply of good tobacco. Yet if I didn't go right down to the tobacco farms and check the crops for myself, I'd never be able to offer you the cigars I do. And I certainly would never have found the priceless bales of wrapper I brought back from my last trip to Central America.
>
> And I never would have been able to come up with a superior cigar like the Granada, either — a cigar that was born of first-hand, on-the-spot adventure in the kind of country I didn't know existed any more.
>
> Getting to the Hidden Valley of the Jalapa River is like going through boot training in the Marines all over again — only rougher. There are 15 rivers to cross and only 7 bridges. We had to ford the streams with four-wheel drive jeeps to get around down there — and the locals had to build a special airport to fly their tobacco crops out to civilization.
>
> I was tracked by a jaguar, avoided the embrace of an amorous boa constrictor, was jeered at by monkeys and stared at by a suspicious mountain lion. I ate the eggs of the baby dinousaur (that's what they call their iguanas) and they were delicious. I sampled the dinosaur meat, too, and it's even better than the eggs.

I was even stopped and frisked as a suspicious character by the local gendarmerie. And when I asked them why they carried both six-shooters and shovels, they carefully explained their "six-by-six" justice to me. When they find a bandit, they use the six-shooter first — then the shovel to put him six feet under. It's civil rites, instead of civil rights down there, and there's a high turnover —or turn-under — in the bandit population.

And so the story goes, leading to the discovery of great cigar tobacco and bringing it back to make Thompson Cigars.

15 rivers to cross... *and only 7 bridges!*

Here's how we were able to bring you...

The GRANADA!

In spite of bandits, jaguars, baby dinosaurs and high water... *at a price that will make a happy bandit out of YOU!*

I used to think that the only way to have a real adventure anymore was to be an astronaut or something. But that was before my recent trip to the Hidden Valley in Honduras, where the alluvial soil is six feet deep and everybody and his brother carries a six-shooter for bandit insurance.

Maybe you thought I just sit around writing letters to my good customers and wrapping cigar boxes to take to the Post Office. Not so. You don't get the best tobacco settin' at home on your resources. And, believe me, you don't always find the comforts of home elsewhere.

Sometimes I wonder why I'm in this business at all -- and why I go all over Hell's half-acre to insure my supply of good tobacco. Yet if I didn't go right down to the tobacco farms and check the crops for myself, I'd never be able to offer you the cigars I do. And I certainly would never have found the priceless bales of wrapper I brought back from my last trip to Central America.

And I never would have been able to come up with a superior cigar like the Granada, either -- a cigar that was born of first-hand, on-the-spot adventure in the kind of country I didn't know existed any more.

Getting to the Hidden Valley of the Jalapa River is like going through boot training in the Marines all over again -- only rougher. There are 15 rivers to cross and only 7 bridges. We had to ford the streams with four-wheel drive jeeps to get around down there -- and the locals had to build a special airport to fly their tobacco crops out to civilization.

I was tracked by a jaguar, avoided the embrace of an amorous boa constrictor, was jeered at by monkeys and stared at by a suspicious mountain lion. I ate the eggs of the baby dinosaur (that's what they call their iguanas) and they were delicious. I sampled the dinosaur meat, too, and it's even better than the eggs.

A RICH, MILD LONG-LASTING CIGAR

SHOWN ACTUAL SIZE

CLK-3620-5

99

I was even stopped and frisked as a suspicious character by the local gendarmerie. And when I asked them why they carried both six-shooters and shovels, they carefully explained their "six-by-six" justice to me. When they find a bandit, they use the six-shooter first -- then the shovel to put him six feet under. It's civil rites, instead of civil rights down there, and there's a high turnover -- or turnunder -- in the bandit population.

But the best is often the hardest to get to -- and I made it to the Hidden Valley, where ex-Cubans plow their way around ancient Mayan monuments to plant some of the very best cigar tobacco in the world.

I bought lots of filler tobacco from the last crop (it'll be ready for shipment in about six months). But one little farm I visited yielded a real bonanza:

> 11 bales of prime sungrown wrapper that's as rich and finely textured as any I've ever seen. It was a small lot and I had to talk fast with both hands in two languages to get the farmer to part with it. He was curing it himself and didn't want to let it go.

I put this wrapper in an old DC3, took off in the rain over a runway full of potholes and brought it back with me to Tampa and locked it up under tight security. Finding those 11 bales of wrappers was enough to make the whole trip a success. That sungrown Cuban seed wrapper is grown without shade or protection. The plant loses about 40% of its leaves through natural causes, so the remaining leaves get all the nourishment, making them even tastier and more satisfying to smoke.

I took this wrapper and used it to finish off some 100% imported filler -- made it in the Palma shape and created a cigar that will give you a real break - through in smoking pleasure. It has no bite. It's got an aroma that's all but hypnotic. And it burns with the long, white ash that's a dead giveaway for a fine wrapper around superior, carefully selected filler.

I think an experience like this is worth sharing with your friends -

And at $16.84 a hundred, they're a steal!

Those 11 bales of sungrown wrapper won't last forever. I put them all around the Granada and when this batch is gone I won't have any more Granadas at this price or any price.

But for a lucky stumble in the jungle, I wouldn't be able to offer them at all. So if you want to enjoy one of the best-smoking cigars you've ever tasted -- a real adventure in smoking that came from a real, foot-sore adventure in a wild and wonderful place -- I'd suggest you get out your ball-point pen and sign up for some genuine and guaranteed smoking excitement on the enclosed order form.

Tom Timmins

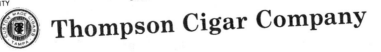

AMERICAN BIBLE SOCIETY "YOUR FAITH CAN MOVE MOUNTAINS" LETTER

For many years, direct mailers assumed fund-raising mailings had to look inexpensive or potential contributors would assume the organization had so much money they really didn't need another contribution. But then along came a tradition-breaking mailing from The American Bible Society that dispelled this idea and created a new trend in direct mail fund-raising.

The mailing utilized all the elements of successful product-selling commercial mailings. The envelope had a die-cut oval with a four-color picture of a snow-covered mountain peeking through. Teaser copy read:

> Your faith can move mountains . . .
>
> Start with this one please.

The mountain was a token on the perforated stub of an enclosed reply card. Recipients were asked to detach it and put it in a "yes" slot on the attached card to become members of the Bible-a-Month Club.

Included in the package was a slick paper brochure, a temporary membership card, and a classic letter. It began:

> Dear Fellow Christian:
>
> Your faith can move mountains. And the enclosed card is your surest way to do it.
>
> Return the mountain to the "YES" slot today and you can do something about the spiritual hunger stalking the emerging continents — Africa, Asia, South America, Oceania. The Scriptures are creating new spiritual age.

Throughout the letter were many elements picked up from successful commercial mailings. For example:

> Send no money, but just signify your willingness to help in this sacred task by returning the enclosed Membership Application.
>
> You may terminate your Membership any time it is necessary.

Benefits weren't overlooked either:

> Your principal reward as a Member will be the inner glow of knowing that each month Holy Scriptures will be sent in your name to someone in a spiritually foresaken outpost of the world — in his own language.
>
> Also, you personally will receive:
>
> 1. Your Membership Card, testifying to your participation.*

2. A free subscription to "The Record," our monthly magazine. This lively publication will keep you informed about your Bible Society family throughout the world.

3. Each month you will receive a facsimile page of the Scriptures you have donated in the strange language of its printing.

The asterisk on the first point led to the letter's postscript, another technique adopted from commercial mailings:

*P.S. For your convenience, I've enclosed your Membership Card with this letter. Just sign it and keep it as evidence of your participation. If you cannot join Bible-a-Month Club, check the "NO" box on the application, and return it with the Membership Card in the envelope provided. Thank you.

Although it was perhaps the most costly fund-raising mailing ever used at that time, it generated substantially great response, and continued to work exceedingly well for many years. Direct marketing expert Paul Sampson comments: "While this was an exciting package, the key factor in its success wasn't so much the format as a great idea — the moving of mountains."

We offer you this opportunity to help bring God's Word to the ends of the earth in all its diverse tongues — through accepting Membership in the rewarding new

"Bible-a-Month Club"

(You give the Bibles...You spread the Light)

Dear Fellow Christian:

Your faith can move mountains. And the enclosed card is your surest way to do it:

Return the mountain in the "YES" slot today and you can do something about the spiritual hunger stalking the emerging continents -- Africa, Asia, South America, Oceania. The Scriptures are creating a new spiritual age.

In the Congo a young man traveled three days on foot to obtain the Bible in his native tongue.

In Burma, the driver of our Bible van is greeted everywhere with joy... joy which could be likened to that which met our Lord on His triumphal entry into Jerusalem.

High in the Andes in Peru, an Indian Bible class meets tonight, memorizing Proverbs translated into their ancient Inca dialect.

Out of the hearts of the new nations being born across the world, we hear souls crying out for salvation. The insatiable demand for Scriptures in native languages runs into the millions.

Helping to fill this need is a holy work in which you are hereby invited to participate.

Send no money, but just signify your willingness to help in this sacred task by returning the enclosed Membership Application. You may terminate your Membership any time it is necessary.

Your principal reward as a Member will be the inner glow of

knowing that each month Holy Scriptures will be sent in your name to someone in a spiritually forsaken outpost of the world -- <u>in his own language.</u>

Also, you personally will receive:

1. Your Membership Card, testifying to your participation.*

2. A free subscription to "The Record", our monthly magazine. This lively publication will keep you informed about your Bible Society family throughout the world.

3. Each month you will receive a facsimile page of the Scriptures you have donated in the strange language of its printing.

Your share of the cost of the Bible will be a modest $2.00 a month... billed only after it is shipped to its recipient. This bill is also your record for Scriptures already sent in your name. Naturally, all contributions are tax deductible.

We need your help. For just $2.00 a month you can play a vital part in this world-saving work. And you may cancel at will.

We do not speak in our own name. We speak in the name of the twelve-year-old Tanzanian boy who comes to the door of your Missionary every day and asks, "Has my Bible arrived yet?"

In the name of that lad, and millions like him, I hope you will seize this unique opportunity to witness for your Lord.

Return the enclosed application today, please, with your mountain moved to the "YES" slot.

Faithfully yours,

John D. Erickson

John D. Erickson
Executive Secretary

*P.S. For your convenience, I've enclosed your Membership Card with this letter. Just sign it and keep it as evidence of your participation. If you cannot join Bible-a-Month Club, check the "NO" box on the application, and return it with Membership Card in the envelope provided. Thank you.

American Bible Society

1865 Broadway • New York, New York 10023

HEWLETT-PACKARD POCKET CALCULATOR LETTER

One of the greatest business-to-business direct marketing success stories was written by Hewlett-Packard and their direct response agency, Stone & Adler. The popularity of pocket calculators started a trend that has become the primary way business marketers beat the high cost of personal selling.

Hewlett-Packard's sales force has always been geared toward high-ticket sales. But in 1972, the firm announced the HP-35 — a $395 multifunction pocket calculator that could perform not only routine mathematical functions but a host of log and trig functions. Engineers and scientists were using time-consuming slide rules or desk-top machines — which then sold for $1,000 or more — to perform these same functions. Selling by traditional methods was too costly and the obvious answer was to reach the market without involving expensive personal selling.

Jim Kobs, then executive vice president of Stone & Adler and now president of his own direct response agency, tells the story behind this classic direct mail program:

■ H-P needed a direct marketing package that could explain the product's technical capability without the aid of a field engineer to answer questions. Second, the firm had to convince prospects to order a $395 product by mail, sight unseen. Third, marketers had to find or develop enough specialized mailing lists to make the volume interesting.

The result was a rather elaborate mailing package with each component doing part of the selling job. A 9x12, two-color envelope established identity with engineers by showing a wide variety of handwritten log and trig problems. The copy was simple: "Now there's a better way to solve problems like these. Hewlett-Packard has the answer."

The four-color brochure was die-cut to dramatize how the HP-35 fit into a shirt pocket. It also showed the product in use, explained its features, and illustrated the complete accessory package.

Another insert was an eight-page Capability Report. It was done in the style of an engineering report complete with line drawings of the product. For convincing skeptical readers of product performances, it even included three typical problems with a comparison of the solution times using a slide rule versus the HP-35.

The order card was 8 ½"x11". To invite action, it had an actual-size illustration of the HP-35 that could be punched out and slipped in a shirt pocket. The copy invited the reader to test the real thing by detaching and mailing the card.

The product was so new and revolutionary that most writers would have used a 3- or 4-page letter to cover the subject. Yet this one does the job very effectively in only one page . . . and lets the other enclosures provide the nuts and bolts selling story.

It's also unusual to see a 300-year-old quotation used as a headline, but it turned out to be very appropriate here.*

*Profitable Direct Marketing, *Jim Kobs, Crain Books, Chicago, 1979.*

The quotation Jim mentions was from Gottfried Wilhelm Leibniz:

> "It is unworthy of excellent men to lose hours
> like slaves in the labor of calculation."

The classic one-page letter began:

> If you concur in this 300-year-old opinion, meet the first pocket
> calculator that speaks your language.

The mailing package pulled 300% better than the break-even quota of two orders per thousand. It received so much attention that it convinced many other companies to use direct mail to sell their products, which were becoming uneconomical to sell through expensive sales forces.

HEWLETT **hp** PACKARD

ADVANCED PRODUCTS • *10900 Wolfe Road, Cupertino, California 95014, Telephone 408-257-7000*

> **"It is unworthy of excellent men**
> **to lose hours like slaves**
> **in the labor of calculation."**
> Gottfried Wilhelm Lebibniz (1646-1716)

If you concur in this 300-year-old opinion, meet the first pocket calculator that speaks your language.

We've christened this tiny, nine-ounce brainchild the HP-35 Pocket Calculator. I like to think of it as an electronic slide rule. But as the enclosed literature will indicate, comparing this new working tool to a slide rule or ordinary calculator simply does not do it justice.

The HP-35 offers a whole lot more in terms of advanced mathematical capability than any hand-held calculator we know about. In fact...

> ...it comes close to being a computer that fits
> in your shirt pocket.

It's as portable as your faithful slide rule. But it's easier to use. It does more, does it faster, does it without reference to cumbersome tables, without the need to write down intermediate results. It gives you answers with the accurate 10-place precision that's especially welcome when you're running out a close calculation, and even keeps track of the decimal.

The HP-35 has just gone into production after many months of exhaustive tests and refinements. During this introductory period, available production is being allocated under my supervision.

However, we'd be pleased to have you try this remarkable little answer machine at our expense--so that you can evaluate its extraordinary capabilities. The price is just $395, and you can take your choice of several purchase and payment options.

To do so, simply fill out and mail the card enclosed. You are welcome to "shirt-pocket-test" the HP-35 for 15 days while you determine for yourself how many hours, errors, and dollars it will save you.

Sincerely yours,

Alexis Sozonoff
Advanced Products Manager

AS:c
Encl.

HEWLETT-PACKARD POCKET COMPUTER LETTER

Two years later, Hewlett-Packard was ready to introduce another new product — the HP-65, a $795 programmable pocket "computer." Taking advantage of the lessons it had learned with its HP-35 mailing, it developed another elaborate mailing package. This time, however, there were more points to cover, and a four-page letter was created by Stan Holden. The mailing package was so successful it created a five-month backlog of orders for the HP-65.

Jim Kobs suggests two primary reasons for the letter's success:

> ■ First, the opening section, which dramatizes "the future is here now" with this product. Second, unlike some other long letters I have seen over the years, it is tightly written throughout . . . to hold the reader's interest.

The letter began:

> Imagine a "computer" that fits in your pocket! Imagine that it is no bigger — and looks very much like — an ordinary pocket calculator . . . but doesn't cost very much more! Now imagine this miniature marvel in your hands, as you try it out for 15 days and cut your problem-solving time down to seconds!

The letter was laden with benefits. Here are some typical paragraphs:

> To solve a problem, just feed in the known data by pressing a few keys on the HP-65's own keyboard. No other equipment is needed. Then start the program running. In seconds, the HP-65 uses computer technology to solve your problem, with up to 10-digit accuracy. You can even program it to skip steps or to select alternate steps — automatically — if intermediate solutions dictate such action! It couldn't be easier . . . or faster.

> The HP-65 can be used literally anywhere — at a meeting, out in the field, up in a plane, down in a mine — wherever your work takes you. It delivers the answers you need the minute you need them — not hours or days later.

> You don't have to go to computer programming school — or hire someone who did. You don't even have to learn "computer language," or invest in accessory hardware. All you need to write and record your own program is your HP-65, a pencil, some paper, and one of the blank program cards supplied.

HEWLETT hp *PACKARD*

19310 Pruneridge Avenue · Cupertino, California 95014 · Telephone (408) 996-0100

<u>Now you can have your own personal "computer"!</u>

Introducing: The HP-65

--the first and only <u>fully-programmable</u> pocket calculator that you can use to solve extremely complex, lengthy or repetitive problems in seconds--<u>anywhere</u>...<u>anytime</u>!

Imagine a "computer" that fits in your pocket! Imagine that it's no bigger than -- and looks very much like -- an ordinary pocket calculator ... but doesn't cost very much more! Now imagine this miniature marvel in <u>your</u> hands, as you try it out for 15 days and cut your problem-solving time down to <u>seconds</u>!

But why imagine? Now -- thanks to Hewlett-Packard's newest state-of-the-art technology -- there <u>is</u> a pocket-sized "computer" ... the HP-65!

> Just like a computer, it's <u>fully programmable</u>.
> And it uses <u>computer logic</u> to solve even
> extremely complex, lengthy or repetitive problems
> in seconds -- anywhere, anytime -- at the touch
> of a few keys!

No, this personal "computer" doesn't use tiny little reels of tape or miniature keypunch cards. It uses small (approximately ½" x 3") magnetic cards. Each card can store a program -- a sequence of keystrokes -- up to 100 steps long. (And, if additional steps are needed to handle an unusually long program, you can do it in stages.)

> To insert a program into the HP-65, just run a pre-
> recorded program card through it. All it takes is
> two seconds! The information from the card is
> duplicated in the HP-65's program memory, where it
> remains for as long as you leave your personal
> "computer" turned on.

To solve a problem, just feed in the known data by pressing a few keys on the HP-65's own keyboard. No other equipment is needed. Then start the program

(over, please)

running. In seconds, the HP-65 uses computer technology to solve your problem, with up to 10-digit accuracy. And you can even program it to skip steps or to select alternate steps -- automatically -- if intermediate solutions dictate such action! It couldn't be easier ... or faster!

Actually, the HP-65 is three "answer machines" in one:

1. It operates on pre-recorded program cards (available from Hewlett-Packard) ...

2. It operates on cards you program yourself (and you don't have to learn "computer language") ...

3. It's also an advanced scientific pocket calculator (with numerous built-in functions that may be incorporated into a program or used independently).

Whichever way you use the HP-65, you'll be amazed at how much time and effort it saves you, and how it helps to reduce computational errors.

Equally important, it enables you to handle complex, lengthy or repetitive problems that would be inconvenient, difficult or time-consuming to handle without using devices many times larger, much more expensive and nowhere near as portable as your personal "computer."

Because it operates on rechargeable batteries as well as on AC, the HP-65 can be used literally anywhere -- at a meeting, out in the field, up in a plane, down in a mine -- wherever your work takes you. It delivers the answers you need the minute you need them -- not hours or days later.

What makes the HP-65 even more incredible is that it's easy to operate! It can be used even by persons who know absolutely nothing about computers (or about calculators, for that matter). The illustrated Owner's Handbook clearly explains every detail, and the Quick Reference Guide offers a how-to-do-it summary.

Briefly, here are the three ways you can use it:

1. Use it with pre-recorded program cards ...

You don't need a scientific or engineering background to benefit from the HP-65's capabilities. But let's assume, for the moment, that you're involved in some project concerned with the surface area of the human body. Perhaps you're a medical technician ... a designer of apparatus for astronauts ... or a chemist working on a suntan lotion.

All you need do is take one of the pre-recorded program cards that come with the HP-65 -- the card labeled "Body Surface Area (Boyd)" -- and feed it through a slot on one side of your personal "computer." The information on the card -- the step-by-step sequence of keystrokes required to solve the problem -- is duplicated in the HP-65's program memory.

Next, using the HP-65's own keyboard, feed in the height and weight of the particular body you're measuring.

Now start the program running by pushing a single key on the HP-65.

In less time than it takes to read this sentence, the answer you're seeking will appear on the HP-65's light-emitting diode (LED) display!

To calculate the surface area of a different body, just feed in that person's height and weight ... and you get the answer just as quickly.

And in case you are a medical technician, and you also want to find out the cardiac index (the ratio of blood pumped per unit of body surface area), simply key in the cardiac input, and the HP-65 gives you the additional answer.

Dozens of pre-recorded program cards are available ...

... and more are on the way. They're packaged in Application Pacs containing up to 40 cards, and you'll find complete information on them in the literature accompanying this letter. In addition ...

2. You can create your own HP-65 program cards!

No, you don't have to go to computer programming school -- or hire someone who did. You don't even have to learn "computer language," or invest in accessory hardware. All you need to write and record your own program is your HP-65, a pencil, some paper, and one of the blank program cards supplied.

Simply prepare a step-by-step sequence of the HP-65 keys you would press to solve your particular problem. If you wish, this program can include conditional tests, skips or other techniques (all of which are clearly explained in the Owner's Handbook).

Turn on the HP-65, press the appropriate keys in sequence, and run a blank card through the machine to record the program.

And that's all you do!

You may use the card again and again, whenever you need it, to cut problem-solving time down to seconds and reduce the possibility of keystroke errors. You can even edit the card, to change or delete any part of the program. Or you can erase the card and record an entirely different program on it.

(If you would rather not work out your own program, you may find exactly what you need among the hundreds of programs -- in a variety of fields -- in the HP-65 Users' Library. See the literature enclosed.)

By creating your own program cards, or by adapting an existing program to your

(over, please)

own specific needs, you greatly extend the versatility of the HP-65 while -- at the same time -- you transform it into a highly specialized, truly personal "computer."

3. **And you can also use the HP-65 as an advanced scientific pocket calculator!**

Already pre-programmed into the HP-65 are the most commonly used scientific functions. Included are log and trig functions, the constant for π, the conversion of decimal angles to degrees/minutes/seconds, the conversion of rectangular coordinates to polar coordinates (or vice versa), and numerous other functions as shown in the enclosed brochure. These built-in functions may be used independently, or incorporated into any program.

> So there you have it -- the totally unique
> three-in-one, pocket-sized personal "computer"
> -- with the "super power" you need to solve
> just about any problem ... anywhere ... anytime!

After you read the enclosed literature, you may agree with us that the HP-65 is pretty fantastic. But only a personal trial can prove how valuable -- how indispensable -- it can be to you.

That's why I invite you to try it for 15 days!

See how it can save you hours - - or perhaps days -- of valuable time and effort, by quickly, easily and accurately solving hundreds of your complex, lengthy or repetitive problems. And see how it can free you from devices that are many times larger, much more expensive and nowhere near as portable as your personal "computer."

You might expect to pay $2,000 or more for an answer machine as incredible as the HP-65 ... but it's only $795.00 (U.S.A. only), complete with accessories as shown in the literature. And if you're not absolutely fascinated with owning and using your own pocket-sized personal "computer," return the HP-65 within 15 days for a full refund or credit!

With a product this unique, it's possible we may not be able to keep up with initial demand. Therefore, if you are interested in the HP-65, I strongly suggest you take advantage of this 15-day trial offer now.

Cordially,

Ray King

Ray King, General Manager
Advanced Products Division
Hewlett-Packard Company

P.S. If you send for your HP-65 now, you'll receive -- at no extra cost -- a year's subscription to the Users' Library Catalog of Contributed Programs, to greatly extend the usefulness of this personal "computer." Please see the enclosed literature for details.

RK:an

THE WALL STREET JOURNAL "TWO YOUNG MEN" LETTER

Another great direct mail letter, written by Martin Conroy, is mailed regularly by *The Wall Street Journal*. It compares the success of two college graduates. Although the letter doesn't claim that reading *The Wall Street Journal* made the difference in their careers, the thought is strongly suggested.

> On a beautiful late spring afternoon, twenty-five years ago, two young men graduated from the same college. They were very much alike, these two young men. Both had been better than average students, both were personable, and both — as young college graduates are — were filled with ambitious dreams for the future.
>
> Recently, these men returned to their college for their 25th reunion.
>
> They were still very much alike. Both were happily married. Both had three children. And both, it turned out, had gone to work for the same Midwestern manufacturing company after graduation, and were still there.
>
> But there was a difference. One of the men was manager of a small department of that company. The other was its president.
>
> Have you ever wondered, as I have, what makes this kind of difference in people's lives? It isn't always a native intelligence or talent or dedication. It isn't that one person wants success and the other doesn't.
>
> The difference lies in what each person knows and how he or she makes use of that knowledge.
>
> And that is why I am writing to you and to people like you about *The Wall Street Journal*. For that is the whole purpose of *The Journal*: To give its readers knowledge — knowledge that they can use in business.

The letter closes:

> About those two college classmates I mention at the beginning of this letter: They were graduated from college together and together got started in the business world. So what made their lives in business different?
>
> Knowledge. Useful knowledge. And its application.
>
> I cannot promise you that success will be instantly yours if you start reading *The Wall Street Journal*. But I can guarantee that you will find *The Journal* always interesting, always reliable, and always useful.

Author Dennison Hatch calls this letter "the most successful single piece of advertising in the history of the world." He estimates this letter has been directly responsible for producing $1 billion in revenues for *The Wall Street Journal*.*

*Million Dollar Mailings, *Dennison Hatch, Libbey Publishing, Inc., Washington, DC, 1992.*

THE WALL STREET JOURNAL.
The daily diary of the American Dream.
22 Cortlandt Street/New York, New York 10007

Dear Reader:

On a beautiful late spring afternoon, twenty-five years ago, two young men graduated from the same college. They were very much alike, these two young men. Both had been better than average students, both were personable and both—as young college graduates are—were filled with ambitious dreams for the future.

Recently, these men returned to their college for their 25th reunion.

They were still very much alike. Both were happily married. Both had three children. And both, it turned out, had gone to work for the same Midwestern manufacturing company after graduation, and were still there.

But there was a difference. One of the men was manager of a small department of that company. The other was its president.

What Made The Difference

Have you ever wondered, as I have, what makes this kind of difference in people's lives? It isn't always a native intelligence or talent or dedication. It isn't that one person wants success and the other doesn't.

The difference lies in what each person knows and how he or she makes use of that knowledge.

And that is why I am writing to you and to people like you about The Wall Street Journal. For that is the whole purpose of The Journal: To give its readers knowledge—knowledge that they can use in business.

A Publication Unlike Any Other

You see, The Wall Street Journal is a unique publication. It's the country's only national business daily. Each business day, it is put together by the world's largest staff of business-news experts.

Each business day, The Journal's pages include a broad range of information of interest and significance to business-minded people, no matter where it comes from. Not just stocks and finance, but anything and everything in the whole, fast-moving world of business... The Wall Street Journal gives you all the business news you need—when you need it.

Knowledge Is Power

Right now, I am reading page one of The Journal. It combines all the important news of the day with in-depth feature reporting. Every phase of business news is covered, from articles on inflation, wholesale prices, car prices, tax incentives for industries to major developments in Washington, and elsewhere.

(over, please)

And there is page after page inside The Journal, filled with fascinating and significant information that's useful to you. A daily column on personal money management helps you become a smarter saver, better investor, wiser spender. There are weekly columns on small business, marketing, real estate, technology, regional developments. If you have never read The Wall Street Journal, you cannot imagine how useful it can be to you.

Much of the information that appears in The Journal appears nowhere else. The Journal is printed in numerous plants across the United States, so that you get it early each business day.

A $28 Subscription

GREAT INTRODUCTORY PRICE! Put our statements to the proof by subscribing for the next 13 weeks for just $28. This is the shortest subscription term we offer—and a perfect way to get acquainted with The Journal. Or you may prefer to take advantage of a longer term subscription for greater savings: an annual subscription at $107 saves you $20 off The Journal's cover price. Our best buy—two years for $185—saves you a full $69!

Simply fill out the enclosed order card and mail it in the postage-paid envelope provided. And here's The Journal's guarantee: Should The Journal not measure up to your expectations, you may cancel this trial arrangement at any point and receive a refund for the undelivered portion of your subscription.

If you feel as we do that this is a fair and reasonable proposition, then you will want to find out without delay if The Wall Street Journal can do for you what it is doing for millions of readers. So please mail the enclosed order card now, and we will start serving you immediately.

About those two college classmates I mention at the beginning of this letter: They were graduated from college together and together got started in the business world. So what made their lives in business different?

Knowledge. Useful knowledge. And its application.

An Investment In Success

I cannot promise you that success will be instantly yours if you start reading The Wall Street Journal. But I can guarantee that you will find The Journal always interesting, always reliable, and always useful.

Sincerely yours,

Peter R. Kann
Executive Vice President/
Associate Publisher

PRK:vb
Encs.

P.S. It's important to note that The Journal's subscription price may be tax deductible.

AMERICAN EXPRESS "QUITE FRANKLY" LETTER

Another letter that has stood the test of time is the membership solicitation letter written by William J. Trembath of Ogilvy & Mather Direct. It was mailed from 1976 through 1988, and was finally replaced by a new control. But it took 150 test letters to find one that finally produced greater response. Trembath reports the only changes made over the years were those to update the list of benefits, as new services were introduced by American Express. The letter was not only the control in the United States for many years, it was also rolled out in 12 other countries. During the time it was used, it was mailed to over 280 million names, and if you were to project the volume of charges made by the card members it produced for American Express, it also represents a "billion dollar" letter.

The letter begins:

> Quite frankly, the American Express Card is not for everyone. And not everyone who applies for Cardmembership is approved.
>
> However, because we believe you will benefit from Cardmembership, I've enclosed a special invitation for you to apply for the most honored and prestigious financial instrument available to people who travel, vacation, and entertain.
>
> The American Express Card is the perfect example of the old adage, "You get what you pay for."

A good straight-forward lead into a list of benefits that fills most of the two-page letter.

AMERICAN EXPRESS TRAVEL RELATED SERVICES COMPANY, INC.
AMERICAN EXPRESS PLAZA, NEW YORK, NY 10004

Diane Shaib
Vice President
Marketing

R. S. Hoogscn
Box 46
Westtown, PA 19398

Dear R. Hoogson:

Quite frankly, the American Express® Card is not for everyone.
And not everyone who applies for Cardmembership is approved.

However, because we believe you will benefit from Cardmembership, I've enclosed a special invitation for you to apply
for the most honored and prestigious financial instrument
available to people who travel, vacation, and entertain.

The American Express Card is the perfect example of the old
adage, "You get what you pay for."

For example, you get a truly impressive array of extra
privileges, all designed for your convenience and security:

- A Worldwide Network of Travel Service Offices* is
  at your Service. Enjoy personal attention at any
  of the nearly 1,000 American Express Offices --
  your "homes away from home" -- around the globe.

- Cash your Personal Check at Thousands of Locations.
  Cash up to $250 at participating hotels and motels,
  and up to $1,000 at most American Express Travel
  Service Offices all over the world. (Subject to
  cash availability and local regulations.)

- Card Lost or Stolen? You'll Get a Quick Replacement.
  If the Card is lost or stolen, an emergency replacement will be provided at any Travel Service Office in
  the world, usually by the end of the next business day.

- Obtain Emergency Funds Instantly. Once you've en-
  rolled in this convenient service, our network of
  automated Travelers Cheque Dispensers lets you obtain
  up to $500...in 60 seconds or less!

- Carry $100,000 of Travel Accident Insurance. Just
  charge your tickets to the Card, and you, your spouse
  or dependent children under the age of 23 are automatically covered when traveling by common carrier
  on land, sea, or in the air. It's underwritten by
  Fireman's Fund Insurance Companies, San Rafael,

(over, please)

*Of American Express Travel Related Services Company, Inc., its affiliates and Representives.

California, for approximately 35¢ of the annual Cardmembership fee.

- Your Hotel Reservations are Assured. As an American Express Cardmember, if you request, your hotel room will be held for you until check-out the following day, at nearly 8,000 participating hotels.

- Enjoy Special Express Hotel Service. Speedy check-in and check-out is available to Cardmembers at more than 1,000 hotels, including Hilton, Hyatt, Marriott, Sheraton, and more.

Extras like these only begin to tell the story of American Express Card security, emergency protection, and convenience. You'll also enjoy:

- Unequalled Mobility. The Card is welcomed by the world's major airlines, car rental agencies, railroads, and cruise lines. Plus it pays for auto parts and servicing at thousands of locations nationwide.

- A Worldwide Welcome. Fine restaurants, hotels, resorts, and a host of other establishments around the world, and right in your hometown, recognize the Card and welcome your patronage.

- Purchasing Power. No need to carry large amounts of cash. The Card takes care of shopping needs, whether you're choosing a wardrobe, buying theater tickets, sending flowers, or hosting a dinner (even if you can't be there!)

- Financial Freedom. Unlike bank cards, the American Express Card imposes no pre-set spending limit. Purchases are approved based on your ability to pay as demonstrated by your past spending, payment patterns, and personal resources. So you are free to make your own decisions about when and where to use the Card.

In a few words, American Express Cardmembership is the most effective letter of introduction to the world of travel, entertainment, and the good life yet devised. Yet surprisingly, these benefits are all yours to enjoy for the modest fee of just $35 a year.

Why not apply for Cardmembership today? All you have to do is fill out and mail the enclosed application. As soon as it is approved, we'll send along the Card, without delay.

Sincerely,

Diane Shaib

Diane Shaib
Vice President

P.S. Apply today, and enjoy all the benefits of Cardmembership. Those listed here are just a handful of what's available. A full listing is included in the Guide to Cardmember Services you'll receive along with the Card.

GREYSTONE PRESS "FRANKLY I'M PUZZLED" PUBLISHER'S LETTER

Most of today's direct mail action-increasing devices are products of the 1960s. In just the space of a few years, a number of techniques appeared on the scene and were quickly adopted by a large number of direct mail advertisers. Suddenly there was widespread use of sweepstakes, tokens and stamps, and computer personalization — all of which had been around in one form or another for many years but had been used only infrequently until the 1960s.

But one exceptional new device became popular almost overnight. It was the addition of an extra letter or memo to a mailing — a second voice encouraging immediate action. Because it first appeared in mailings from Greystone Press and was signed by publisher Paul M. Greystone, it was dubbed "The Publisher's Letter."

A typical Greystone "Publisher's Letter" was used to promote a book series called "Discovering Antiques." In addition to the usual enclosures, there was a simulated sealed envelope with the teaser:

> PLEASE DO NOT OPEN THIS ENVELOPE
> UNLESS YOU HAVE ALREADY DECIDED
> NOT TO SEND IN FOR YOUR FREE VOLUME 1

When the seal was opened, a printed message was inside. It began:

> As the publisher of this Encyclopedia I am puzzled!
>
> Frankly, I do not understand why everyone does not send in for free
> Volume 1 — since it is absolutely free (we even pay the postage) and
> since there is never any obligation to buy any volumes, now or ever.

Word quickly spread of the extra response being generated by mailings with this enclosure, and suddenly everyone in direct marketing seemed puzzled. The three most copied words in direct mail became "Frankly I'm puzzled." Similar enclosures appeared in hundreds of different mailings. As it turned out, the success of this device wasn't so much the words but the idea of adding another voice — from "a higher authority."

There are always a certain number of recipients of a mailing who have almost decided to accept the offer, but need an extra "push" — and the so-called publisher's letter provided that push. This pioneer publisher's letter is most often credited to Paul Michael, although I've been told the basic idea was the brainchild of Henry Goldsmith, general manager of Greystone.

Dear Friend:

As the publisher of this Encyclopedia I am puzzled!

Frankly, I do not understand why everyone does not send in for free Volume 1 -- since it is absolutely free (we even pay the postage) and since there is never any obligation to buy any volumes, now or ever.

Once you see how good the first volume is, I hope you will want the rest. It's a sample. Of course, if you don't want further volumes, just tell us to stop. You never return Volume 1 -- you never pay for it -- no one will call you or come to your home to try and change your mind.

We don't send books to people who don't want them. It would be just as silly as if your grocer sent you five pounds of apples you didn't want. You would only send them back and not pay him for them. It's the same for us in the book business. Sending unwanted books simply doesn't make sense.

Perhaps you do not believe that you never have to pay a single penny for Volume 1. Many people must feel that there is a hidden charge of some kind.

Perhaps you say to yourself: "Why should I send for free Volume 1 if I don't intend to get the rest of the Encyclopedia? What is the good of owning a single volume of an Encyclopedia?"

The answer to that question is simple. There is so much interesting material in the free Volume 1 that it will make an exciting addition to your home library whether or not you ever take another volume.

Perhaps you say to yourself: "I know all about buying books by mail." If so, just bear in mind that this is not a Book Club. There are no monthly cards to return. Once you CANCEL, your subscription is cancelled. You never receive another book.

There may be other reasons for not sending in for your free Volume 1 -- but for the life of me I can't think what they might be. So, if you have decided not to send in for free Volume 1, perhaps you would take just a minute to send me a card to tell me why? I would appreciate it a great deal.

Cordially,

Paul M. Greystone

Paul M. Greystone
for the Publisher

PMG:lk

A QUESTION FROM THE PUBLISHER FOR THOSE OF YOU WHO
HAVE DECIDED NOT TO SEND IN FOR YOUR FREE VOLUME 1

Paul M. Greystone, Publisher

PLEASE DO NOT OPEN UNLESS
YOU HAVE ALREADY DECIDED NOT
TO SEND IN FOR YOUR FREE VOLUME 1

P.M.G.

DIRECT MARKETING EDUCATIONAL FOUNDATION
PERSONALIZED LETTER FROM BOB STONE

The old saying, "The shoemaker's children have no shoes" isn't necessarily true when it comes to the labor of love of many top names in direct marketing. In searching for letters to be included in this book, I wrote to many of my colleagues for nominations for the best classic direct mail letter. The winner was written by Bob Stone to raise funds for what was then called the Direct Mail/Marketing Educational Foundation. It was five pages long, and every sentence helped draw more contributions than had ever before been obtained by this group.

The letter has won many awards. But its greatest award was that the funds it raised led to the establishment of the first degree-program in direct marketing at a major university and inspired dozens of other colleges and universities throughout the country to develop their own programs in direct marketing.

The opening is truly classic:

> Remember when you were a kid? A "dreamer" was put down as someone who would never amount to anything — destined to be a "non-achiever" for life.
>
> What a myth!
>
> Let me tell you about some "dreamers" who became super achievers in direct marketing. They succeeded beyond their wildest dreams.

Bob went on to describe such "dreamers" as L. L. Bean, Len and Gloria Carlson, and Lester Wunderman. Then he added:

> But of all the dreams-come-true which I have witnessed over the years there is one which supersedes all others. A dream-come-true which has touched all our lives, a dream which will live beyond our lifetimes.
>
> The year was 1965. Lewis Kleid, a leading list broker in his day, was a close friend of Edward N. Mayer, Jr., known around the world as "Mr. Direct Mail."
>
> Lew made a proposition to Ed. He said, "Ed, if you will devote time to teaching the rudiments of direct marketing to college kids, I'll provide the seed money to make it happen."
>
> Thus, with the simplicity that was a trademark of Ed Mayer, the Lewis Kleid Institute was launched. Today, almost 17 years later, the Direct Mail/Marketing Educational Foundation, a non-profit organization which sponsors Kleid Institutes, continues in the Ed Mayer image.

> Over the past 17 years, over 1,000 bright college students have
> taken the 5-day intensive course, sponsored by the Foundation . . .
> all expenses paid. It is estimated that over 50% of these students have
> entered into a direct marketing career.

The letter went on to describe the dreams of creating the first Direct Marketing Center at a major university and asked for contributions to a $1.2 million capital fund to make it happen. The letter ended with this postscript:

> P.S. It is my fondest dream that you and I will be there to witness the
> commencement exercises of the first graduating class with a
> degree in Direct Marketing.

Not only did the letter raise the necessary funds, but Bob Stone and many others were present when those commencement exercises were held at the University of Missouri in Kansas City. The students not only had a degree in direct marketing, but they had had the benefit of weekly lectures from one of the greatest pros in the field — Bob Stone.

STONE & ADLER INC.

150 NORTH WACKER DRIVE • CHICAGO, ILLINOIS 60606 • TELEPHONE 312/346-6100

ROBERT STONE, *Chairman of the Board*   July 28, 1982

Mr. John Jones
Jones Manufacturing Co.
1621 Main Street
Ottumwa, Iowa 52501

Dear John,

Remember when you were a kid. A "dreamer" was put down
as someone who would never amount to anything -- destined
to be a "non-achiever" for life.

What a myth!

Let me tell you about some "dreamers" who became super
achievers in direct marketing. They succeeded beyond
their wildest dreams.

There's the thrilling story of L. L. Bean in Maine. For
years they ran a successful mail order business...catering
to outdoorsmen.

But Leon Gorman dreamed of new horizons...a new world out
there of men and women who never fished or hunted -- dressed
the way outdoors people dress. A pipe dream? Hardly. Leon
Gorman turned dream to reality. Sales - plateaued at the
$50 million level - boomed past the $100 million level in a
few short years.

What about the legendary "kitchen table" people? Len
Carlson, out in California, is a part of the legend.

Len and his wife Gloria shared a dream. They dreamed they
could put together a catalog of hard-to-find gadgets that
would appeal to the masses. Thus Sunset House was born.

Fifteen years and a customer base of 6.5 million names
later, the press announced Sunset House had been acquired
by a major corporation for a price reported to be in the
millions.

The most remarkable dream story on the agency side is that
of Lester Wunderman. Les was an account person with the
Max Sackheim agency. He dreamed of having his own agency.

But an agency that would apply sophisticated direct response

-2-

techniques to all media -- including a "new" medium called television. Today his firm - Wunderman, Ricotta & Kline - has billings in excess of $100 million, with offices in New York and 12 foreign countries.

As you read of these dreams-come-true I hope you are recalling your own. The dreams you have had which have helped you to get to where you are today.

But of all the dreams-come-true which I have witnessed over the years there is one which supersedes all others. A dream-come-true which has touched all our lives, a dream which will live on beyond our lifetimes.

The year was 1965. Lewis Kleid, a leading list broker in his day, was a close friend of Edward N. Mayer, Jr., known around the world as "Mr. Direct Mail."

Lew made a proposition to Ed. He said, "Ed - if you will devote time to teaching the rudiments of direct marketing to college kids, I'll provide the seed money to make it happen."

Thus, with the simplicity that was a trademark of Ed Mayer, the Lewis Kleid Institute was launched. Today, almost 17 years later, The Direct Mail/Marketing Educational Foundation, a non-profit organization which sponsors Kleid Institutes, continues in the Ed Mayer image.

Over the past 17 years over 1,000 bright college students have taken the 5-day intensive course, sponsored by the Foundation...all expenses paid. It is estimated that over 50% of these students have entered into a direct marketing career.

As one of the privileged few who has had the honor of lecturing each new group of candidates over many years -- I only wish you could witness, as I have, the excitement that comes to each as they are introduced to the wonders of direct marketing disciplines.

"I learned more in five days than in my four years as a marketing major," is a somewhat typical statement from one of these exuberant students.

But let me give you just a few quotes from hundreds in file.

"I learned so very much -- the week just set my spark for direct marketing into a big roaring fire!"

Marilee Gibson Yorchak
New Mexico State University

-3-

"The Institute has greatly increased my awareness and understanding of direct marketing, and furthered my career interest."

                    Tim Harrison
                    University of North Carolina

"If one of your objectives was to stimulate young, ambitious
people to enter your field, you succeeded with me."

                    Paula Miante
                    College of William and Mary

I guess from all of this one would have to conclude our dream
has truly come true. Well - not exactly.

None of us ever dreamed that direct marketing would have the
explosive growth we have all experienced. (As an aside -
when I wrote my first book I trumpeted that total sales of
goods and services via the direct marketing method had reached
the staggering figure of $300 million. The estimated figure
for 1981 is $120 billion!)

So now we realize that if our true dream is to be realized -
growing our own at the college level to people our future
growth - we are going to have to raise our sights beyond the
far horizon.

Where we are bringing the gifted student to the Institute -
only one each from about 35 colleges twice each year - we've
got to get Direct Marketing taught on the college campus in
full semester courses. Not to three score and ten for five
days. Instead - to hundreds for full semesters.

Is this "The Impossible Dream"? No!

I'm now going to tell you about what some regard to be an
emerging "miracle," which is in the process of happening as
I pen this letter.

At a Board of Directors meeting a few months ago in the
offices of The Direct Mail/Marketing Educational Foundation,
Richard L. Montesi, President, made a startling proposal.
A proposal which he stated would make our ultimate dream
come true.

The ultimate dream, as he expressed it, is to establish a
Chair for a Direct Marketing Center in three major universities: one in the Middle West; one in the East; and one in
the West.

The full-scale curriculums will be structured to earn a
degree in Direct Marketing for each graduate, carrying with

them a stature similar to that enjoyed by a graduate from the Wharton School of Business or Harvard Business School.

"An exciting idea," we said. "But how are we going to fund these centers?" "From a capital fund of $1.2 million," Dick said. "$1.2 million. Good God!" was the reaction.

Well then the miracle started happening. Andy Andrews, one of the directors, said - "Why don't we go around the table right now and see how much commitment we can get over the next three years from the small group of directors at this table?"

Would you believe we raised $120,000.00 - 10% of our goal - within five minutes!

When we left that day a few of us agreed to write some letters and make some phone calls. And what happened as a result surpasses anything in my experience.

Remember those "dreamers" I talked about earlier? Well let me tell you what happened with some of them.

Remember Leon Gorman of L. L. Bean? He's committed $15,000 over three years. And Len Carlson - another $15,000. And Les Wunderman - $15,000. They're putting their money where their dreams are.

The list goes on. "Dusty" Loo of Looart Press - a major commitment. John Flieder of Allstate Insurance - "Count us in." Kiplinger Washington Editors. The Kleid Company. Jim Kobs of Kobs & Brady - "Absolutely!" Publishers Clearing House. Grolier. Colonial Penn. Rodale Press. Spiegel. American Express.

John Yeck of Yeck Brothers Group - "You can count on us." Eddie Bauer. Rapp & Collins. Ogilvy & Mather. Alan Drey. The DR Group. Hanover House. And on and on.

To this moment, these people and some others we have contacted bring total commitments to $725,000. So we have reached 60% of our goal!

This is exciting in itself, but equally exciting is the fact that we have two formal proposals from two major universities detailing how a Chair would be established for Direct Marketing. And the cost.

One proposal is from UMKC - University of Missouri, where Martin Baier of Old American has taught Direct Marketing classes for a number of years. The other proposal is from

-5-

New York University. Both universities are ready when we are.

So we are this close to bringing off a 20th Century miracle!

Now we come to you to ask you to share in this dream of dreams. There is a pledge card inside of the enclosed envelope. The amount suggested is just that. A suggestion. You are the best judge of what your company should pledge against the future.

I have asked for and have gotten approval to have your response come back to me personally. I'd like to hear from you even if there is some unforseen circumstance under which you cannot make a pledge.

We must decide very soon upon the first university to establish a Direct Marketing Center. Therefore I will appreciate it if you will reply within the next 10 days. Thank you so very much.

                    Sincerely,

                    Bob Stone

P.S. It is my fondest dream that you and I will be there to witness the commencement exercises of the first graduating class with a degree in Direct Marketing.

DIRECT MARKETING EDUCATIONAL FOUNDATION BOB DALE LETTER BY JOHN YECK

What do you do for an encore when a direct mail classic has everyone talking — and contributing? Turn to another world champion copywriter.

That's what happened for the Direct Marketing Educational Foundation (DMEF).

Fortunately that world champion was already on hand — DMEF's long-time chairman, John Yeck. Anyone who has attended a convention of the Direct Marketing Association for the past couple of decades has been treated to a special platform appearance of this direct marketer extolling the virtues of the industry's educational arm. About the only thing that can beat a John Yeck fund-raising speech is a John Yeck fund-raising letter. And in 1984, he created my personal favorite classic direct mail letter.

It came over the letterhead of Bernie Fixler, a former chairman of the board of the Direct Marketing Association, and a personal friend of thousands of people in the field. It talked about his former business partner, the late Bob Dale, who is fondly remembered by almost everyone who has been in the direct mail field.

John Yeck's copy made Bob Dale come alive once again for everyone who knew him:

> Direct marketing is a popular term today, but you and I can remember, not all that long ago, when it wasn't too highly thought of by the marketing "elite" or, I guess, the public at large.
>
> And very few of us stood up in front of others to praise it.
>
> But one who did was a wiry, peppery, enthusiastic little fellow who, when he stepped in front of an audience to talk about direct mail
>
> . . . grew giant high.
>
> He moved, barked, shouted, whispered, coaxed and finally mesmerized those audiences into believing in direct mail, too.
>
> Of course, you know who I mean. Bob Dale.
>
> He'd laugh if I called him a Giant, but that's what he was.
>
> He had presence. When Bob stepped into the room, you knew things were going to be different.
>
> He was full of vitality and enthusiasm-plus. Even writing about him now peps me up.

John's copy went on to describe a DMEF memorial fund "to keep Bob Dale's memory alive." And in the fashion of the man the letter was about, it included this close:

> Naturally, I've enclosed a card — and a stamped, addressed envelope — Bob wouldn't have me do it any other way. In fact, he'd

probably have made me add some kind of extra "goodie" for quick response and a lift letter of some sort.

I won't do that exactly, but you can be sure that your name, as a friend of Bob's, will be tied to whatever memorial is established which, of course, will depend upon the amount we finally raise. As for a "lift," I think you can probably get that, instantly, just by shutting your eyes and remembering Bob in full flight, on the platform, in front of a fascinated audience.

. . . eyes sparkling, feet moving, arms punctuating and those colorful, exciting, enthusiastic words pouring out of his mouth.

Just think about that for a minute, then open your eyes . . . and fill in the card.

Don't you wish you, too, had known Bob Dale? But perhaps you do, thanks to John Yeck's inspired "labor of love" copy.

Bernie Fixler

care of DMEF
6 E. 43rd Street
New York, New York 10017

October 24, 1984

Mr. Richard Hodgson
Sargeant House
P. O. Box 46
Westtown, PA   19395

Dear Dick:

Direct marketing is a popular term today, but you and I can remember, not all that long ago, when it wasn't too highly thought of by the marketing "elite" or, I guess, the public at large.

And very few of us stood up in front of others to praise it.

But one who did was a wiry, peppery, enthusiastic little fellow who, when he stepped in front of an audience to talk about direct mail

... grew giant high.

He moved, barked, shouted, whispered, coaxed and finally mesmerized those audiences into believing in direct mail, too.

Of course, you know who I mean. Bob Dale.

He'd laugh if I called him a Giant, but that's what he was.

He had <u>presence</u>. When Bob stepped into the room, you knew things were going to be different.

He was full of <u>vitality</u> and <u>enthusiasm-plus</u>. Even writing about him now peps me up.

And he had <u>commitment</u>. He'd talk to students, to meetings, to business groups, to anyone who was willing to listen about his favorite subject - direcf ghaweting.

Bob's been gone from us for some time now, but I think about him often. He was a real pioneer in educating others to the value of what we and our friends do or did.

People like Bob - Giants like Bob - shouldn't be forgotten.

But that can easily happen unless those who knew him do something concrete to keep his memory alive ... A "Robert Dale Memorial" that really amounts to something.

Giant size, to match Bob.

I think the right place for a memorial like that is in the Direct Marketing Educational Foundation. Bob helped the Foundation a great deal in its early days, when it needed help badly. He taught at Collegiate Institutes with Ed Mayer and Paul Sampson and enjoyed the give and take with college students. He'd love the way direct marketing education has spread in the colleges today.

So I'm calling on you, and the many other friends of Bob, to join with me in setting up a substantial fund to establish a permanent memorial to him.

I've started the fund with a $10,000 gift and I hope I get a basketful of others to match that - or put it in the shade. But the size of your gift is less important than the size of your interest, for I'd like to ask you, also, to do what I cannot ... locate others who knew Bob and encourage them to join with us.

Naturally, I've enclosed a card - and a stamped, addressed envelope - Bob wouldn't have me do it any other way. In fact, he'd probably have made me add some kind of extra "goodie" for quick response and a lift letter of some sort.

I won't do that exactly, but you can be sure that your name, as a friend of Bob's, will be tied to whatever memorial is established - which, of course, will depend upon the amount we finally raise. As for a "lift", I think you can probably get that, instantly, just by shutting your eyes and remembering Bob in full flight, on the platform, in front of a fascinated audience

... eyes sparkling, feet moving, arms punctuating and those colorful, exciting, enthusiastic words pouring out of his mouth.

Just think about that for a minute, then open your eyes

... and fill in the card.

Bernie Fixler
Bernie Fixler

TOM COLLINS' "GEORGE McGOVERN" LETTER

One of the most difficult writing assignments is the political fund-raising letter — particularly when millions must be raised to support an unpopular candidate. As election results showed, George McGovern turned out to be such a candidate. But Tom Collins' fund-raising letter for George McGovern's presidential campaign is a classic.

The letter introduced many voters to George McGovern and set forth in powerful fashion why he believed he deserved the Democratic party's nomination to run against Richard Nixon in 1972. It also raised a substantial amount of money to promote his candidacy.

Although writers usually avoid using the pronoun "I" in direct mail letters, this letter is loaded with "I's" — and appropriately so since the signer, himself, was "the product." But what really distinguishes this letter are its short, pithy paragraphs. Consider the opening:

> You are one of a number of people whose help I am asking in the most important effort any American can ever undertake.
>
> After mailing this letter to you, I will, on Monday, January 18, declare to the Nation my candidacy for the office of President of the United States.
>
> In so doing, and in writing you to inform you of my decision, I am deliberately breaking political precedent in several ways.
>
> It is unprecedented for a presidential candidate to make a formal declaration almost two full years before the next presidential term begins.
>
> It is unprecedented for such a declaration of intent to be made in a letter to thousands of potential supporters across the country.
>
> And it is unprecedented for the candidate himself to invite the many thousands who respect his positions on the major issues to help finance the organization of his campaign headquarters and staff.
>
> But I am taking these unusual steps because these are unusual times.
>
> I am making my intentions known now because the times call for the greatest forthrightness and the clearest commitment.

The letter goes on for seven pages, with no paragraph longer than five lines and most only two or three lines long. But each paragraph makes a strong point and leads into the next.

This great direct mail letter's heritage is a letter written 22 years earlier by Walter Weintz. In a 1972 speech at a Direct Mail/Marketing Association conference, he described this experience, which laid the groundwork for most of today's political direct mail:

■ To the best of my knowledge, the Republicans started using direct mail on a scientific, mass basis back in 1950. At that time, Senator Robert Taft was running for his life for re-election.

The big unions had announced that they had earmarked a war chest of several million dollars for a campaign in Ohio to defeat Taft, because he was co-author of the Taft-Hartley Act, which gives the federal government the power to halt strikes that hurt the national interest. Senator Taft was a friend of De Witt Wallace, the head of *The Reader's Digest*, and of Al Cole, who was then the *Digest's* general manager.

They volunteered my services (I was then circulation director of the *Digest*) to do a direct mail campaign to help get Senator Taft re-elected.

Senator Taft was convinced that he should take his stand on Taft-Hartley Law, and, of course, we tried to talk him out of that because we knew that blue-collar workers would be against him on the basis of the Taft-Hartley Act.

Fortunately, in direct mail you are able to test almost anything, including political appeals. We mailed out, as I recall, a half-dozen different letters, each one putting forth a different central idea on why the recipient of the letter should support Senator Taft.

Since we needed some way to measure the effect of our different appeals, in each mailing we included a contribution card, keyed to the letter it went with. Thus, we were able to count returns from each letter and tell which pulled the best.

We sent out about 20,000 copies of each letter. I was astounded when the letter which was built around a positive presentation of the Taft-Hartley Act was far and away the most successful.

We subsequently mailed hundreds of thousands of Taft-Hartley letters into the blue-collar worker sections of the industrial cities of Ohio: Cincinnati, Cleveland, Akron, and so on. The blue-collar workers responded by voting overwhelmingly for Taft against the urging and advice and the three million dollar campaign fund of their union leaders.

This same technique was used by Walter Weintz two years later for the Dwight D. Eisenhower presidential campaign. Ten letters — each with a different theme — were mailed. Nine out of the ten pulled almost exactly the same. But the tenth, which talked about the seemingly never-ending war in Korea, outpulled the others by 250%. As a result, that became a key campaign theme for General Eisenhower — "I shall go to Korea" — and played an important role in his victory the following November.

GEORGE McGOVERN
SOUTH DAKOTA

United States Senate
WASHINGTON, D.C. 20510

January 15, 1971

My Dear Friend:

You are one of a number of people whose help I am asking in the most important effort any American can ever undertake.

After mailing this letter to you, I will, on Monday, January 18, declare to the Nation my candidacy for the office of President of the United States.

In so doing, and in writing you to inform you of my decision, I am deliberately breaking political precedent in several ways.

It is unprecedented for a presidential candidate to make a formal declaration almost two full years before the next presidential term begins.

It is unprecedented for such a declaration of intent to be made in a letter to thousands of potential supporters across the country.

And it is unprecedented for the candidate himself to invite the many thousands who respect his positions on the major issues to help finance the organization of his campaign headquarters and staff.

But I am taking these unusual steps because these are unusual times.

I am making my intentions known now because the times call for the greatest forthrightness and the clearest commitment.

Today's issues need to be defined and addressed <u>now</u> -- fully and honestly -- so that the voters of America can make the judgment of 1972 with the benefit of a considerable period of testing and deliberation.

The stakes are too great, our national problems are too grave, to ask our people to make that judgment hastily in the last weeks before the election, while the bands are playing and the crowds are roaring.

Because the present Administration has deepened the sense of depression and despair throughout our land, the Democratic nominee in 1972 will in all probability be the next President.

2.

For this reason, he should be chosen carefully from the various contenders only after meeting, in a broad range of public forums, the most critical tests of character, performance, and understanding.

I am prepared to submit my record and myself to that kind of critical comparison and test.

Having campaigned successfully twice for Congress and twice for the United States Senate as a Democrat in my heavily Republican native state of South Dakota, I seek the presidency with the confidence that I can be nominated and elected.

I seek the presidency with the conviction that I can provide the sense of history, the toughness of mind and resolve, and the spirit of deep compassion which this highest office demands.

I seek the presidency because I believe without reservation in the American promise and because I can no longer tolerate the diminishing of that promise.

The remarkable architects of the Declaration of Independence and the Constitution of the United States endowed this nation with founding ideals that have never been surpassed.

These ideals -- grounded in the Judeo-Christian ethic -- affirm the sacredness of each individual and the bonds that bind him to his fellow creatures.

I can neither add to nor detract from these enduring principles. Indeed, they constitute my philosophy of government.

But in this decade, as we approach the 200th anniversary of the Declaration of Independence -- the beginning of a revolution devoted to "life, liberty, and the pursuit of happiness" -- we need a second American revolution.

Not a revolution of violence, but a quiet determination to square our nation's policies and priorities with the ideals of our founding documents.

In fact, I believe this is our only hope for avoiding the ugly violence that now tempts many desperate people.

We cannot reconcile the deep divisions in our society by merely patching over them. We can only reconcile them by instituting the reforms so urgently needed and persuading the majority of the American people to accept them.

3.

I want to lead our nation along this path of reconciliation and rededication.

And although the Democratic Party is fortunate, as it always has been, in possessing a wealth of leadership talent, I believe that I am uniquely qualified to meet the special requirements of today.

There were, I believe, two factors that cost our party the presidency in 1968.

The first was the war in Vietnam.

The second was the conviction of many Democrats that our party was not responsive in 1968 to their views and concerns.

I have sought to the best of my ability to meet both of these central challenges to our party and our nation.

As you are undoubtedly more aware than most, my major energies since coming to the Senate in 1963 have been directed to ending the war in Southeast Asia, reducing our excessive military outlays, and developing a positive foreign policy that would create the conditions necessary for peace.

As a young bomber pilot in World War II, I vowed that if I survived the war I would devote the balance of my life to the cause of peace. I have kept that pledge and will keep it no matter what else transpires.

It was the pursuit of peace that led me into graduate studies in history, government, and international relations at Northwestern University.

It was the conditions of peace I sought to convey to my students when I assumed my professorship at Dakota Wesleyan University.

I sought the works of peace as a U.S. Congressman from 1956 to 1960, and as President Kennedy's Food for Peace Director in 1961 and 1962.

And beyond my personal grief, it was my commitment to peace that led me to mourn with special sorrow the deaths first of President Kennedy, and then of Robert Kennedy and Martin Luther King in that tragic spring of 1968.

4.

Since 1968, I have been carrying on the fight against President Nixon's needless prolongation of the war in Vietnam.

In addition, I have given my energy to the revitalization and reconciliation of the Democratic Party.

It has been my privilege to serve as Chairman of our party's Commission on Party Structure and Delegate Selection.

That Commission, in accordance with the instructions from the last national convention, has developed guidelines to insure that every Democrat will be given a "full, meaningful, and timely opportunity" to participate in the selection of our presidential candidate in 1972.

I believe that these guidelines, when fully implemented, will go a long way toward healing the deep wounds our party suffered at the 1968 convention.

And I believe that my nomination as our party's presidential candidate offers the best chance of heading off a fourth-party movement by Democrats still fuming with impatience over the mistakes of past leadership.

These Democrats -- and you may be one of them -- have always known exactly where I stand. They know that I have opposed these mistakes longer and more consistently than any other presidential prospect in our party.

At the same time, I want, and I believe I enjoy, the respect and good will of all other elements of our party leadership.

My dream and my goal is to unite our party and lead it to victory without giving up one inch of my own integrity and total commitment to the ideals of "life, liberty, and the pursuit of happiness" for all Americans. I am certain it can be done.

Undoubtedly I will be frequently advised to soft-pedal the passionate concern I have expressed as a Senator for our poor, our neglected sick, our hungry, our minority citizens with black or brown or red skins, our troubled young people.

But as much as I welcome advice, this is advice that I cannot and will not accept. I intend to be as completely forthright as a presidential candidate as I have been as a Senator.

5.

I believe the times demand this. I believe the people want it. And I know that I must do it.

I believe that the next President of the United States must possess and demonstrate this kind of quiet inner strength.

Our intervention in Vietnam's civil war was not an act of national strength but rather a drifting with the tide of old ideas and illusions.

President Nixon's failure to pull us out of the Vietnam quicksand promptly and decisively is not an act of strength, but rather reveals a lack of the strength needed to face up to the enormity of our error and the seriousness of our predicament.

Vietnamization is not a formula for ending the killing in Vietnam. It is a clear design to keep the war going by ending criticism in the United States. It is merely prolonging the bad dream from which our nation is attempting to awake.

To arouse our people and lead them back along the path of true peace will take the kind of strength and clarity that President Lincoln exhibited during another time of grave national error, the error of permitting human slavery in our midst.

I say now what he said then: "We must disenthrall ourselves."

And I am inspired by the profile of courage he exhibited as a young Congressman, when he gambled and lost his seat in the House of Representatives by daring to speak up against the immorality of our war with Mexico.

Another great American president, Franklin Roosevelt, told us nearly forty years ago, during our last great national crisis, "We have nothing to fear but fear itself."

Today, in this winter of our discontent, our greatest enemy is not fear but despair.

I believe that this despair stems from the fact that our great and powerful nation has wandered so far away from its ideals that it has almost lost the way.

An America which launched its own independence with "a decent respect for the opinions of mankind" now wastes its blood and substance in the jungles of Southeast Asia in open defiance of the common sense of the civilized world.

6.

An America founded on a belief in the sacredness of life now endangers the very basis of life by polluting the air, water, and land which sustains us. We are standing in garbage up to our knees while hurling rockets to the moon.

An America whose early pioneers opened the doors of Harvard College six years after landing at Massachusetts Bay now is led to believe that we cannot afford adequate funding to strengthen our schools.

An America founded on the belief that "all men are created equal" has been so slow to grant full equality to its racial minorities that it is driving some among them to acts of desperate and self-destructive violence.

An America whose dollars were once so sound they were recognized as a standard around the world now finds that its dollars are so weakened by "guns and butter" inflation that even working Americans find it hard to afford butter, to say nothing of meat on the table for dinner.

An America of law is cursed by rising crime, dangerous neighborhoods, and an underworld drug traffic that is jeopardizing the future even of children in grade school.

An America with a Constitution that placed its war-making power in an elected Congress now finds that power wrested away by the CIA, the Pentagon, and impetuous chief executives.

An America which has always renewed itself through the vigor and idealism of its youth now finds many of our most sensitive and intelligent young people losing their faith in our system and turning to drug addiction, exile, or dangerous fantasies of domestic guerilla warfare.

And an America which has prided itself on the opportunities for individual fulfillment now has millions of working men and women who are trapped in unrewarding jobs, or can't even find a job because the demand for their particular skill has disappeared.

I want to provide a second chance for these latter Americans, through a peacetime G.I. Bill which will make it possible for any American to go back to school and get the additional training he wants or needs.

7.

I want to provide a second chance for all Americans who feel that they have somehow been left behind and forgotten.

I want to provide a second chance for America itself to realize the dreams embodied in our Constitution and Bill of Rights.

I want to dispel the heavy smog of despair that is choking our usual optimism and social vigor.

Many people will say that I don't have a chance. And it is true that, standing alone, I _would_ not.

But together, you and I have the best chance of all. If you will join with me now, I pledge that we will _make_ that chance.

To fulfill that pledge, I need sufficient funds to staff and operate a campaign headquarters and start bringing my case to the people all across the country throughout 1971.

I am confident that this 1971 effort will generate sufficient additional support to enable me to mount a successful campaign in 1972.

But the time to start is now.

In the ancient wisdom of Ecclesiastes, "To every thing there is a season, and a time to every purpose under the heaven."

I believe this is a time to heal. A time to build up. A time to cast away the stones of war, and gather together stones for building. A time to speak. A time for love, not hate. A time for peace.

If you agree, won't you join hands with me now?

Very sincerely yours,

George McGovern

P.S. If by accident you received an extra copy of this letter, please pass it on to a friend.

NATIONAL REPUBLICAN SENATORIAL COMMITTEE
"REPUBLICAN PRESIDENTAL TASK FORCE" LETTER

Probably the most successful political direct mail letter of recent vintage was one signed by Ronald Reagan inviting selected Republican voters to become members of the Republican Presidential Task Force. Unlike Tom Collins' letter for George McGovern, it had a more conventional "you" — rather than "I" — orientation. It also used short, pithy paragraphs, and began:

> As your President, I am calling upon you to make a most unusual sacrifice.
>
> Not the kind of sacrifice that a national emergency might require of you or your children or your grandchildren to protect our shores from invasion.
>
> I pray that will never happen — but today I still must ask you to volunteer.
>
> And I must ask you to sacrifice for your country — in order to keep our Republican majority status in the Senate.
>
> For this reason, I am personally inviting you to become a member of the "Republican Presidential Task Force."

The concept of getting a core customer group to become members of a "club" is one of the most powerful strategies for many commercial direct marketers. Its adaptation for political causes shows how commercial techniques can be effectively adapted to fund-raising. The member benefits — not unlike many used commercially — were described in the personalized letter:

> I am calling upon you to become a charter member of the Task Force.
>
> In honor of this occasion, I have ordered a special Medal of Merit to be struck.
>
> And Senator Bob Packwood, Chairman of the Task Force, will present you with your Medal of Merit.
>
> I think it's beautiful and impressive . . . though a bit large for informal wear, so there's a lapel pin (an exact reproduction of the Medal of Merit) to be worn proudly every day.
>
> Also, your name will be entered in my "Honor Roll" book and remain with my permanent papers.
>
> I am placing a copy of this Honor Roll on file so that everyone can see your name on this vital document, along with the other true Republicans who are making this country strong again.
>
> Equally exciting, I've commissioned Senator Packwood to dedicate a full size American flag at a special ceremony in the Rotunda of our Nation's Capitol Building.

And I've asked Bob to send this personal memento to you so that you can proudly fly it as I will on every day that's important to America.

And as a member of the Task Force, Senator Packwood will also be sending you a Task Force Membership Card with a toll-free, unlisted, members only Washington hot-line number on the back.

It's not for constituent services . . . there are regular channels for that.

But Task Force members can call or write any day to get an accurate up-to-date report on issues that are being discussed in the Senate.

You will also be receiving a special insider's report called "The Force" so you can know exactly what is happening on Capitol Hill and across the country.

And Bob is planning on writing you special personal letters to keep you informed of any issues that he feels the Task Force should be taking immediate action on.

REPUBLICAN PRESIDENTIAL

TASK FORCE

RONALD REAGAN
Founder

BOB PACKWOOD
Chairman

September 4, 1981

Mr. John D. Sample
Epsilon Data Management
24 New England Executive Park
Burlington, Massachusetts 01803

Dear Mr. Sample:

As your President, I am calling upon you to make a most unusual sacrifice.

Not the kind of sacrifice that a national emergency might require of you or your children or your grandchildren to protect our shores from invasion.

I pray that will never happen -- but today I still must ask you to volunteer.

And I must ask you to sacrifice for your country -- in order to keep our Republican majority status in the Senate.

For this reason, I am personally inviting you to become a member of the "Republican Presidential Task Force."

And you are urgently needed. Here's why:

Right now we Republicans only have a slim 4 vote majority lead in the Senate. That's all!

It took us 26 long years to gain 16 Senators to get that narrow majority. But the Democrats need only gain four states in the November '82 elections to win it back from us!

This means that all the programs I am trying to get through on your behalf may be in jeopardy if we don't act fast.

Believe me, I'm not asking everyone to join this club -- only proud, flag waving Americans like you who I know are willing to sacrifice to keep our nation strong.

I am working with the National Republican Senatorial

-2-

Committee...our Party's only official committee that
concentrates exclusively on the United States Senate...
in an effort to build a Task Force of grass-roots Republicans...who are willing to join together to build a war
chest to help us keep a Republican majority in the Senate.

Remember -- November 2, 1982 is just around the corner!

And the "Republican Presidential Task Force" is a
must for every Republican who is serious about keeping a
Republican majority in the Senate.

I am calling upon you to become a charter member of
the Task Force.

In honor of this occasion, I have ordered a special
Medal of Merit to be struck.

And Senator Bob Packwood, Chairman of the Task Force,
will present you with your Medal of Merit.

I think it's beautiful and impressive...though a bit
large for informal wear, so there's a lapel pin (an exact
reproduction of the Medal of Merit) to be worn proudly
everyday.

Also, your name will be entered in my "Honor Roll"
book and remain with my permanent papers.

I am placing a copy of this Honor Roll on file so
that everyone can see your name on this vital document,
along with the other true Republicans who are making this
country strong again.

Equally exciting, I've commissioned Senator Packwood
to dedicate a full size American flag at a special ceremony
in the Rotunda of our Nation's Capitol Building.

And I've asked Bob to send this personal momento to
you so that you can proudly fly it as I will on every day
that's important to America.

And as a member of the Task Force, Senator Packwood
will also be sending you a Task Force Membership Card with
a toll-free, unlisted, members only Washington hot-line
number on the back.

It's not for constituent services...there are regular
channels for that.

But Task Force members can call or write any day to
get an accurate up-to-date report on issues that are being
discussed in the Senate.

-3-

You will also be receiving a special insider's report called "The Force" so you can know exactly what is happening on Capitol Hill and across the country.

And Bob is planning on writing you a special personal letter each month to keep you informed of any issues that he feels the Task Force should be taking immediate action on.

I believe that the "Republican Presidential Task Force" will be one of the strongest action groups in America.

That's why Bob Packwood and I decided to launch the "Republican Presidential Task Force." We must maintain our Republican majority status in the Senate!

And that's why I'm asking you to become a Task Force member and send $120 a year (i.e., $10 a month) and more when possible. I realize this is a sacrifice -- but sacrifice is what made this country great.

I cannot carry this burden alone. I am only one man. It will be your regular monthly contribution that will carry us to victory.

So I urge you to check the "YES" box on the enclosed Acceptance Form and mail it with your check today.

Remember, this is an exclusive club -- and every member is dedicated to keeping a Republican majority in the Senate. And the Democrats are coming after us in 1982. They want to defeat our 12 Republican incumbents up for re-election.

So tough days are ahead...days that call for sacrifice!

That's why I'm hoping you'll accept my personal invitation now to join this Task Force by sending your contribution of $120 (or $10 for the first month) without delay.

Sincerely,

Ronald Reagan

Ronald Reagan

P.S.   If you truly share my vision of America then I urge you to join the "Republican Presidential Task Force."

Thanks so much for reading my letter, and, please, I need your answer within 10 days.

Ronald Reagan

HUMOR IN DIRECT MAIL: THE HABAND LETTERS

For the majority of mailers, humorous letters are a dangerous gamble. All too often, what seems funny to the writer fails to draw laughter from recipients. And when it does tickle readers' funny bones, the laughter may easily distract from the selling message.

It takes an exceptional writer to consistently turn out lighthearted messages that produce sales. And M.H. Habernickel was just such a writer. For 50 years, he kept producing letter after letter that not only built a following of dedicated readers, but became the cornerstone of his business as well.

The Haband letter selected for this book is just one of hundreds of masterpieces turned out over the years by M.H. Habernickel. We could have selected most any of the 100 or so Haband letters in our files since they, too, are true classics. The real magic of these letters was their continuity. They had a personal style all their own. They kept readers "up to date" on the Habernickel family and the Haband staff — particularly Miss Feeney, Mr. Habernickel's long-time secretary. The letters often brought a host of personal replies from recipients. But, most important of all, they produced millions of orders.

Operating Through THE UNITED STATES MAILS Exclusively Since 1925

HABAND COMPANY

FAMOUS FOR TIES

PARCEL POST ASSN.

Men's Wear

M. HABERNICKEL, JR.

PATERSON, N.J.

Dear Haband Customer:

My oldest and dearest friend, Bill Griffin, a retired Episcopal minister, challenged my son Duke to an automobile race around the block — Backwards!

Here's how it came about. When Bill was a kid and before he was old enough for a license, he acquired a broken-down jalopy. He finally got the thing running, but he couldn't take it out on the road. The only place he could drive it was on the wagon turn-around between his house and the barn.

Eventually when he got tired of circling around frontwards, he drove around in reverse. It got so he could travel around that circle backwards at full throttle! For hours on end! The result is that Rev. Bill (ret.) is still the best backer-upper around the State.

Well that challenge suited Duke exactly. He couldn't wait. So the two of them decided to make the race around the block next Saturday morning at daybreak. That way, they figured, they would settle the argument before the cops came out of the diners and before the kids, dogs and bicycles got out on the street.

When the women heard about it, the best they could do was induce the boys to just race around the block one at the time. Against the stopwatch.

When Miss Feeney, my secretary for 25 years, heard about it, she said, "Dear old Father Murphy will roll over in his grave." When I heard about it, I said, "You will have me in my grave before my time, but Bill why don't you confine yourself to wearing your collar backwards, and you Duke, if you can drag yourself out of bed that early, why don't you get up to the office in the morning for once and find out how the rest of the world lives." Well, that was the end of that.

But y' know what? I can't back up a car, as proven by the well-rolled lawn on both sides of my drive-way. And again, y' know what? I don't give a hoot! I have my own specialty in doing things backwards. I have my own specialty in doing things backwards. I reverse fashion trends! It works two ways. In the first place I don't expose my customers to every freak fashion that comes down the pike. Secondly I reject the idea that fash-ion starts at the top price lines and then has to trickle down to the rest of us when all the glamour is gone.

You take, for example, the new Leisure Suit. Here's a men's outfit that has everything the American Male is looking for. Solid Comfort. Plus, a new, very physical, handsome Good Looks. It makes a man look younger, chestier, slimmer-waisted, very much alive and up to date. Would I say sexier? I'll leave that up to you. But what a long overdue release from the dull old dress code established by my father and President McKinley! Frankly I feel 15 years better-looking when I wear a Leisure Suit, and I think absolutely everyone else looks better in them too!

Now I am sure you have read how Leisure Suits were all dreamed up by some great international design-er who put a $200 price tag on it, and who already has every playboy on the Riviera, every major movie star in Hollywood, and all the rich sport figures showing off in these new Leisure Suits. But maybe you can tell me.

What I don't understand is this: Why doesn't anybody ever come out with these things for the ordinary guy like you and me? While they are at the peak of fashion! AT PRICES THAT MAKES SENSE! Well, folks, maybe good old Haband can be the one to reverse the routine this time. Just take a look at our certified prospectus.

To begin with, you notice, we don't insult you by asking a hundred dollars for one of these suits — that's what everybody seems to be charging now. Even in the ho-hum national chain stores. Maybe 6 years from now the rest of them will come down to match Haband's price but right now everybody is out of sight.

And it's not fair! Next to the dashing good looks of a Leisure Suit, practical economy is their strongest appeal. They cost less to make than an old-fashioned suit and they should cost you less to buy. Look at all the fine details we show you on our color pictures enclosed. Like the 4 button-down pleated pockets. The shoulder epaulets. The full collar. The easy split side seams!

And look at the splendid two-way, non-snag knit, 100% polyester fabric. Take a minute to examine the sample swatches we've enclosed. It keeps its shape, holds its crease, and performs really beautifully. Rain or shine, hot or humid, and wherever your travels take you. With all of that style, detail and fabric, our Haband price for the complete Leisure Suit is only $29.95! Right, Twenty-Nine, Ninety-five and not $89 or $100! $29.95!

Am I beginning to speak your language? Does this combination of Good Looks and Dramatic Economy whet your appetite? Then hold on to your hat and let me tell you even more!

You can kiss your Dry Cleaner goodbye! Now, for once and for all, not just your slacks but the whole outfit, top and bottom, pants and jacket, need only an easy spin through your home wash machine to get a full Permanent Press No Iron Restoration! You know how easy wash and wear knit slacks come out. Now you can do your whole Haband Leisure Suit the same way! The savings can pay for the whole suit in a single season!

Well, there it is. I was just gathering my notes to enumerate for you, stitch-by-stitch and feature-for-feature all the technical details like Talon® zipper, two-way stretch, BanRol® linings and sleeve wiggins when Miss Feeney, my secretary for 25 years chirped, 'Hold it boss, I never bought an outfit for its technical features. Either I just "gotta have it" or I don't.'

Well, if you have been around lately, or if you have been watching the celebrities on television, if you have been to a big convention, if you have been to the theatre, or the resorts,—you know you gotta have a Leisure Suit. If you sense how others respond when a good looking man walks into a room, you gotta have a Leisure Suit. You absolutely must or you are going to feel out of it. And maybe, up till now, your common sense said you couldn't afford it. But now, my friend, at Haband's $29.95, and with all that no-iron wash and wear, you gotta have a Leisure Suit. And why not — you'll never get a better deal.

Very truly yours,

MH/BF

HABAND OF PATERSON

JOHN YECK'S "LET'S HAVE BETTER MOTTOES ASSOCIATION" LETTERS

Some years ago, an ex-circus bandsman, Fred Gymer, decided to go into advertising copywriting. To attract clients, he created the mythical Let's Have Better Mottoes Association and began a series of tongue-in-cheek letters, each accompanied by a motto of-the-month to be hung on recipients' walls. The series became quite popular, and many companies asked Gymer to adapt his letters for their own mailings.

In many businesses, the biggest job for direct mail is to keep the company name in front of customers. This is a case that often calls for lighthearted copy. And no syndicated mailing series has done this job so well over such a long period as the Let's Have Better Mottoes Association.

When Fred Gymer died some years ago, most everyone thought the series would die along with him. Writing such letters month after month requires a very special talent. Fortunately the one person uniquely talented to keep the series going decided to acquire the business and today new motto cards continue to be hung each month in homes and offices throughout the world. And a new generation of readers eagerly awaits the monthly letters which flow from the talented pen of John Yeck.

While we've included just one of the monthly Let's Have Better Mottoes Association letters and accompanying motto created by John Yeck, it's typical of the long-running series.

2222 Arbor Boulevard · Dayton, Ohio 45439 · 513/294-4000

THE LET'S HAVE BETTER MOTTOES ASSOCIATION, INC.

As part of one of its rare forays into economics, the Let's Have Better Mottoes Association, Inc.'s official board has chosen a motto submitted this month by Bill Anderson:

POVERTY IS CATCHING
you can get it from your wife

The motto will be conspicuously displayed as the icing on the prize-winning lemon cake at our annual picnic on the 18th. Ladies are particularly invited and even wives are admitted. However, husbands of female members will be well advised to stay home.

A vacation is what you take when you can't take what you've been taking any longer.

Taking his cue from this month's motto, Joe has turned his attention to the world of business. His astonishing discoveries include such intelligence as: a) an expert knows just about as much as you do but is better organized and uses slides; b) punctuality at meetings is the art of guessing how late the rest of the committee will be; c) that the computer has revolutionized business ... there are just as many mistakes as ever but now they're nobody's fault; and d) free advice is worth every cent it costs.

Money won't buy love but it sure puts you in better field position.

Other mottoes which lost out but probably bear repetition if only because of the weather include: "I'M NEVER TOO BUSY TO SAY GOODBYE," from George Bucko; "A CLEAN DESK IS THE SIGN OF A FRIGHTENED MAN," from John Eckels, and "IT IS MORE BLESSED TO GIVE, THEN RECEIVE," from R. F. DeLay.

Business is what if you don't have enough of you get out of.

Cordially,

John D. Yeck

Secretary
The Let's Have Better Mottoes Association, Inc.

SECTION III

CONSUMER MAIL ORDER LETTERS

We see them almost every day. We open our mailboxes and discover the store has come to us. You name it. Someone is trying to convince us we should buy a product or service from them — sight unseen. This is no small task for the copywriter. The customer can't touch, feel, or see the product. They can't see the "store." They don't know what the salesperson looks like. Words alone must create a convincing picture.

Although photographs or drawings in a brochure or booklet will help do the job, testing has shown that the words in a direct mail letter most often make the difference between success and failure.

To supplement the classic direct mail letters shown in the preceding chapter, I've chosen a number of additional consumer mail order letters to show how copywriters have handled other difficult mail order selling situations.

THE FRANKLIN MINT "NORMAN ROCKWELL PLATE" LETTER

Franklin Mint letters (in addition to the classics used to introduce The Franklin Library) are among the contemporary classics of direct mail because each successfully introduces another new series of collectibles.

The first, a one-page letter announcing the first Christmas plate by Norman Rockwell, is particularly notable because it created today's boom in collectible plates. While plate collecting had been enjoyed throughout the world since Bing & Grondahl of Denmark introduced its first Christmas plate in 1895, it was a rather quiet hobby with only a limited number of participating collectors.

But by bringing America's favorite artist into the act and producing etched plates of silver, The Franklin Mint started a trend that has been growing ever since. This single letter produced 18,321 orders at $100 each.

One thing The Franklin Mint had learned through research was that the "big" market was made up not of dedicated collectors, but of people who wanted some kind of collection —without having to work at it. The primary interest of most buyers wasn't in potential appreciation value — that would involve constantly tracking the market, involving special knowledge and "work."

Thus, the typical Franklin Mint letter doesn't lead off with an "investment" approach, although something about the history of appreciation of similar collectibles is usually woven into the copy to establish the type of item being offered as worthy of collecting. The key emphasis in this letter was that this was a "first" — an important selling point in the collectibles field. And, of course, there was strong emphasis on the "limited edition." A few years before, The Franklin Mint had introduced the idea of using an order deadline as a means of establishing the limit of an edition.

At the time, true collectors scoffed at the idea of letting the number of orders decide an edition limit. But The Franklin Mint was dealing with "non-collectors" — those who didn't have the foggiest idea of what quantity constituted a limited edition. However, a deadline date was something they could understand. Today, an edition limited by deadline has become relatively common.

THE FRANKLIN MINT
FRANKLIN CENTER, PENNSYLVANIA 19063

August 10, 1970

Dear Subscriber:

Norman Rockwell, the most famous American artist of our time, has just created his first Christmas Plate.

The Franklin Mint will issue it as a limited edition work of art in solid sterling silver.

You, as an established Franklin Mint collector, are the first to be informed of this.

Christmas Plates have always been very popular with collectors, and it is interesting to note that the more limited issues have greatly appreciated in value over the years. Some limited first editions in china and crystal, only a few years old, are now selling for $1000 and more — even though they are not made of precious metal and are not the work of a major artist.

While we cannot guarantee the extent to which our first plate will appreciate in value, we believe that it has a lot going for it. Being made of solid sterling silver, it has a basic intrinsic value to start with. And it is the work of a major artist, his first work in this medium. In addition, it is the first Christmas Plate to be issued by The Franklin Mint, the first of a new annual series. At the original issue price of $100, which includes a deluxe presentation case, it is a rather remarkable value.

There will undoubtedly be a great demand for this plate from museums and collectors around the world. But since we will produce this design only in 1970, and each plate must be individually etched, we feel certain that the supply will fall far short of the demand.

Consequently, the prestige gift stores invited to sell this plate will each have a very limited allocation, and no reorders will be accepted.

Furthermore, we will accept no direct orders from anyone except established Franklin Mint collectors like yourself — and these individual orders will be accepted only if postmarked by August 23, 1970. No more than one plate can be sold to any subscriber, and we must reserve the right to cut off the acceptance of orders even earlier if necessary.

Therefore, if you would like to acquire one of these plates for your home, please be sure your order is postmarked as early as possible and is submitted on the enclosed special order form.

Sincerely yours,

Joseph M Segel

Joseph M. Segel
President

JMS/jg

THE FRANKLIN MINT "GALLERY OF AMERICAN ART WESTERN ART" LETTER

The other classic Franklin Mint letter introduced its first non-metallic collectible — a limited edition collection of western art prints. The challenge of this letter was to convince non-collectors (who had previously purchased more easily understood coins, medals, ingots, and plates) to buy a collection of art prints.

The whole concept of print collecting — and the value of western art — had to be introduced in this letter. No mention of anything related to appreciation value of limited edition prints appeared until the middle of the second page of the letter. Even then, there was a strong qualifier for the non-collector audience:

> This doesn't mean that all prints will increase in value. Indeed, this is not the best reason to build a collection of fine prints. You should only purchase those prints which you truly admire.

A suggested reason to acquire the collection — easily understood by Franklin Mint collectors — was added near the close of the letter:

> For you and your family, this collection will become a lasting heirloom — a portfolio of fine art to be enjoyed and admired for many years to come.

This "benefit" wasn't just a copywriter's whim. Constantly monitoring customer correspondence had shown this to be one of the key reasons why non-collectors had purchased previous Franklin Mint products.

The letter also clearly established an action-compelling deadline:

> There is only one time you can acquire The Franklin Mint Gold Medal Portfolio of Western Art. That time is now. The very last date by which subscriptions may be placed is May 15, 1973. Any subscriptions postmarked after that date must, regretfully, be returned. I suggest you mail the enclosed subscription form as early as possible.

This mailing won a host of awards. But its most important "award" was that 4,333 Franklin Mint collectors responded to the single mailing, producing over $2 million in sales. And it quickly established The Franklin Mint as a multifaceted collectibles company rather than simply a maker of coins and medals.

The Franklin Mint Gallery of American Art

FRANKLIN CENTER, PENNSYLVANIA 19063

April 30, 1973

Dear Collector:

In the late 1800's a struggling young artist by the name of Charles M. Russell traveled the Montana countryside painting pictures. If he was lucky, he got $25 apiece for them.

Recently a museum in the Southwest received an offer for one of the paintings in its collection -- a painting by the same Charles M. Russell. The offer was $230,000. The museum turned it down.

And just a few weeks ago, a gallery in Sedona, Arizona staged a one-man show of contemporary Western Art. Collectors were lined up when the doors opened. Within twenty minutes more than $75,000 worth of art was sold.

The increasing demand for Western Art is no mystery. There are good reasons for it. Western Art, more than any other, symbolizes the traditions of our American heritage. It recaptures the pioneering spirit many people have lost -- but now long for. In its realism, its honesty, it portrays the rugged individualism of American life.

Now, for the first time, the best works of ten leading Western artists are available to you on a systematic monthly acquisition plan, at a price you can afford.

The Franklin Mint Gallery of American Art has obtained the exclusive right to issue a limited edition of signed prints of the ten award-winning paintings featured in the enclosed brochure. The Franklin Mint Gold Medal Portfolio of Western Art is a truly exceptional collection. One you can be proud to own and display.

It is important to note that these are signed prints. Each will be individually signed by the artist -- and that makes all the difference in the world. A signed print of a major work by a prominent artist is a significant work of art.

Because the term "print" itself is often misunderstood, a few words of explanation are in order. There is an important distinction between a fine print versus a piece of printing. Ordinary color printing utilizes just four colors. But in creating fine prints, the skilled printmaker uses as many colors as necessary -- often as many as ten or twelve -- to fully capture the rich tones, fine detail and subtle hues which the artist has so carefully blended in creating his work.

Fine prints have been treasured for centuries. Louis XIV of France was an avid print collector. So was Thomas Jefferson. And in our own time, Cornelius Vanderbilt and J. Pierpont Morgan assembled print collections which are now highly valued.

Like original paintings, prints frequently become increasingly valuable over the years. You are probably aware that original Currier & Ives prints, which originally sold for less than a dollar in the nineteenth century, are now commanding auction prices of as much as $5,000. Audubon bird prints sell for even more. And a signed print by Renoir recently brought $13,160.

This doesn't mean that all prints will increase in value. Indeed, this is not the best reason to build a collection of fine prints. You should only purchase those prints which you truly admire.

The prints in The Franklin Mint Gold Medal Portfolio of Western Art are distinctive for several reasons. But three in particular:

1. They are prints of <u>museum quality</u>

2. They are exclusive <u>limited editions</u>

3. They are <u>signed prints</u>

MUSEUM QUALITY means that these prints will be produced by the Triton process -- the printmaking process preferred by leading museums because it captures the full tones of the original. Unlike ordinary lithographic reproductions, you won't see the image broken up into a lot of small dots if you look at it under magnification.

EXCLUSIVE LIMITED EDITION means that the subscribers to this portfolio will possess <u>the only signed prints of these works of art that will ever be produced.</u>

What's more, there will be no unsigned prints. Once the prints for the Gold Medal Portfolio have been made, the plates will be destroyed. Only smaller size reproductions will be permitted for books and other reference publications.

And, since the privilege of subscribing is being extended exclusively to a select group of collectors -- and only until May 15, 1973 -- the number of prints will be EXTREMELY LIMITED.

Thus, you will own a most unusual collection. Museum quality prints of Western paintings which have been awarded Gold Medals for excellence. An edition limited exclusively to a small group of collectors. And each print individually hand-signed by the artist.

These are the true hallmarks of a fine collection. A collection you will want to share with your family and show to your friends. For it can be enjoyed by anyone who appreciates the beauty of fine art.

To get just an impression of the beauty of these paintings, look at the illustrations in the accompanying prospectus. Even though they are greatly reduced in size (the actual prints measure 22" x 30"), the great character of these works is evident.

Signed prints of this quality frequently cost $100 or more apiece. But because we are issuing the Gold Medal prints only as a complete collection the offering costs are substantially lowered -- and you get the benefit of acquiring these fine prints at just $50 each.

The prints will be sent to you at the rate of one per month, beginning in June 1973. As part of your subscription, you will receive a magnificent library portfolio to protect and display the complete collection of ten signed prints.

Each print is separately matted in the portfolio. One of the great advantages of this arrangement is that you can hang any of the prints any time you wish ... and you can easily alternate your collection on the wall of your home or office.

For you and your family, this collection will become a lasting heirloom -- a portfolio of fine art to be enjoyed and admired for many years to come.

There is only one time you can acquire The Franklin Mint Gold Medal Portfolio of Western Art. That time is now. The very last date by which subscriptions may be placed is May 15, 1973. Any subscriptions postmarked after that date must, regretfully, be returned. I suggest you mail the enclosed subscription form as early as possible.

Please note that no advance payment is necessary. You will receive an invoice with each of the signed prints as they are sent to you on a monthly basis.

Sincerely,

Richard S. Hodgson
Managing Director

RSH:lrt

P.S. As a subscriber to The Franklin Mint Gold Medal Portfolio of Western Art, you will receive a complimentary First Edition copy of the art book that will be published about these ten award-winning paintings and their artists. You will be able to order additional copies, if you wish, so you can share with your friends the book about your personal collection.

National Wholesale Company "Sarah Smith" Letter

Although it's sometimes effective to have a celebrity present a message, most letters are more believable when they come from a noncelebrity. Eddie and Sarah Smith are celebrities within direct mail circles, but they aren't a couple you read about in the national news. The pantyhose letter, written by John Lyle Shimek, is a direct mail classic. It begins:

> I'm Sarah Smith, and want to share something my husband said the other day that just about sums up the reasons why you may be disappointed with most panty-hose made today. Eddie said:
>
> "Most other panty-hose come in two or three sizes today but some of the prettiest and most shapely legs don't!"
>
> This is so true. He couldn't be more right!
>
> Most of us switched to panty-hose a few years ago and then what happened?
>
> The manufacturers started switching sizes on us — now some make only one size and expect the woman who buys them to jump for joy and think she will get a comfortable fit and look like a fashion model.
>
> Honestly, I just don't know how most women put up with the hit-or-miss fit, poor quality and dime store appearance they get when they buy panty-hose today.

The letter continues in the same personal tone. On page 2, for example, "Sarah" writes:

> I just wish you could see all the nice letters we get from women of all ages who write to tell us how much trouble they have had with store bought panty-hose that don't fit, and how they love their new found National Panty-Hose.

And on page 4:

> When our customers from out-of-state stop by to say "hello" and pick up a few boxes of hosiery, Eddie always likes to give them something free — kind of like the free gifts offered on the coupon enclosed.

Do your Panty Hose make you feel pretty? Do they fit perfectly and wear and wear?

Hello,

I'm Sarah Smith, and want to share something my husband said the other day that just about sums up the reasons why you may be disappointed with most panty-hose made today. Eddie said:

"Most other panty-hose come in two or three sizes today but some of the prettiest and most shapely legs don't!"

This is so true. He couldn't be more right!

Most of us switched to panty-hose a few years ago and then what happened?

The manufacturers started switching sizes on us-- now some make only one size and expect the woman who buys them to jump for joy and think she will get a comfortable fit and look like a fashion model.

Honestly, I just don't know how most women put up with the hit-or-miss fit, poor quality and dime store appearance they get when they buy panty-hose today.

Even the 99¢ "Grocery Store" type is too much to pay for something that doesn't make you look and feel good!

I love panty-hose and hope they are here to stay- but they certainly should be made to fit properly and give

Eight into three won't go!

Size A Size B Size C

you stylish good looks--and last a while--and if we pay quality <u>prices</u>, we should get <u>quality</u> hosiery.

Eddie started selling quality hosiery by mail, by the dozen, over 30 years ago. Now he has over 500,000 satisfied customers--many who have been regular customers for over 30 years. So--

If you are fed up with baggy, ill-fitting hose--

If you find you can't get the same size twice--

If the quality is poor or inconsistent--

If you'd like to try something better,something that is different and really worth the money you pay--

I'd like to invite you to try our National brand. See for yourself what a pleasure it is to have panty-hose that fit like a smooth second skin--but don't come apart or fade after the second wearing.

I just wish you could see all the nice letters we get from women of all ages who write to tell us how much

trouble they have had with store bought panty-hose that don't fit -- and how they love their new found National Panty-Hose.

They tell us how nice it is to have sheer panty-hose at last, that have crotch pieces and panels--and are made of the most expensive materials. They say our panty-hose give them the beauty, the comfort, long wear, and confidence they have needed for years.

Over and over again, they say in so many, many ways --

8 into 3 just won't go!

When you try to make 8 sizes of women fit into only 3 sizes of panty-hose--nobody gets a good fit. If you are short they sag and if you are tall they pull down. If you are slim they bag and if your figure is full they bind. Even someone in the middle doesn't get a good fit because the panty-hose were designed to fit everybody--which means we all end up with ill-fitting panty-hose that does nothing for our figures or morale.

That's why Eddie insists on only the finest quality made in eight sizes -- Yes EIGHT separate sizes. When you come to National for your panty-hose -- you are abso- lutely sure of getting a perfect fit. You'll look great, feel good and will be well dressed and attractive. Take your choice from four <u>regular</u> sizes and four <u>queen</u> sizes.

You don't ever need to worry when you order from National. Our money-back guarantee protects you completely. If you should ever get a pair that is not perfect in every way -- Eddie just doesn't argue. He simply sends you another pair -- no questions asked. (I've seen him send a whole dozen, just to be sure the customer was repaid for her trouble and for calling an error to his attention.)

When our customers from out-of-state stop by to say "hello" and pick up a few boxes of hosiery, Eddie always likes to give them something free -- kind of like the free gifts offered on the coupon enclosed.

Your free pair coupon will do more than just bring you some nice free gifts -- buying the National way will bring you <u>freedom</u> -- freedom from being forced to take something less than you deserve -- freedom to choose exactly what you want from National's complete line - 30 styles of panty-hose and stockings.

So if you would like to test wear hosiery that's "tailor made" for YOU -- not for <u>everybody</u> and <u>anybody</u>--

Why not try the National way for yourself. You'll be so glad you did. Why not get a trial order in the mail today. Then you'll see why more than 500,000 women buy with confidence from National.

Sincerely,

Sarah Smith

Sarah Smith

P.S. Remember we ship all orders within 24 hours, too!

NATIONAL *Wholesale Co.* INC.
HOSIERY DIVISION

Lexington, North Carolina 27292
(704) 246-5904

BANKER'S LIFE "ONE WOMAN TO ANOTHER" LETTER

Even after the women's liberation movement came into being and mailings to businesswomen increased dramatically, there was a continuing tendency to disguise the fact that the writer of a letter might have been a woman. For example, when Joan Manley was named Publisher of Time-Life Books, she initially signed all the promotion letters, "J. Daniels Manley." Today, however, many direct mail advertisers have found it pays to use woman-to-woman letters (and few even hesitate to have a female signature on letters going to male audiences if the logical signer happens to be a woman).

A pace-setting woman-to-woman letter was created by Sheila Stogol for Banker's Life. Selling life insurance to women has long been a problem. "Perhaps," Sheila Stogol suggests, "companies just were not able to see their female prospects as these prospects see themselves." So she started out with an intriguing headline:

>   From one woman to another . . .

>   Here's one Fact of Life your mother probably never told you!

The letter then eases into the subject, building interest for three paragraphs before starting to sell insurance:

>   When you and I were growing up, financial security planning was probably the last thing a woman thought of for herself. If your childhood was like mine, when the subject of life insurance came up, Mother usually stayed in the kitchen and let Dad handle everything.

>   But our lifestyles are different now! Not only are women concerned with running the household and raising children, many mothers are also holding a job to help make ends meet.

>   Because you care so much about your family's economic security, you put in many long, hard hours keeping up with home, children and work. And your family depends on you for that support. Your income is an important part of your family's present and future resources.

**Bankers Life
and Casualty Company**
4444 Lawrence Avenue • Chicago, Illinois 60630

From one woman to another...
Here's one Fact of Life your mother probably never told you!

Dear Friend:

When you and I were growing up, financial security planning was probably the last thing a woman thought of for herself. If your childhood was like mine, when the subject of life insurance came up, Mother usually stayed in the kitchen and let Dad handle everything.

But our lifestyles are different now! Not only are women concerned with running the household and raising the children, many mothers are also holding a job to help make ends meet.

Because you care so much about your family's economic security, you put in many long, hard hours keeping up with home, children and work. And your family depends on you for that support. Your income is an important part of your family's present and future resources.

That's why today <u>women</u> as well as men urgently need enough life insurance protection to help see their loved ones through a very difficult time. To help replace their income <u>and</u> provide household help to keep the family together. And that's where Bankers can help with our ...

<u>$20,000 Life Up-Date Plan for Women</u> (Policy L-54F) -- the economical, easy-to-apply-for protection.

Of course, nothing could <u>replace</u> you! But this $20,000 term life protection would greatly ease the <u>financial</u> burden your family would face if they had to try to make it without you. And the additional $20,000 can help bring your coverage up to 1980 standards, in light of your growing responsibilities.

Now you can get $20,000 protection at a price that will fit even the tightest budget -- because you pay only for pure term life protection. And if you wish, you can keep this protection all the way up to age 70 -- for coverage through the years you need it most. There are no expensive frills to increase the cost.

Imagine -- $20,000 protection can cost less than a couple of pounds of beef. For a woman of 29, it's just $4.00 a month.

What's more, this protection couldn't be easier for you to apply for. All you have to do is fill out the enclosed application and mail it to us.

(over, please)

There's no need for an embarrassing, time-consuming physical exam. There are just three health questions to answer to determine whether you qualify.

Everything is handled the modern, no-fuss way. You can do it all by mail, and you get a policy written in no-nonsense language that's easy to read and understand.

You don't even send any money when you apply -- so you risk nothing!

If you're between ages 18 and 59, you can apply for all this protection right now, without cost, without obligation. Just complete and mail the simplified application in the enclosed postage-paid envelope.

That's right! It won't cost you anything to apply! You don't send a cent until your application is approved and you actually receive and look over your policy. In other words, you pay nothing until you decide if it's exactly what you want and need.

The sad fact is that old notions die hard. Many women today still don't realize the growing need for life insurance, even though they are responsible for a major part of their family's income.

Consider that the average woman has only a little over $7,000 life insurance, as compared to $29,000 for the average man, according to the American Council of Life Insurance.

Then ask yourself just how far your own present life insurance would take your family. The simple answer to bringing your coverage up-to-date is Bankers economical $20,000 Life Up-Date Plan for Women. That's why I urge you to apply for this valuable coverage right now.

Sincerely,

Cheri Wahlund

Cheri Wahlund
Bankers Life and
Casualty Company

P.S. Here's one more good reason to apply now. As soon as we hear from you, we'll rush your free copy of Cashing In at the Checkout, a remarkable book packed with ideas to help you slash your grocery bills and receive cash refunds, too. See the enclosed Free Gift Certificate for full details.

Personal Improvement Corporation "Lover of Life" Letter

One of the toughest selling jobs a letter writer faces is promoting a book by mail. Often there is no colorful brochure to be enclosed. You're faced with the job of selling words with only words.

Copywriter Bob Matheo faced such a challenge when Personal Improvement Corporation asked him to create a letter to sell *Keeping Young & Living Longer*. He describes the challenge:

■ To assess the letter, you must consider first the message the reader received on the outer envelope. It was:

"TURN THE TABLES ON FATHER TIME! A noted gerontologist reveals: 1. How to turn back the clock and feel, look and act years younger; and 2. How to slow down the aging process and add 25 vigorous years to your life span."

This is a whale of a promise. It is so big, in fact, that I feared two adverse reader reactions: the first was disbelief; the second was rejection (who wants to live to 100 if you're going to be senile, incontinent, and bedridden?).

So my first task was to deal with those two negative reactions. I dispelled disbelief in a display area at the top, by quoting book reviews and citing the author's credentials.

And I dispelled rejection with my opening.

Here's what he wrote:

> Dear Lover of Life:
>
> I myself am middle aged. I really enjoy life. But when I heard that Dr. Hrachovec could help me live past 100, my first reaction was, "Who wants to?"
>
> I was thinking of some old people I've seen. Senile. Incontinent. So weak they can hardly walk. If that's what old age is, I don't want it.
>
> But I soon discovered that isn't the kind of old age Dr. Hrachovec has in mind.

"NO WIDE-EYED VISIONARY...his credentials are impeccable."
—OAKLAND (Cal.) TRIBUNE

"A NO-NONSENSE HEALTH BOOK full of practical, sensible advice...no gimmicks, no fancy foods and vitamins, no extremes in exercise...all designed for staying 'Active and Healthy Past 100.'"
—HARTFORD (Conn.) COURANT

"A NOTED GERONTOLOGIST proves it is entirely possible to live past 100 and still enjoy an active, healthy, worthwhile life. Dr. Hrachovec tells us precisely what we must do and what we must not do...he makes many vital points that will bring hope to sufferers of allergies, circulatory problems, heart trouble, obesity and other chronic ills."
—LIBRARY JOURNAL

Author JOSEF P. HRACHOVEC, M.D., D.Sc. (pronounced Rash-o-vek), until a few years ago he was Senior Research Scientist in Molecular Biology of Aging, and Research Associate at the Gerontology Center at the University of Southern California. Currently, he is a practicing physician-geriatrician, in Beverly Hills, California. (For more details on his credentials, see back of Order Form).

Dear Lover of Life:

I myself am middle aged. I really enjoy life. But when I heard that Dr. Hrachovec could help me live past 100, my first reaction was, "Who wants to?"

I was thinking of some old people I've seen. Senile. Incontinent. So weak they can hardly walk. If that's what old age is, I don't want it.

But I soon discovered that isn't the kind of old age Dr. Hrachovec has in mind. His wish for all of us is:

LIVE YOUR LIFE FULLY
TO THE LAST DAY OF YOUR ALLOTTED TIME.

And he shows us how to make that allotted time last 25 years longer than you might ordinarily expect.

How? By eliminating or reducing disease-inducing, life-shortening errors before they do you irreversible harm.

He does not want you to buy injections or treatments.
He does not want you to buy vitamins or medications.
He does not want you to buy fancy exercise equipment.

He only wants you to "buy" the idea of avoiding errors.
And it costs you nothing -- except discipline.

-- turn page, please

START GETTING YOUNGER -- AT ONCE!

Unless you are severely impaired, you can start turning back the clock as soon as you've read Chapter 18. On page 129, Dr. Hrachovec explains a completely natural way to reverse the aging process. He calls it the "closest thing to an anti-aging pill." And a few pages later, he gives you a method to figure how many years you can add to your own life expectancy by following the program.

Here's a clue. Age-reversal is accomplished through exercise. But some kinds of exercise are bad, even downright dangerous, for middle aged people. Improperly done, exercise can kill you! On pages 141-142 you'll learn what kinds of exercise you should avoid -- and what kinds are safe, healthful and beneficial.

And on pages 149-156 he explains exactly how to start an exercise program in middle age. You get a formula for measuring your present state of fitness, a method of calculating the number of minutes a day you should exercise, and a way to assess your capacity to improve.

And improve you will! Even if you have led a sedentary life for years, you will be able to recapture your youthful physical fitness -- and the joyous, vital sense of well-being that goes with it.

EATING MISTAKES TO AVOID

Exercise is one of three critical areas in which you can make serious, life-shortening errors. Another is nutrition.

Many of us commit a dangerous error by eating too much at a single meal. Do you? There is a simple test you can perform that shows whether you are straining your heart by overeating. Read it on pages 51-52.

Another kind of bad eating habit, reports Dr. Hrachovec, creates a "traffic jam" in the blood that prevents nutrients from traveling to tissues that need to be restored or replaced. When this happens, your tissues -- and you -- age too fast.

One of the most serious and life-shortening consequences of eating errors is middle-age diabetes. In fact, it is estimated that about 2-million Americans have diabetes and don't even know it! If any of your relatives have had diabetes, you are probably susceptible to it. If you are overweight, you are also susceptible. But, susceptible or not, diabetes is always a danger in middle age. On page 62 you'll find 5 rules to help prevent the danger from becoming a reality.

Page 2

HOW TO "KICK" YOUR ADDICTION TO SUGAR

Sugar is closely associated with diabetes as well as other health problems. Indeed, many people are actually addicted to it -- they have a physical craving that has to be satisfied. If you are a sugar addict, it is doubtful that you can go more than two or three days without sweets.

Now there is a proven way to cure this addiction. It's on pages 81-82.

But some sugars are worse for you than others. You'll learn which kind builds dangerous triglycerides and cholesterol in the blood. Which kind turns directly into fat in your body. And which kinds don't.

AFTER ELIMINATING ERRORS -- THEN WHAT?

There is one more important step after eliminating errors in nutrition and exercise. Preventive Maintenance. You should keep a watchful eye on yourself. Dr. Hrachovec says: "I do not intend to turn a carefree you into a hypochondriac. I intend to keep you carefree, enjoying vigorous health ... past 100. Preventive Maintenance does not call for constant worry about health ... just a little attention to problems at the right time."

So he tells you what danger signals to be alert for -- what things to check from time to time. There is a simple test, for example, which you can give yourself to determine whether you have the beginnings of emphysema (which even non-smokers can get). He tells you how to avoid disease-inducing stress, and how to relieve it if it does occur. He shows you how to enjoy to the utmost those extra years you've added to your life.

Because life to 100 is your birthright! Even if your parents died young, even if you are susceptible to all the major chronic diseases ... you have as good a chance as others to live past 100. But you need to know what you're susceptible to ... and what specific errors to avoid.

YOU SET THE CLOCK BACK -- OR YOU GET YOUR MONEY BACK

The book is yours for just $13.00 plus shipping. And you won't have to wait till you're 100 to see if it works. Follow Dr. Hrachovec's program and you will start to look and feel younger in days. And it won't be a one-shot pick-me-up -- the good feeling will keep growing, month after month.

I therefore give you not the usual 7 - or 15-day guarantee -- but an IRONCLAD 90-DAY GUARANTEE! You must be personally satis-

-- turn page, please

fied that you have in effect set back the clock -- or you may return the volume for a refund in full (less postage & handling costs). Could anything be fairer?

The sooner you start, the better you'll feel. So order today.

Most sincerely,

Lon Charles

P.S. Don't miss Dr. Hrachovec's supplementary chapter, "How to Survive a Heart Attack."

As you probably know, coronary heart disease needn't be the killer it is. Simply by following the book's advice, you not only reduce your chance of heart attack; you also reduce your chance of dying from a heart attack you might get by 90%!

But, in case you should suffer a heart attack <u>before</u> this program has had its full beneficial effect, it would be good to know how to recognize the symptons (including those tricky "silent" attacks). And you should also learn the two critical things you must do in the first 15 minutes to ensure survival.

1122 1/83

MORE NUGGETS FROM THIS 242-PAGE GOLDMINE

A dangerous eating pattern that can trigger heart attacks. (p. 70)

Another eating pattern that can add years to your life. (p. 72)

Why Rand Corporation and Smith, Kline & French both predict a 50% increase in the human life span for the near future. (p. 7)

How the author has already prolonged animal life by 40% with various anti-oxidants, including one that's available without prescription in any drug store. (p. 24)

What you can do now to ensure longer, healthier lives for growing children. (pp. 80-81)

The simple diet that reduces high blood pressure. (p. 178)

How to test yourself for heart strain. (pp. 196-198)

How the technique that makes groceries last longer on the shelf has already prolonged animal life. (pp. 8-9)

Why rapid weight loss at the start of a diet is misleading. (p. 93)

How to lose weight without counting calories—train yourself to listen to signals your body sends you. (p. 99)

The Food Exchange System—a way to compute calories without actually counting them. (chapter 15)

How long should you exercise after you start to huff and puff. (p. 145)

A way to figure the minimum number of minutes a day you should exercise. (p. 157)

How stress causes chronic diseases. (p. 167)

How to build an exercise program up to full fitness from a sedentary start. (chapter 22)

How even non-smokers can get emphysema; and a simple test to see if you have the beginnings of this dread disease. (p. 188)

Strategies for survival…and for living a rewarding life. (chapter 26)

The secrets of progressive relaxation. (pp. 203-205)

How to make your heart stronger. (chapter 20)

Strategies to avoid overeating and overweight. (chapter 13)

Why standard weight tables can give you a bum steer. (pp. 85-87)

Why, with some people, "everything they eat turns to fat." (p. 66)

Another publication from
PERSONAL IMPROVEMENT CORP.
160 FARMINGDALE ROAD. WEST BABYLON. NEW YORK 11704

CALHOUN'S COLLECTORS SOCIETY "MY STOCKBROKER HUSBAND" LETTER

There are two ways to sell collectibles: as a unique personal possession (the technique favored by The Franklin Mint) or for their appreciation potential. A classic direct mail letter using the second approach was created by Herschell Gordon Lewis for Calhoun's Collectors Society.

A handwritten teaser on the envelope read:

> My stockbroker husband laughed at my "investment" but I knew better!

The letter inside began:

> Being married to a stockbroker, I hear more about the ups and downs of the stock market than most women.
>
> Back in April 1971, I bought my first "collector's plate" for $25.00. To be honest, I didn't buy it as an "investment" and my husband Gene certainly didn't even think of it as such. I bought the plate because I liked it. It reminded me of some collector's plates my mother had which were handed down to my oldest sister (and which, incidentally, were appraised for quite a bit of money just about the time I bought my first plate). So, I guess I had that word "investment" in the back of my mind as I displayed that plate for the first time. I even made the mistake of mentioning to my husband that one day it might be worth a lot more than I paid for it. He laughed and suggested if I had spare money to invest, he could recommend a good stock broker.
>
> Well, getting to the "last laugh" department — that $25.00 plate now lists for $580.00. That's an increase of 2,320 percent in just six years. The Dow-Jones in that same time has actually gone down from 950.82 as of April 28, 1971 to 769.92 on January 31, 1978. Of course, certain stock issues have done very well but overall I'm sure Gene wishes the market had done as well the past six years as my beautiful plate (besides, my investment pays a big dividend — I can enjoy looking at it every day).

Calhoun's Collectors Society, Inc.

Calhoun's means quality.

I'm repeating this offer to you one last time. Please read the enclosed note from Mr. Calvin... there's a good reason.

Dear Member,

Being married to a stock broker, I hear more about the ups and downs of the stock market than most women.

Back in April, 1971, I bought my first "collector's plate" for $25.00. To be honest I didn't buy it as an "investment" and my husband Gene certainly didn't even think of it as such. I bought the plate because I liked it. It reminded me of some collector's plates my mother had which were handed down to my oldest sister (and which, incidentally, were appraised for quite a bit of money just about the time I bought my first plate). So, I guess I had that word "investment" in the back of my mind as I displayed that plate for the first time. I even made the mistake of mentioning to my husband that one day it might be worth a lot more than I paid for it. He laughed and suggested if I had spare money to invest, he could recommend a good stock broker.

Well, getting to the "last laugh" department -- that $25.00 plate now lists for $580.00. That's an increase of 2,320 percent in just six years. The Dow-Jones in that same time has actually gone down from 950.82 as of April 28, 1971 to 769.92 on January 31, 1978. Of course, certain stock issues have done very well but overall I'm sure Gene wishes the market had done as well the past six years as my beautiful plate (besides, my investment pays a big dividend -- I can enjoy looking at it every day).

But just for the fun of it, I asked my husband to tell me what would have happened if I'd bought IBM stock in 1971. It turned out that the stock increased about 26%, and the dividends added 18% more. I couldn't resist remarking that this seemed a bit pale compared to the 2,320 percent increase in value on my plate. In this period of raging inflation I know quite a few people who, realizing that $25.00 invested at 5% in 1971 would now be worth only $33.75, wish they'd bought a few plates like mine.

One Appletree Square • Minneapolis, Minnesota 55420

Since that day six years ago when I first became interested in plate collecting, I've learned a lot. I'm now working for a company that's in the very thick of collectibles, and everyone here is excited about a new series of plates by the artist Yiannis Koutsis called "The Creation". This series is yours at a huge discount if you join Calhoun's Plate Collectors Club. The experts tell me this may be the most important plate series of the past ten years. But I don't want you to think I'm an expert. I'm still just a collector, but I've learned this lesson very well:

> Some plates, like some stocks, shoot up in value quickly.
> But even if they don't, collector's plates are works of
> art that you can enjoy as objects of beauty.

I think that's the best of all worlds. We can enjoy the plates, show them to our friends, even give them as the most treasured of gifts. And if they increase in value, what a lovely way to "invest"! Besides, who of us would ever enjoy displaying a stock certificate or a savings passbook?

Recently there was a plate collectors' convention here in Minneapolis. Much to my surprise, Gene suggested that why didn't "we" attend. A few years ago, he would have settled down with the Wall Street Journal or practiced his putting while I browsed through the plates. This certainly brought home one fact I had learned at work: Plate collecting is becoming the number one form of collecting in this country. This is important news for all of us who are collectors or who are thinking about becoming collectors. Over the next few years, as more and more people become collectors, the plates that are being issued now just have to become more valuable. That old law of supply and demand will really be at work, with more collectors bidding for the same number of limited editions.

> That's why I asked the president of our company, Stafford
> Calvin, if I could write this letter to invite you to acquire
> the Charter Edition of "The Creation" Series at $29.50 for
> each plate in the series.

If you're already a collector, you know that there are many plates available today, some of them costing as much as $1,250 at issue price. Some others are issued by the hundreds of thousands at a very low price; I think these are better called "souvenir plates" than collector's plates.

> When my husband asked me, learning of this new "Creation"
> series, "How does anyone know which plates will increase in
> value quicker than others?" I answered without thinking:
> "I guess you'd consult the experts -- the ones who really
> study the field."

I didn't know. So I discussed the matter with Mr. Calvin. It turned out he had been thinking along the same lines. The result is that one of the leading authorities in collectibles has become Advising

Consultant to Calhoun's. Roy Shoults owns Albatross Antiques, is president of the National Association of Limited Editions Dealers, and is generally regarded as one of the world's most knowledgeable people in this field.

What he says about this series is important. In his report to Mr. Calvin, Mr. Shoults felt that series presented an unusual opportunity for collectibles. He indicated a very high degree of public acceptance and that the aftermarket projection "seems permanent and assured".

Mr. Shoults went on to say that "The Creation" was one of "the most outstanding concepts of this decade".

OF ALL COLLECTIBLES EVER MADE AVAILABLE THROUGH CALHOUN'S -- WHETHER STAMPS, FIGURINES, BELLS, OR WHATEVER -- THE PLATE SERIES "THE CREATION" HAS BROUGHT THE GREATEST RESPONSE WE'VE EVER RECEIVED.

Don't miss the expiration date.

This invitation to obtain the Charter Edition of "The Creation" Series is open to you for just 21 days. This may be the only notification you will receive. Please don't miss out. Return your reservation promptly. (You may use one of your credit cards if you wish.)

When you return the enclosed reservation form, you will be assured of receiving each and every plate in the series "The Creation" at $29.50.

I do hope that you'll take advantage of this offer. Since I've become a plate collector, I've seen or read about almost every new issue. This is the one -- perhaps the only -- series which is truly timeless. "The Creation" carries a theme that will be as important to your great-grandchildren in 2078 as it is to you in 1978. And porcelain itself is ageless. Hundreds and hundreds of years from now, your collection will be as perfect as they will be the day you get them. What a wonderful family legacy! I plan to leave my set to one of my children, with instructions to hand it down to the next generation. You might choose to sell yours, or give it as a gift; mine will be a family heirloom.

Please do return your reservation within the 21-day period. You'll then be sure of owning the Charter Edition, which I believe will be far more coveted than even the First Edition.

You should know that any collectible you ever get through Calhoun's carries an unconditional 15-day examination period. If, after examining "In the Beginning", living with it, and showing it to your friends and relatives, you decide not to keep it, you may return it to us at any time up to 15 days after receipt for a full refund.

I realize that this letter will probably be read by some men. According to statistics, they're plate collectors too. (About half our Society's members are men.)

My husband Gene isn't as avid a collector as I am -- yet. But he did pay "The Creation" what for him is the ultimate compliment: Looking at Plate I the other night, he said, "That really <u>is</u> an unusual piece of art. Can we get a set for my sister?"

Sincerely,

CALHOUN'S COLLECTORS SOCIETY, INC.

Rhoda Engelson

RE/afu

P. S. The answer to the question in the last paragraph is on your reservation form. We must limit you to one set.

NATIONAL LIBERTY "CANCER INSURANCE" LETTER

Almost as difficult as writing political fund-raising letters is the task of selling insurance by mail. Not only is it primarily selling an idea, but what you can and can't say is controlled by many regulations that differ from state to state.

The late Arthur S. DeMoss refined the whole process of selling insurance by mail; his firm, National Liberty, consistently turned to the nation's most skilled direct mail writers to create masterpieces for its mailings.

A true classic was written for Arthur DeMoss' signature by Chris Stagg. The subject was difficult, but handled with exceptional skill. The letter began:

> This is a letter that is not like any you have ever received or I have ever written. My subject is not pleasant, but it is serious.
>
> My subject is cancer.

The letter went on to cite cancer statistics, and then stated:

> Until now, there have been only two things you could do to help fight this dread disease:
>
> 1. You can be sensible about your health. Annual checkups, stop smoking, etc.
>
> 2. You can be generous, by giving freely to the American Cancer Society, among many outstanding charities.
>
> But charity should begin at home, and now it can.

The letter lost no time talking about the cost of the cancer insurance plan being offered, but did it in a meaningful way. It explained why families of cancer victims need extra funds:

> You will need the money.
>
> John Wayne had lung cancer and beat it. So did Arthur Godfrey. So have millions of others, thanks to early detection and dramatic improvements in medical techniques.
>
> But movie and TV stars are rich. They can afford the very best care and never ask what the bill will come to. It doesn't matter when life is at stake.
>
> Or does it?
>
> We've designed this Cancer Expense Protection Plan because too many folks we know of recovered from cancer only to find themselves a burden to their families. And because of the enormous costs of cancer treatment, the security from a lifetime of honest work had evaporated as though it had never been there at all. Before cancer,

there had been independence. Now there was almost total dependence. And their spirits, frankly, died.

You can help prevent that, if you will take just one prudent step.

The letter concluded with a strong close:

> There is no reason anymore to be frightened about the cost of treating cancer. For National Home is ready to help. And, as I said, it takes but one prudent step on your part.
>
> Fill in and mail us the enclosed application today . . . along with 25¢. (The return envelope is postpaid.) We'll send you your policy, with an Effective Date shown on it. Read it carefully, please. If you don't like it . . . if you feel, for any reason at all, that it doesn't meet your requirements, send it back within 15 days of receiving it, and we'll return your money.
>
> That's all; there's absolutely no risk on your part. Under our 15-day money-back offer, you don't risk one cent!
>
> If you decide not to take advantage of this offer, I'll understand. But do think it over carefully. Who knows when you'll get an opportunity as good as this again?

National Home Life Assurance Co.

ARTHUR S. DeMOSS
PRESIDENT

Dear Friend:

This is a letter that is not like any you have ever received or I have ever written. My subject is not pleasant, but it _is_ serious.

My subject is cancer.

One out of every four Americans will get it, according to the 1975 Facts and Figures of the American Cancer Society, despite the truly excellent work of the medical profession. In fact, 53,000,000 of us now living will eventually have cancer. This means that it will strike about two out of three American families. Families like yours. Families like mine.

Until now, there have been only two things you could do to help fight this dread disease:

1. <u>You can be sensible about your health</u>. Annual checkups, stop smoking, etc.

2. <u>You can be generous</u>, by giving freely to the American Cancer Society, among many outstanding charities.

But charity should begin at home, and now it can.

Most sincerely, I urge you to read my letter carefully. It describes a plan that helps protect you against the menace of cancer. It helps protect you against having your life's savings, and those of your family, wiped out because of the almost incredible <u>costs</u> of cancer care.

And yet the cost of this plan is low. In fact, if you're 54 years old or under, the monthly premium is only $2.90. And if you're 55 or older the monthly premium is only $4.70. Yet we'll pay you, no matter what your age, $33.33 a day cash ($1,000.00 a month) if you're hospitalized due to cancer. That's in addition to what <u>anybody</u> pays you.

You will need the money.

John Wayne had lung cancer and beat it. So did Arthur Godfrey. So have millions of others, thanks to early detection and dramatic improvements in medical techniques.

<u>But movie and TV stars are rich</u>. They can afford the very best care and never ask what the bill will come to. It doesn't matter when life is at stake.

Or <u>does</u> it?

We've designed this Cancer Expense Protection Plan because too many folks we know of recovered from cancer only to find themselves a burden to their families. And because of the enormous costs of cancer treatment, the security from a lifetime of honest work had evaporated as though it had never been there at all. Before cancer, there had been independence. Now there was almost total dependence. And their spirits, frankly, died.

<u>You</u> can help prevent that, if you will take just one prudent step.

As you can see, the enclosed Enrollment Form is not transferable; no one but you may use it. In addition, we've made your first month's coverage just 25¢. If you have not had cancer, then I urge you to fill in and mail us the application along with your 25¢ today. In return, we will send you the policy to examine yourself, so that you can make your own independent decision about it. If you like the policy, keep it and continue your cancer protection at the rates now in effect: $2.90 a month if you're 54 or under . . . or $4.70 a month if you're 55 or older. However, if for any reason at all, you decide it isn't just what you need, then just return the policy to us within 15 days, and we'll return your quarter. No questions asked.

<u>You</u> can cancel. <u>We can't</u>.

Regardless of how often you have been treated for cancer, just pay your premiums on time and we can't cancel you out.

And we won't.

And remember, <u>your rate can be changed only if there's a rate adjustment on all policies of this class in your whole state</u>. You will never be singled out for a rate increase, regardless of how much you've collected.

We at National Home have over 50 years of experience in the insurance business. We're currently paying claims of $35,000,000.00 a year, to policyowners, under our various life, accident, and health plans.

As a thoughtful consumer, you probably have some good solid questions to ask. I will do my best to answer them forthrightly.

<u>"What are the benefits of your policy?"</u>

1. <u>Every day</u> you're hospitalized because of cancer, you'll collect $33.33 cash (that's $1,000.00 a month) paid <u>direct to you</u> unless <u>you</u> tell us otherwise. Up to a maximum of $12,000.00.

2. <u>Every daily visit</u> from your doctor while you're hospitalized for cancer will entitle you to $10.00. Limit: $1,200.00. 120 visits.

3. <u>In-Hospital Expenses for cancer treatment up to a maximum of $2,000.00</u>. These include reasonable and customary charges for diagnostic <u>X-rays</u>, <u>operating rooms</u>, <u>drugs and medicines</u>. <u>private duty nurses</u>, <u>blood and plasma</u> (unless it's replaced by your donors), <u>ambulances</u>, <u>X-ray</u>, <u>Radium</u>, and <u>Radioactive Isotope therapy</u>.

Another part of this benefit is well worth mentioning here. Many folks live in communities where the local hospital simply <u>doesn't have</u> the proper treatment facilities. If your doctor says that you must go to a hospital outside your area for special treatment, your airline or railroad fare is covered, too.

4. <u>Your surgeon's fee</u> will also be paid by us up to the limits shown on the schedule I've enclosed. The maximum here, for combined surgeon's and anesthesiologist's fees is $1,200.00. (Be sure to check the little folder carefully.)

And there is more. Suppose you need a nurse at home after a covered hospital stay? Well, if you've been hospitalized for cancer for a period of 5 days or more . . . and if your doctor says you must have a full-time nurse within 5 days of your discharge . . . then National Home will pay you $14.28 a day (that's $100.00 a week) for as many days as you received hospital benefits -- up to <u>50 weeks</u>.

And as I said, this protection is now available to you for just 25¢ for your first month . . . and then only $2.90 a month if you are 54 or under; $4.70 if you're 55 or older.

<u>Note well, please</u>: despite the fact that all this money will be paid direct to you (unless <u>you</u> tell us otherwise), it is <u>not taxable</u>. It is <u>not</u> income, and the IRS has ruled that it cannot be taxed.

You may wish to cover your family, too. After all, it makes good sense because -- blindly -- cancer strikes the young as well as the mature.

If you decide on family protection, the single premium for your <u>whole</u> family (<u>including you</u>, your <u>spouse</u> and <u>all</u> your unmarried, dependent children from birth up to age 19) is far less than you'd expect. For example, if you're 54 or under, the total family premium per month is just $5.40. If you're 55 or older, it's $7.60 a month. That's it; that's all. Regardless of how many dependent children you have. And 25¢ covers <u>all</u> your insured family for the first month. (It's a sad, but true fact that leukemia -- a cancer of the blood -- attacks children and young adults, but seldom bothers with people like you and me. Consider this, please, as a word to the wise.)

<u>"What are the exclusions and limitations?"</u>

Just as you should thoroughly understand the benefits . . . you should also understand the exclusions.

- 3 -

over please . . .

specifically with the <u>costs</u> of cancer in mind. For example, many of these plans may not cover all the costs of --

chemotherapy, radiation and cobalt treatments, private nursing care, special medicines, ambulances, surgery, etc.

Yet this is the extra help than can save your life, or the life of someone dear to you. But these medical techniques are expensive, and National Home wants to <u>help you keep what you've saved</u>.

That's why the benefits from this cancer policy are paid to you <u>over and above</u> what you collect from anyone else. And they're paid direct to <u>you</u>, unless you request otherwise. You spend them as you wish.

These benefits are <u>not</u> taxable, nor can anyone tell you how to spend them.

After all, while you're sick in the hospital with cancer, <u>life goes on</u>. Expenses continue, even go up. And who is going to pay <u>those</u> bills? Just because you're hospitalized doesn't mean that the on-going bills stop.

There is no reason anymore to be frightened about the cost of treating cancer. For National Home is ready to help. And, as I said, it takes but one prudent step on your part.

Fill in and mail us the enclosed application today . . . along with 25¢. (The return envelope is postpaid.) We'll send you your policy, with an Effective Date shown on it. <u>Read it carefully, please</u>. If you don't like it . . . if you feel, for any reason at all, that it doesn't meet your requirements, send it back within 15 days of receiving it, and we'll return your money.

That's all; there's absolutely no risk on your part. Under our 15-day money-back offer, you don't risk one cent!

If you decide <u>not</u> to take advantage of this offer, I'll understand. But do think it over carefully. Who knows when you'll get an opportunity as good as this again?

Sincerely yours,

Arthur S. DeMoss
President
National Home Life Assurance Co.

ASD:st

P.S. "People Are Funny," as my good friend Art Linkletter has said so often. But they're <u>also</u> funny about believing that cancer always happens to the "other guy". <u>It doesn't</u>.

Please think about it. Then send us your completed Enrollment Form.

Established 1920—Over 50 Years of Reliable Service

National Home Life Assurance Company • Adm. Offices: Valley Forge, Pennsylvania 19481
LH5534

OMAHA STEAKS "PROSPECTING" LETTER

One of the most successful direct marketers is Omaha Steaks International. Executive vice president Fred Simon is a strong believer in constant testing to seek out new approaches that will beat his long-running control letter. But so powerful is his classic prospecting letter, even the nation's top letter writers have been unable to beat it. The mailing features a check made out to the recipient, and a "Johnson Box" at the top of the letter:

> USE THE ENCLOSED CHECK IN YOUR NAME — in the amount of $23.00 to get more than a 43% discount on your first box of succulent Omaha Steaks. Treat yourself to the world's most tender beef, guaranteed to please you . . . at attractive, introductory savings. So please read this letter right now. If you love good steaks, you'll find my story interesting — and my offer very tempting!

The letter begins:

> Can you recall the best steak you ever tasted in your life? One that was tender, juicy and just full of flavor? I'll bet you can. Most likely, it was served at an exclusive restaurant or supper club.
>
> I'm writing to you because I believe you would enjoy a box of my "fork-tender" Omaha Steaks . . . the same steaks I sell to fine restaurants . . . shipped frozen, directly to you. Here's my story.

The letter goes on to explain where fine restaurants get their fine steaks (Omaha Steaks, of course) and ends with a powerful close:

> To order by mail, just endorse the enclosed check, fill in the order form, enclose your payment — then use the postage-free envelope before the date shown on your check. After that date, I'll select a new group of people to receive this rare offer — and your chance will be past. So please respond now.
>
> Your satisfaction is fully guaranteed.

Frederick J. Simon
4400 South 96th Street • P.O. Box 3300
Omaha, Nebraska 68103

****

USE THE ENCLOSED CHECK IN YOUR NAME -- in the amount of $23.00 to
get more than a 43% discount on your first box of succulent Omaha
Steaks. Treat yourself to the world's most tender beef, guaranteed
to please you ... at attractive, introductory savings. So please
read this letter right now. If you love good steaks, you'll find
my story interesting -- and my offer very tempting!

FOR STEAK LOVERS ONLY

F.J.S.

****

Dear Friend,

Can you recall the best steak you ever tasted in your life? One
that was tender, juicy and just full of flavor. I'll bet you can. Most
likely, it was served at an exclusive restaurant or supper club.

I'm writing to you because I believe you would enjoy a box of my
"fork-tender" Omaha Steaks ... the same steaks I sell to fine
restaurants ... shipped frozen, directly to you. Here's my story.

TOP QUALITY

Have you ever wondered why the steaks fine restaurants serve taste
so good? It's simple, really. The chefs in fine restaurants know that
all their skill in food preparation is absolutely useless -- unless they
begin with first quality cuts of meat.

Where do smart chefs get this superb beef? From suppliers like me
in the heart of America's beef country -- the Midwest -- who select and
cut steaks to their exacting specifications. We specialize in fine
quality meats for elegant restaurants and clubs. In such places,
customers pay a premium price. So the meat has to be the very best.

My company, Omaha Steaks International, has been a beef supplier to
fine restaurants since 1917. That's the year we began supplying a few
of Omaha's posh steak houses. Today, we supply USDA Prime and Top
Choice Omaha Steaks to restaurants in every part of America. In fact
it's quite possible that you've enjoyed one of our steaks at a fine
restaurant, without even knowing it.

MAGNIFICENT STEAKS~ AT HOME!

But that's only half our business. Over the years, we found people
who wanted our magnificent steaks for personal use. We had to charge
them a premium price. But, to these people, quality was their greatest
concern. They simply wanted to enjoy our top quality steaks at home --
and share them with family and friends.

This gave us the idea of actually seeking out discriminating steak
lovers, especially in places where aged, corn-fed, Midwestern beef was
not available. So we sent out our first mail order catalog. And the
response was tremendous. As a result, about half of our business is now
devoted to supplying people all over America with the best steaks money
can buy ... for their dining, entertaining and gift needs.

To introduce you to Omaha Steaks ...

ALL THE WAY FROM THE HEART OF BEEF COUNTRY U.S.A... TO YOUR DOOR!

... I have a very special offer. An introductory discount, typical of the specials we offer to our regular customers all year long.

I'll send you 6 (6 oz.) Filet Mignons, each 1-1/4" thick -- (the regular price of these fine steaks is $52.95) -- for only $29.95, plus $4.00 for shipping and handling. You save $23.00; that's more than 43% off the usual price.

SAVE $23.00

As soon as I receive your order, I'll send you a confirmation by First Class mail. Then, within two or three weeks, your Omaha Steaks will be delivered right to your door. (They're boxed and wrapped for your freezer, placed in an insulated, reusable cooler, packed with over 20 pounds of dry ice ... and shipped out freight prepaid.)

With your order, I'll enclose, FREE, our full color catalog of succulent steaks and gourmet foods you may order by mail or phone.

Also -- you get the Omaha Steaks Cookbook FREE. This booklet contains recipes and instructions by food expert James Beard. So you'll be certain to cook your steaks to perfection.

In addition -- I want you to enjoy these steaks at no risk. So I offer you this guarantee:

NO-RISK GUARANTEE

IF YOU ARE NOT PLEASED FOR ANY REASON, WE WILL REPLACE YOUR ORDER OR REFUND YOUR MONEY, WHICHEVER YOU PREFER.

So place your order now, while everything is right in front of you. The fastest way to get your steaks is to call us TOLL FREE at 1-800-228-9055 and charge to your American Express, Visa, MasterCard, Diners Club or Carte Blanche account. You may phone 7 days a week, day or night. (Nebraska residents call 0-402-391-3660, COLLECT.)

CALL TOLL FREE TO ORDER

To order by mail, just endorse the enclosed check, fill in the order form, enclose your payment -- then use the postage-free envelope I've provided. Whether you phone or write, I must receive your order before the date shown on your check. After that date, I'll select a new group of people to receive this rare offer -- and your chance will be past. So please respond now.

Your satisfaction is fully guaranteed.

Sincerely,

Frederick J. Simon

Frederick J. Simon
Executive Vice President

DOUBLE OFFER ~ FOR EVEN MORE GOOD EATING!

P.S. To more than double your enjoyment, you may order 12 (6 oz.) Filet Mignons -- at the special price of $58.95 plus $4.00 for shipping and handling.

CALL FREE WITH YOUR CREDIT CARD ORDER ... 1-800-228-9055

G2440-0783

FRANK LEWIS "MIRACLE GRAPEFRUIT" LETTER

Another classic food letter has been used with success for many years by Frank Schultz of Royal Ruby Red Grapefruit in Alamo, Texas. The key element of the letter is a story:

> It happened in a grove owned by our family doctor, Dr. Webb, back in 1929. One of the men who was picking fruit came up to the Webb house holding six of the strangest grapefruit anyone had ever seen! A single branch of an ordinary grapefruit tree had produced these six unusual fruit — truly a "miracle."
>
> These were big grapefruit, unusually big. And they had a faint red blush on their skin. The amazing thing was that when Dr. Webb sliced open the grapefruit, the fruit was brilliant ruby red in color.
>
> The good doctor decided to taste this strange new grapefruit. With his first spoonful his eyes opened wide! The fruit was perfect, juicy and luscious. It wasn't sour like other grapefruit either — it was naturally sweet without sugar.
>
> For some reason, we'll never know why, nature had chosen to produce an entirely new kind of grapefruit here in our Magic Rio Grande Valley. It was incredible — men had labored for years to produce the ideal grapefruit, and had failed. But suddenly on a single branch of one tree in one grove, Mother Nature had done it all herself!

The letter goes on for four pages telling how Frank Lewis now grows and harvests similar ruby red grapefruit, continuing in narrative form. Then an unusual offer:

> When your shipment arrives (remember, it will be delivered prepaid) here is what I want you to do: Just place four Royal Ruby Reds in your refrigerator until they are thoroughly cool. Then cut them in half and have the family sample this unusual fruit.
>
> The treat is on me! You decide whether or not Royal Ruby Reds are everything I say. You determine whether or not eating a Royal Ruby Red is the fantastic taste experience I promise.
>
> You decide. I'm betting that you and your family will want more of this superb fruit — and on a regular basis too. If the Royal Ruby Reds make you say "yes," then keep the remaining fruit. Otherwise return the unused fruit (at my expense) and you won't owe me a single penny.

Phone 512 • 787-5971
P O BOX 517

Frank Lewis
ROYAL RUBY RED GRAPEFRUIT . . . ALAMO, TEXAS
78516

Dear Friend,

Have you heard of the "miracle" grapefruit? I am going to
send you a package of them so you can enjoy them for
Christmas and the Holidays.

That's right. I'm going to send you a package
(with all charges prepaid) of 16 to 20 of these
"miracle" grapefruit. In fact your fruit is
tree-ripening right now.

These grapefruit are most unusual. Not one man
in a thousand has ever tasted one. They are so
naturally sweet they don't need any sugar. Each
weighs a pound or more.

But wait a minute. Let me tell you the story of the "miracle"
that produced these grapefruit.

Actually it happened in a grove owned by our family doctor,
Dr. Webb, back in 1929. One of the men who was picking fruit
came up to the Webb house holding six of the strangest grapefruit anyone had ever seen! A single branch of an ordinary
grapefruit tree had produced these six unusual fruit - truly
a "miracle."

These were big grapefruit, unusually big. And
they had a faint red blush on their skin. The
amazing thing was that when Dr. Webb sliced open
the grapefruit, the fruit was a brilliant ruby
red in color.

The good doctor decided to taste this strange new grapefruit.
With his first spoonful his eyes opened wide! The fruit was
perfect, juicy and luscious. It wasn't sour like other grapefruit either - it was naturally sweet without sugar.

For some reason, we'll never know why, nature had chosen to produce an entirely new kind of grapefruit here in our Magic Rio Grande Valley. It was incredible - men had labored for years to produce the ideal grapefruit, and had failed. But suddenly on a single branch of one tree in one grove, Mother Nature had done it all herself!

You can imagine the excitement! And from that one branch, grove after grove has been budded and grafted to our own Texas Ruby Red Grapefruit. Now when I say not one man in a thousand has ever tasted this grapefruit - you can easily understand why.

To begin with, Ruby Reds are rare. You can look for them in stores, but I doubt if you'll find one. You may find pink grapefruit, but seldom if ever do you see the genuine Ruby Reds.

So you start with the rarity of Ruby Reds, and to get to ROYAL Ruby Reds you have to get rarer yet. Only 4 to 5 percent of the entire crop will qualify as a "Royal Ruby Red."

Each Royal Ruby Red weighs a pound - or more! Each has a rich red color, flowing juices, luscious naturally sweet flavor, and the ability to keep perfectly for many weeks.

Why, we won't even consider harvesting a grove until I've checked out the fruit for tree-ripened maturity in my own testing laboratory. I check for "natural sugar," low acid balance and high juice content. I check to see that the fruit is plump and meaty, and I even check to see that the skin is thin. Not only does each factor have to check out, but all the factors have to be in a proper relationship to each other before I'll harvest a grove.

And when we pick the fruit we're as fussy as a lady trying on an Easter bonnet! Every one of us takes a "picking ring" when we harvest. If the fruit is small enough to pass through this ring - we don't pick it! It simply isn't big enough to qualify as a Royal Ruby Red!

Even after picking there are other careful inspections each fruit must pass before I'll ship it to you. I size the fruit. And I grade it for beauty. Sometimes the fruit will be wind scarred. I won't ship it to you. Or sometimes it will have a bulge on the stem end that we call "sheep nose." I won't send it to you. You can see I really mean it when I say I ship you only perfect Royal Ruby Reds.

When your shipment arrives (remember, it will be delivered prepaid) here is what I want you to do: Just place four Royal Ruby Reds in your refrigerator until they are thoroughly cool. Then cut them in half and have the family sample this unusual fruit.

This treat is on me! You decide whether or not Royal Ruby Reds are everything I say. You determine whether or not eating a Royal Ruby Red is the fantastic taste experience I promise.

You decide. I'm betting that you and your family will want more of this superb fruit - and on a regular basis too. If the Royal Ruby Reds make you say "yes," then keep the remaining fruit. Otherwise return the unused fruit (at my expense) and you won't owe me a single penny.

But you are never going to know just how wonderful genuine Royal Ruby Reds are unless you sign and mail the enclosed postage-paid card right quick.

That way you are sure to receive your package containing 16 to 20 Royal Ruby Reds for you and your family to sample a few days before Christmas.

Now suppose you do like Royal Ruby Reds - suppose you love them - can you be sure of getting more?

You surely can. By saying "yes" to my first shipment you have the privilege of automatically joining my Winter Fruit Club. Please be assured you pay nothing in advance. But each month during the winter I'll ship you a pack of 16 to 20 orchard-fresh, hand-selected, hand-packed Royal Ruby Reds.

Every Royal Ruby Red you receive will have passed my tough tests. Each will weigh a pound or more. Safe delivery is guaranteed. This fruit is picked, packed and shipped each month, December through April.

You pay only _after_ you have received each shipment. And you may skip or cancel any shipment, simply by telling me your wishes.

> So sign and mail the postage-paid card today. Remember, it obligates you to nothing, except making a taste test of the best grapefruit that has ever been grown. And that taste test is on me!

Of course, as you can well imagine, when I say supplies are limited - I'm not kidding! There's a strong demand for Royal Ruby Reds, and the crop is extremely limited.

So to taste this "miracle" grapefruit, and have the opportunity to savor it each month during the growing season, please be sure to mail the order card now.

Sincerely,

/CA

P.S. Mr. Harry B. Walsh wrote me recently from Connecticut saying, "... in a world so full of mass production and synthetic substitutes, it's really a privilege to be able to enjoy one of nature's most marvelous creations." Amen!

SECTION IV

CIRCULATION AND BOOK PROMOTION LETTERS

When I asked America's leading direct mail copywriters to send me their all-time best letters, the vast majority chose letters they had created to sell magazine subscriptions or books. Perhaps this is not surprising since writers are also readers and thus, all have a very special interest in books and magazines. In addition, magazine and book publishers tend to pay top dollar for direct mail letters, and copywriters consider such an assignment a real plum.

There's also a tremendous amount of competition in this field. Letters are most frequently mailed in the millions over a period of time and publishers keep testing to find letters that will beat their control — the letter that won in previous testing. From nearly 1,000 different circulation and book promotion letters, I've chosen the "control-beaters" shown in this chapter to demonstrate a variety of successful techniques that have produced outstanding results.

ORGANIC GARDENING "FIVE MISTAKES" LETTER

Opening a letter with a question often backfires, particularly if the question asked can be answered in the "wrong" way. But a classic question-asking letter did an outstanding job for *Organic Gardening* magazine. The envelope had a picture of a gardener at work and this teaser:

> Can you spot the five mistakes here that make
> you work more and enjoy your garden less?

The letter inside had a number-keyed line rendering of the envelope photograph with a near repeat of the envelope teaser and this lead:

> If you're working harder and enjoying your garden less . . .
>
> . . . could be, you're making a few common mistakes like our friend
> in the color photograph on our outside envelope — mistakes that
> may be causing you extra work and added frustration.
>
> Could be. Because one trait that the world's best gardeners have in
> common is how little physical labor they actually do.
>
> It's true.
>
> After all, it's not how much you do that leads to garden success, it's
> how much you know.

This led into selling copy for a premium booklet, "The Best Gardening Ideas I Know," which was offered with a trial subscription to *Organic Gardening*. The letter outlined the five mistakes, one by one, with a line drawing to illustrate each mistake.

Bulk Rate
U.S. Postage
PAID
Rodale Press, Inc.

ORGANIC GARDENING®
Emmaus, PA 18049

Can you spot the five mistakes here that make you work more and enjoy your garden less?

CAR RT SORT**RR 05
75026
S S HODGSON
1433 JOHNNYS WAY
WEST CHESTR   PA 19380

THE ANSWERS ARE INSIDE, BUT WE'VE ALSO GOT THREE FREE GIFTS FOR YOU—SEE BACK OF THIS ENVELOPE FOR NEWS ABOUT IT . . .

How many of these common gardening mistakes are causing you to work harder than you really have to?

Dear Gardening Friend:

If you're working harder and enjoying your garden less ...

... could be, you're making a few common mistakes like our friend in the color photograph on our outside envelope — mistakes that may be causing you extra work and added frustration.

Could be. Because one trait that the world's best gardeners have in common is how <u>little</u> physical labor they actually do.

It's true.

After all, it's not how much you <u>do</u> that leads to garden success, it's how much you <u>know</u>.

And, right now, if you'd like to know more and work less ...

... we'd like to send you — absolutely free — a copy of THE BEST GARDENING IDEAS I KNOW, THE ORGANIC GARDENING HARVEST BOOK and BUILD-IT-YOURSELF HOMESTEAD ... these wonderful work-saving guides are yours just for taking a no-obligation look at ORGANIC GARDENING magazine.

AFFIX STAMP ON CARD AND MAIL TODAY

These FREE guides can save you work and mistakes.

To get your gifts ... just tear off the stamp on this page, affix it to the enclosed reply card and drop it in the mail. As soon as we hear from you, we'll send you the latest issue of our magazine and all three booklets ...

... and you'll be on your way towards eliminating the common mistakes that could be taking the fun and pleasure out of your gardening. Mistakes. that our friend in the photo is making like ...

... <u>MISTAKE NUMBER ONE</u> weeding. You'll never have to do it again ...

(over please)

... because weeding is wasted work that's rough on your back and even rougher on your garden soil. And the surface feeder roots of your plants.

Our free booklets will show you a quicker, better way to keep the weeds down: <u>mulch</u>! Mulch is a thick layer of spoiled hay, grass clippings, old leaves — anything — that you put down to smother weeds once and for all. It's easier on your back ... takes less time than weeding ... and give's your garden a neat appearance. But more important: it protects your precious topsoil from the harsh sun and dry weather. And as it rots, it continually builds more topsoil and more fertility.

If you can recall those hours spent pulling weeds on a sweltering July afternoon, I'm sure you'll eagerly remedy this mistake. And here's another:

<u>MISTAKE</u> <u>NUMBER</u> <u>TWO</u> is our friend's long, straight planting rows. What a waste of your space and steps! Only a small portion of the garden gets used for plants this way. The rest of the space is wasted on bare rows and empty spaces that you must dutifully weed. If <u>you</u> garden this way ...

... THE BEST GARDENING IDEAS I KNOW will help you put an end to that waste and work with the "raised bed method" — a technique from China that enables you to grow more vegetables much closer — so close that their leaves almost touch, thus shading and crowding-out weeds. Raised beds mean less bending, fewer steps. Now you can have a big garden in a few attractive, easily managed, intensely fertile plots!

And what else is our friend in the photo doing wrong?

<u>MISTAKE</u> <u>NUMBER</u> <u>THREE</u> is mono-cropping — he's segregating each variety of vegetable from all the others. Not only is it an inefficient technique, but he's asking for a lot of insect and disease trouble if a little should develop.

A smarter way is "companion planting" — a centuries-old garden technique that is now backed-up with a heap of scientific evidence. Tests show that certain vegetables and plants <u>should</u> be planted together because they can stimulate each other's growth ... repel other's insects and diseases ... and generally help each other "do better." One example is corn planted with beans. The beans give nitrogen to the corn's roots and the corn stalks provide "climbing poles" that save you work. There are plenty more ...

... and you'll find a complete listing of companion plants in THE BEST GARDENING IDEAS I KNOW: all the plants that should go together ... and those that shouldn't.

And did you spot this common mistake...?

MISTAKE NUMBER FOUR is the chemical fertilizer bags lurking in the background. Why are they a mistake? Because, first of all they're expensive. But worse, they could do more harm than good in your garden — they may destroy inhibit the bacteria in your soil whose job it is to produce free, natural fertilizer from the air and the soil. That's why it seems the more chemical fertilizers you use, the more you need the next season.

Chemical fertilizer can break down the structure of your soil, too, rendering it "inert dirt" that turns into a sloppy mudball when it rains and bakes rock hard under the hot sun. Makes plowing and tilling a real chore!

You'll read about a better, cheaper, more natural way to build deep-down, long-lasting soil fertility in THE BEST GARDENING IDEAS I KNOW. It's compost! You don't buy it, you make it yourself from free materials that most people waste. It really works, too. The deep, dark rich soil that you build will be proof. Living proof that follows you into old age!

But the greatest mistake of all is ...

... MISTAKE NUMBER FIVE the poison sprays and dusts that our friend is using to get rid of insect pests. Little does he realize that those poisons are really making his bug problems worse — not to mention the ecological havoc and health dangers he's spreading in the environment.

In THE BEST GARDENING IDEAS I KNOW, you'll learn why scientists believe insect pests attack: the popular theory is that insects prefer to attack weak plants, culling out the unfit according to Nature's plan. Thus, the healthier your soil, the healthier your plants. Weak soil (as can happen with chemical fertilizer use), produces weak plants. And that's where the bug problem begins.

Poison sprays complicate matters. They kill everything along with the pests: soil bacteria, earthworms, songbirds and all the "good bugs" — the praying mantis, ladybug, the green lacewing and many other garden friends — whose normal function is to keep pests under control naturally. Once the ecological balance is upset, the pests return unchecked. Each time they get a little more resistant to the pesticide, forcing you to find something stronger.

It's a deadly cycle that you can break with the know-how you'll find in the free guides and ORGANIC GARDEN-ING magazine. You'll learn how to recognize and attract armies of "good bugs" and natural predators.

You'll discover simple homemade recipes for safe, non-toxic and non-polluting sprays and repellents that really work. Plus many other ways to help your plants become more insect and disease-resistant, <u>naturally</u>.

And <u>MISTAKE NUMBER SIX</u> ... well, we <u>could</u> go on and on, because so does THE BEST GARDENING IDEAS I KNOW — <u>there</u> <u>are</u> <u>19</u> <u>helpful</u>, <u>work-saving</u> chapters in all, with tips on starting seeds right ... harvesting and storing fruits and vegetables ... saving more time, money, mistakes and work in nearly every aspect of your garden operation.

Hundreds of thousands of good gardeners have become better gardeners thanks to this "best ideas" book ...

... and now, the Editors of ORGANIC GARDENING magazine want to send <u>you</u> not only a free copy of THE BEST GARDENING IDEAS I KNOW — but two other equally helpful booklets — THE ORGANIC GARDENING HARVEST BOOK and BUILD-IT-YOURSELF HOMESTEAD, too. Here's why ...

We want you to have these three free booklets because we're certain that once you see how much easier and enjoyable your gardening can be ... you'll want to go deeper and deeper into the fulfilling and rewarding experience of the organic gardening world. And that's where ORGANIC GARDENING magazine comes in. Because no other magazine can get you more personally involved in the natural world all around you.

Each and every issue of the magazine is chock-full of the best gardening ideas from our experimental farms ... the latest discoveries and techniques ... and the plots and patches of some of the world's most experienced gardeners.

So when we send you free copies of the guides, THE BEST GARDENING IDEAS I KNOW, THE ORGANIC GARDENING HARVEST BOOK and BUILD-IT-YOURSELF HOMESTEAD we'll also send you the latest issue of ORGANIC GARDENING magazine.

So act right now. The postage is paid and you've got nothing to lose (except a litany of unnecessary, back-breaking garden mistakes!).

Waiting to mail your book,

Robert Rodale
Publisher

Business Week "Invitation" Letter I

For many years, *Business Week* magazine has used various invitations to bring in new subscriptions. Two of the longest-running control packages were created by Dick Neff. One of these control packages started off with a script type heading:

> You are cordially invited to receive a free
> Executive Portfolio with your name stamped in gold
> prepared by the editors of Business Week

The letter began:

> As a management executive, you're one of a select group invited to accept a potentially profitable "double-header" offer.
>
> First, you will receive — FREE — a 135-page Executive Portfolio containing 12 reports to management on major American business problems. This invaluable volume, compiled by the editors of *Business Week*, is packed with profit-building ideas and will make a significant contribution to your professional library.
>
> Second, you will receive a full year of *Business Week* for only $18.50, a savings of $32.50 over the newsstand price.

The invitation was enclosed in a separate inner envelope with the recipient's name handwritten on the face.

You are cordially invited

to receive

a free Executive Portfolio

with your name stamped in gold

prepared by

the editors of Business Week

Dear Reader:

As a management executive, you're one of a select group invited to accept a potentially profitable "double-header" offer.

Your name stamped
in gold here

First, you will receive – FREE – a 135-page Executive Portfolio containing 12 reports to management on major American business problems. This invaluable volume, compiled by the editors of Business Week, is packed with profit-building ideas and will make a significant contribution to your professional library.

Second, you will receive a full year of Business Week for only $18.50, a savings of $32.50 over the newsstand price.

Not for sale anywhere, the handsome, free portfolio, embossed with your name in gold leaf on the cover, is available only to Business Week subscribers. Its contents include solid facts and vital insights into such subjects as:

Productivity: Our Biggest Undeveloped Resource (Winner of the National Magazine Award for General Excellence)... The Scramble

(over please)

for Resources ... the Spectacular Rise of the Consumer Company ... Can U.S. Industry Find the Money it Needs? ... and New Products: The Push is on Marketing (Winner of the John Hancock Award for Excellence in Business and Financial Journalism).

Whatever your professional interests - marketing, finance, production, R&D, computers, transportation, sales - you'll like the vivid, in-depth reporting on them in Business Week.

You get inside looks at the Washington scene, Wall Street and the other markets, foreign business, and regional business news. A weekly index wraps it all up in a 90-second review. "Personal Business," a column of tax, insurance, and family finance tips, helps you hang onto more of what you earn. The whole magazine is an aid to you and your business in getting ahead, staying ahead of your competition and in making prof-itable decisions.

In the time you spend each week with Business Week you get more usable information than you might get if you spent days reading newspapers, general news magazines, newsletters, and consultants' reports.

<u>And instead of spending $200 to $300 or more you spend only $18.50 a year. About 36¢ a week ... for business intelligence that could increase your earnings by a quantum leap.</u>

The writing in Business Week is crisp, concise, businesslike -- yet with colorful and human touches. And Business Week brings rewards out of all proportion to its cost. Nearly 4-1/2 million readers, managing billions of dollars worth of business, turn to it because they know Business Week does the best job of business reporting in America.

In today's economy can you afford <u>not</u> to subscribe?

You risk nothing. For, if you're not convinced Business Week is worth far more than it costs, you may cancel at any time and we will refund the unused portion of your subscription to you. The Executive Portfolio is yours to keep in any case. Why not return the reply form in the postage-paid envelope before it slips your mind?

Cordially,

Charles C. Randolph

Charles C. Randolph
Publisher and Vice-President
McGraw-Hill Publications Co.

CCR/inv

P.S. No need to send money. We'll bill you or your firm later, if you prefer.

Business Week 1221 Avenue of the Americas, New York, New York 10020

Business Week "Invitation" Letter II

Although the previous *Business Week* Invitation Letter was used longer, copywriter Neff personally likes a later variation. He says:

■ I like this one better because its copy is livelier and more interesting. Letters longer than two pages rarely work for *Business Week*, but this one did because it doesn't put you to sleep; it nudges you now and then.

Another good point: the personalization device I used here was less costly than a handwritten name. Two initials were all it called for.

The copy began:

> Management executives like you are a special breed. They couldn't care less about free gifts just because they're free. But if they see one that can help them be more effective, put more black ink in the company's books, and put more money in their own banks and investment portfolios, their minds are wide open. That attitude is one reason they hold the jobs they do.
>
> I think in a moment you'll agree with me that an Executive Portfolio I have reserved in your name is such a gift.

Copy throughout the three-page letter continued in a lighter vein. Consider these examples:

> Now, as you might expect, we are not in business just for the purpose of delivering presents. We wouldn't be making this offer if we didn't want you to try something. That something, to nobody's surprise, I'm sure, is *Business Week*.
>
> If you're still waiting for the bad news from the cockpit, don't. It's all good news today. You may cancel your subscription at any time; we will gladly refund your money on the unused portion, and you may still keep your Executive Portfolio. (We're not terribly worried about free loaders, because this offer is being made only to a very select group.)

Here's the better news: You can keep this
gift even if you don't buy a sizeable
bargain we're offering.

```
* * * * * * * * * * * * * * *
*                           *
*     FREE EXECUTIVE PORTFOLIO   *
*   WITH YOUR NAME STAMPED IN GOLD  *
*                           *
*      - prepared by the editors  *
*        of Business Week    *
*                           *
* * * * * * * * * * * * * * *
```

Dear Reader:

    Management executives like you are a special breed. They couldn't
care less about free gifts just because they're free. But if they see
one that can help them be more effective, put more black ink in the
company's books, and put more money in their own banks
and investment portfolios, their minds are wide open.
That attitude is one reason they hold the jobs they do.

    I think in a moment you'll agree with me that an Execu-
tive Portfolio I have reserved in your name is such a
gift.

Your name stamped
in gold here

    It is Business Week's 160-page Executive Portfolio, containing 13
special reports to management on major business promblems. Packed with
profit-building ideas, it will be an invaluable addition to your library
- at home or at work.

    Not for sale anywhere, the handsome, free portfolio, embossed with
your name in gold leaf on the cover, is a gold mine of management intelligence. Its contents include priceless information and fascinating
insights into such subjects as:

    Reappraising the Seventies: Scenario for Survival
    (Winner of an INGAA - University of Missouri Busi-
    ness Journalism Award). The Office of the Future.
    The Debt Economy (Winner of the John Hancock Award
    for Excellence in Business and Financial Journalism).
    Price-Fixing: Crackdown Under Way. The Corporate
    Woman: Up the Ladder, Finally (Winner of the
    National Magazine Award for Public Service).

(please turn)

-2-

Now, as you might expect, we are not in business just for the purpose of delivering presents. We wouldn't be making this offer if we didn't want you to try something. That something, to nobody's surprise, I'm sure, is Business Week.

But if you're still waiting for the bad news from the cockpit, don't. It's all good news today. You may cancel your subscription at any time; we will gladly refund your money on the unused portion, and you may still keep your Executive Portfolio. (We're not terribly worried about free loaders, because this offer is being made only to a very select group.)

If you do decide to go ahead with a year's subscription, which is what more than 95 percent of executives do once we have sent them their first issue, you will save a modest little pile of money, $29.50 to be exact, on the newsstand price. For the latter runs to $51.00 a year, compared to only $21.50 for a year's trial subscription.

And you'll save a less modest pile of money if you let Business Week be your business-intelligence source instead of spending the $200 to $300 a year it could cost you to get LESS usable information from newsletters, consultant's reports, and general news magazines...not to mention assorted newspapers.

You'll also save an enormous pile of reading. You could spend days combing such sources and not do as well as with a few short hours each week with Business Week.

Finally, while I hate to make such an unscientific prediction, Business Week just might help you MAKE a pile of money.

It's certainly true that the better-informed you are on business matters, the better choice you have of making it big. And nothing keeps you informed on business like Business Week.

Business leaders everywhere, managing billions of dollars worth of business, turn to it because they know Business Week does the best job of business reporting in America. One reason: no other business magazine has so many reporters or so many editors.

Published weekly, not monthly as many business magazines are, it brings you the news fast. In fact, one special section covering fast-breaking late developments is inserted only minutes before press time. Moreover, you can read BW fast. A weekly index wraps it all up in a 90-second review. Charts, tables, and graphs give you statistics at a glance. The writing is crisp. Concise. Colorful and lively, but straight to the point.

Whatever your business interests - Marketing, Finance, Production, R&D, Computers, Transportation, Sales - you'll find them covered in

-3-

depth in Business Week.

You get really <u>inside</u> looks at the Washington scene, Wall Street and the other markets, foreign business, regional business news. And "Personal Business", a column of tax, insurance, and family finance tips, helps you hang onto more of what you earn.

In today's economy can you afford <u>not</u> to subscribe?

Getting your own copy instead of having Business Week routed to you lets you be on top of things, and look it. Lets you get valuable business ideas <u>ahead</u> of - not <u>after</u> - competitors in and outside your office. Lets you cut out articles or save the issues for more thorough reading without arousing resentment in others.

If you'd like to take advantage of this inexpensive offer, we'd suggest you act without delay. For there's no telling how long we will be making it. And it may not come to your attention again.

Since there's no risk, why not return the reply form in the postage-paid envelope before it slips your mind?

Cordially,

Charles C. Randolph
Publisher and Vice-President
McGraw-Hill Publications Co.

P.S. No need to send money. We'll bill you or your firm later, if you prefer.

Business Week 1221 Avenue of the Americas New York, New York 10020

Business Week "Invitation" Letter III

A totally different package, developed by the innovative team of Bill Jayme and Heikki Ratalahti, went all-out for a lighter touch than even Dick Neff's second letter. It featured one of the most unique envelopes ever used for a subscription promotion mailing. Across the top in 2"-high bold letters it said:

DAMN!

As if this wasn't a strong enough teaser to make anyone want to find out what's inside, there was a round window showing a token on the order card. It said:

I want to quit cussin' and start crowing

The letter inside was headed by a "Johnson Box":

By agreement, our magazine solicits subscriptions from men and women in middle and upper management positions.

With this letter, the Editors now invite you to join this exclusive and knowing circle . . . to save yourself or your company $37.75 on the newsstand price with a year's subscription to *Business Week* at the regular rate of $26.00.

. . . and to receive free as a welcoming gift one of the most valuable business handbooks that's ever been privately printed.

The five-page letter began:

Hasn't it happened to you in business? It sure used to happen to me.

Let's say you go into a meeting. Everyone present has lots to say — ideas, opinions, news. Finally you put in your own two cents' worth. You mention something you've just heard . . .

. . . only to discover that everybody else has known about it for days. So you find yourself saying "Damn!"

Or let's say you finally get the money together to make an investment for your family. The stock looks good. The time looks right. You buy . . .

. . . only to have the market the very next day start sinking lower and lower. So you find yourself saying "Damn!"

If you've experienced frustrations like these . . . if every once in a while, you really blow it, and each time, you vow "never again" . . . welcome to *BUSINESS WEEK* — the magazine that knows. The magazine that tells you.

The magazine that can help you quit cussin' your luck — and start you crowing instead!

Another interesting feature of the letter is the effective use of a postscript to emphasize the premium:

> P.S. I hope I've got your name spelled right — but check the enclosed card to make sure. If it's wrong, forgive me — and please make corrections. The way it finally appears on the card is exactly how your desk handbook will be embossed on the cover in gold leaf — compliments of the Editors.

DAMN!

BusinessWeek
1221 Avenue of the Americas
New York, N.Y. 10020

BusinessWeek

By agreement, our magazine solicits subscriptions from men and women in middle and upper management positions.

With this letter, the Editors now invite you to join this exclusive and knowing circle...to save yourself or your company $37.75 on the newsstand price with a year's subscription to Business Week at the regular rate of $26.00...and to receive free as a welcoming gift one of the most valuable business handbooks that's ever been privately printed.

With our compliments

Dear Colleague:

Hasn't it happened to you in business? It sure used to happen to me.

Let's say you go into a meeting. Everyone present has lots to say -- ideas, opinions, news. Finally you put in your own two cents' worth. You mention something you've just heard ...

... only to discover that everybody else has known about it for days. So you find yourself saying "Damn!"

Or let's say you're called upon to make a really important decision. You spend some restless nights mulling your options. You check out the available data. Finally, you make up your mind ...

... only to learn too late that your data is incomplete or out-of-date. So you find yourself saying "Damn!"

Or let's say you finally get the money together to make an investment for your family. The stock looks good. The time

(over, please)

-2-

looks right. You buy ...

... only to have the market the very next day start sinking lower and lower. So you find yourself saying "Damn!"

If you've experienced frustrations like these ... if every once in a while, you really blow it, and each time, you vow "never again" ... welcome to BUSINESS WEEK -- the magazine that knows. The magazine that tells you.

The magazine that can help you quit cussin' your luck -- and start you crowing instead!

No other business reading so succinctly, so thoroughly, and so reliably gives you the information you need week-in and week-out to keep on top of the people you work with, the job you handle, and the security you're building for yourself and your family.

With this letter, I invite you to join the executive elite of this country as a subscriber to BUSINESS WEEK ...

. to save yourself or your company an immediate and impressive thirty-seven dollars and thirty-seven cents...

. and in the bargain, to receive free with our compliments a privately-printed new handbook for your desk that could be among the most important volumes you've owned in all of your business career.

More about your free gift in a moment. First, let me tell you some of the reasons that I personally find BUSINESS WEEK so helpful -- and why I think you will too. It can help keep you better-informed all-around. It can help keep you from making mistakes. It can help give you more confidence, more assurance, more savvy ...

... and it can take an awful lot of the worry out of your working hours. I know. I was once in your boat.

Worry about all the up-and-comers? Nobody helps you keep tabs on other people as candidly as BUSINESS WEEK. You learn what the competition is up to. What your counterparts in other companies are doing. You meet the people who might do you some good. The people to stay away from. You get to know who may be gaining on you. You see the people you've overtaken.

Before you know it, you've enlarged your circle -- new contacts, new prospects, new faces to keep an eye out for. You know who is who -- and who isn't.

-3-

<u>Worry about falling behind?</u> Never before has it been so exciting to be in the business you're in. Look around you. New challenges. New ideas. New breakthroughs. New solutions. New markets. New opportunities. New opportunities for the people who work for you. New opportunities for you.

BUSINESS WEEK gives you a <u>manageable</u> way of keeping on top of it all -- not just the news in the field you're in, but wherever things go on that concern you. In the regulatory agencies. The union councils. The upstairs rooms at the banks. The boardrooms. The think tanks. The courts. The B-schools. The media. The marketplace. Whenever and wherever in the world there's someone talking about you.

<u>Worry about whether you're doing as right as you could by your family?</u> BUSINESS WEEK is not only your professional counsel -- but your personal mentor as well. Is now a good time to stay heavy in cash -- or to try to beat new inflation by investing? In the market? In bonds? In property? In gold? In art? In what?

Where are the great vacation places -- easy-to-get-to, fun, inexpensive? What business books should you maybe take along? What new advances in health should you be aware of -- diets, exercise, drugs? How can you best the IRS? Who's got the good buys in insurance? Where should you aim for next in your career? How's your pay compare with theirs?

<u>Worry about your time?</u> You should. From birth to retirement, each of us has only 35 million minutes in which to do it all. To learn. To grow. To make it. It's my honest feeling that BUSINESS WEEK can assist the process measurably. It can help you learn. It can help you grow. It can help you make it bigger and better than you've ever dreamed. And it doesn't take that much out of you:

Our magazine comes to you weekly -- not daily. Issues won't pile up unread. And <u>in just one agreeable hour and 52 minutes (last issue I timed cover-to-cover), you'll have the answers to almost everything</u>:

What's new. Who's new. Where it's at in business. And what it all means to you. To your continuing success in your field and your company. To achieving your goals -- professionals and personal. To your happiness -- and that of your family. Like me, you've probably worked hard to give them the lifestyle they now enjoy. Isn't it worth insuring? Especially when keeping informed costs so little?

As you may or may not know, subscriptions to BUSINESS WEEK are not sold at cut rates. No "special introductory offers." Company policy.

-4-

So if you're waiting for a better offer, be forewarned -- this is it. And because you do save quite a sizable amount of money, our best offer is really quite generous:

If BUSINESS WEEK is not already sold out on the relatively few newsstands that carry it, individual issues cost $1.25 apiece, or $63.75 a year. Use the enclosed card to subscribe now, however, and your price is

ONE FULL YEAR (51 issues) just $26.00
Includes all Supplements and Annual Round-ups

By placing your order today at the regular rate of $26.00, you save a full $37.75 over the single-copy price. Your subscription fee may be tax deductible, too, when you use BUSINESS WEEK for business or investment purposes. And in addition, you receive as a gift with our compliments

PRIVATE EXECUTIVE PORTFOLIO -- YOURS FREE

What's the economic scenario to 1980, and how can you jump on the bandwagon now? If you own a small business -- or yearn to start one -- how can you avoid certain hassles? How deep should you get in commodities and options? What are some alternatives to bankruptcy? If you've got a great new idea or invention, what problems should you anticipate these days in getting it to market?

How is the Middle Class now getting the go-around -- and how can you fight back? If you're a woman, how well are you doing these days, and how might you do even better? Where can you go now for venture capital? How would your pricing stand up under FTC scrutiny, and what can they do to you personally? What can you adapt from revolutionary new word-processing techniques to save yourself time and money?

In BUSINESS WEEK's all-new Executive Portfolio, you'll find the answers to hundreds of questions like these -- an overview of virtually the entire business climate today, prepared in cooperation with our full editorial staff, and privately printed for your eyes only.

As soon as your subscription order is received, your own personal desk copy will be shipped free -- an illustrated handbook that is not for sale anywhere, and that could be one of the most rewarding business tools in your possession.

Send no money. You can charge your subscription to your company, to your credit card, or I can arrange to bill you privately -- whichever is more convenient. And you don't need a pen to order. Just punch out the token on the enclosed card, slide it into the holder opposite, then mail the card in the enclosed envelope. Postage, of course, is on us.

Note, however: Only so many copies of the free
Executive Portfolio are being printed -- no more.
In fairness, copies are being made available on
the basis of first-come, first-served.

To avoid delay or disappointment, your request
should be postmarked quickly -- if at all possible,
by tonight.

May we look for your reply by return mail? Thank you -- and welcome
to BUSINESS WEEK, and to America's executive elite.

Cordially yours,

R. B. Alexander

R. B. Alexander
Publisher and Vice President
McGraw-Hill Publications Company

P.S. I hope I've got your name spelled right -- but check the
enclosed card to make sure. If it's wrong, forgive me -- and
please make corrections. The way it finally appears on the card
is exactly how your desk handbook will be embossed on the cover
in gold leaf -- compliments of the Editors.

BusinessWeek

1221 Avenue of the Americas
New York, New York 10020

BON APPETIT "SANGRIA" LETTER

The control letter Bill Jayme wrote for Knapp Communications to launch *Bon Appetit* magazine in 1976 remained unbeatable for many years until Jayme wrote another that beat it. The original letter began:

> First, fill a pitcher with ice.
>
> Now pour in a bottle of ordinary red wine, a quarter cup of brandy, and a small bottle of Club soda.
>
> Sweeten to taste with a quarter to half cup of sugar, garnish with slices of apple, lemon, and orange . . .
>
> . . . then move your chair to a warm, sunny spot. You've just made yourself Sangria — one of the great glories of Spain, and the perfect thing to sit back with and sip while you consider this invitation. It's from all of us here at
>
> *BON APPETIT.*

Enjoy food and drink? Enjoy discovery?
Want to sample new dishes, new cuisines?
Want to add more *life*, more *style*, to your
lifestyle? Here's the token that can help you:

**Send my
FREE
copy**

You'll find this token on the enclosed card.
Send it back by return mail and you'll get
free — no cost, obligation or commitment —
the current issue of a new magazine that's
dedicated to the innovative you.

Bon Appétit

Dear Reader:

First, fill a pitcher with ice.

Now pour in a bottle of ordinary red wine, a quarter cup of brandy,
and a small bottle of Club soda.

Sweeten to taste with a quarter to half cup of
sugar, garnish with slices of apple, lemon, and
orange....

... then move your chair to a warm, sunny spot. You've just made
yourself Sangria -- one of the great glories of Spain, and the

perfect thing to sit back with and sip while you consider this invitation. It's from all of us here at

BON APPETIT

... the new magazine about wining, dining, entertaining, the good life at home and abroad. The magazine for the innovative you. The magazine that's designed to help you put even more life, even more style, in your lifestyle.

Enjoy new places? New experiences? Come board the Northern Pacific with us and journey back to the 30's -- when dining cars served you for breakfast such eye-openers as fresh oysters on toast, and mutton chops with mushroom sauce.

Come cruise the Thames as we dine at the Anchor Inn at Shepperton, established in 1158, and maybe the only place in the world where you can still have authentic Entrecote de Vigneron --- steak in a sauce made with wine, herbs, chopped onions, and snails, topped with a perfectly poached egg.

Enjoy people? Parties? The good life? Come join the Captain's table with BON APPETIT aboard the Royal Viking Star when they open the "line" aquavit -- the fiery Norwegian schnapps that must, by definition, have traveled aboard the ship for a year, and have crossed the Equator at least once.

Come watch the wizardry of Chuen Look Chang. In a matter of minutes, using only his hands, he can transform a thick ball of heavy flour dough into 265 perfectly symmetrical noodles as fine as angel hair just by pulling, stretching, and throwing.

Enjoy discovering new restaurants? New dishes? Try the Beef Wellington at The Bakery in Chicago. The Scampi alla Griglia at the Ristorante Chianti in Los Angeles. The Oysters Bienville at the Commander's Palace in New Orleans. The Rack of Lamb at Tony's Wife in New York. The Mandarin Duck at Kona Kai in Kansas City.

In San Francisco, sample the Coquille St. Jacques at the Ritz Old Poodle Dog. In Boston, the Lobster Savannah at Locke-Ober's. In Detroit, the Dover Sole at the London Chop House. In Fort Lauderdale, the Filet Mignon at The Wharf.

Or try any of the dozens upon dozens of culinary experiences BON APPETIT tips you off to each month. Wherever you're dining, whatever you choose, you'll be in good hands -- we promise. We know the places. We know the people. They're good, or we wouldn't send you!

Enjoy fine wines? Come tour the châteaux of Bordeaux, where they've been exporting "les grands seigneurs" since 1152 A.D. Come tour the wineries around Lodi, California, where the soil is so rich in organic matter that you can set it afire, and where they grow the fabled Flame Tokay grape.

Come learn from a professional taster some pointers for keeping track of them all -- more than 5,000 different wines from France, half again as many more from Germany, and at least 1,500 from Italy, not to mention all the reds, whites and pinks we produce here at home.

In BON APPETIT's wine pages, you'll not only become more knowledgeable about varieties you've already tried, but also discover new labels and vintages. You'll meet the growers, tasters, collectors. You'll go to auctions, get tips on investing!

Enjoy puttering about the kitchen? Entertaining? Next time, spring this on your guests -- BON APPETIT's Chilled Avocado Soup:

3 fully ripe avocados	1/4 teaspoon onion salt
1 cup chicken broth	Pinch of white pepper
1 cup light cream	1 teaspoon lemon juice
1 teaspoon salt	Lemon slices as garnish.

Halve avocados lengthwise, remove seeds and peel. Blend with chicken broth in electric blender until smooth. Combine and mix with cream and seasonings. Pour into glass container, cover and refrigerate for three hours or overnight. Stir in lemon juice, garnish with lemon slices, and serve chilled.

It's different, delightful, delicious -- and see how easy BON APPETIT makes preparation? No fancy foreign phrases you don't know. No exotic ingredients to go searching for. Our recipes are written in easy-to-follow English. They call for materials you can find in any properly stocked market. And what a range they cover.

With BON APPETIT, you'll expand your repertoire in no time to include new appetizers, new breads, new desserts, new sauces, new ways with meat, fowl and fish. You'll get a better hold on the world's great cuisines -- French, Italian, German, Scandinavian, Mexican, Japanese, Chinese, Indian, and regional American cooking!

You'll hit on new ways to give parties -- with new foods and drinks to serve up! You'll discover new places to go -- and learn what to try when you get there! You'll pick up new ideas, broaden your perceptions, gain added sophistication and expertise. And we also predict -- you'll enhance your lifestyle.

No other magazine is more passionately dedicated to fulfilling the inner you --the you that gets satis-

faction out of inventing, experimenting, creating ...
and in the process, bringing pleasure to others. And
isn't pleasure what it's all about? <u>Making life more
rewarding for your family? Gratifying and gladdening
good friends?</u>

BON APPETIT comes to you monthly in one of the most stunning formats
of any magazine we know. But don't take our word -- see the folder.
Color portfolios showing food, table settings, beverages, international
cuisine and celebrity recipes. Color candids of people and parties!
How-to sequences to help you learn! Drawings! Sketches! Nostalgia!

<u>This magazine is for collecting.</u> Save your issues,
and in no time, you've got yourself a permanent, near-
encyclopedic source of recipes and reference -- a
lasting fount of ideas!

Where (and when) you can find it on newsstands, BON APPETIT costs 75¢
a copy. A year's subscription is regularly nine dollars. But by
mailing the enclosed card promptly

YOU CAN SAVE $1.05!

Instead of nine dollars, your special price
is only $7.95. You pocket a full $1.05 --
better than 10% off!

To reserve your subscription and save ... just place the token in the
slot on the card, and use the postage-paid envelope to mail. May we
look for as early a postmark as possible -- in order to avoid disappointment?

Cordially yours,

Cleon T. Knapp

Cleon T. Knapp
Publisher

CTK:jg

FREE GIFT. If you already know that you're going to like BON APPETIT,
you can enclose your payment now, in advance, and get yourself a useful
free gift -- a handsome wall chart for your kitchen that lists and describes the world's great cheeses, and that tells you which wines go well
with them. See the enclosed leaflet for details.

Quest/78 "Charter Subscription" Letter

Another intriguing Bill Jayme lead is a must for any book on classic direct mail letters. It was used to help launch *Quest/78* magazine.

Dear fellow adventurer:

Remember how great it felt that first time?

You were ten, maybe eleven or twelve. They'd given it to you for your birthday. They held it steady while you climbed into the saddle. They pushed. And then they let go.

You picked up speed. The wobbling ceased. Suddenly, you were off — hair streaming, wind in your face, biking away to China, and you loved it!

Or maybe it was when you were older. Finally, Friday came. Three o'clock. Four o'clock. Ten minutes to five. At last, there it was — the envelope.

You ripped it open. Your first paycheck ever! All yours! And you'd earned every penny! You were richer than Rockefeller, and you loved it!

Or maybe it was the time you got through all three acts without forgetting a line. Or when you first had your picture in the paper. Or succeeded in cooking a meal from start to finish entirely by yourself.

Or when you first wrote a poem that wasn't half bad. Or proudly signed your name to a painting. Or shot par golf. Tossed a winning touchdown. Or welcomed your first-born to the world . . .

If it's been too long since you've experienced thrills and chills like these — moments of exhilaration, elation, accomplishment . . .

If you're ready to become enthralled again — with challenge, with achievement, with yourself . . .

. . . then welcome to *QUEST/78*. The new magazine that brings out the best in you. The magazine that says "try it!" The magazine that engages you, challenges you, urges you on. The magazine that makes you feel good all over.

Ever expect a dozen or so— and have a multitude show up? That's what happened to us not long ago when we published our very first issue. At a time when our country was supposedly wallowing in gloom and doom—corruption, violence, porn—how many people, we wondered, would go for a magazine about quality, excellence, achievement. 100,000? 200,000? Wrong! The minute Volume I, Number One came off the presses, the lines began to form. And by today, they stretch cross-continent—from New York to California, from Texas to Illinois. Lo and behold, a magazine *about* success is *itself* a success without parallel!

Quest/78

This letter invites you to find out what all the hoopla is about . . . to get in on this unusual new publication *without* having to stand in line . . . and to *save a substantial amount of money* . . . by becoming a

CHARTER SUBSCRIBER

Dear fellow adventurer:

Remember how great it felt that first time?

You were ten, maybe eleven or twelve. They'd given it to you for your birthday. They held it steady while you climbed into the saddle. They pushed. And then they let go.

You picked up speed. The wobbling ceased. Suddenly, you were off--hair streaming, wind in your face, biking away to China, and <u>you loved it</u>!

Or maybe it was when you were older. Finally, Friday came. Three o'clock. Four o'clock. Ten minutes to five. At last, there it was--the envelope.

You ripped it open. Your first paycheck ever! All yours! And you'd earned every penny! You were richer than Rockefeller, and <u>you loved it</u>!

Or maybe it was the time you got through all three acts without forgetting a line. Or when you first had your picture in the paper. Or succeeded in cooking a meal from start to finish entirely by yourself.

Or when you first wrote a poem that wasn't half bad. Or proudly signed your name to a painting. Or shot par golf. Tossed a winning touchdown. Or welcomed your first-born to the world...

If it's been too long since you've experienced thrills and chills like these--moments of exhilaration, elation, accomplishment ...

If you're ready to become enthralled again--with challenge, with achievement, with yourself ...

... then welcome to QUEST/78. The new magazine that brings out the best in you. The magazine that says "try it!" The magazine that engages you, challenges you, urges you on. The magazine that makes you feel good all over.

With this letter, I invite you to have a look at QUEST/78 under our 100 percent refund guarantee. And if you like it, to become a Charter Subscriber.

You'll save yourself an immediate $3--a discount of 25 percent off. And this savings is only the first of many. Keep reading for how you'll save more!

Almost since Adam and Eve first woke up under the apple tree, poets, philosophers and pundits have been attempting to define human existence. To some, life is dismal and dreary. Samuel Butler found it "one long process of getting tired." Victor Hugo called it "an abyss."

Napoleon found it "a bore" and "a cross." Voltaire, "a combat." Shakespeare, "a walking shadow." One eminent Victorian, P. J. Bailey, went to the extreme of comparing it to "a bridge of groans across a stream of tears." Desperation!

Others, mercifully, find living more fun. America's own Ralph Waldo Emerson called life "a series of surprises ... an ecstasy." And QUEST/78 cries, "Hear, Hear!" Just lift back that elegant cover, and you'll see:

Pages upon pages about people who are enjoying their lives to the fullest--making each minute count, getting the most out of every hour, every day, every week. Plus pages upon pages about you--and how you can go do the same.

Want to find out how to make it in the world of getting and spending? In QUEST/78, come learn from Saul Zabar. He happens to run the world's best delicatessen. But his zeal, dedication, and enthusiasm would make him a success at almost anything--president of a steel company, president of a university, President of the United States!

Or come get to know anthropologist Margaret Mead at age 75-- up and about at 5 a.m. in her Manhattan apartment to rehearse a speech she'll be giving that afternoon, then settling in to her typewriter, where by day's end she may just add yet another line or two to the 49 she already commands in Who's Who!

-2-

Toying with changing your lifestyle? In QUEST/78 learn why and how James Brown, Yale '56, gave up a seat on the Stock Exchange and $168,000 a year to free-lance as a photographer! Why and how Stephanie Wallach abandoned a successful career as a film editor to become one of the nation's few female airline pilots!

Why and how Jim Patterson cut out from investment banking in New York City to go run a country inn in Vermont with his wife! Why and how Richard Gill gave up a lifelong career as a lecturer at Harvard to become, in his middle forties, one of the Metropolitan Opera's more promising basso profundos!

Want to try your hand at something different? Come lift off with QUEST/78 in the AX-7--the balloon that lets you fly free! Come look over Bob Summer's shoulder as he fashions the world's finest bamboo fly rod. Come trek the primal landscape with Lawrence Osgood--a journey across the Arctic tundra!

Come learn what shapes the creative imagination as QUEST/78 interviews such artists as Saul Steinberg, Mary Frank, Joan Mitchell, George Segal. Come find out how Stan Lee did it--make Spider-man the world's best fantasy trip! Come discover how Anthony West resolved it--the dilemma of the conscientious objector!

All these stories and more have appeared in recent issues. First-person accounts--intimate, revealing, one-to-one. Interviews--candid, honest, forthright. Fiction. Verse. Reviews. All set amidst some of the most stunning illustration you've ever seen.

On the basis of its preview issue alone, in fact, QUEST/78 has been honored with a prestigious Gold Medal from the Society of Publication Designers--the highest possible accolade for graphics, design, illustration!

I truly believe that QUEST/78 will grip you like no other magazine ever. Boggle your imagination. Turn you on. Help you achieve what you've always wanted. Help you realize your fullest potentials. Help you fall in love again with life ...

... but why not come see for yourself under our 100 per-cent refund guarantee. You've got nothing to lose but the blahs. And you've got everything to gain. New experi-ences! New people! New ideas! New excitement! New inspiration! New challenges!

QUEST/78 comes to you every other month. When and where it's not sold out on newsstands, single copies cost two dollars each. A year (six issues) is regularly $12 by subscription. But when you return the enclosed reservation card now, your price as a Charter Subscriber is only $9.

-3-

Right away, you save a welcome $3.00.! And you also assure yourself of these added, valuable Charter Benefits:

Preferential rates in perpetuity. As a Charter Subscriber, you're guaranteed perpetual savings--always the lowest possible price on all renewals, and on any and all gift subscriptions you may wish to give.

100 Percent Refund Guarantee. If ever QUEST/78 lets you down, just cancel and get all your Charter Subscription money back--not just a portion, but everything you've paid for a full refund of 100 percent.

May we look for your acceptance by return mail? Charter Reservations are being accepted on the basis of first-come, first-served. To avoid delay or disappointment, your reservation should be postmarked just as quickly as convenient. Thank you--and welcome to QUEST/78!

Cordially yours,

Jack Martin
Publishing Director

JM:wj

P.S. Send no money. Just tuck the token into the slot on the order card--that's all. We'll bill you at a less pressing moment, after QUEST/78 starts coming.

Quest/78

1133 AVENUE OF THE AMERICAS NEW YORK, NEW YORK 10036

PSYCHOLOGY TODAY "HITLER" LETTER

Before the classic "bathroom door" letter was created by Bill Jayme for *Psychology Today* magazine (see page 29), the long-running control letter was another classic by John P. Walsh.

On the outer envelope was a picture of Adolf Hitler and this teaser:

> The year, 1930. The place, Berlin. You are a practicing psychoanalyst confronting an interesting new patient. His name is Adolf Hitler. He is a professional politician regarded as one of the country's rising young men. Now he has come to you because
>
> (continued inside)
>
> he is troubled by persistent anxieties. He speaks confidently about his plans for Germany, yet he admits to fear of failure and therefore punishment by "lesser" beings. Lately, however, when he considers some of the harsh deeds demanded by his grandiose plans, he has been bothered by feelings of guilt. Nevertheless, he is convinced that the ends justify the means. He is bothered only because his increasing anxieties and guilt feelings may impede him in the execution of his designs. Hitler asks you to put an end to these disturbing feelings. Can you help him?

By all means a classic "grabber." Of course, that alone won't sell magazine subscriptions. But Walsh's excellent letter copy picked up where this quotation from a *Psychology Today* article left off:

> You don't have to be a a professional to be interested in — even fascinated by — this hypothetical problem. Not a professional doctor, psychologist or minister. All it takes is a normal amount of curiosity and interest in how and why people act as they do.
>
> Because I believe that description embraces you, you see here an invitation and a fleeting offer. It is to . . .
>
> become a subscriber to the magazine that bridges
> the gap between laboratory and living room . . .
> *PSYCHOLOGY TODAY*

(continued from outer envelope)

he is troubled by persistent anxieties. He speaks confidently about his plans for Germany, yet he admits to fear of failure and therefore punishment by "lesser" beings. Lately, however, when he considers some of the harsh deeds demanded by his grandiose plans, he has been bothered by feelings of guilt. Nevertheless, he is convinced that the ends justify the means. He is bothered only because his increasing anxieties and guilt feelings may impede him in the execution of his designs. Hitler asks you to put an end to these disturbing feelings. Can you help him?

from Psychology Today's
"Morality in Psychotherapy"
by Marvin Frankel

Dear Reader:

You don't have to be a professional to be interested in -- even fascinated by -- this hypothetical problem. Not a professional doctor, psychologist or minister. All it takes is a normal amount of curiosity and interest in how and why people act as they' do.

Because I believe that description embraces you, you see here an invitation and a fleeting offer. It is to . . .

become a subscriber to the magazine that bridges
the gap between laboratory and living room . . .
PSYCHOLOGY TODAY

The benefits of subscribing are more rewarding than they are tangible . . . but nonetheless real.

Psychology Today is not abstract, disconnected, academic theory but, rather, an assessment of fascinating, logical, senseless, consistent, erratic, down-to-earth life as it is. With little regard for how it should be.

It is a bracing hour of thought for a bad TV night, a conversational reference point during cocktails, an unassuming authority on how not to bring up the kids, an inspiration for students that can be literally upgrading.

And it's fun.

No matter if you've graded more blue books that you've filled -- or if to you a blue book is only something to save a particular brand of trading stamps in -- Psychology Today is fun. The best kind of fun . . . fun with a point.

The fact that you read this far indicates that for you, fun can be stretching the brain, challenging the mind, doubting the apparent. And that's what I promise you, month after month, in Psychology Today. Articles such as these:

"Amnesia: A World Without Continuity." How you visit the amnesiac's lost worlds when you say "It's right on the tip of my tongue."

"The Psychopharmacological Revolution." Advantages and disadvantages of pills that have replaced straight jackets and restored ability to function.

"The Small-World Problem." Why you know someone who knows someone who knows someone who knows someone who knows Elizabeth Taylor ... or Joe Namath ... or even Spiro Agnew!

"Pain and Aggression." Why they are often a cause and effect ... and why that is probably the reason you're around to read this.

"Parapsychology: New Neighbor or Unwelcome Guest." Why scientists are taking the study of psychic phenomena seriously ... and what they are learning about it.

"Are I.Q. Tests Intelligent?" Why you may be a lot smarter (or otherwise) than your I.Q. test scores have indicated. New insights into fluid and crystallized intelligence ... how present I.Q. tests fail to differentiate ... and what it can mean.

The archaic idea that some men are "born criminals" may have some validity after all. The culprit may be an extra chromosome.

Every month, you'll enjoy Psychology Today's conversations with eminent psychologists, educators, philosophers, writers and others who are commenting incisively on the human condition. People like Margaret Mead, Rollo May, Herbert Marcuse, Harvey Cox.

Ours is a magazine that is obliged to only one ideal -- researched, authenticated facts. The truth as we know it today. Fully cognizant that is not the way it will necessarily be tomorrow.

We accept no taboos in our monthly quest for enlightenment, save one: Don't bore the reader. We talk about sex clinically and, if necessary, carnally; we are neither doting nor derisive about children; and with religion we treat both the blasphemous and the beatific.

How do we do all of this? Very, very lucidly.

You don't have to be a Ph.D. to know that knowledge is often cloaked in jargon, circumlocution and (alas!) pomposity. But not in Psychology Today. Our editors are just that . . . editors. As ruthless with a blue pencil as they are sensitive to your ennui threshold. We don't think that, just because a fair percentage of our subscribers hold scientific degrees, our pages have to read like it.

And this is our approach to graphics. If you've never heard of a responsible magazine of science using four-color photography and art with boldness and skill ... glance at the folder enclosed. And then at the order form, with its "Happy to Oblige" token. By putting the token into the "yes" slot, you and Psychology Today will become acquainted.

(Please turn the page . . .

You couldn't pick a better time than right now, because now you can subscribe under the terms of a special introductory offer. Mail the enclosed card and we will send you a complimentary copy of the current issue plus the next 11 for just $6 -- 50% off the regular subscription price of $12!

There's only one hitch . . . Promptness counts. That's the reason we require no payment now; you don't even have to take the time to write a check. You can mail the card immediately.

How about right now.

Sincerely,

T George Harris

T George Harris
Editor

TGH/dca

P.S. Even if your decision is not to try Psychology Today, will you tell us by putting the token in the "no" slot? Thank you.

psychology today DEL MAR, CALIFORNIA 92014

PREVENTION MAGAZINE "MEMORIES OF GRANDMOTHER" LETTER

One of America's most successful publishers is Rodale Press in Emmaus, Pennsylvania. Their books and magazines are oriented to self-sufficient living and aimed at those who have a personal interest in health, ecology, and natural ways. Many of Rodale's promotion letters are masterpieces of addressing a specific audience in language tuned to its special interests, but one of the best is this classic for *Prevention* magazine. It begins:

> My Grandmother lived with us when I was growing up.
>
> She used to give me camomile tea when my stomach was upset. She insisted that the family use vinegar to rinse hair and made a cucumber cleanser for my face. As I grew older, I decided Grandmother was hopelessly out of date.
>
> Then a few years ago, I began remembering how it was when I lived with her. How shiny and healthy our hair had always been. How beautiful my skin remained throughout adolescence. How full of energy and vitality all of us were without our soft drinks, candies and snack foods (she wouldn't allow them in the house — "empty foods," she'd snort . . . and hand me a box of raisins or dried apricots).

Sound like your grandmother (or one you knew when you were growing up)? For Rodale's audience, everyone at least wishes they had had a grandmother like that . . . and the mood is set to sell a magazine that takes its readers back to Grandmother's sage advice.

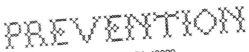

EMMAUS, PA 18099

Dear Reader:

My Grandmother lived with us when I was growing up.

She used to give me camomile tea when my stomach was upset. She insisted that the family use vinegar to rinse hair and made a cucumber cleanser for my face. As I grew older, I decided Grandmother was hopelessly out of date.

Then a few years ago, I began remembering how it was when I lived with her. How shiny and healthy our hair had always been. How beautiful my skin remained throughout adolescence. How full of energy and vitality all of us were without our soft drinks, candies and snack foods (she wouldn't allow them in the house — "empty foods," she'd snort ... and hand me a box of raisins or dried apricots).

I was reminded of Grandmother when I noticed how often the government removed a chemical from the market after everyone had been eating it for years. I began wondering whether the products I was using today would be forbidden tomorrow.

And that started me thinking about how many chemicals I used and ate. Almost everything contains chemicals! I kept reading how scientists thought some of them caused serious medical problems. How simple things like headache remedies could create other troubles.

I was stunned by the number of foods that were almost completely "fake" — most of the good things had been taken out and chemical substitutes put in.

You read about threats and dangers to your health like these everyday. In almost every newspaper and magazine you open.

But I know of only one publication that tells you — sincerely and consistently — how you may combat these problems ... what you may do to try to live healthier in this often unhealthy world of ours: PREVENTION magazine.

If you've ever seen PREVENTION, you know its style. Understandable. Practical. Down-to-Earth. It's the magazine that over two million Americans regularly turn to for the help and advice that they often cannot find from any other source — sometimes doctors included.

If you haven't seen the magazine ... I'd like to send you the latest issue so you can take a good look. I'm sure you'll find its "feel better" ideas as stimulating as a breath of fresh air.

(over, please)

To get your no-risk, no obligation copy of PREVENTION magazine ...

　1.　Just mail the enclosed postpaid card. BUT SEND NO MONEY NOW.

　2.　We'll send you PREVENTION and enter a <u>trial</u> no-risk 12-month subscription in your name.

　3.　If you like what you see and want to subscribe to PREVENTION magazine's unique brand of "feel better" advice, simply pay the $6.99 invoice.

　　　If not, just mark "cancel" on our bill, return it and owe nothing. You keep the first issue free of charge.

Now, that's a fair offer, isn't it?

And we're making it so easy because we want you to take <u>just one look</u> — so you can see just how valuable PREVENTION magazine may be in your life.

Why so <u>valuable</u>?

Because PREVENTION is the cheapest, most easily accessible source that you have to much of the latest medical research findings ... to some of the alternative ways to try to "get better" and "stay better" without resorting to drugs and surgery ... to the basic, earthy, natural approach to better health and better living that my Grandmother (and perhaps, <u>yours</u>, too) knew almost intuitively.

WHY DO <u>YOU</u> NEED PREVENTION?

It's an honest question. And, basically, the answer is three-fold:

1.　<u>PREVENTION tries to help you even-out the increasing odds against your better health</u>. Open any newspaper or magazine and you're likely to read about another chemical in your environment ... another additive in your food ... another way that may shorten your life span; another way perhaps leading to diseases like cancer or heart trouble.

It's getting so depressing that many people block it out of their minds. They "grow accustomed" to the new dangers. They try to pretend they don't exist. But that doesn't make these potential dangers disappear; it doesn't make life any healthier, longer ... or even happier.

PREVENTION tries to alert you to the dangers, too. But we don't stop there. Every issue tells you what you may do to try to avoid them ... possibly correct them ... and, in some cases, even perhaps repair some of the damage that they may have already done.

2.　<u>PREVENTION tells you more than your doctor perhaps can or will</u>. Today, surgery and drugs are not the only "get better" alternatives available to you. There are other options open. Options that, often, are safer, cheaper, gentler than those of "traditional medicine." Time after time, we've found that a number of today's physicians may not even be aware of these alternatives. So how can you expect to know of them?

PREVENTION tries to be your link. You learn about how your body functions ... what it needs for better well-being ... how you may, many times, correct a minor illness or ailment <u>yourself</u>. PREVENTION may help you be a more intelligent, more aware medical consumer. (After all, your health is <u>your</u> responsibility.)

<u>3. PREVENTION seems to work well</u>. The PREVENTION System for Better Health apparently gets results. If it did not, we would most certainly not be <u>the number one health magazine in the world today</u> — which we are — with over two million regular subscribers.

We make no miracle claims; offer no instant results. All we say is if you truly want better health ...

    ... if you want to try to live a longer, more active life ... if you want to treat what may be the source — not symptoms alone — of your health problems ... if you want to know more about what you may do to live healthier in this, unhealthy world of ours ...

... PREVENTION may show you — step-by-step — the things that you may do to help achieve these desires.

Isn't it worth a <u>free look</u>? And if PREVENTION works for you, isn't it well worth the $6.99 subscription price? We think so. Over two million monthly readers think so.

But what do <u>you</u> think? Look first (at <u>our</u> risk) and then decide. Here's how ...

<u>REMEMBER OUR NO-RISK OFFER: LOOK NOW, DECIDE TO SUBSCRIBE LATER</u>

Of course, I could go on and on about PREVENTION. Sharing with you the many ways the PREVENTION System has helped me personally ... telling you about specific natural healing techniques ... quoting some moving testimony from PREVENTION readers ...

... but I'll spare your time.

One free look is worth a thousand words of advertising. And PREVENTION speaks for itself — <u>powerfully</u>.

So you be the judge.

Just mail the enclosed card to inspect PREVENTION — the modern "get better, feel better," natural health system whose roots go very deep indeed.

I'm on the PREVENTION System. And I've got to tell you, I feel better — and look better — because of it. It <u>has</u> helped me. It may help you, too.

I hope you try PREVENTION. I hope everybody does. We need a little more "real" in our lives and a few less substitutes.

Sincerely,

Sandy Gibb

Sandy Gibb

P.S.   <u>ACT NOW AND GET A FREE BOOK ABOUT THE PREVENTION SYSTEM!</u>
For all those who mail the enclosed card ...

Yours free!

... we have a free bonus: a copy of THE PREVENTION SYSTEM FOR BETTER HEALTH — the book that explains in plain language, how this natural health method works. Here are the basics of the 35-year-old system that has helped improve the well-being of so many over the years.

You can't buy a copy of this remarkable book anywhere. But it's yours free — whether you subscribe to the magazine or not — so take action now, while you're thinking about it.

P.P.S.   AN EXTRA FREE BOOKLET ... AND ADDED SAVINGS!

If you're planning to give PREVENTION a try, why not try 24-months? There are plenty of good reasons why you should:

1.   THERE'S NO EXTRA RISK. Our money back on unmailed copies privilege assures it.

2.   GUARD AGAINST PRICE INCREASES. They're almost inevitable with our present economy. Buying a 24-month subscription could be an insurance policy against higher prices.

3.   GET THIS BOOK AS A BONUS. In addition to your <u>free</u> copy of THE PREVENTION SYSTEM FOR BETTER HEALTH, we'll send you a copy of our HERBS FOR HEALTH when you subscribe for 24 months.

Now you can get acquainted with one of the alternatives to drugs and medications: the healing herbs. Here are the "medicines of yesterday" that are making a comeback. You'll find Herbal treatments and folk "remedies" for dozens of common ailments. And you'll learn to know and use 70 wonderful plants and herbs in HERBS FOR HEALTH. You can't buy it anywhere, but it's yours <u>free</u> from PREVENTION with this trial subscription.

PUBLISHERS CLEARING HOUSE "TRANSPARENT" LETTER

Long before anyone in direct mail had heard of transparent poly envelopes, Marvin Barckley had discovered the magic of a transparent surface for renewal letters he created for the old *Quick* magazine. He later adopted this technique for the Publishers Clearing House (PCH) letter shown here. It was printed in black, blue, and yellow on a sheet of clear cellophane. Copy began:

> It is transparently clear to you as a Clearing House customer . . .
>
> . . . that you get up to twice as many copies for your magazine dollar when you order your new subscriptions at Clearing House prices instead of paying regular publisher prices.
>
> And it is crystal clear, too — we hope — that the bulletins we send you are designed to keep you well-informed on current Clearing House prices . . . not to pressure you to buy.

When you mail as frequently as PCH mails to its house list, a change of pace is a must; this "transparent" letter was a great way to get renewed attention.

Dear Customer:

It is transparently clear to you as a Clearing House customer ...

... that you get up to twice as many copies for your magazine dollar when you order your new subscriptions at Clearing House prices instead of paying regular publisher prices.

And it is crystal, too — we hope — that the bulletins we send you are designed to keep you well-informed on current Clearing House prices ... not to pressure you to buy.

(After all, you don't buy a new car or TV every time you see a newspaper ad. And we surely don't expect an order from you every time we write you. — That just wouldn't make sense.)

But we can't help getting mighty enthusiastic at times about the great savings you can make at Clearing House new-subscriber prices. For it is a genuine pleasure to be able to send you Discount Coupons like the ones I'm enclosing with this letter.

And you can see why. This month, for instance, we are ready to send you:

TV GUIDE for only 8-1/3¢ a copy (72 issues, $5.97)

LOOK for only 8¢ a copy (39 issues, $3.00)

LADIES' HOME JOURNAL for only 12-1/2¢ a copy (23 issues, $2.88)

SATURDAY EVENING POST for only 7-2/3¢ a copy (39 issues, $2.98)

... and there's OUTDOOR LIFE for less than 17¢ — NEWSWEEK, only 11¢ — SPORTS ILLUSTRATED for only a dime — and many, many others.

This is a fine time to make sure you and your entire family have good stay-at-home reading for leisure hours in the weeks ahead. Your Discount Coupons cover a broad range of magazine riches from fiction — to hobby helps — to homemaking — and the whole world of news and ideas and information.

The enclosed certificate made out in your name makes ordering easy. You simply pick out the magazine or magazines you want — paste the Coupons on the card — "charge it" — and PAY-AS-YOU-READ if you like. You just pay 1/3 each month for three months after your magazines start coming.

We've served you before, and we'd be delighted to serve you again. So why not make up an order now — and then mail it to us today.

Best wishes,

Robert H. Treller

RHT: jhb

Publishers Clearing House "Advance Notice" Letter

There are two basic package formats used in direct marketing — the "KISS" package ("Keep It Simple, Stupid" or "Keep It Sweet and Simple") and the so-called "RIC" package, loaded with bells and whistles. (I don't know who came up with the acronym, but it stands for "Readership, Involvement, Commitment.")

No one has created more effective RIC packages than Henry Cowen and Marvin Barckley, whose loaded envelopes consistently kept Publishers Clearing House selling more magazine subscriptions than anyone else.

It might seem that the busy PCH mailing packages put little emphasis on letters. A bit of history, supplied by Barckley, helps explain why letters continue to play a vital role:

■ Before 1960, Clearing House letters were simple and warm notes that were basically designed to create a friendly ambience to induce studying the stamp sheet and using the order form.

After Henry Cowen and I came, we worked hard at punching up product, elaborating on value and service, emphasizing savings . . . with the me-to-you personal-I-care style.

The letter then became a much more important part of the package — ranking right next to the stamp sheet on getting attention. It still is very important, but with the advent of contest and computer personalization, it moves further down the line in the sales-sequence pattern.

Where we formerly grabbed attention with "Umpty-ump titles at less than 7 1/3¢ a copy" on the envelope and elaborated on that idea in the letter, we now grab their attention with our Giveaway on the envelope, prize brochure, and computer form . . . and then we have to sell like hell in the letter while we have their attention!

One of my favorite Barckley letters for PCH was used as a follow-up to their big "everybody gets it" January mailing. It was aimed at customers . . . and said so:

Good customers deserve the best. That's why keeping you informed about everything new at the Clearing House is Top Priority business with us.

A couple of weeks ago we sent you our latest bulletin — and alerted you to watch the EARLY EVENING NEWS on TV, March 1, 1982, to learn the names of our most recent top winners, including the $250,000.00 winner of SuperPrize II!

Hold your breath, cross your fingers, and keep a chair by the phone because, if we call, it's for a really BIG one. But meantime . . .

. . . we want you to be the first to get your entry in for still another QUARTER MILLION DOLLAR PRIZE . . . SuperPrize III. Announcement to the general public will be out in another 3 to 4 weeks, but you are special to us so we want you to have a head start.

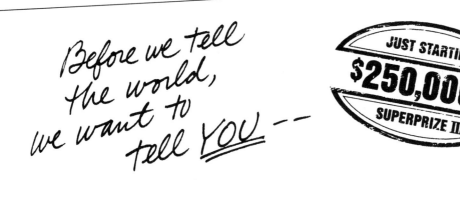

Before we tell the world, we want to tell YOU --

Dear Friend of the Clearing House:

<u>Good customers deserve the best</u>. That's why keeping you informed about everything new at the Clearing House is Top Priority business with us.

A couple of weeks ago we sent you our latest bulletin -- and alerted you to watch the EARLY EVENING NEWS on TV, March 1, 1982, to learn the names of our most recent top winners, <u>including the $250,000.00 winner of SuperPrize II</u>!

Hold your breath, cross your fingers, and keep a chair by the phone because, if we <u>call</u>, it's for a really BIG one. But, meantime ...

)) ... we want you to be first to get your entry in for still another QUARTER MILLION DOLLAR PRIZE ... SuperPrize III. Announcement to the general public will be out in another 3 to 4 weeks, but you are special to us so we want you to have a head start. ((

That $250,000.00 <u>IS</u> a dazzler ... but your enclosed Entry/Order form, sent back by February 26, 1982 also puts you in the race for thousands of other exciting prizes ... from $5.00 to $2,500.00 ... to $25,000.00 ... to $75,000.00 ... and yes, even to $125,000.00!

You'll see this bulletin is unusual in another way, too. Along with lots of America's popular favorites, we've included many, many special interest titles that are hard to find anywhere else. Most are offered only once or twice a year, so if you see one (or more) that you like, order now -- while you can!

Here are just a few of the fascinating titles you're going to find:

✓<u>AUDUBON</u>   ✓<u>OVATION</u>   ✓<u>ALL CATS</u>

  ✓<u>CONNOISSEUR</u>   ✓<u>GOLDMINE</u>   ✓<u>IT'S ME</u>

    ✓<u>TAX HOTLINE</u>   ✓<u>TECHNOLOGY</u>   ✓<u>FARM WIFE NEWS</u>

    ✓<u>NEW SHELTER</u>   ✓<u>MOVING IMAGE</u>   ✓<u>DANCEMAGAZINE</u>

     ✓<u>COUNTRY PEOPLE</u>   ✓<u>GAMBLING TIMES</u>   ✓<u>BOTTOM LINE PERSONAL</u>

Something for everyone! And, in the case of FIFTEEN of our titles, something EXTRA for everyone ... FREE-gift-with-subscription without a penny of extra cost! Look at these:

TAX HOTLINE   6 iss/$9.99   PLUS - TAX AVOIDANCE STRATEGIES *Free!*

SPRING   12 iss/$9.97   PLUS - GOOD HEALTH/GOOD LOOKS *Free!*

FAMILY HANDYMAN   10 iss/$8.95   PLUS - HANDYMAN'S NEW ANSWER BOOK *Free!*

CHANGING TIMES   15 iss/$9.87   PLUS - HOW TO GET MORE FOR YOUR MONEY *Free!*
                                    AND - THE NEW TAX LAW AND YOUR TAX RETURN

GAMBLING TIMES   6 iss/$11.97 PLUS - GAMBLING AROUND THE WORLD: *Free!*
                                           WHAT, WHERE, & HOW

KIPLINGER   26 iss/$11.97 PLUS - INFLATION FIGHTING *Free!*
WASHINGTON LETTER   NEWSLETTER

NEW SHELTER   9 iss/$8.97   PLUS - APPROACHING FREE ENERGY *Free!*

REFUNDER'S DIGEST   6 iss/$8.95   PLUS - IT'S EASY MONEY WHEN YOU *Free!*
                                           KNOW HOW TO GET IT

THE SATURDAY   9 iss/$9.95   PLUS - Saturday Evening Post FAMILY *Free!*
EVENING POST   COOKBOOK

And lots more! Many old reliables available, too. You'll know them when you see them.

So, by all means, as you get your Giveaway entry ready to mail to beat the deadline, look over the enclosed sheet of SIX DOZEN coupons. All unbeatable values ... with low prices ... free credit ... PAY-AS-YOU-READ ... and all the other great customer services you know you can count on at The Clearing House.

By now, you know you don't have to order to be a winner. So -- the next most important thing is this: Get your entry in the mail by February 26 -- and then keep on sending entries regularly as your bulletins continue coming in for the rest of the year. Remember, if at first you don't succeed ... enter, enter again!

Take advantage of your head start now and send your entry without delay.

Good luck,

Robert H. Treller

Robert H. Treller, for
The Clearing House

RHT:kgg

Remember -- ONE lucky number can win you more than one prize and when one of them can be A QUARTER-MILLION DOLLARS, you just have to go for it!

FLY FISHERMAN MAGAZINE "TROUT SPOKEN HERE" LETTER

John Francis Tighe is not only one of the top writers of book and circulation promotion letters, but he is also one of the most prolific writers about writing. Two of his circulation promotion letters are included in this section. He comments:

■ These letters demonstrate the importance of establishing credibility for your sales pitch by talking to the prospect in his own language.

What makes letter writing a unique advertising medium is its *personal* quality. A good sales letter is essentially a first person communication from one human being to another. It is vital for that one-to-one feeling to come through, even in cheap off-set letters such as these — and even though the prospect *knows* he is reading a form letter.

The *Fly Fisherman* mailing uses language so specialized that after several years, I no longer know what some of the words mean. But because one wrong connotation would have torpedoed the mailing by revealing its author as a smartass copywriter instead of an angler, I went to great lengths to learn the vernacular — which was something like learning Portuguese. However, it paid off. The mailing became the control, and may still be.

Actually, although the letter is filled with "fishing talk," the language is really quite down-to-earth and understandable by almost everyone. It begins:

> There's bait casting. There's spin fishing. And then there's fly fishing —
>
> — what Robert Traver (author of *Anatomy of a Murder* but best known to fishermen for his love affair with trout) called "one of the more amiable forms of an incurable madness."
>
> If the hairs on your neck tingle at the vision of a dusk-rising brown gently finning as he looks upstream for hors d'oeuvres, you've got the madness.
>
> I know I do. I'm the Editor of FLY FISHERMAN. Like Robert Traver I fish because . . .

It's worth taking special note of the postscript at the end of this outstanding letter. I like a P.S. (often read first) that introduces a "what's that all about" element. This encourages the reader to search the body copy to discover an answer.

> P.S. We've ordered enough FREE CREELS — we think — to meet the anticipated response. But they are likely to go fast, so why risk waiting months while we re-order? Since your creel will be shipped as soon as you pay for your subscription, why not get it immediately by enclosing payment now?

Trout Spoken Here.
Also Bass. Salmon. And Bonefish.

CRAZY FOR FLY-FISHING? SEND FOR YOUR

COMPLIMENTARY ISSUE OF FLY FISHERMAN --

THE BEST THERAPY FOR VICTIMS OF THE

"INCURABLE MADNESS" DESCRIBED BELOW.

There's no obligation. But we'll throw in a FREE CREEL if you accept our subscription offer.

Fellow Angler:

There's bait casting. There's spin fishing. And then there's fly fishing --

-- what Robert Traver (author of Anatomy of a Murder but best known to fishermen for his love affair with trout) called "one of the more amiable forms of an incurable madness."

If the hairs on your neck tingle at the vision of a dusk-rising brown gently finning as he looks upstream for hors d'oeuvres, you've got the madness.

I know I do. I'm the Editor of FLY FISHERMAN. Like Robert Traver I fish because ...

"... in a world where most men seem to spend their lives doing things they hate, my fishing is at once an endless source of delight and an act of rebellion ...

"... because trout do not lie or cheat and cannot be bought or bribed or impressed by power, but respond only to quietude and humility and endless patience ..."

I've got it bad; this amiable madness. And so do all of us here at FLY FISHERMAN magazine.

When we're not hipdeep in New York's Beaverkill, Montana's Bighorn or California's Hat Creek, we're planning our next trip -- swapping stories about our last one -- or writing about it in FLY FISHERMAN.

When we're not waiting for a hatch along Michigan's Au Sable ... skimming the boneflats of the Florida Keys ... casting to smallmouths in Virginia's Shenandoah River, we're writing about it in FLY FISHERMAN.

When we're not debating the merits of the Light Cahill, Gray Midge, Royal Wulff, Rusty Spinner, Leadwing Coachman, Tan Caddis Pupa, Marabou Streamer, Muddler Minnow, Black-Nosed Dace...

    ... or inventing better imitations of mayfly nymphs, duns
        and spinners, caddisflies, stoneflies, minnows ...

    ... creating artificials from ostrich, goose or peacock
        feathers; beaver, muskrat, or skunk fur; badger, bear
        or antelope hair ...

    ... selecting, stripping and winding hackle ... perfecting
        our whipfinish knot ... polishing our roll-casting
        technique ...

    ... comparison-testing the latest single-action reels,
        checking the "feel" of a state-of-the-art boron rod
        (or rolling our own) ...

    ... we're writing about it in FLY FISHERMAN.

Share the expertise of our small army of field editors and streamside reporters. In each issue --

Our Fly-Tiers Bench reveals how to tie the "perfect fly" you've dreamed of. Our Casting About column leads you to pristine lakes and crystal streams. Our New Products section reports the latest in fly fishing gear and clothing and our equipment features help you in selecting that ideal fly rod, reel, lines, and other things you'll need to improve your fishing.

The enclosed postage paid reply card will bring your complimentary issue of FLY FISHERMAN -- with no obligation to subscribe.

If you love it -- love the cameraderie of anglers trading tips, techniques and tall tales; love the glowing photos of misty lakes and mountain streams, rainbow trout and rainbow-colored flies -- take advantage of our generous reduced-rate subscription offer.

If you don't -- ?

Simply write "cancel" on our invoice and mail it back without paying or owing anything. Worth a try? Then mail the reply card today.

Cordially,

John Randolph

John Randolph

P.S. We've ordered enough FREE CREELS -- we think -- to meet the anticipated response. But they are likely to go fast, so why risk waiting months while we re-order? Since your creel will be shipped as soon as you pay for your subscription, why not get it immediately by enclosing payment now?

JDR/jbb

Popular Mechanics Encyclopedia "Dirty Hands" Letter

The other letter by Tighe that demonstrates his use of "the recipient's own language approach" was written for the *Popular Mechanics* Do-It-Yourself Encyclopedia and remained its control for many years. It opens with a Johnson Box and then moves into an intriguing opening:

> This invitation isn't for deadbeats, rip-off artists or "gentlemen" who hate to get their hands dirty.
>
> It's for the rest of us.
>
> It's for the average guy who works hard for a living (and wants to live better). Who knows the value of a buck (about 50¢ these days). Who is willing to trade a few drops of sweat for the chance to save big bucks.
>
> It's for guys who aren't afraid to get down under the sink with a pipe wrench. Guys who don't mind sticking their hands in the toilet tank to adjust a ball cock (because they know it's going to save a $16 plumber's bill).

It even adds a note of patriotism:

> Our country was built on the sweat and hard work of do-it-yourself guys. And from *POPULAR MECHANICS*, the #1 do-it-yourself magazine, we'd just like to say THANK YOU.

An interesting addition is a second Johnson-like box below the postscript:

> OUR PROMISE
>
> When Popular Mechanics says free, it really means free.
>
> Unlike some of those book and record club deals that promise something special at the beginning, and then commit you to expensive purchases later on in the fine print, this free offer does not obligate you in any way. This is not a book club. You'll receive your free book with no obligation — ever — to accept anything else.

Popular Mechanics

250 WEST 55th STREET, NEW YORK, N.Y. 10019

```
************************************************
*                                              *
*    If you want to live better...             *
*                                              *
*    Don't mind hard work...                   *
*                                              *
*    Like to pay your own way...               *
*                                              *
*    Let me ship you VOL. I of the exciting    *
*    POPULAR MECHANICS DO-IT-YOURSELF          *
*    ENCYCLOPEDIA.                             *
*                                              *
*    And I want you to keep it.  FREE!         *
*                                              *
************************************************
```
(because you're my kind of guy!)

Good Friend,

This invitation isn't for deadbeats, rip-off artists or "gentlemen" who hate to get their hands dirty.

It's for the rest of us.

It's for the average guy who works hard for a living (and wants to live better). Who knows the value of a buck (about 50¢ these days). Who is willing to trade a few drops of sweat for the chance to save big bucks.

It's for guys who aren't afraid to get down under the sink with a pipe wrench. Guys who don't mind sticking their hands in the toilet tank to adjust a ball cock (because they know it's going to save a $16 plumber's bill).

Pardon me for "waving the flag" but that's the way I feel!

Our country was built on the sweat and hard work of do-it-yourself guys. And from POPULAR MECHANICS, the #1 do-it-yourself magazine, we'd just like to say THANK YOU.

Our big, illustrated POPULAR MECHANICS DO-IT-YOURSELF ENCYCLOPEDIA was written with "shirtsleeves" guys in mind. Guys like you.

So please -- let me ship you Volume I FREE. (No strings attached. No purchase necessary.)

It's BIG -- 168 oversized pages crammed with up-to-date money-saving plans, photos, diagrams and articles about how-to-do just about EVERYTHING!

From fixing your car's alternator to improving your gas mileage by 30 percent!

From drilling an angled hole accurately, to resurfacing your asphalt driveway or fixing a small appliance.

It's PRACTICAL -- oversized pages lay down flat so you have them right there on your shop table or car fender to refer to. Sturdy hard-covers laugh at dirt!

Type is LARGE so it's easy-to-read.

Each article is generously illustrated -- Volume I alone has more than 600 step-by-step drawings, photos and diagrams.

SPEAKING OF SAVING, HAVE YOU BEEN TO A BODY SHOP LATELY? If it was within the past 12 months you know the cost of auto body repairs has zoomed out of sight!

So we got the manager of a big body shop near our office to share his trade secrets with us. The results? An article illustrated with how-to-do-it photos that shows you how to get rid of scratches, dents, rust and rotten spots yourself -- make your fender look like new!

All this, and much more, is in Volume I of the POPULAR MECHANICS DO-IT-YOURSELF ENCYCLOPEDIA.

But remember -- you don't pay a cent for it. Now or ever. And there's no obligation -- NO PURCHASE NECESSARY!

"Well, come on," you're probably saying, "There's gotta be a catch."

MAYBE THERE IS. *You be the Judge!*

Sure, I'd like to sell you the whole POPULAR MECHANICS DO-IT-YOURSELF ENCYCLOPEDIA.

But I know from experience that I can't "sell" someone like you. You've got to prove for yourself it's worthwhile. So accept our FREE book and examine Volume I, then make up your own mind.

VOLUME I IS YOUR FREE SAMPLE. AND I WANT YOU TO USE IT FOR ALL IT'S WORTH.

Got kids? Turn to page 50 for complete plans and instructions for making your own hockey tabletop game. (You'll have a ball with it, too.) It would cost you plenty in a store. But you can make it with a few dollars' worth of lumber, particleboard, and an old range exhaust fan.

Want a greenhouse? On pages 30-32 you'll find plans for an elegant addition -- an add-on Greenhouse.

How about valuable antiques? Why not build your own authentic reproduction pine and maple bench...for a fraction of what an original would cost. Complete plans and instructions start on Page 30.

Turn to page 178 to see how easy it is to do all your own routine auto service and maintenance. (If you're spending $200 a year to have a pro do it, you could save $150!)

Cool your house in the summer (and cut your air conditioning electric bills) by installing an attic fan. The article starting on page 156 shows you how.

I could go on and on. But why should I? Volume I of POPULAR MECHANICS DO-IT-YOURSELF ENCYCLOPEDIA is yours for the asking.

You don't even pay to send for it. Postage paid Reply Card enclosed.

So what are you waiting for? Say YES today! *the price is right!*

When your "Free Sample" arrives, keep it. And use it. And see for yourself why POPULAR MECHANICS is usually considered the world's leading source of "do-it-yourself" information.

NOW LISTEN TO THIS.

If Volume I isn't everything I've promised, just drop us a note saying "No more!" That will be the end of it (of course, you keep Volume I). But if you're as pleased as I expect, just sit back and enjoy your Free Volume. Then, eight weeks later, you'll receive Volume II of the POPULAR MECHANICS DO-IT-YOURSELF ENCYCLOPEDIA -- just as big, beautiful, husky and crammed with plans and information as the first one. For example:

HOW TO TEST & RECHARGE MOST BATTERIES...BUILD YOUR OWN BARBECUE BAR... FINISH YOUR BASEMENT LIKE A PRO...PUT IN A STAIRWELL...INSTALL A HALF-BATH ANYWHERE. PLUS EVERYTHING YOU OUGHT TO KNOW ABOUT BANDSAWS ...HOW TO REMOVE A BEARING WALL...ALL ABOUT BELT SANDERS...CHOOSING THE RIGHT BIKE...AND MUCH, MUCH MORE!

That's just a sample of Volume II. But remember --

YOU HAVEN'T YET SPENT OR RISKED A PENNY!

Because Volume II is yours to examine and use freely for 14 days! Then, if you're not completely "sold" on the POPULAR MECHANICS DO-IT-YOURSELF ENCYCLOPEDIA, just return it before the Free- Examination Period is over, and owe nothing.

By now, however, if you're the kind of guy I think you are, you should be itching to get your hands on the remaining 18 volumes of the POPULAR MECHANICS DO-IT-YOURSELF ENCYCLOPEDIA. If so, when Volume II arrives, simply remit the low subscriber price of only $5.95 plus a small charge for shipping & handling and any applicable sales tax.

Don't return Volume I. It's yours to keep!

Then, the remaining volumes will be sent to you over a five-month period -- each shipment strictly "on approval." Pay for each volume (one payment a month) at the low subscriber price of only $5.95 -- or return it within the 14-day Free-Examination Period and owe nothing.

BUY AS FEW OR AS MANY VOLUMES AS YOU WISH. CANCEL ANY TIME!

Remember -- Volume I of the POPULAR MECHANICS DO-IT-YOURSELF ENCYCLOPEDIA is your "Free Sample" -- yours to keep, even if you decide not to buy anything.

But to get it, you have to sign and mail the enclosed Reply Card.

Do it today.

Cordially,

J.M. Walters

what have you got to lose?

J. Michael Walters
For POPULAR MECHANICS

P.S. If you take pride in work well done, want to give your family the better things in life...then you need POPULAR MECHANICS how-to-do-it information on AIR CONDITIONERS...BARBECUES... BOATS...BIRDHOUSES...BOOKCASES...BURGLAR ALARMS...CAULKING... CAMERAS...CONCRETE...CLOCKS...DOORS...DRILL PRESSES...ENGINES... FAUCETS...FENCES...GUNS...GETTING IN SHAPE...HEATERS... INSULATION...KITCHENS...KITS...LANDSCAPING...METAL-WORKING... OUTBOARDS...PAINTING...PLUMBING...PLYWOOD...REMODELING...ROOFS ...RAIN GUTTERS...SEPTIC TANKS...SEWING CENTERS...SKIN DIVING... SOLAR ENERGY...SWIMMING POOLS...TILE...TOOLS...TOYS...TRAILERS ...TREES...UPHOLSTERY...VACATION HOMES...VACUUMS...WINDOWS... WOODWORKING. These are just a few of the subjects covered in the 20 volume POPULAR MECHANICS DO-IT-YOURSELF ENCYCLOPEDIA. And Volume I is yours to keep -- but only if you mail the Reply Card NOW!

OUR PROMISE

When Popular Mechanics says free it really means free. Unlike some of those book and record club deals that promise something special at the beginning, and then commit you to expensive purchases later on in the fine print, this free offer does not obligate you in any way. This is not a book club. You'll receive your free book with no obligation -- ever -- to accept anything else.

THE POPULAR MECHANICS ENCYCLOPEDIA IS PUBLISHED BY HEARST BOOKS, A DIVISION OF THE HEARST CORPORATION

9/82-PME-L

TIME-LIFE BOOKS "COWBOY" LETTER

When it comes to creating great letters to sell books by mail, nobody tops Time-Life Books. They regularly use colorful envelopes and big, beautiful brochures; however, it's their letters that close the sale.

Many consider a package developed to sell a series called "The Old West" as Time-Life's best of all time. The letter started with three "survival tips" for life in the Old West. They were intriguing enough to encourage further reading:

> When two cowboys approach each other on the trail, both are expected to keep course and perhaps pass a friendly word; to veer off is to suggest furtiveness — or even danger. A wave of greeting is bad form — it may scare the horse.
>
> "Milk is relished upon the plains," wrote J. L. Campbell in his 1864 Emigrant's Guide Overland. "In case of a storm when cooking cannot be done, it serves a tolerable purpose." Surplus milk can always be churned into butter simply by hanging pails beneath the jolting wagon; at day's end the butter is ready.
>
> Watch what you say to a Westerner. An Englishman visiting a friend on a ranch in Wyoming inquired of the foreman, "Is your master at home?" The foreman looked him straight in the eye and replied, "The son of a bitch hasn't been born yet."

With those teasers in a Johnson Box at the top of page one, readers were primed for more details. They began:

> Someone once had the guts to ask Clay Allison what he did for a living. He must have been smiling when he asked the question, because he lived to repeat the answer. Allison said, "I am a shootist," and with those four words he eloquently summed up a long career dedicated to blasting his fellow men to smithereens.
>
> Allison was one of a special breed in the old West — a gunfighter — and you can read his story, along with those of dozens of other heroes and rascals, in the exciting pages of The Gunfighters, the fascinating introductory volume in THE OLD WEST series. You are invited to examine this book for 10 days FREE, without obligation to buy it.

Here are some survival tips for life in the Old West of the 19th Century:

--When two cowboys approach each other on the trail, both are expected to keep course and perhaps pass a friendly word; to veer off is to suggest furtiveness -- or even danger. A wave of greeting is bad form -- it may scare the horse.

--"Milk is relished upon the plains," wrote J. L. Campbell in his 1864 Emigrant's Guide Overland. "In case of a storm when cooking cannot be done, it serves a tolerable purpose." Surplus milk can always be churned into butter simply by hanging it in pails beneath the jolting wagon; at day's end the butter is ready.

--Watch what you say to a Westerner. An Englishman visiting a friend on a ranch in Wyoming inquired of the foreman, "Is your master at home?" The foreman looked him straight in the eye and replied, "The son of a bitch hasn't been born yet."

These are just three samples of the salty, entertaining reading you'll find in a lively, lavish new library from TIME-LIFE BOOKS called

T H E   O L D   W E S T

Dear Reader:

Someone once had the guts to ask Clay Allison what he did for a living. He must have been smiling when he asked the question, because he lived to repeat the answer. Allison said, "I am a shootist," and with those four words he eloquently summed up a long career dedicated to blasting his fellow men to smithereens.

Allison was one of a special breed in the old West -- a gunfighter -- and you can read his story, along with those of dozens of other heroes and rascals, in the exciting pages of The Gunfighters, the fascinating introductory volume in THE OLD WEST series. You are invited to examine this book for 10 days FREE, without obligation to buy it.

Allison and men like him lived (and usually died) with six-gun in hand. They were seldom the glamorous figures the movies and television later made them, but lonely, bitter, frequently psychotic killers who belonged on a psychiatrist's couch. Some were outlaws and some were lawmen; frequently

it was hard to tell the difference. But they all had one thing in common --
they were bad news.

--Take John Wesley Hardin, out of Bonham, Texas. He
    had 44 notches on his gun, including one for a snoring
    hotel guest who disturbed his rest.

--Or Jim Miller, another friendly gent. He gunned down
    51 people during his career, starting with his own
    grandparents when he was only eight years old.

--Bill Longley, from Austin County, Texas, had killed
    32 men by the time he was 27 years old. The last
    was one too many, and Bill was hanged.

But there were good guys, too. Sheriff Pat Garrett, six feet four
and fast on the trigger, who killed Billy the Kid with a shot in the
dark. Wild Bill Hickok, a lawman known occasionally to exaggerate his
own prowess. Dodge City lawman Bat Masterson, who eventually fell from
public favor for excessive gunplay. And Wyatt Earp, whose reputation
rests mostly on 30 seconds of gunplay at the O.K. Corral.

In The Gunfighters you'll ride with Jesse and Frank James when they
pull off the first daylight bank robbery in American history, and feel the
frustration of Allan Pinkerton and his detectives as they fruitlessly chase
the outlaw band around the Midwest for years. You'll walk the streets of
Tombstone with the Earps and Doc Holliday as they stalk the Clantons and
McLaurys in the most famous shoot-out in the history of the West.

I could go on and on, but I'll let the book do that. The Gunfighters
is big, beautiful and brimming over with enjoyment: 8 1/2 by 11 inches, 240
pages, 40,000 words. It's a book to lose yourself in -- and to rediscover
a part of America that has long since vanished. There are more than 250
photographs, paintings and drawings, many in color, to help you understand
the era of the gun.

A series as big as all outdoors -- THE OLD WEST

Gunfighters, good and bad, played their role in America's development.
And the West of 70, 90, and 150 years ago was full of other interesting people
and places. So full, in fact, that we've filled a series of fascinating
books with them and called it THE OLD WEST.

Here are volumes crackling.with the excitement of men and women pushing out beyond the frontier, raising children and Cain, busting sod and
staking out ranches in a land as wild and rugged as the open sea, hunting
buffalo and bear, building the railroads, and finally becoming that marvelous blend of fact, legend and myth that has fascinated all of us since two
men named Lewis and Clark first crossed the country.

The Gunfighters -- which you can now examine without cost for 10
days -- is the introductory volume of THE OLD WEST. Hard on its heels

-3-

comes The Pioneers, the story of the men, women and children who started pouring out of Independence, Missouri, in 1841. They were headed west, walking beside the covered wagons that held their possessions, going across 2,000 miles of country to the Pacific coast. Mostly American born, they were home seekers, determined to find the fertile paradise that missionaries and mountain men had sworn existed on the other side of the Continent. They were innocent, and braved the wilderness because they did not know its hazards -- its forbidding mountains and pitiless deserts, ruinous fires and frequently predatory Indians. But they met the perils with courage, and most of them won through to become the West's new settlers. The Pioneers will make you proud to be an American.

In The Indians, a book that will be a revelation to most readers, you'll see the first inhabitants of this country as they really were: men and women with complex cultures thrown into conflict with strangers who took their land and livelihood and left them beaten, bewildered and bitter. In this sensitively written, magnificently illustrated volume -- you will find out about the great diversity of Western Indian life -- how many tribes there were, where they were located, how they were organized and how they lived. You'll observe how a buffalo hunt was conducted; how a hide was tanned; how a tepee was made. You'll find out about the great variety of religious practices, tribal taboos, idols, fetishes, superstitions, Indian sign language. You'll meet the great warriors of the various tribes, including such famous Sioux leaders as Red Cloud, Sitting Bull, Spotted Tail, Crazy Horse and many others. You'll study the Indian's concept of land ownership and land use, as well as his methods of warfare, and you gain an entirely new perspective on the conflicts of the old West.

Later on you'll meet The Trailblazers -- a bold, strong-willed breed of men who, in their quest for fame, fortune, knowledge and adventure, helped open the West. There were those two bright, young early explorers Meriwether Lewis and William Clark, who, with their 30-man, $40,000 Corps of Discovery, changed the course of history. Sweaty, grizzled mountain men like John Colter, Zenas Leonard and Jedediah Smith, who in addition to their fur trading helped fill in the holes of the map. General William Ashley, who, after some botched and bloody forays with the Arikaras, sent his men overland, invented the rendezvous and turned fur trading into a wheeling-dealing business. Big Joe Walker, the best nuts-and-bolts trailblazer, who sighted and followed the Humboldt River southwest, scaled the Sierra passes, discovered Yosemite and painted the image of California as the promised land.

You'll delight in The Cowboys, to understand perhaps for the first time these intriguing, complex men -- products of a particular time and place, living by a code compounded of hard-fisted frontier desperation and Victorian-era social values. They were tough because their life was hard. And they unbent once in a while because they had to. Sure, they were a hard-driving lot...but there was humanity in them and a great love of the big country. So judge them and their way of life, if you must, but do it by their standards. You can do just that with The Cowboys.

-4-

<u>The introductory volume comes to you on a 10-day FREE trial</u>

To receive your copy of <u>The Gunfighters</u> for 10 days' FREE examination, just affix the book token to the enclosed postage-paid card and drop it in the mail. When your copy arrives, look it over, show it to your family and friends. Then, if you don't find yourself caught up in this book... if you don't learn hundreds of new and fascinating facts...and meet some mighty interesting people, just return <u>The Gunfighters</u> within 10 days and that ends it.

If you decide you want to keep this introductory volume, the price is $7.95 plus shipping and handling, which for a book of this high quality and content is exceptionally low.

If you keep <u>The Gunfighters</u>, then forthcoming volumes in THE OLD WEST will be sent to you, one at a time, approximately every other month. Each volume, of course, will be sent on the same 10-day free-examination basis and at the same price of $7.95 plus shipping and handling. But each volume will have to stand on its own merits. You may reject any book within 10 days simply by returning it. You are never under any obligation to purchase any minimum number of books and you may cancel this free-examination privilege at any time simply by writing to us. No further books will be sent.

I do hope that you will take this opportunity to be introduced to <u>The Gunfighters</u>. In 240 pages, 40,000 words and over 250 fascinating pictures, it will plunge you into a part of our past that's well worth poring over. Just mail the enclosed postpaid card today. Send no money. There's no risk, no gamble -- just the promise of good, down-to-earth, hearty adventure.

Sincerely,

Joan D. Manley
Publisher

JDM/GFE

P.S. If you're interested in our 10-day free-trial invitation to see <u>The Gunfighters</u>, I urge you to act at once. Every indication is that this will be among the most popular books ever published by TIME-LIFE BOOKS, and I would like to be able to rush you your copy immediately.

GOOD HOUSEKEEPING "33 WAYS" LETTER

Milton Pierce originally wrote this long-running letter in 1960, and it turned out to be the winner in test after test, and is still used today in special situations. The letter begins on the envelope with the teaser "33 Ways to Save Time & Money" followed by the first nine ways. The two-page letter inside continues the list:

> How many of these 33 articles can help you?
>
> They're just a few of hundreds which have appeared in *Good Housekeeping*. You'll find more, every issue, in "The Better Way" — a magazine within a magazine — that *Good Housekeeping* readers are so enthusiastic about.
>
> Every month a staff of experts writes about medical and legal problems and advises on education, jobs, insurance, budgets and government benefits. You get information to protect your rights — earn more income for your family — guard your purse against shrinking dollars. On the envelope are 9 of the articles. Here are 24 more:

The list of articles, of course, changes from time to time, but Milton Pierce's original copy theme continues to work year after year.

Good Housekeeping saves you money with this great special offer...

> 14 MONTHS FOR ONLY $2.97

33 WAYS TO SAVE TIME AND MONEY . . .

Dear Reader:

How many of these 33 articles can help you?

They're just a few of hundreds which have appeared in Good Housekeeping. You'll find more, every issue, in "The Better Way" — a magazine within a magazine — that Good Housekeeping readers are so enthusiastic about.

Every month a staff of experts writes about medical and legal problems and advises on education, jobs, insurance, budgets and government benefits. You get information to protect your rights — earn more income for your family — guard your purse against shrinking dollars. On the envelope are 9 of the articles. Here are 24 more:

10. Income Tax Law Changes that Save You Money
11. Meat Buying Guide: The Kindest Cuts of All
12. When Crime Victims Are Paid For Losses
13. 75 Ways You Can Help Clean Up the Environment Now
14. What To Consider Before Buying a House
15. The Facts About Those New Waterbeds
16. Unit Pricing in Markets: What It Means to Shoppers
17. Liability Insurance: Is Your Family Fully Protected
18. How To Protect Your Appliances When Power Is Reduced
19. A Guide For Stretching Your Buying Dollar
20. Menstrual Problems: Causes and Treatment
21. What To Do If You Lose Your Handbag
22. Where To Get The Most Interest on Your Savings
23. Caring For The Ill At Home
24. Need A Loan? First Check Those Interest Rates
25. The Vitamins You Really Need
26. How To Prevent Most Home Accidents
27. Joint Ownership: Advantages And Disadvantages
28. A Laundering Guide For The Newer Fabrics
29. Noise in The Home: A Growing Health Menace
30. How To Lay Vinyl Floor Tiles
31. Are Weight-Loss Belts Effective
32. What To Do if Your Auto Insurance Is Not Renewed
33. A Guide To New "Meatless" Meat Products

The way to get HUNDREDS more (and start saving money today) is to subscribe to Good Housekeeping for the next 14 months for only $2.97! This offer is good for 20 days only, and may never be repeated. So take advantage of it now.

Over a million readers who buy Good Housekeeping month-by-month at the single-copy cost of 60¢, pay $8.40 for 14 issues. At the regular subscription price, you would pay $5.83 for 14 issues. But you can receive these same 14 valuable issues for only $2.97. Today's Good Housekeeping is a bargain at any price.

Over, please...

As soon as you receive your first copy of Good Housekeeping, you are bound to be surprised at the number and variety of homemaking features — MORE than ever before — MORE than in any other woman's magazine. And each feature is illustrated with greater use of color.

You get expert help on child care, teen problems, beauty, fashions and critical health problems. You get pages and pages of tempting, easy-to-prepare recipes — more than enough to fill a costly cookbook. And each of these tasty dishes is prepared first in our famous kitchens. Good Housekeeping also brings you additional bonuses such as the 16-page "Special Occasion Cookbook." And to make sure you eat wisely, our staff will report every month on "You and Your Diet." You'll get other helpful tips on needlework, sewing, appliances, decorating and building.

Exciting contributors are Charlotte Montgomery, Speaker for the House, with news and opinions on products, ads and services, Dr. Joyce Brothers, one of America's best known psychologists, and Barbara Yuncker reporting on the latest developments in medicine. Homemakers, like yourself, report on "My Problem and How I Solved It."

The attractively illustrated long features coming soon — smart Decorating Sections you'll use to pretty up your home — a preview of the newest in low-cost appliances — dozens of new hairdos to try, are alone well worth the special reduced price.

Then count up the value of the dozens of compelling stories you'll enjoy, such as the recent "Wheels," a vivid and eye-opening novel about Detroit's inner circle by Arthur Hailey, the best-selling author of "Airport" and "Hotel;" "Escape," a stunning new novel of grand romance and high suspense by Madeleine Brent; and "A Question of Time," an exciting novel of political intrigue by Pierre Salinger, the author of "With Kennedy." You'll read outstanding stories like these before they become best-sellers and film hits.

There will be outspoken articles on issues of the day that affect you and your family, such as: "When the Paychecks Stopped," "The Secret Family of Father Duryea," "How Organized Crime Invades the Home," and "The Population Bomb and How To Defuse It." Good Housekeeping readers also shared intimate close-ups of Pat Nixon, Robert Young, Dick Van Dyke, Shirley Jones, Mr. and Mrs. Paul Newman, and Jimmy Stewart.

Take advantage of this opportunity now to enjoy...14 issues of Good Housekeeping for only $2.97! You save $5.43 from the single-copy cost, and $2.86 from the regular subscription value.

Send no money now; we'll gladly bill you later. But remember, this special offer can be guaranteed only for the next 20 days. To make this saving, be sure to check and mail the enclosed order card today.

Cordially yours,

Anne Ward

for Good Housekeeping

GH72S-BAS

Good Housekeeping 250 WEST 55TH STREET, NEW YORK, N. Y. 10019

SECTION V

FUND-RAISING LETTERS

The second favorite of direct mail copywriters is the creation of letters for their favorite charities and other fund-raising organizations in which they have a special interest. Writing letters to raise funds is demanding — a task that must come from the heart as well as the head. Many of America's top copywriters specialize in writing fund-raising letters, and have produced some real gems. The following letters are representative of the different types of fund-raising letters, and supplement the classics shown in Section II.

YMCA "ERNIE BANKS" LETTER

If you've ever lived in Chicago, or are a Chicago Cubs fan, you've probably had a long-time love affair with one of the most popular men to ever wear the Cub uniform — Ernie Banks. So when a letter arrives with his signature, it has special pulling power. And that's what happened when Ernie Banks requested support for the YMCA of Metropolitan Chicago. The copy was actually written by one of the nation's leading fund-raising letter writers, Dick Trenbeth, and went to 50,000 Chicagoans. The letter began:

> No fast ball, high and inside, could come close to producing the terror most of us felt during the grim weekend of April 4–7. Except for the work of 77 remarkable young men, the fire bombs and gunfire that ravaged a number of ghetto neighborhoods might have spread through the city and into the suburbs.
>
> Few roaring cheers in the ball park have pleased me as much as the news that several powerful youth gangs were working on the side of the law in keeping the looting and burning from spreading. The leaders of these gangs, some 200 of them throughout the city, have been working closely with the dedicated 77 young professionals who carry on the work of the Youth Action Program.

The letter explained the Y's role in the Youth Action Program and other activities, and then ended with this appeal:

> Right now, before you're reminded by another frightening newscast or smoke clouds rising skyward, won't you walk to your desk and write a check to the YMCA of Metropolitan Chicago? It's one positive way you can share in this urgent business of saving lives and perhaps even our city. You'll sleep more soundly than ever with the reassurance and satisfaction that comes from doing the right thing before time runs out.

The combination of a noted personality and a message built around a recent news event worked wonders and produced nearly double the number of contributions of previous direct mail efforts.

ERNIE BANKS
Board of Managers
YMCA of Metropolitan Chicago

Dear Concerned Citizen:

No fast ball, high and inside, could come close to producing the terror most of us felt during the grim weekend of April 4-7. Except for the work of 77 remarkable young men, the fire bombs and gunfire that ravaged a number of ghetto neighborhoods might have spread throughout the city and into the suburbs.

Few roaring cheers in the ball park have pleased me as much as the news that several powerful youth gangs were working on the side of the law in keeping the looting and burning from spreading. The leaders in these gangs, some 200 of them throughout the city, have been working closely with the dedicated 77 young professionals who carry on the work of the Youth Action program.

Most of these young men in Youth Action are not far removed from their own recent pasts as gang leaders or members. Now, though they've turned away from violence to more constructive ways of problem solving, they are still accepted and respected by the young people they're trying to help. Wise in the ways of the gang, they mix with the members and control violence at the source, in the dark streets and alleys of the slum neighborhoods which many of them still call their own.

Serious trouble in the inner city is often being prevented <u>right</u> <u>now</u> because the gang leaders trust the Youth Action workers enough to tip them off when the lid is about to blow. As one of them said,"There's no percentage in having my own 'hood burned down, and maybe my own people shot up!"

Not long ago John W. Gardner, former Secretary of Health, Education and Welfare, asked voluntary agencies here in Chicago to help. He asked them to work with neighborhood people in a closer way than the government can hope to do. That's just what Youth Action has done. In a voluntary, combined attack, the YMCA of Metropolitan Chicago, working with the Chicago Boys Clubs, Chicago Youth Centers, and the Hull House Association, is dealing first-hand with the explosive problems of the inner city streets. The YMCA provides nearly two-thirds of the total effort of Youth Action.

- 2 -

And this is just one of the many, many ways the YMCA is providing you and me with <u>preventive</u> social services. Some of these services, such as unique educational opportunities, job training for dropouts, and certain camping programs, generate part of their own funds. But in addition to these and other sources of financing, the YMCA's share of Youth Action, at its present level, is about $500,000 which it must raise this year. As tension increases, a million dollars might not be enough.

We're all "concerned citizens" these days. Willingness to help all we can now could mean saving millions in money, and possibly our homes and businesses as well as saving potentially useful lives.

The other day I was talking with a very down-to-earth business man who rather impatiently accused the YMCA of not letting enough people know about its many programs to reduce the boiling point of the inner city. He mentioned the extensive camp programs, many of them for boys and girls who had never seen a camp, had never even been in the country. He was especially high in his praise for the Central YMCA's dropout high school. He paid tribute to the Y's "open door" Community College where some of the toughest gang leaders are getting a last-chance education. Many of these former delinquents are returning to their neighborhoods and encouraging others by their own example to rise above their problems and solve them constructively.

In case we have made the mistake of not letting you know about these things before, we invite you now to join in this crusade to prevent a recurrence of the ghastly events of early April. We need both your interest and your generous gift of money. And if you have even a few hours a week to spare, let us show you how you can help as a volunteer.

Right now, before you're reminded by another frightening newscast or smoke clouds rising skyward, won't you walk to your desk and write a check to the YMCA of Metropolitan Chicago? It's one positive way you can share in this urgent business of saving lives and perhaps even our city. You'll sleep more soundly than ever with the reassurance and satisfaction that comes from doing the right thing before time runs out.

Sincerely,

Ernie Banks

Ernie Banks
Member, the Board of Managers
YMCA of Metropolitan Chicago

NEW YORK ZOOLOGICAL SOCIETY "ZOOFER" LETTER

I suspect a number of the classic letters in this book, where the writer is not identified, may easily have been written by Linda Wells. This direct mail copywriter, consistently turned out control-beating letters for a wide variety of different organizations.

One of her classics was built around a new word she coined for the New York Zoological Society — "zoofer." She puts the new word right to work in the Johnson Box at the top of page one:

> ZOOFER! It's a noun that means a member of the New York Zoological Society — an insider who gets free admissions . . . free parking . . . free Safari, Skyfari, and Bengal Express rides . . . invitations to previews, films and lectures . . . invitations to garden parties and local events . . . travel opportunities here, there, and everywhere . . . plus a subscription to *ANIMAL KINGDOM!*

> ZOOFER! It's a verb that means having fun, learning, growing and making a major contribution to the protection and preservation of wildlife . . . environmental research . . . and conservation education!

> ZOOFER! It's the two-fer ticket enclosed that entitles you to the zoofiest fashion item since designer jeans — the one-and-only, members-only Z shirt created for animal lovers like you by one of New York's most zooperb zanies. With the zoofer inside this envelope and your new membership card, you can get two Z shirts for the price of one! You buy one. You get one FREE!

Wells continues to weave "zoofer" and other newly-coined fun words throughout the letter, all enhancing the two lead-in sentences of the letter:

> Do zoofers have more fun?

> Yes, I certainly believe we do.

Such lighthearted copy continues right down to the close:

> The sooner you join, the sooner you can zoofer in your Z shirt! So be one of the very first people in the tri-state area to sport the fun fashion of the year. Come now! Join now! Zoofer with the zoofers of the New York Zoological Society now!

Linda Wells (212) 753-3069

New York Zoological Society
Letter -- page 1
February 7, 1983

ZOOFER! It's a noun that means a member
of the New York Zoological Society -- an
insider who gets free admissions...free
parking...free Safari, Skyfari and Bengal
Express rides...invitations to previews,
films and lectures...invitations to garden parties and local events...travel opportunities here, there and everywhere...
plus a subscription to ANIMAL KINGDOM!

ZOOFER! It's a verb that means having
fun, learning, growing and making a major
contribution to the protection and preservation of wildlife...environmental research...and conservation education!

ZOOFER! It's the two-fer ticket enclosed
that entitles you to the zoofiest fashion
item since designer jeans -- the one-and-
only, members-only Z shirt created for animal lovers like you by one of New York's
most zoo-perb zanies. With the zoofer inside this envelope and your new membership
card, you get two Z shirts for the price
of one! You buy one. You get one FREE!

Dear Member-Elect:

    Do zoofers have more fun?

    Yes, I certainly believe we do. My name is Howard Phipps, Jr.
I am President of the New York Zoological Society, and if you join
our 000,000 members today, I can promise you not one, but three,
very special and unusual kinds of enjoyment.

    First of all, your membership is the best entertainment value
in the tri-state area. One membership buys your whole family unlimited free admissions to both the Bronx Zoo and the New York
Aquarium at Coney Island. You get 10 tickets for free parking at

259

Linda Wells (212) 753-3069

the Zoo and Aquarium. Twenty tickets for free animal rides, Safari, Skyfari and Bengal Express rides and free admissions to the Children's Zoo where your youngsters have a chance to get acquainted with more than 200 animals in their native habitats.

But that's only the beginning of the fun you'll have when you start to zoofer with us!

. As a zoofer, you can give children's parties at the Zoo -- parties with ice cream and birthday cake, zoovenirs and "Please Touch" animal demonstrations.

. As a zoofer, you'll be invited to the Society's Annual Meeting in Lincoln Center, where you'll be first to see fabulous wild animal and marine exhibits.

. As a zoofer, you'll get four free tickets to the gala Spring Garden Party, where you'll sip punch with your fellow members and see the newest animals in the Zoo.

. As a zoofer, you'll have weekend use of the Zoo's private staff dining room -- a zooper place to meet and eat any time of the year.

The fun of learning and growing

Part of the fun of zoofering is your new opportunity to meet and make friends with other people in the area who care as much as you do about the protection and preservation of wildlife, environmental research and conservation education.

Another part -- and a large part -- of the value of membership is your whole family's new chance to learn and grow.

When you join the New York Zoological Society, you're welcome to members-only previews of all our new exhibits. You'll have first chance to get tickets to our annual film-lecture program given by world-famous zoologists. You and the family will be invited to join us on daytrips to nearby wildlife preserves and longer tours to wilderness areas like the Galapagos Islands, conducted by New York Zoological Society scientists.

But that's not all!

You'll receive one year (six issues) of ANIMAL KINGDOM Magazine, the excitingly-written, wonderfully-photographed magazine that tells you more about wildlife and wildlife preservation than you can find anywhere else!

As beautiful as Smithsonian...as informative as Natural History...as up-to-the-minute as Science 83, this ex-

Linda Wells (212) 753-3069

traordinary members-only publication comes to you from the cutting edge of scientific discovery. It takes you and your whole family to the frontiers of the future!

The excitement of shaping the future

Entertainment is one good reason for joining the New York Zoo-logical Society today. The learning opportunity is another. But the greatest satisfaction of all is knowing that you are <u>doing</u> something to make the world a better place to live.

The New York Zoological Society is a private, non-pro-fit organization chartered in 1895 to conduct zoologic-al research and promote environmental education. Our four components are the Bronx Zoo, the New York Aquar-ium, the Osborn Laboratories of Marine Science and the Animal Research and Conservation Center.

As a member, you'll be making an important contribution to the largest urban zoo in America and one of the world's major centers of zoological and environmental research. You'll be aiding scien-tists in pioneering work on animal behavior, animal husbandry and zoo animal habitats. You'll be supporting new animal breeding pro-grams to save rare and exotic animals from extinction. You'll be providing a home where more than 3,500 animals can live, breed and raise their families in safety.

<u>You'll be helping the New York Aquarium</u> at Coney Island, where more than 14,000 aquatic creatures live in replicas of their natural habitats. Aquarium education programs are national models, and the collection is the basis for important new work being done at our third facility, the respected and renowned Osborn Laboratories.

<u>You'll be helping the Osborn Laboratories</u>, where scien-tists focus on a wide range of problems in the basic and applied sciences. The effects of pollutants on marine or-ganisms. Analysis of the marine food chain. The role of disease processes in the ecology of the sea. The ef-fect of man's intrusion into the aquatic environment.

<u>You'll be helping the Animal Research and Conservation</u> <u>Center</u>. From our local facilities, Society scientists go out around the world to demonstrate the need for wild-life refuges...provide basic wildlife information...and suggest the direction of prudent land development.

Closer to home, you'll be helping more than 2,200,000 people who come to the Bronx Zoo and Aquarium every year for education and recre-ation. You'll be helping more than 350,000 school children who come to augment their classroom experience. You'll be helping more than

Linda Wells (212) 753-3069

850 men and women earn their livings or get their first work experience. The Zoo is the largest employer of youth in the Bronx.

Zoofering is _fun_ -- good, clean, healthy family fun! And it's not as frivolous as it sounds. As a Family Member of the New York Zoological Society, you are supporting education and scientific research...making your voice heard about ecology and the environment...taking action to help create a better world for your children and theirs.

<u>Come zoofer with us today!</u>
<u>Get your members-only Z shirt free!</u>

So join for the _fun_ of it, the _learning_ of it, the _importance_ of it! Join one of the area's most distinguished groups of local leaders as a Family Member today!

Your annual dues as a Family Member are only $35 for all those valuable benefits. So mail the enclosed acceptance card in the postpaid envelope right away. There's no need to send any money; we'll bill you later if you prefer.

When you receive your permanent membership card, bring it with the enclosed zoofer ticket to the zoofer kiosk at the Zoo. You've parked free. You've entered free. Now you can get your members-only designer Z shirt free! It's a $10 value, but with the zoofer ticket and your card, you can buy one for $5 and get a second one absolutely free!

The sooner you join, the sooner you can zoofer in your Z shirt! So be one of the very first people in the tri-state area to sport _the_ fun fashion of the year. Come now! Join now! Zoofer with the zoofers of the New York Zoological Society now!

Thank you -- and welcome!

Sincerely,

Howard Phipps, Jr.
President

CHAMPAIGN COUNTY COUNCIL ON ALCOHOLISM "LONELY MAN" LETTER

Many of today's top copywriters learned their letter-writing skills in the business letter classes taught at the University of Illinois for many years by Jack Maguire. But Maguire is more than just an outstanding educator, he writes great letter copy. One of his classic letters was originally written for a local Council on alcoholism, but was subsequently copied by similar organizations in many other areas. It begins:

> There's a lonely man . . .
>
> Tonight he's quietly resting in a clean hospital bed. He has the best of medical and psychiatric care — all from professional volunteers.
>
> No more D.T.'s. No more hemorrage. No more of that cold, hollow, empty feeling of fear and futility.
>
> He's thinking thoughts that speak of gratitude to man and thankfulness to God.

The letter describes another lonely man whose alcoholism remains untreated. It then closes with a strong bid for contributions:

> Your contribution could tilt the scales so one human life moves on to dignity and thankfulness.
>
> Instead of . . . Well-l-l . . .

And this postscript:

> P.S.   The envelope will bring your check quickly. Please?

There's a lonely man ...

tonight. He's quietly resting in a clean hospital bed.
He has the best of medical and psychiatric care -- all
from professional volunteers.

No more D.T.'s. No more hemorrhage. No more of that
cold, hollow, empty feeling of fear and futility.

He's thinking thoughts that speak of gratitude to man
and thankfulness to God.

There's another lonely man ...

tonight. He's quietly sitting on a dirty stool at a foul-
smelling bar. His home, his love, his all ... are gone.
And soon can be his life.

Ahead are D.T.'s. Convulsions. A final gutter - peace.

Both are Alcoholics, one we got to in time. The other
desperately needs a life-line ... to pull him out of his
personal hell.

Once before we asked you for the kindness and understanding
which would help us reach the second man in time.

So far ... we haven't heard. And we're seriously short of
our goal of only $6,000. And we can't qualify for United
Fund for another year.

May we ask again for your help? May we ask for $100, $50,
$25, $10 -- _any amount_ -- from you.

Your contribution could tilt the scales so one human life
moves on to dignity and thankfulness.

Instead of ... Well-l-l ...

W. Kenneth Porter

W. Kenneth Porter
President

P.S. The envelope will bring your check quickly. Please?

HARRY S. TRUMAN LIBRARY INSTITUTE FUND RAISING LETTER

Tom Collins is best known as the creative genius behind many commercial direct marketing campaigns. However, two of his fund-raising letters will probably be long remembered after much of his great commercial work has passed into history.

Among the choices for the all-time classic direct mail letters in Section II was his memorable letter for the George McGovern presidential campaign. An equally deserving choice could have been the letter he created to launch the Harry S. Truman Library Institute. The opening six paragraphs of this highly productive letter show how effective the "you" approach can be in fund-raising as well as other types of direct mail letters:

> Your name is on a list of a selected group of especially aware people to whom we are extending an invitation.
>
> By this letter, we are inviting you to become an Honorary Fellow of the Truman Library Institute.
>
> Please let us know within 14 days, by return of the enclosed card, whether you wish to accept or decline this designation.
>
> In accepting, you will be joining such distinguished Americans as Arthur Schlesinger, Jr., I.W. Abel, Arthur Goldberg, David E. Lilienthal, Hubert Humphrey, Clark Clifford, Georgia Neese Clark Gray, William H. Hastie, and many others in helping to make the Truman Library a vital part of America's political heritage.
>
> Your tax-deductible annual dues of twenty-five dollars will make it possible for students, scholars, and authors from everywhere to come to Independence, Missouri, and avail themselves of the incredibly rich resource materials the Library contains.
>
> At this crucial point in our history, when our nation is groping for rededication to honesty, integrity, and credibility in government, you will be making a significant contribution to keeping alive the spirit of Harry Truman.

The letter was signed by W. Averell Harriman and John W. Snyder, and had a very effective postscript:

> P.S. For those whose good fortune or achievement permit them to contribute $100, we have created a special category, Honorary Associates. New members in this category will receive, in addition to all of the privileges of Honorary Fellowship listed above, (1) an exact replica of the famous sign, "The Buck Stops Here," that sat on Mr. Truman's desk in the Oval Office of the White House, and (2) "The Man From Missouri," a little book of memorable words, wisdom, and wit of Mr. Truman, culled from his speeches, letters and remarks.

HARRY S. TRUMAN LIBRARY INSTITUTE

HARRY S. TRUMAN LIBRARY   •   INDEPENDENCE, MISSOURI, 64050

TELEPHONE AREA CODE 816/833-1400

Dear Nominee:

Your name is on a list of a selected group of especially aware people to whom we are extending an invitation.

By this letter, we are inviting you to become an Honorary Fellow of the Truman Library Institute.

Please let us know within 14 days, by return of the enclosed card, whether you wish to accept or decline this designation.

In accepting, you will be joining such distinguished Americans as Arthur Schlesinger, Jr., I. W. Abel, Arthur Goldberg, David E. Lilienthal, Hubert Humphrey, Clark Clifford, Georgia Neese Clark Gray, William H. Hastie, and many others in helping to make the Truman Library a vital part of America's political heritage.

Your tax-deductible annual dues of twenty-five dollars will make it possible for students, scholars, and authors from everywhere to come to Independence, Missouri, and avail themselves of the incredibly rich resource materials the Library contains.

At this crucial point in our history, when our nation is groping for rededication to honesty, integrity, and credibility in government, you will be making a significant contribution to keeping alive the spirit of Harry Truman.

As time passes, President Truman's place in history is rising. To the eminence of Washington, Jefferson, Jackson, and Lincoln, historians now add as great American Presidents not only Theodore Roosevelt, Woodrow Wilson, and Franklin Roosevelt, but also the name of Harry Truman of Independence, Missouri.

(continued)

Mr. Truman made no attempt to shroud himself in the grandeur of the office of the President of the United States. He remained as unpretentious after he became President as he was throughout his career.

But he called the shots as he saw them. He had a deep reverence for history, and placed his respect for the Office of President far above his own ego needs. He made outstanding appointments to high level positions and trusted them to do their jobs.

And he steered the nation with a steady hand through the dramatic days of winding up World War II... formation of the United Nations...quick recognition and warm support of the newly declared State of Israel... the Marshall Plan for rebuilding Western Europe...his 1948 "Whistle Stop" campaign and his stunning upset victory over Thomas E. Dewey in the face of seemingly impossible odds...the Berlin Airlift...bold American leadership of the United Nations' response to the invasion of South Korea by North Korea.

On his desk sat a homely sign given to him by an admirer. Its words have since passed into history, indelibly associated with President Truman's strong sense of personal responsibility for the actions of his subordinates: "The <u>buck stops here</u>."

When President Truman retired, he wished to preserve the papers and other historical material of his administration and make them available to all the people in a place suited for study and research. In addition, gifts from heads of state and ordinary citizens, as well as other items associated with him and his career, filled many rooms and needed a large museum facility in which to be properly displayed.

To realize this dream, The Harry S. Truman Library and Museum was built in Independence with funds contributed by thousands of individuals and organizations throughout the United States. The building and its contents were then donated to the U.S. Government. It is administered by the National Archives and Records Service as an integral part of the nation's record-keeping system.

But this does not provide any funds for encouraging research and authorship and for financing additional acquisitions, two essentials to the continuing vitality of the Library in the stream of American history and culture.

(continued)

So the Truman Library Institute was formed to provide funds for these worthwhile objectives.

About two hundred fifty deserving students, scholars and authors have been able to come to the Library for research through grants-in-aid by the Library Institute for travel and living expenses. From these and other researchers have come hundreds of graduate papers and over 80 published books. But more funds are needed to continue and expand this program.

As an Honorary Fellow, you will receive recognition and appreciation for your support in the following:

1.   An individually inscribed annual membership card, permitting free admission to the museum of the Library for you and your family accompanying you. Approximately three million people have visited the museum. Appointments may be made for a guided tour of the exhibit galleries and behind the scenes in the research area.

2.   The Library Institute Newsletter, "Whistle Stop," published throughout the year to keep the Honorary Fellows informed of the fruits of their support.

3.   A three-inch, half-pound, solid bronze Truman presidential medallion, obtainable only from the United States Mint, the Truman Library, collectors, and rare coin dealers.

4.   Your name recorded in a leatherbound Register of Honorary Fellows, as one of the exhibits viewed by the millions of Americans who will visit the Library museum for generations to come.

5.   Unexpected little privileges of Fellowship from time to time will include invitations to special programs and addresses and to receptions at the openings of new exhibits, or the printed programs of a Truman memorial occasion which you cannot personally attend.

(continued)

SPECIAL FUND COMMITTEE

I. W. Abel
Clinton P. Anderson
Joseph Anthony Beirne
Charles F. Brannan
David K. E. Bruce
Rufus Burrus
Thomas C. Clark
Clark M. Clifford
Oscar L. Chapman
Margaret Truman Daniel
Cyrus S. Eaton
George M. Elsey
James A. Farley
Abraham Feinberg
Edward H. Foley
Georgia Neese Clark Gray
Gordon Gray
John S. Graham
W. Averell Harriman
Edgar F. Kaiser
Joseph Daniel Keenan
Leon H. Keyserling
W. John Kenney
David E. Lilienthal
Robert A. Lovett
John J. McCloy
Joseph J. McGee, Jr.
Charles S. Murphy
Robert Nathan
Frank Pace, Jr.
Edwin W. Pauley
John W. Snyder
John L. Sullivan
Stuart Symington
Harry H. Vaughan
James E. Webb
A. Lee M. Wiggins

But, of course, far more important to you than any of these tokens of appreciation will be simply the inner satisfaction you will have in keeping the Truman spirit alive and enriching our political process with a better understanding of his contributions to the American democratic tradition.

We do hope you will accept this invitation. It will mean a great deal to us if you do so, and we are certain it will mean a great deal to you.

But whether you wish to accept this invitation to become an Honorary Fellow or not, please let us know within 14 days. We have contracted for a special clerical task force which will be available for processing new memberships, and your prompt reply will help them complete their tasks within the time allotted. Thank you for the courtesy of your reply.

Sincerely yours,

W. Averell Harriman

John W. Snyder

P.S. For those whose good fortune or achievement permit them to contribute $100, we have created a special category, Honorary Associates. New members in this category will receive, in addition to all of the privileges of Honorary Fellowship listed above, (1) an exact replica of the famous sign, "The Buck Stops Here," that sat on Mr. Truman's desk in the Oval Office of the White House, and (2) "The Man From Missouri," a little book of memorable words, wisdom, and wit of Mr. Truman, culled from his speeches, letters and remarks.

T-73

UNITED REPUBLICAN FUND OF ILLINOIS "DEMONSTRATION" LETTER

Many of the best political direct mail letters originate at a local rather than national level. Because of their limited distribution, however, they often go unseen by those in the broader direct mail field. A classic created for a local political group was one written by the late Bill Gregory for the United Republican Fund of Illinois. It was called to our attention by Jim Kobs, his partner at Kobs Gregory Passavant, who comments:

> ■ Fund-raising letters present a difficult copy challenge. Because you are really selling an idea instead of a product. This is one of my favorites. The challenge was to raise funds from conservative donors, in a period when the liberals were getting all the media coverage. It is a good example of where an illustrated letter probably comes across more strongly than one without an illustration.

The illustration was one familiar to Illinois Republicans, to whom the letter was sent. It was a news photo of Chicago police officers breaking up the rioting at a Democratic National Convention. A more conventional copywriter would probably have used the photo to condemn the opposition party in some way. But Bill Gregory took a more positive approach. His copy began:

> Must "demonstration" be a monopoly of the New Left?
>
> Some of us, members of the United Republican Fund, have an answer. It is:
>
> "Not by a damn sight!"
>
> Our members are proud to consider themselves "activists" in an old-fashioned, uniquely American way. We've been demonstrating, many of us, since before most of today's young radicals were born.
>
> Ours is a different kind of demonstration . . .
>
> . . . not with bricks or fire bombs, but with words, work, ideas, and dollars.
>
> . . . not for revolution, anarchy, and chaos, but for responsible government, two-party government, and orderly change.

And the three-page letter comes back to this beginning for its close:

> Your membership dues, whatever the rate you assign yourself, will be something more than a contribution toward a stronger party and a stronger demonstration by your party's candidates for the things you believe in.
>
> They will also be a contribution — perhaps a vital one — to making your state and your country a better place to live . . . because that is really what is at stake today!
>
> So make your personal dues check just as generous as you can, and mail it today.
>
> We will be pleased indeed to welcome you as a activist in an ongoing demonstration for responsible government.

The United Republican Fund invites you to take part in a <u>different</u> kind of demonstration.

Dear Fellow Republican:

Must "demonstration" be a monopoly of the New Left?

Some of us, members of the United Republican Fund, have an answer.
It is:

"Not by a damn sight!"

Our members are proud to consider themselves "activists" in an
old-fashioned, uniquely American way. We've been demonstrating,
many of us, since before most of today's young radicals were born.

Ours is a <u>different</u> kind of demonstration ...

    ... not with bricks or fire bombs, but with words, work,
ideas, and dollars.

    ... not for revolution, anarchy, and chaos, but for
responsible government, two-party government, and <u>orderly</u>
change.

In short, we have been demonstrating since 1934 for the things you
and I believe in.

Our brand of responsible "activism" seldom makes the headlines or the 10:00 O'clock news. But ...

... it has helped elect men like Dwight Eisenhower, Richard Nixon, and Everett McKinley Dirksen. It has helped elect Republican governors, congressmen, and legislators. It has helped keep Illinois a two-party state — despite the stranglehold of the Democratic machine in Cook County.

Our kind of "activism" is a lot older than the Fund's 36-year history. It is as old as the Republic itself. In fact, we believe it is one of the things that makes possible an orderly government in a society of free men.

Today, this kind of orderly government, shaped by responsible debate of concerned citizens, is threatened as never before:

1. It is threatened, all-too-obviously, by those who believe in debate by rocks and obscenities hurled across a barricade, in a "dissent" or arson and dynamite, or simply in "freedom" without responsibility.

2. It is threatened, less obviously, by politicians whose unthinking, unquestioning radicalism makes them unwitting dupes of "the new politics."

3. It is threatened most of all by those who believe as we do in orderly government but who are just too uncaring to demonstrate these beliefs.

In times like these, I think you will agree, the responsible citizen has something more than the right to demonstrate his beliefs.

He has a positive obligation to do so.

That, really, is what the United Republican Fund is all about.

It is one key reason why our majority is no longer a silent one. It is a proven, effective way for you to add your views to many views, your voice to many voices, your dollars to many dollars — and to play an active, informed role in the way your country and your state are governed.

If this kind of activism sounds like the kind you'd be proud to share in, we would be proud to count you as one of our members.

How much does it cost to enroll in this distinguished company of Republican activists?

You may be surprised to learn that your annual membership dues are entirely up to you.

In total, this year, our members will share in the task of making over $1,000,000 available to Republican national, state and county committees — plus candidates whose job is to demonstrate in your behalf.

How much of this total you wish to assume is a question you alone can decide. But perhaps these brief facts will help you in reaching a decision:

1. Your dues as a URF member will work harder than any other contribution you can make at every level — national, state, and local.

2. Your dollars will go to support the campaign of not just one candidate in one district but to every Republican candidate in Illinois.

3. The earlier you make your contribution the more effective you will make the efforts of every candidate who is working and speaking for you.

Finally, here is one more vital fact to consider.

Your membership dues, whatever the rate you assign yourself, will be something more than a contribution toward a stronger party and a stronger demonstration by your party's candidates for the things you believe in.

They will also be a contribution -- perhaps a vital one — to making your state and your country a better place to live ... because that is really what is at stake today!

So make your personal dues check just as generous as you can, and mail it today.

We will be pleased indeed to welcome you as an activist in an ongoing demonstration for responsible government.

                              Sincerely yours,

                              THE UNITED REPUBLICAN FUND

                              W. H. Fetridge

                              William Harrison Fetridge,
                              President

United ☆ ☆ ☆
Republican Fund
of Illinois   *Serving the whole Republican party . . .*

80 EAST JACKSON BOULEVARD
CHICAGO, ILLINOIS 60604

THE MIAMI UNIVERSITY FUND "EDDIE RICKENBACKER" LETTER

The best fortune any group seeking funds could find would be to discover that Direct Marketing Hall-of-Famer John Yeck was interested in their cause. One organization that has benefited mightily from Yeck's interest is The Miami University Fund. Over the years, he has written many classic fund raising letters to support the University. All are equally deserving of recognition as very special direct mail letters, but the one shown opposite is typical of his golden touch.

Yeck loves to weave thought-provoking stories into his letters — like the one in this letter about Eddie Rickenbacker's rescue in the Pacific during World War II. He doesn't spend a lot of time spinning a tale, but gets to the point quickly. Note his use of quick, short sentences — point-making thoughts you can't miss:

> Whose check did that?
>
> Somebody's. Waves of checks, really. Through the Fund, small gifts combine to do great things.

THE MIAMI UNIVERSITY FUND

April, 1974

Just the right instant:

When Eddie Rickenbacker was adrift on that raft in the Pacific, without food or water and all but dead, a ship sailed by in the east. Those on the raft could see the ship, but it was far away. From shipboard they were but a tiny speck on a broad, broad sea.

And the sun was setting on their 22nd - and probably last - day.

Each wave would lift the raft for just an instant, then fall. But there were times during the minute or so while it crossed before the setting sun - when, _if_ someone on the ship had glanced toward it for just one lifted instant, he would have seen, in silhouette, the men on the raft.

Someone glanced!

We know about that instant because someone did look; saw; and acted. So seven lives continued and contributed greatly to the world in the future. Without the look, that moment would have passed unknown.

Now I don't want to seem to overstate the effect of The Miami University Fund on future lives. But honestly, it works just that way.

For one student after another, some Fund action changes lives for the better. Sometimes they know. They tell us. Often no one knows. They can't. A library book opens a mind without the slightest thought of the Fund, but someone's money put it there. A teacher, his technique improved because of a gift from who-knows-who, sparks a student's lifelong interest. Miami's Institute of Environmental Sciences, now making real changes in real communities, began with a study paid for with undesignated Fund dollars. Whose check did that?

Somebody's. Waves of checks, really. Through the Fund, small gifts combine to do great things.

Nothing at Miami today is as desperate as Rickenbacker was on the raft. But the opportunities ahead are just as broad, the value to the future just as great, when someone looks; sees; and acts ... with a gift that lifts the student at just the right instant.

Is the chance worth the glance?

Now?*

John E. Dolibois

John E. Dolibois, Vice President

JED/dgd

*A response from you now - with contribution, pledge, or even a "no" - will save Miami the cost of follow-up mailings for this 1974 fund effort. Thank you!

NATIONAL FEDERATION OF THE BLIND PENNY LETTER

One of the oldest direct mail fund-raising devices is to tear a dollar bill in half and send one half to a potential contributor with a letter that says: "We've sent you half of a dollar. We have the other half. But we can't put it to work unless you send your half back to us. And, while you're doing that, how about putting another dollar of your own in with it?"

It's a technique that in one form or another, has worked well over the years. Who's greedy enough to keep a piece of paper they can't use and, by not returning it, keep a needy charity from having a dollar they need? And very few who return the "half dollar" fail to add at least another dollar in the envelope.

What's at work is a guilt process. All of us have been trained from childhood not to throw away government currency. It's valuable. But what are you doing to do with a torn dollar bill? The easiest way to escape your "guilt trip" is to send it back to the one who sent it to you.

One of today's modern versions of the old torn dollar bill technique is an effective "penny" letter from National Federation of the Blind. Attached is a shiny new penny. The copy begins:

> Lisa wants you to have this shiny penny.
>
> The penny tells the story of each blind child's hope . . . the story of every blind person's search for the understanding which leads to freedom.

On page 2 of the letter, it explains:

> Please hold the penny in your hand.
>
> Remember, it's not what the penny is worth which gives us blind people a break. A couple dozen pennies, a few nickels and dimes in a blind man's cup hardly buy a loaf of bread anymore.
>
> What's important to us blind people is the penny's one word message: LIBERTY!
>
> I'm sure you'll agree LIBERTY means FREEDOM and EQUALITY for all Americans, sighted and blind alike.
>
> What we blind citizens want is LIBERTY! What we want is FREEDOM! Freedom from dependency and welfare programs. We don't want handouts . . . pennies thrown in a tin cup with pity. We want the chance to pay our own way . . . do an honest day's work for an honest living.

A postscript on the letter reinforces the penny idea:

> P.S. I sincerely hope you'll keep the penny Lisa sent you as a symbol of your commitment to help us blind people in America find FREEDOM and EQUALITY. Blind children especially need the opportunities your gift provides. Please send it as soon as possible!

Although the Federation doesn't ask you to return the penny, the recipient is still faced with the problem of what to do with it. He can't just throw it away. So it has to be removed from the letter, with the letter's message coming once more to mind.

Sometimes it hurts to be blind...

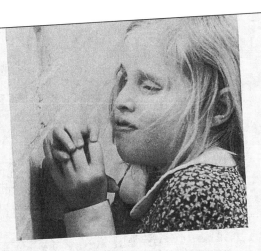

Dear Friend,

Lisa wants <u>you</u> to have this shiny penny.

I hope you'll keep it as a very important reminder of her urgent, compelling need.

The penny tells the story of each blind child's hope... the story of every blind person's search for the understanding which leads to freedom.

Because people like <u>you care about us</u>, we've come a long way since the tin cup days. We thank you sincerely for the positive role you play in our lives... and hope, you'll never stop your support.

<u>I think you understand the truth</u> about us:

★ BLIND people can waterski, bowl, dance!

★ BLIND people can cook, garden, repair their children's toys or the kitchen sink!

★ BLIND people can go to college, vote, participate in community affairs!

★ BLIND people can be secretaries, lawyers, machinists, farmers, nurses aides!

★ BLIND people can do normal, productive, interesting things!

★ BLIND PEOPLE CAN SUCCEED IF THEY CAN GET SOMEONE TO GIVE THEM A CHANCE. That's why <u>we still need your continued support.</u>

Sad to say, there's still many miles to go for thousands of blind people who struggle against the current. Our blindness is grossly misunderstood, by friends and neighbors, even family. <u>Sometimes it hurts to be blind.</u>

In God We Trust...

-2-

Well-meaning people put us down on a daily basis. Intelligent people show prejudice they would be ashamed to admit.

Some people wonder if we get married, make love, bear children. We have difficulty with adoptions, restaurants, passports, train and plane rides, insurance. Saddest of all 70% of us have no jobs.

In the meantime, we must count on people like you, almost for our very existence. Your right attitude, your open-mindedness, and your regular financial support can help us bring about better lives for blind men, women and children. Please agree to help us!

Only kind people who understand our urgent needs, who give generously, will make the difference in the length of time it will take those of us who are blind to be accepted as normal human beings in society.

Please hold the penny in your hand.

Remember, it's not what the penny is worth which gives us blind people a break. A couple dozen pennies, a few nickels and dimes in a blind man's cup hardly buy a loaf of bread anymore.

What's important to us blind people is the penny's one word message: LIBERTY!

I'm sure you'll agree LIBERTY means FREEDOM and EQUALITY for all Americans, sighted and blind alike.

What we blind citizens want is LIBERTY! What we want is FREEDOM! Freedom from dependency and welfare programs. We don't want handouts... pennies thrown in a tin cup with pity. We want the chance to pay our own way... do an honest day's work for an honest living.

What we blind citizens want is EQUALITY! The biggest problem we face is not the lack of eyesight but the lack of understanding. Lack of understanding leads to lack of opportunity and the 70% unemployment rate.

Blindness affects only our eyes not our competence, intelligence, skills, aptitudes or ability. We know from experience our blindness need not be a handicap as far as any aspect of life is concerned.

Please focus your eyes on the urgent needs of blind children

-3-

We know how to handle our blindness. It is inconvenient, but, not incapacitating. We are confident in our abilities to perform many of the jobs in our community and perform them well. BUT, WE NEED A CHANCE TO DEMONSTRATE OUR SKILLS!

We'll prove with proper training, we can show superior performance on the job. Sighted people will exchange their fear and their pity for understanding and acceptance. They'll recognize us as friends, neighbors and co-workers they want to know and love, to live and work with, recreate and share with.

A few years back some of us blind people got smart. We decided to act on the penny's message -- to make LIBERTY work for us. We pulled ourselves up from the sitting position and grouped together to form the largest nationwide organization of blind people, the NATIONAL FEDERATION OF THE BLIND.

We blind leaders are more determined than ever to find life-fulfilling opportunities for all blind people and especially for blind children who deserve better lives than some of us have known. We can't do it alone. We need your help more than ever before. We need it desperately right now.

Your gift makes it possible for us to assist a young blind student through law school, inform blind persons of their rights and responsibilities under the law, counsel and inform a young mother who learns her newly-born child is blind, assist a blind senior citizen cut through red tape to receive Social Security benefits, and many other direct services.

With your contribution we also work to wipe out old-fashioned attitudes which destroy rather than build. Radio, TV, films, speeches, newspapers, magazines and the mail shout the truth about the abilities of blind people... because you help!

The truth about blindness can be heard in Congress, on the street, in homes, factories, and stores... wherever people are present to hear it. Someday, hopefully soon, because you care enough to help spread the word, blind people will get their chance and be treated as equals.

Help open the door of opportunity for blind children today

-4-

<u>Your generous gift today can help:</u>

    BLIND students receive scholarships for
          college educations
    BLIND parents find jobs which pay at
          least the minimum wage
    BLIND workers learn to use talking
          typewriters and computers
    BLIND people receive articles in Braille,
          on cassette tapes, and records
    BLIND persons obtain watches, travel canes,
          talking clocks and calculators,
          adapted tools at or below cost
    BLIND individuals attend leadership seminars
          at the National Center for The Blind

    <u>Please don't delay!</u> Send $55.00, $27.50, $17.25,
$11.50, $8.25, or as much as you can share with us -
the NATIONAL FEDERATION OF THE BLIND. I've enclosed a
special envelope for your tax-deductible gift which
goes directly to our bank in Maryland.

    The message on the penny is our challenge! We
blind leaders won't rest until all blind people, men,
women, and children enjoy true FREEDOM and EQUALITY.

    There's another message on the penny! IN GOD WE
TRUST! We pray He'll inspire you to have faith in our
abilities. We <u>blind people want and need your help</u> in
our struggle for LIBERTY. Thank you in advance for
your most generous gift ever.

**Blind kids
really need
your help
right now,
dear friend!**

Sincerely,

Ralph Sanders

Ralph W. Sanders
Finance Chairman

RWS:pnc

P.S. I sincerely hope you'll keep the penny Lisa sent
you as a symbol of your commitment to help us blind
people in America find FREEDOM and EQUALITY. Blind
children especially need the opportunities your gift
provides. <u>Please send it as soon as possible!</u>

NATIONAL FEDERATION OF THE

Blind

1800 JOHNSON STREET, SUITE 300
BALTIMORE, MD 21230

Southern Poverty Law Center "Klanwatch Project" Letter

Some years ago, Morris Dees, an enterprising young student at the University of Alabama, came up with a direct mail program that has been copied thousands of times by other college students throughout the country. His idea: Write parents and offer to deliver a cake to their son or daughter away at school on their birthday.

After graduating, Dees developed a successful publishing business, which he eventually sold to the Times-Mirror Publishing Company.

The following mailing for the Southern Poverty Law Center was written by Dees. It has a "lift memo" labeled "A Message from Gregory Peck." It reads:

> I hope that you will give your support to the important KLANWATCH Project of the Southern Poverty Law Center.
>
> One of my earliest and most vivid memories is of a Klan incident, the burning of a cross in front of a house rented by a black family in the small town of La Jolla, California. It was in the early 1920's, when I was about five years old, but I remember it well. It must have been my first awareness that hate and violence existed in the world. The incident shocked me, and I suppose the concept of resisting and fighting racial injustice took root and became part of my character.
>
> The effort being waged by KLANWATCH against the Klan deserves our vigorous support, and I urge you to join in this cause.

In addition to the four-page letter from Dees, shown on the next page, the letter also had a sealed brown envelope with this message on the outside:

> ### WARNING
>
> The enclosed photograph is very disturbing. It shows the victim of a lynching by the Ku Klux Klan in Alabama — not in the 1880s but in the 1980s.
>
> The purpose of the picture is to awaken you to the horrifying reality of Klan violence in the South today. You can do something to stop this Klan savagery. Read the letter to find out how.

SOUTHERN POVERTY LAW CENTER
KLANWATCH PROJECT
1001 South Hull Street   Montgomery, Alabama 36195

Morris Dees
Chief Trial Counsel

Dear Friend,

I hope you will take the enclosed police photograph very seriously.

The family of Marvin Davis* will forever remember their visit to the Mobile, Alabama, morgue to identify his body. Only a few hours earlier, he had been laughing with friends and planning a happy future after graduation from junior college.

Members of the Mobile Klavern of the Ku Klux Klan had other plans for 19-year-old Marvin Davis. Even though these Klansmen had never met Marvin and had nothing against him personally, they kidnapped him at gunpoint from a city street as he was going to a convenience store.

The next morning, Marvin Davis's body was found hung by the neck from a tree in a black neighborhood.

A Klansman, James Knowles, confessed to being a part of this lynching. It was done, he said, "to show Klan strength in Alabama." On December 10, 1983, a jury convicted one Klansman for Marvin's murder.

I watched this trial. Grown men in the audience openly wept as Marvin Davis's confessed lyncher told how Marvin begged for his life while Klansmen prepared the noose for his neck. It was obvious to me and our investigators that many more Klansmen were involved in the conspiracy to lynch Marvin Davis than have been arrested.

If this recent Klan violence were just an isolated incident, we would not be nearly as concerned. But the lynching of Marvin Davis is just one of a series of modern day Klan attacks on blacks and Jews.

There is a new wave of violence sweeping the Deep South and it is being led by the Ku Klux Klan.

And the Southern Poverty Law Center's KLANWATCH Project has taken the lead in bringing the Klan to justice.

To help find all the killers of Marvin Davis, we have filed

(over, please)

*name changed to protect family privacy

- 2 -

a massive Federal civil rights suit against the nation's most violent Klan group, the United Klans of America. This Klan faction has been found guilty of some of the most heinous Klan crimes of this century.

Members of the United Klans of America have a bloody record of violence, including:

- burning a Greyhound bus carrying Freedom Riders in 1961.

- bombing the Birmingham Sixteenth Street Baptist Church in 1963, killing four black children.

- murdering civil rights worker Viola Liuzzo in 1965 as she shuttled marchers from Selma to Montgomery.

- shooting into the home of Alabama's NAACP President in 1979.

Now, as admitted by Klansman James Knowles, we know that members of the United Klans lynched young Marvin Davis.

The enclosed _Newsweek_ article dramatically illustrates how effective our work has been in tracking down Klansmen guilty of racial violence.

KLANWATCH lawyers and investigators obtained a Federal court injunction in 1982 stopping the Texas Klan from harassing Vietnamese fishermen from using Galveston Bay.

Working with the Texas Attorney General, we also obtained a court order in 1982 banning the Klan's paramilitary army, the Texas Emergency Reserve.

In December, 1983, KLANWATCH lawyers obtained a similar court order halting the Invisible Empire's Klan Special Forces from conducting paramilitary activities in Alabama.

And in May of 1984, we filed a Federal civil rights suit against the Carolina Knights of the Ku Klux Klan to stop their harassment of innocent blacks and to disband their private Klan army.

The battles we have had with the Klan in the past will be small compared to the fights ahead. The Klan is getting desperate as blacks gain political power in the South, and they will stop at nothing.

The massive voter registration drives planned by blacks in the Deep South will cause Klansmen to resort to the night riding tactics of the past. A black church was burned by arsonists in Humphries County, Mississippi, just two days before the August

- 3 -

1983 Democratic runoff.

We must keep our lawyers poised to help in stopping voting rights violations.

We must continue our legal representation of those like Roy Patterson, the decorated black Marine Sergeant we saved from the electric chair for killing two white Georgia law enforcement officers who maliciously attacked him and his family.

We must keep our Klan investigative program in full force and continue publishing the KLANWATCH "Intelligence Report" for law enforcement agencies and the public media.

We must continue our KLANWATCH educational programs and distribute our Academy-Award-nominated documentary film, The Klan: A Legacy of Hate in America, to schools and civic groups.

We are engaged in a tremendous amount of work, and we must have your help to continue.

That is why I hope I can count on you to send a contribution of at least $25 or more by Thursday or Friday of next week.

Last summer our offices were burned by arsonists, and Federal authorities believe they were Klansmen.

Every time we pick up a law book that was not destroyed in the blaze, the soot and darkened bindings remind us that we face an enemy who will stop at nothing to disrupt our work.

For the first time, we feel what the Freedom Riders must have felt when they rode into Birmingham in 1960 and were welcomed by a club-swinging mob of Klansmen.

As guards protect our homes and offices at night, we understand a little of the fear unprotected civil rights workers in the 1960s must have felt as bully Southern sheriffs and night riding Klansmen took the law into their own hands.

I was born in Alabama and I love the South. Our people are basically friendly and loving. You would feel at home with most of my neighbors. But I am ashamed of the small group of mean-spirited racists whose hatred of blacks and Jews has given our region a bad name.

Like Dr. King, we too have a dream.

Since the late 1960s we have fought a lonely and sometimes discouraging battle. I have come to realize that historic

(over, please)

- 4 -

advances in human rights are not made by the masses but by the determined few who dedicate their time and resources in hopes that some day all our brothers and sisters can walk proudly in the sunshine of justice.

I feel sure you share this dream with us and that you are not willing to sit idle while the gains in human rights are trampled by the Ku Klux Klan and their allies.

We hope you will send a tax-deductible gift of $25, $50 or whatever amount you can afford so we can carry on this vital work.

Please help us find and bring to justice all those responsible for the lynching of Marvin Davis.

Sincerely,

Morris Dees
Chief Trial Counsel

MD:sk

P.S. I want to share with you a moving letter the Center received recently from one of our supporters:

"Thank you for never giving up despite the long hours of work, depressing setbacks, and now this vicious [arson] attack [on your building]. Thank you for accepting my minuscule check and giving me in return the immense pride of knowing in some way I'm taking a stand against bigotry. Every time I read an update from you, I realize that no other organization that I contribute to makes me feel that the money is so well spent. I only wish I could give more."

-- Kathy Reisch
Tipton, Iowa

CHRISTINA L. WOODS MEMORIAL FUND LETTER

When you ask fund raisers to name the top letter writers among their ranks, one name is repeated over and over: Bob Westenberg. And when you ask Bob about his favorite fund-raising letter, he quickly brings out one he wrote for a local charity — the Christina L. Woods Memorial Fund. It's simple, straightforward, warm, and human:

> Cancer took Chris Woods a year ago Christmas. She was 16 . . . a brave young lady whose courage simply couldn't overcome her disease.
>
> Today there's a special living memorial for her . . . The Christina L. Woods Memorial Fund.
>
> When families have to rush seriously ill children to St. Joseph's Hospital in Phoenix, they often forget cash or credit cards in their haste. As a result, they find themselves with no place to stay, and no means of paying. Some simply can't afford any place.
>
> So Chris' fund pays for their lodging up to one week. It's an on-going fund with just one purpose: to help people out when they really need it . . . at a time of tremendous stress and worry.

6018 Highway 179
Sedona AZ 86336

Tom Smith
RFD 3
Top Ledge Road
West Redding CT 06901

Dear Tom,

Cancer took Chris Woods a year ago Christmas. She was 16...a brave young lady whose courage simply couldn't overcome her disease.

Today there's a special living memorial for her...The Christina L. Woods Memorial Fund.

When families have to rush seriously ill children to St. Joseph's Hospital in Phoenix, they often forget cash or credit cards in their haste. As a result, they find themselves with no place to stay, and no means of paying. Some simply can't afford any place.

So Chris' fund pays for their lodging up to one week. It's an ongoing fund with just one purpose: to help people out when they really need it...at a time of tremendous stress and worry.

<u>No one is ever asked to pay back.</u>

The fund is running low. I wonder if you'll help us replenish it? If you could send $30, or $50 or $100 or any amount at all it would be much appreciated, and well used.

We've arranged for some of these people to stay in private homes for just $15 a night. That stretches the money further, and enables us to help still more people.

Think of it this way...each $15 you can give will be one night for a family, compliments of you, and Chris.

It's a worthwhile thing to do. And a fitting memorial for Chris. She would have liked the idea of helping other people this way.

Please send what you can. Every penny goes in the fund. Nothing is used for any other purpose.

Thanks,

Bob Westenberg
Fund Administrator

P.S.   Please make checks payable to Christina L. Woods Memorial Fund.

THE NATIONAL TRUST FOR HISTORIC PRESERVATION "DRAYTON HALL" LETTER

One of the most unique fund-raising letters is a six-page letter written by Mal Decker to obtain funds to support the work of The National Trust for Historic Preservation.

When the Trust acquired Drayton Hall, considered the finest untouched example of Georgian architecture in America, it needed additional funds considerably beyond those that could be provided by selling additional memberships. So it turned to Malcom Decker Associates for a solution.

Decker came up with the idea of a series of five porcelain boxes featuring design motifs found within Trust properties and then created a classic mailing package to sell a limited edition of 2,500 sets of the boxes. The package included a four-color brochure plus the six-page letter. The letter opened with this Johnson Box:

> This letter is concerned with the serious state of one of the finest 18th century houses in America — and an intriguing plan whereby you can help us save it. It also offers an opportunity to acquire a most unusual limited edition.
>
> If we succeed, with your help, you will be invited to a very special preview of this great house and a reception along with a highly distinguished group of guests.

The letter described, in great detail, Drayton Hall and asked for support to preserve this historic home. It told how supporters will be invited, along with many dignitaries, to a special reception and will receive a specially commissioned medallion to mark the occasion.

The letter described the unique fund-raising method — a limited edition collection of five fine porcelain boxes — and then described the boxes, how they came into being, and how they may be acquired.

If anyone still believes "nobody reads long copy," consider this: the six-page letter brought in $1,500,000 — more than double the goal of The National Trust, and more than required for restoring Drayton Hall. It also won a Gold Mailbox from the Direct Mail/Marketing Association as the "Best Single Mailing Piece of 1975."

The National Trust for Historic Preservation
740-748 Jackson Place, N.W. ★ Washington, D.C. 20006

This letter is concerned with the serious state of one of the finest 18th century houses in America --- and an intriguing plan whereby you can help us save it. It also offers an opportunity to acquire a most unusual limited edition.

If we succeed, with your help, you will be invited to a very special preview of this great house and a reception along with a highly distinguished group of guests.

Dear Friend,

I think this is important.

George Washington was two years old when John Drayton, a member of the King's Council for the Colony of South Carolina, broke ground for a two-story brick mansion on the Ashley River, 12 miles upstream from Charleston. It stood sturdily through the Revolutionary War and the War of 1812, and is one of the few great Carolina houses to escape the ravages of the Civil War.

And although Drayton Hall has stood the tests of time since 1738 and is celebrated as one of the great architectural and historical treasures of America, its survival is threatened. Deterioration and vandalism have taken a heavy toll and extensive preservation is urgently required.

Drayton Hall was purchased by the National Trust as the only means of saving it from development. It was the Drayton family's wish that the property they cherished for seven generations pass directly from the family to an organization that would preserve the house for the public benefit. Very substantial funds -- up to $2,000,000 -- must now be expended for preservation and to create an endowment which would insure the proper long-range support of the property.

If we succeed in raising half this sum, we can request an equal amount of federal funds for this vital work: for every dollar you contribute we will be able to get a matching dollar.

If you join us in this cause, you will be invited to attend a preview of Drayton Hall this Spring. Lunch will be

- 2 -

provided at the Plantation followed by a reception at the Russell House, the headquarters of the Historic Charleston Foundation. There we will celebrate the rescue of Drayton Hall and mark the completion of our Twenty-fifth Anniversary as the only non-governmental organization chartered by Congress to safeguard America's cultural and historical heritage.

The invitation list will include our five Honorary Members, Mrs. Nixon, Mrs. Johnson, Mrs. Onassis, Mrs. Eisenhower and Mrs. Truman. The Secretary of the Interior and members of Congress will be invited, as will eminent architects, historians and preservationists.

A specially commissioned medallion will be struck to honor this significant milestone in the history of preservation, and each guest attending will receive a serially numbered copy. More about the medallions later. Let me now tell you how you can help to save Drayton Hall and --- at the same time--- make what I believe is an excellent investment.

Prior to accepting the presidency of the National Trust for Historic Preservation, I was curator of the American Wing of the Metropolitan Museum of Art in New York. Among the vast treasures of that great museum is a large collection of European eighteenth-century hinged boxes. Some are fashioned from precious metals studded with jewels; others are enamelled silver or copper. A few are Limoges porcelain from France -- an ideal medium for multicolor decoration.

Last winter we began searching for a suitable medium to raise funds for Drayton Hall, and to mark our first quarter-century. We considered a wide range of limited editions. None seemed exactly right. Our qualifications were extremely demanding. We insisted on an edition of the finest quality, a high level of aesthetics, a genuine possibility for appreciation, and the widest possible appeal among those who cherish our history and cultural traditions.

Then one day I remembered the porcelain boxes.

We visited Tiffany and Cartier in New York and obtained the names of their finest resources before we commissioned the design of the porcelain boxes we are pleased to be offering you today.

The National Trust Collection of Fine Porcelain Boxes consists of five extraordinary examples celebrating some of our most distinguished properties: Cliveden, Woodlawn, Shadows-on-the-Teche, Lyndhurst, and Decatur House.

In the course of my letter I will provide you with more information on these boxes --- sufficient, I believe, to enable

- 3 -

you to decide whether you wish to purchase them for aesthetic, charitable, or investment reasons. Or, very possibly, all three.

I mentioned earlier that our requirements were extremely stringent --- that among them was the insistence on a very high level of aesthetics. It was our feeling that nothing less would be suitable in portraying properties of the National Trust. We feel we have been true to our dedication.

We selected for this project the finest of the few crafts- men in the world capable of meeting our standards: the famous and venerable Porcelaine de Paris.

Each box is different in shape, made from models over 100 years old, and is decorated in exquisite detail from original oils, watercolors, and design motifs found within our Trust properties. The artists include E. L. Henry, Edward Savage (1789), Adrian Persac (1861), John Robert Murray (1824), Alonzo Chappel (1863), Alexander Jackson Davis (1838), Currier & Ives (1875).

Of course, fine art cannot be transferred directly to porcelain but must be repainted for the medium by highly skilled artists. Two were selected for this delicate assignment, each with 25 years of experience at Porcelaine de Paris. After you inspect the boxes, you will recognize why both have been named "Best Worker of France," an extraordinary award given but once every three years to a handful of workers in the entire nation. These artists were apprenticed to a man who was, himself, a "Best Worker of France." He, in turn, learned the art of miniature painting from his father.

The secret of making porcelain was guarded by its Chinese originators for 1200 years. It was not until 1709 than an alchemist in Meissen discovered the Chinese formula, but he kept it only 10 years. During this short span, artisans in Meissen developed porcelain as an art form, and when other European centers learned the secret, they contributed to the state of the art.

Paris was one of these centers, and outstanding among its many factories was Porcelaine de Paris, established by Jean Baptiste Locre in 1773 --- the year of our Boston Tea Party. It has been, since 1860, the sole surviving porcelain factory in the City of Paris.

Why, you may ask, was this extraordinary effort made to produce museum-quality art objects? Beyond our concern for beauty and quality we also wished to offer works with the greatest possible chance for appreciation. It was our clear purpose to produce porcelain of heirloom quality. While there is, of course,

- 4 -

no absolute guarantee that these boxes will increase in value, it has become abundantly clear in recent years that the greatest increase among collector's items is obtained by limited editions with specific characteristics:

- The artistic merit and total aesthetic value must be exceptionally high.

- The craftsmanship and quality of manufacture must be impeccable.

- The quality of materials used should simply be the best obtainable.

- The issue must be officially sanctioned or underwritten by an authorized source.

- The size of the edition must be strictly limited: it must not exceed 10,000 and, if it is to become truly rare within a reasonable period of time, it should be smaller. (Our edition is limited to 2,500.)

It is my opinion that these boxes meet our exacting requirements in every respect, and we commend them to your consideration.

For your information, antique porcelain boxes, especially those from the Eighteenth century, are bringing extremely high prices as collectors vie for the choicest pieces available. In the past five years, prices have more than tripled. At one recent Sotheby Parke Bernet auction, a 1745 gold-mounted porcelain box from Meissen fetched $2,400, and at another auction, 11 boxes were knocked down at prices ranging from $175 to $30,000 each. And a New York dealer is currently asking $36,000 for a very rare French porcelain box.

The National Trust Collection is being offered first to members and friends who have demonstrated a clear interest in historic preservation. The edition is strictly limited to 2,500. Each set is serially numbered. Only one set will be available to each subscriber. Orders will be filled in the exact sequence in which they are received. (Should we offer a second series of boxes at some future date, the first opportunity to purchase a set bearing the same serial number will be reserved for you.)

The first set will be presented to the Smithsonian Institution for its permanent collection. The last set will remain on display here in our headquarters. The remaining 2,498 sets

- 5 -

of five boxes will be available for sale at $600 the set. Upon completion of sale, the litho plates used to prepare the series will be defaced, thus assuring protection to all subscribers.

Important tax information: Due to the non-profit, tax-exempt status of the National Trust 66 2/3% of the $600.00 purchase price (or, $400.00) is deductible for income tax purposes.

The enclosed folder printed in four colors approximates the amazing depth and value of the 16 different colors used in the production of these pieces. Please examine it closely.

If you agree that these boxes are outstanding, that prospects for their appreciation are indeed bright, and that our work to save Drayton Hall and preserve America's heritage is worthy of your support --- then I urge you to act promptly.

Send us your order today with your check for $600 to purchase your set of The National Trust Collection of Fine Porcelain Boxes. Your payment will be acknowledged and you will be informed of your number in the limited edition. For those who appreciate low numbers, please remember: assignment will be made strictly in order of receipt.

In consideration of your full payment in advance, you will receive a .999 fine silver medallion struck to commemorate our Twenty-fifth Anniversary and the rescue of Drayton Hall.

If you prefer, you may purchase the first two boxes in the set now for $250 and the remaining three for $125 each. You will be billed prior to each monthly shipment. With your final box you will receive the serially numbered limited edition medallion in bronze.

Because these boxes are hand-crafted and your serial number is fired into the porcelain, please allow 30 to 60 days for delivery from the date you receive your acknowledgement.

You will have two weeks following receipt of the National Trust Collection to make your own independent appraisal and decide if you wish to keep it. If you decide against The Collection, simply return it insured. Your payment will be refunded in full and there will be no further obligation.

If you decide to keep The Collection, you will be elected (or re-elected) a Sustaining Member of the National Trust. Your

- 6 -

name, as the original purchaser, will be entered in a special bound volume which will be maintained in the National Trust Archives.

And, of course, you will be a guest of honor this Spring at Drayton Hall when we salute our first 25 years with the rescue of this magnificent property. It will be a memorable gathering.

Please let me hear from you promptly. I would like you to have the pleasure of examining The National Trust Collection at the earliest date. By agreeing to examine it, you risk only the time it takes you to decide whether or not you share our high opinion of these unique boxes.

Won't you place your order now?

Sincerely,

James Biddle
President

P.S. Please consult the Order Card for an illustration of the medallion commemorating the rescue of Drayton Hall and the Twenty-fifth Anniversary of the National Trust. It will be struck in .999 fine silver expressly for those subscribers who elect to make full payment for their subscription at this time.

COVENANT HOUSE LETTERS

The primary element that distinguishes most great fund-raising letters is the close personal involvement of the writer with his or her subject. Very often, the best letters are written not by professional copywriters, but by someone actively working for the cause being promoted. And when that individual is a natural writer, some truly great copy can result.

Such was the case with a series of letters from Covenant House, the exceptional facility dedicated to serving the thousands of "street kids" in Manhattan. Those letters were written by Father Bruce Ritter, the founder of Covenant House. He wrote not only of his successes, but also his frustrations, failures, and ambitions. The letters read like pages from a great novel. But there was never any question they were not works of fiction.

There was never a question that he needed more financial support than he received. But his letters, unlike so many fund-raising letters, were not emblazoned with that too-often repeated word, "EMERGENCY." They didn't cry the blues about empty coffers. Even though the stories he related were often tragic, they weren't filled with tears.

Through each letter, you got a feeling of "being there" — and wanting to help. While Father Ritter later got into trouble and had to abandon his leadership of Covenant House, the foundation of support he laid through his exceptional letters has continued to serve the institution well.

OCTOBER 1982

460 WEST 41 STREET
NEW YORK, N.Y. 10036
(212) 613-0300

Hello, my friends,

It was 1:30 in the morning of a warm, starry night when Craig stole out of the large, quiet house in suburban Maryland, down the long winding drive running through acres of manicured lawn to the waiting taxi. At the airport the boy discovered there were no early morning flights to New York so he grabbed another cab to the bus terminal in Baltimore, just in time to hop a bus for the Big Apple. Craig arrived in New York City's mammoth Port Authority Bus Terminal at 6:00 A.M. He was barely 12.

At that hour in the morning even Times Square and 42nd Street are fairly quiet. Not knowing what to do and trying to kill some time, Craig hopped into a cab. "Give me a tour," he ordered the driver. For the next hour Craig got an early morning ride around Manhattan from the George Washington Bridge to the Battery through Central Park, to the Bowery and Chinatown. The driver finally collected 40 dollars from the sleepy boy and dropped him off at a pay phone near the Empire State Building on 34th Street.

"Can you give me the number of a good hotel where I can stay until I get a job," Craig inquired rather plaintively of the operator, adding that he was on his own and had no place to go. God had His eye on this kid. The briskly professional voice of the operator changed magically into that of a warm, concerned adult. "Listen, kid. Do exactly what I say. Get another taxi and go to 460 West 41st Street. There's a place there called UNDER 21 and they'll be able to help you. Don't go anywhere else and don't go with anybody else!"

Craig, suddenly very much alone and scared, did exactly that.

Now most of my kids are street kids. Good kids, but they know things nobody should ever have had to know. Most of my kids have had to survive in ways they're not exactly proud of. Most of them are very skilled in the theory and practice of survival in their Times Square jungle. So I couldn't blame them very much for salivating hungrily when this 12-year-old lamb walked in our front door about 9:00 A.M. on Tuesday. I mean, a tiger is a tiger, right? I mean a wolf doesn't exactly feel affection for the possum that he had for lunch. Gratitude, maybe, but not affection. Maybe someday the lion will lie down with the lamb but until that day arrives my staff at Covenant House keep a special and very protective eye out for the lambs that come to us.

One hundred pairs of eyes lit up at the sight of the expensive matched luggage, the carefully understated designer clothes, the Gucci shoes. A top-of-the-line Sony Walkman radio was plugged into Craig's head. It took Clarence Coles, our experienced Supervisor on duty, about five seconds to size up the situation. Settle down, Clarence warned an assorted gaggle of wolves, tigers and lions that had immediately encircled their prey, offering instant friendship and an in-depth tour of 42nd Street. (Forty-deuce is a blast, man!)

Don't let this kid out of your sight for a moment, Clarence warned Pat Atkinson, a member of our Covenant Community from North Dakota, and one of our staff on duty that morning. Be like glue to this kid.

Craig was a really neat kid, about five feet high, with short brown hair and very alive friendly brown eyes. Pat whisked him, all 90 pounds worth, upstairs to the floor where we keep our younger, more vulnerable kids. Craig drew another admiring crowd there. He obligingly opened his matching suitcases and showed them his "extras": 250 dollars in cash, an AC/DC portable color T.V., a Canon AE-1 camera and a complete wardrobe of designer clothes. Pat sighed, gathered Craig's things together and locked everything up tight. Let's talk, he said.

It turned out that Craig had been planning on running away from his home in Southern Maryland for about 3 weeks. The night he finally left home he scrawled a hurting and thoughtless note (a little kid kind of note) on a page he had ripped from a Mercedes-Benz catalog his Mother had given him to choose the kind of car he would receive when he got his driver's license. On the torn photograph of a 45,000 dollar car Craig had written: "I hate this car as much as I hate you."

By now, Pat and Craig were getting along real well. (Pat has a great talent for getting through to kids like Craig.) A few well chosen examples of what happens to 12-year-old unstreetwise kids in Times Square had left Craig silent and shaken. So when Pat suggested that they call his Mother and let her know that Craig was alright, Craig liked the idea a lot. His face lit up momentarily and then fell quickly: "My Mother isn't home very much," he said quietly. "You can always talk to the maid, I guess."

Pat called the boy's home. The maid didn't know where his Mother was and volunteered that Craig's Father was yachting off Malibu. Pat talked to the gardener who wasn't much help either. The chauffeur referred Pat to the housekeeper who thought she could locate the Mother. Thirty minutes later, frantic and crying with relief, Craig's Mother called UNDER 21. We then began the happy process of getting an equally relieved Craig back home to parents who wanted him back very much and where he wanted to be.

On their way over to the Bus Terminal, Pat and Craig stopped in our main lounge to say goodbye to his host of newfound friends. My by-now-resigned lions and tigers and wolves cast a last wistful look at the color T.V. and the Walkman radio and the 600 dollar camera, and protectively allowed that they were real glad the kid was going to make it home O.K. Pat put Craig on a nonstop bus to Baltimore. He was back home, safe, by 10:00 P.M. -- total elapsed time about 21 hours -- and called Pat right away to let him know that things were O.K. "You've got a great place there," he said. "I guess I was pretty lucky, huh?"

I never really believed in luck very much. I believe in God watching out for little kids, rich or poor, and in kind people -- like that telephone operator -- who took the time to help a kid, and in all of you who care about children and are the real reason why Craig got home alright, unbrutalized, unviolated, unhurt, and with his dignity and his faith in the goodness of people intact.

We don't get many kids like Craig, of course, which is why I'm telling you his story. Craig is only one of the more than 15,000 kids who will come to our UNDER 21 centers this year. For most of them the story will not have a happy ending.

Rich or poor, good or bad, we try very hard to love each one of them, to keep that promise we make to every kid that walks through our doors -- the promise the prophet Ezekiel talks about in his eighth Chapter: "I bound myself by oath, I made a covenant with you . . . and you became mine."

We're not sentimental about it. Hard noses and soft hearts is what I tell my staff.

These past few months have been very rough for a lot of kids, and it's been very rough for my staff, also. We really do need your prayers, and your financial support. When you pray for your own kids, and families, pray for me and my kids, too.

We pray for you all the time.

Peace,

BUSINESS-TO-BUSINESS DIRECT MAIL

One of the most difficult letter writing jobs is creating messages for business executives. These messages not only have to appeal to the intended recipient, they have to get through the so-called "secretarial hurdle" as well.

In business offices, advertising mail is often screened by a personal secretary, an office manager, or in some cases, the mail room. Therefore, a good business-to-business direct mail letter has to seem important. More business-to-business letters are written than consumer mail order letters. But since they go to very select audiences, most are never seen by the majority of people in the direct mail field.

In this section, representative examples of outstanding business-to-business direct mail letters came from my own files and several response agencies who have business clients. The best of these letters follow.

IBM DIRECT RESPONSE LETTERS

IBM, like thousands of other business-to-business marketers, was troubled. It watched as the cost of a traditional personal sales call doubled, tripled, and quadrupled. Something had to be done or the cost of selling would wipe profit potential.

So IBM set up a task force in its Office Products Division, and studied methods of selling many products and supplies by various alternate methods. The answer was "IBM Direct" — a combination of direct mail and telephone marketing to sell many items that had become uneconomical to sell by direct customer contact. When it became obvious that IBM was out of the testing stage, many other companies — who had been watching IBM with an eagle eye — ventured into direct marketing. But IBM gets much of the credit for leading the way.

The letter shown here is typical of many used by IBM's Office Products Division. While it, and many similar letters used by IBM, might not be considered a "classic" strictly from a copywriting standpoint, these letters deserve special recognition for their role in leading other business-to-business marketers into direct marketing.

International Business Machines Corporation

IBM Direct 1 Culver Road
Dayton, New Jersey 08810
800-631-5582

In New Jersey
800-352-4960
In Alaska and Hawaii
800-526-2484

THERE HAS NEVER BEEN A BETTER TIME TO TRADE IN
YOUR OLDER TYPEWRITER...
FOR A NEW HIGH PERFORMANCE IBM TYPEWRITER.

Just call IBM DIRECT at the above number. We offer two IBM
typewriters that meet office typing problems head-on.

The IBM Correcting "Selectric" III Typewriter can actually
lift typing errors off the page as they occur -- eliminating the
need for messy erasures and correction fluid. Your paperwork
is clean, crisp and error-free the first time you type.

The IBM Electronic 75 Typewriter combines the power of
electronic memory with the simplicity of a familiar keyboard.
The result is a typewriter that can store, edit, correct and
assemble your typed documents automatically. That means you
save valuable time -- and money.

The enclosed brochure will tell you more about these remarkable
typewriters, and how easy it is to own one. We think you'll
agree they represent a sound investment in quality, performance
and dependability.

But why not see for yourself? Try one or both models for 15
days in your office. Then, if you are not completely satisfied,
return the typewriter(s) within the 15-day trial period for a
full refund. No other obligation, of course.

To order yours today, just call IBM DIRECT toll free. Or, if
you prefer, mail the enclosed postage-paid reply card. Either
way, you'll like the speed and convenience of IBM DIRECT.

Sincerely,

Joseph Bousa III

Joseph Bousa, III

JB/wf

P.S. If you order through IBM DIRECT before December 31, 1981,
IBM will send you a handsome address file for your office
absolutely free. See the enclosed card for details.

XEROX "USED COPIERS" LETTER

When you want to dispose of used equipment, it's likely the primary benefit is low price. And that's the way Xerox approached the selling of its used Xerox 550 copiers in a letter written by Judy Finerty. It featured a simulated newspaper clipping:

Xerox to sell copiers for under $1200!

Next to this was an attention-getting headline:

Introducing the plain paper copier that's so low in price, you can't afford not to own it!

Copy then builds a strong story for the Xerox 550 copier before easing into the reason for the low price:

This remarkable copier already has proven technology. It's been tested and retested. And it works. These machines have simply been "outgrown" by their previous users. We select only the finest copiers from this supply. Copiers that have received the tender — even loving — care of skilled Xerox technicians throughout their history.

We take these "cream of the crop" copiers, carefully clean and disassemble them, and then rebuild them from the ground up. Defective and worn-out parts are replaced, working surfaces lubricated and adjusted. Once this is done, we run a complete operational check.

We put each copier through the same kind of paces it will receive in your office. Only ones that come out "A-OK" are released for distribution.

These carefully reconditioned 550 copiers look and perform just like new.

In fact, we are backing them with the exact same warranty that we provide with our newly manufactured copiers.

So you get exceptional value — but you pay a very affordable price.

XEROX®

Xerox Corporation
Xerox Square
Rochester, New York 14644

Xerox to sell copiers for under $1200!

Rochester, N.Y.—In a move to better serve the small business community, Xerox Corporation announced today that they now have a plain paper copier that retails for under $1200.

"Our Xerox 550 copier is the first on the market for such a low price that lets a person copy on letterheads, transparencies, colored paper and special forms as well as regular bond paper," said W.R. Diener, Manager, Direct Marketing.

This small machine is just the latest in a series of moves by Xerox to expand its services to all areas of the copying market. "Our 550 copier should provide smaller businesses with the kind of copies they probably felt they couldn't afford to have in-house before," Diener continued. "It gives them the quality of a Xerox copier but with an incredibly low price tag, even lower than most treated paper copiers."

INTRODUCING THE PLAIN PAPER COPIER THAT'S SO LOW IN PRICE, YOU CAN'T AFFORD NOT TO OWN IT!

It's the Xerox 550 copier.
Call (800) 828-9090 toll free to get more information or to order yours and take advantage of our special 15-day free trial.
New York State residents, call (800) 462-2070.
A trained Xerox representative will answer your call.

Dear Decision Maker:

You could be seeing articles like this one in your local newspapers and business publications during the next few weeks.

And it's no wonder. Xerox is making history in the copying industry. That's because we've introduced the first plain paper copier that costs less than $1200!

Now you may be asking yourself, "What does that mean to me?" What it means is that now you can afford to have a real Xerox copier in your office. So you can make copies run on professional-looking plain paper. You don't have to settle for "funny" treated paper that so many small businesses have been forced to use in the past.

NOW, YOU CAN HAVE HIGH QUALITY COPIES
AT A PRICE THAT'S LESS THAN YOU'D
EXPECT TO PAY.

Xerox would like to introduce you to the copier that's ideal for your company no matter how small it is or how few copies you make.

(over, please)

-2-

It's the Xerox 550. It gives you professional
looking plain paper copies. Yet it costs
very little to own...just $1195.

And when we say professional-looking plain paper copies, we
mean it. (After all, that's what we've built our reputation
on over the past 20 years.) The copies are good enough to
compete with the originals you made them from.

In fact, you can make your copies right
on the same kind of paper as your originals.
And the only other small copiers we know
of that can make this claim cost almost
twice as much as the Xerox 550.

Need copies run of bills, receipts, expenses or accounting
work papers for your bookkeeping records? No problem. The
Xerox 550 can handle it. Want to send out copies on your
letterhead? With the 550, it's a "piece of cake."

You just load your letterhead into the paper tray. This means
your secretary doesn't have to spend time retyping the same
proposal, or letter, and all your customers get an "original".
Don't you agree that using the Xerox 550 will save valuable
secretarial time, and add a more professional look to your
correspondence?

Such high quality correspondence can't help but enhance your
own professional image.

EASY TO USE...EASY TO CARE FOR!

The Xerox 550 is a lot of machine for the money. It's sturdy,
yet compact, and fits neatly onto a desk-top or its own stand.

And you don't have to be an electronics genius to run it, either.
The single-sheet feed is triggered automatically when you insert
your originals into the document feed-in slot. There are no
buttons to push or dials to worry about -- no adjustments either.
And this "instant on" feature makes sheet-feed copying of typical
office documents a breeze.

HOW CAN XEROX BRING YOU SUCH A HIGH-
QUALITY COPIER AT SUCH A LOW PRICE?

The answer is simple. First, we opened a new, cost-efficient
distribution channel that is directly linked to the professional,
highly-skilled staff that you may already know as the team
at your local Xerox Branch Office.

The result?

Prompt, knowledgeable personnel just a toll
free phone call away. You'll enjoy the
convenience of shopping by phone (toll free,
of course) or mail. So it will be easy
to ask questions, get more information,
or place an order.

-3-

<u>Knowledgeable, professional service personnel</u>
-- just a few miles away. So if you do
run into a problem, we'll quickly dispatch
a Xerox "trouble shooter" to your door,
ready to solve it.

But now here's the really good part! This new system let's
you "cash in" on big savings.

The money we save by reducing costs, we
pass along to you in lower prices.

But that's just the first step. Secondly, we're very selective
about the copiers that we distribute through this new channel.

We picked the 550. Here's why.

This remarkable copier already has proven technology. It's
been tested and retested. And it works. These machines have
simply been "outgrown" by their previous users. We select
only the finest copiers from this supply. Copiers that have
received the tender -- even loving -- care of skilled Xerox
technicians throughout their history.

We take these "cream of the crop" copiers, carefully clean
and disassemble them, and then rebuild them from the ground
up. Defective and worn-out parts are replaced, working surfaces
lubricated and adjusted. Once this is done, we run a complete
operational check.

We put each copier through the same kind of paces it will
receive in your office. Only ones that come out "A-OK" are
released for distribution.

These carefully reconditioned 550 copiers look and perform
just like new.

In fact, we are backing them with the
exact same warranty that we provide with
our newly manufactured copiers.

So you get exceptional value -- but you pay a very affordable
price.

<u>SO MUCH CONVENIENCE ...</u>
<u>SO MUCH PRACTICALITY -- YOU</u>
<u>SHOULD SEE IT FOR YOURSELF.</u>

The Xerox 550 would make a practical and handsome addition
to any office. It features a distinctive beige metal casing
highlighted with a decorative accent front panel that blends
well with modern or traditional decor.

Now I'm not asking you to buy this copier on faith. Rather,
I'm inviting you to take advantage of a rare opportunity.

When you order the Xerox 550 now, we will make it
available to you with a 15 day <u>FREE</u> trial.

(over, please)

-4-

Once you have the copier in your office, really put it through its paces...enjoy all its conveniences and benefits. Only then do you need to make a final decision. If you decide you can get along without it, simply call our 800 toll free number and we'll come and take it away.

To purchase your Xerox 550 immediately and have it start working for you (and at such a great price, there's no reason not to), simply check the appropriate box on the order card or call toll free today. You can enclose payment in full, we can bill you, or you can charge it to your MasterCard, Visa, or American Express card.

Or, if you prefer, Xerox will help you finance your purchase. There's $140.00 down payment required so you won't be investing a large part of your working capital all at once. You simply pay $39.98 a month for 36 months. This amounts to an annual percentage rate of 21.5%. The finance rates are competitive, and you will have the advantage -- and the convenience -- of being able to rely on one trustworthy source for your copier, service, supplies, and financing. To find out more about our financing plan and if you qualify, simply check the appropriate box on the enclosed order card or call our toll free number today.

NOT CERTAIN? LET US TELL YOU MORE!

To get more details, simply call us at (800) 828-9090 toll free or mail the card today. A highly-trained Xerox 550 expert in our office will be happy to answer all your questions. New York residents call (800) 462-2070.

Remember, the Xerox 550 is one of the lowest priced, high quality plain paper copiers available today. You owe it to yourself and your company to investigate it further.

Sincerely,

Richard J. Benyo

Richard J. Benyo
550 Direct Marketing

P.S. If you already have a copier that you're pleased with, the Xerox 550 is still a great bargain for you. It's the ideal "second" copier on heavy volume days. And it's great as a back-up unit when your other copier is down. Don't forget you can charge it conveniently to your MasterCard, Visa, or American Express card.

XC-2009 L

Printed in U S A

McNeil Consumer Products "Tylenol Crisis" Letters

Direct mail letters can be used for many purposes. But no situation calls for more immediate action than a consumer product recall.

In September 1982, when news reports around the world reported the deaths in the Chicago area resulting from contaminated Tylenol capsules, everyone assumed this disaster spelled doom for one of the most popular over-the-counter medications. But McNeil, the maker of Tylenol, didn't panic — they developed a classic direct mail program. Recognizing the vital role of doctors in rebuilding confidence in Tylenol, they immediately contacted physicans, using a special StatGram format developed by Clark-O'Neil, the medical mailing service, to communicate newsworthy information to health care audiences. The telegram-type message read:

> DEAR DR. SMITH:
>
> MCNEIL CONSUMER PRODUCTS COMPANY HAS CONFIRMED THAT SEVERAL BOTTLES OF ITS PRODUCT, EXTRA-STRENGTH TYLENOL CAPSULES, HAVE BEEN TAMPERED WITH AND CYANIDE POISON ADDED TO SOME OF THE CAPSULES. THESE INCIDENTS HAVE ALL OCCURRED IN THE CHICAGO AREA AND WE ARE TAKING STEPS TO REMOVE FROM SALE IN THE CHICAGO AREA ALL EXTRA-STRENGTH TYLENOL CAPSULES.
>
> THE BOTTLES IN QUESTION, WHICH CONTAIN 50 CAPSULES, WERE FROM TWO LOTS OF PRODUCT WHOSE NUMBERS ARE MC2880 AND 1910MD. PRODUCTS MARKED IN THIS WAY SHOULD NOT BE BOUGHT OR CONSUMED, AND CONSUMERS HAVING SUCH PRODUCT SHOULD RETURN IT TO THE PLACE OF PURCHASE OR TO MCNEIL CONSUMER PRODUCTS COMPANY.
>
> ALTHOUGH WE BELIEVE THE PROBLEM IS CONFINED TO THE CHICAGO AREA, WE ARE TAKING THE PRECAUTION OF WITHDRAWING THESE TWO LOTS EVERYWHERE THEY ARE IN DISTRIBUTION. WE CURRENTLY HAVE NO EVIDENCE THAT ANY OTHER EXTRA-STRENGTH TYLENOL CAPSULE OR OTHER TYLENOL PRODUCT WAS SIMILARLY CONTAMINATED.

This message was followed up with a series of messages, some of which are shown here. The factor that distinguishes these letters is the total lack of panic. Just clear, straightforward, confidence-building copy that kept doctors fully informed.

R6622

FROM

MCNEIL
CONSUMER PRODUCTS COMPANY
CAMP HILL ROAD
FORT WASHINGTON, PA. 19034

STAT/GRAM ™·

Electronic Dispatch

OCTOBER 1, 1982

TO

RICHARD S. HODGSON, M.D.
POST OFFICE BOX 46
WESTTOWN, PA.   19395

DEAR DR. HODGSON:

MCNEIL CONSUMER PRODUCTS COMPANY HAS CONFIRMED THAT SEVERAL BOTTLES OF ITS PRODUCT, EXTRA-STRENGTH TYLENOL* CAPSULES, HAVE BEEN TAMPERED WITH AND CYANIDE POISON ADDED TO SOME OF THE CAPSULES. THESE INCIDENTS HAVE ALL OCCURRED IN THE CHICAGO AREA AND WE ARE TAKING STEPS TO REMOVE FROM SALE IN THE CHICAGO AREA ALL EXTRA-STRENGTH TYLENOL* CAPSULES.

THE BOTTLES IN QUESTION, WHICH CONTAIN 50 CAPSULES, WERE FROM TWO LOTS OF PRODUCT WHOSE NUMBERS ARE MC2880 AND 1910MD. PRODUCTS MARKED IN THIS WAY SHOULD NOT BE BOUGHT OR CONSUMED, AND CONSUMERS HAVING SUCH PRODUCT SHOULD RETURN IT TO THE PLACE OF PURCHASE OR TO MCNEIL CONSUMER PRODUCTS COMPANY.

ALTHOUGH WE BELIEVE THE PROBLEM IS CONFINED TO THE CHICAGO AREA, WE ARE TAKING THE PRECAUTION OF WITHDRAWING THESE TWO LOTS EVERYWHERE THEY ARE IN DISTRIBUTION. WE CURRENTLY HAVE NO EVIDENCE THAT ANY OTHER EXTRA-STRENGTH TYLENOL* CAPSULE OR OTHER TYLENOL* PRODUCT WAS SIMILARLY CONTAMINATED.

*REGISTERED TRADEMARK OF MCNEIL CONSUMER PRODUCTS COMPANY

McNEIL

McNEIL CONSUMER PRODUCTS COMPANY, CAMP HILL ROAD, FORT WASHINGTON, PA 19034, (215) 233-7000

October 8, 1982
11:00 A.M.

Dear Doctor:

On Thursday morning, September 30, 1982, the Cook County, Illinois, Medical Examiner's Office advised the McNeil Consumer Products Company that three deaths due to cyanide poisoning had occurred in the northwestern suburbs of Chicago. At that time, a fourth victim was critically ill and has subsequently died. In each instance, the poisoning was traced to cyanide adulteration introduced through tampering with Extra-Strength TYLENOL® Capsules. Three of the deaths were in one family and involved a single 50-capsule bottle of Extra-Strength TYLENOL Capsules with the Lot #MC2880. The fourth death was associated with a bottle of Extra-Strength TYLENOL Capsules with the same lot number.

McNeil Consumer Products Company immediately notified the Food and Drug Administration and initiated a national recall of all Extra-Strength TYLENOL Capsules with that lot number. In addition, all Extra-Strength TYLENOL Capsules, regardless of lot number, were recalled in the seven county area around Chicago.

Three additional deaths, all in the Chicago area, have subsequently been traced to Extra-Strength TYLENOL Capsules that had been tampered with.

Further, on Friday, October 1, a case of strychnine poisoning due to adulteration introduced through tampering with Extra-Strength TYLENOL Capsules was reported in Oroville, California, a small community approximately 100 miles north of Sacramento. As various lots of Extra-Strength TYLENOL Capsules were identified in these events, they were withdrawn either nationally or regionally as the circumstances indicated.

The situation has rapidly changed over the past six days. McNeil has therefore now established the following policy pertaining to hospital, wholesale and retail customers and consumers:

> In agreement with the FDA, McNeil Consumer Products Company is voluntarily withdrawing all TYLENOL capsule products (including Regular Strength TYLENOL® Capsules, Extra-Strength TYLENOL Capsules, non-blistered CoTYLENOL® Capsules, and Maximum Strength TYLENOL® Sinus Medication Capsules) from hospital, wholesale and retail accounts nationally. In addition, McNeil Consumer Products Company is advising all TYLENOL capsule users to now use TYLENOL tablets until capsules in tamper-resistant packages are available. Consumers are urged to return all TYLENOL capsule products to the place of purchase or to mail bottles to Tylenol Exchange, P.O. Box 2000, Maple Plains, Minnesota 55348. They will receive TYLENOL tablet products in exchange.

(over)

— 2 —

We are assisting local, state and national law enforcement agencies, as well as the FDA, in every way possible to identify who tampered with the Extra-Strength TYLENOL® Capsules and have offered a $100,000 reward for information leading to the arrest and conviction of the person or persons responsible for the murders in Chicago.

We have, of course, thoroughly examined the possibility that Extra-Strength TYLENOL Capsules were tampered with at our manufacturing locations or distribution channels. We have continued to use all of our research and quality assurance capabilities — and those of other Johnson & Johnson subsidiaries — to make certain there is no possibility that cyanide or strychnine poison were introduced during our handling of the product. We are confident that no contamination took place in our facilities.

There is widespread public confusion about which TYLENOL products are involved. Many people do not understand that it is only Extra-Strength TYLENOL Capsules and possibly Regular Strength TYLENOL Capsules that have been implicated and that tablets could not be tampered with in the same manner as capsules.

Because of this confusion, some media have questioned Extra-Strength TYLENOL Tablets, pediatric formulations and all of our other products. There is no evidence indicating that any other products of either McNeil Consumer Products Company or McNeil Pharmaceutical, including TYLENOL® with Codeine, have been tampered with in any manner. We would sincerely appreciate your assistance in reassuring your patients that there is no evidence that the tablet and pediatric forms of our products have been tampered with. If you have any questions, please call me collect at (215) 233-7262.

McNeil Consumer Products Company appreciates the many expressions of confidence in our company and in the quality of our products we have received from every segment of the health care profession. Our company is proud of our ethical image and we will do everything in our power to continue to justify your trust and confidence.

Sincerely,

Thomas N. Gates

Thomas N. Gates, M.D.
Medical Director
McNeil Consumer Products Company

McNEIL

McNEIL CONSUMER PRODUCTS COMPANY, CAMP HILL ROAD, FORT WASHINGTON, PA 19034, (215) 233-7000

November 8, 1982

Dear Doctor:

Because you are the best source patients have for accurate information about the continued use of TYLENOL® products, we would like to update you on our actions and recommendations.

The Food and Drug Administration has thoroughly investigated the McNeil Consumer Products Company manufacturing plants and has concluded that the contamination of Extra-Strength TYLENOL capsules did not occur in our facilities and that our manufacturing processes are consistent with the standards required.

Having withdrawn all TYLENOL capsule products from the market, McNeil is proceeding aggressively with the development of new tamper-resistant packaging for all of our products. In the meantime, TYLENOL tablets, both Extra-Strength and Regular Strength, remain an effective therapeutic alternative for your patients. The Commissioner of the Food and Drug Administration has stated that TYLENOL tablets could not have been tampered with in the same manner as capsules.

Finally, enclosed is a public service announcement by the Commissioner of the Food and Drug Administration. In this statement, Dr. Hayes summarizes the sense of shock experienced by all of us regarding the recent situation. He also notes that effective measures are being taken to help ensure that nothing like this happens again.

McNeil Consumer Products Company appreciates the support of the health care profession and will do everything possible to continue to justify your trust and confidence in our products.

Sincerely,

Thomas N. Gates, M.D.
Medical Director
McNeil Consumer Products Company

McNEIL

McNEIL CONSUMER PRODUCTS COMPANY, CAMP HILL ROAD, FORT WASHINGTON, PA 19034, (215) 233-7000

Dear Doctor:

On November 24, 1982, Mayor Jane Byrne announced that TYLENOL® acetaminophen products in tamper-resistant packaging were approved for sale in Chicago, thus ending a seven-week ban on their availability. New safety-sealed, tamper-resistant TYLENOL packaging will begin appearing in Chicago-area stores shortly and will be widely available by January. Extra-Strength TYLENOL® Capsules will be the first to appear in tamper-resistant packaging, followed by other forms of TYLENOL in early 1983.

Because you may receive questions from your patients about the new tamper-resistant packaging, we have enclosed a sheet that fully describes the new three-phase protection that will be available on all Extra-Strength TYLENOL Capsules.

For your information, all TYLENOL products removed from Chicago-area stores have been destroyed; all TYLENOL products shipped by McNeil Consumer Products Company to Chicago in the future will be in safety-sealed packaging. This applies not only to Regular Strength and Extra-Strength TYLENOL Tablets and Capsules, but to Children's TYLENOL® products, CoTYLENOL® Cold Formula products, Maximum-Strength TYLENOL® Sinus Medication, SINE-AID® Sinus Headache products and COLDMAX® Cold Formula products. The sale of TYLENOL® with Codeine has also been reinstituted in its existing sealed packaging.

While the new safety-sealed TYLENOL packaging will help to reduce the potential for future tampering, McNeil and the FDA are encouraging all persons to carefully examine any medication before using it. We would appreciate your assistance in disseminating this advice, as well as information about our new packaging, to your patients.

McNeil Consumer Products Company wishes to thank you for your continued trust and confidence in TYLENOL. If you have any questions, please call toll free, 1-800-237-9800.

Sincerely,

Thomas N Gates, MD

Thomas N. Gates, M.D.
Medical Director
McNeil Consumer Products Company

DAY-TIMERS, INC. "FREE TRIAL OFFER" LETTER

The first lesson every direct mail writer learns is to stress benefits rather than features. The following letter from Bob Dorney of Day-Timers, Inc. gets right down to benefits before anything else:

> You can increase your work output by 20–40%
>
> Know what you must do each day
>
> Delegate and monitor your work load
>
> Reduce lost time and wasted effort
>
> You can do all these things . . . and more. We guarantee it!

The letter summarizes the product's feature — the famous Day-Timer Time-Planner Diary — and then wraps it together in a unique selling proposition:

> Together, they give you what leading management consultants consider to be the single most important asset you can possess. . . skill in managing your time!

To get the reader to think about using the product, the letter suggests:

> Test yourself: Do you know how to guarantee you'll get top priority tasks finished first? Is your work organized . . . or are you constantly putting out "brush fires"? Can you remember every project you must finish today, tomorrow, weeks ahead? Can you remember details of work you accomplished only yesterday?

After a string of further benefit-laden paragraphs, Day-Timers takes a lead from successful circulation promotion letters:

> Test It Yourself for 30 Days — Then Decide!
>
> You needn't take our word for it. The only sure way to prove the Day-Timer system will work for you is to put it to the test of actual use . . . in your own job situation. Use it at our expense for 30 days — then decide! If the Day-Timer doesn't equal or exceed your expectations, just return the unused portion after 30 days and that will end the matter.

DAY-TIMERS, Inc.
Allentown, Pennsylvania 18001
215 - 395-5884

These are now proven facts . . .

— You can increase your work output by 20-40%
— Know what you must do each day
— Delegate and monitor your work load
— Reduce lost time and wasted effort

You can do all these things . . . and more. We guarantee it!

Yes, these are just a few of the benefits busy executives are achieving each day with a Day-Timer 5-in-1 Time-Planner Diary. Every Day-Timer combines the benefits of five different books:

1. An Appointment Book
2. "Tickler" Reminder System
3. Daily, Weekly and Monthly Work Planner/Organizer
4. Time and Activity Record
5. Expense and Reimbursement Record

Together, they give you what leading management consultants consider is the single most important asset you can possess . . . skill in managing your time!

Test yourself: Do you know how to guarantee you'll get top priority tasks finished first? Is your work organized . . . or are you constantly putting out "brush fires"? Can you remember every project you must finish today, tomorrow, weeks ahead? Can you remember details of work you accomplished only yesterday?

If you've answered "No" to a single one of these questions you're sure to benefit by using what a leading business newsletter has called "one of the best time-management aids ever developed." Today, more than 1,000,000 busy executives and professionals use a Day-Timer to save hours a day, organize their desks, and free their minds for creative thinking and problem-solving.

GIVES YOU AN "AUTOMATIC MEMORY" — WON'T LET YOU FORGET!

Stop scribbling notes on scratch pads and on the backs of envelopes, notes which are easily lost and leave no memory behind. Enter every reminder, every inspiration, every idea in your Day-Timer . . . where it will be preserved . . . along with the record of their execution and follow-through.

Your Day-Timer will give you an automatic memory — organizes everything for you as far ahead as you need plan, as far back as you need records kept. The basic strategy of this highly successful Day-Timer system is to keep all this scattered information in one place — for instant reference whenever needed — so no detail need ever be overlooked or forgotten.

See Other Side for 30-Day PROVE-IT-YOURSELF Free Trial Offer . . .

Free Your Mind for Important Decisions!

Forget Remembering! You'll work more relaxed knowing every important detail is written down in your Day-Timer — for quick and easy recall whenever needed. This frees your mind for creative thinking . . . lets you give full attention to the job at hand . . . because you don't. have to "keep remembering" 1,001 details.

And, just as your Day-Timer helps you keep things humming along on time, you'll understand how it is that certain executives seem to get so much more done than others . . . can attend so many more meetings . . . never seem to forget an important fact, date or commitment. Their "secret" is no secret at all . . . they just use a Day-Timer!

Test It Yourself for 30 Days — Then Decide!

You needn't take our word for it. The only sure way to prove the Day-Timer system will work for you is to <u>put it to the test of actual use</u> . . . in your own job situation. Use it at our expense for 30 days — then decide! If the Day-Timer doesn't equal or exceed your expectations, just return the unused portion after 30 days and that will end the matter.

There's no risk for you . . . or for us. Our records reveal that over 93% of those who begin to use a Day-Timer faithfully continue to use it as a valued partner year after year after year. The reason is simple — it works! And our Guarantee is it will work for you or you can return it and owe nothing.

Now is the best time to find out why Day-Timers have won such overwhelming acceptance. Your reward will be a job that's suddenly become easier and more enjoyable. You'll quickly be convinced that — next to the telephone — it's the best time-saving investment you ever made.
So, order your Day-Timer now . . . today!

Sincerely,

Robert C. Dorney,
President & Gen. Mgr.

P.S.　　When ordering your DAY-TIMER . . . first select the page size and format best suited to your own particular schedule . . . then pick a wallet or binder to complete your set. (Thereafter, you will only need to order the filler pages each year.)

INGHAM HALL, LTD. "LAWYER" LETTER

Probably no top copywriter today has successfully sold more kinds of products than Andi Emerson. The following letter is one of the most unique she has written. It promotes the services of her lawyer in a most intriguing way. Consider her Johnson Box lead:

> If your lawyer always remembers YOU are the employer and
>
> Returns calls promptly
>
> Meets promised deadlines
>
> Thoroughly understands your business
>
> Willingly researches your oddball questions
>
> Writes simplified contracts that fully protect you
>
> And never "surprises" you with an unexpected bill . . .
>
> THEN PLEASE STOP READING HERE.

Immediately, Emerson screens out uninterested readers. For those who are interested in seeking the services of a new lawyer, she brings in her personal experience:

> Running this business has given me some painful lessons on when to be demanding and when to let up a bit — but I never got over being irritated by our lawyers' condescending manner. Not one lawyer, but several over a period of years.
>
> That list at the top of the page comes from my own sad experience, as well as from the complaints of most of my friends. Medium to small companies, it seems, often encounter the same difficulties with outside professional help — the lack of genuine interest.
>
> That's why I offered to write a short letter for the counselor we lucked into — a supremely dedicated woman who actually uses her mind and her ears, as well as her legal background.

Ingham Hall, Ltd.
MARKETPLACE OF THE UNCOMMON
44 East 29th Street, New York, N.Y. 10016
(212) 260-5280

If your lawyer always remembers YOU are the employer and

    Returns calls promptly

    Meets promised deadlines

    Thoroughly understands your business

    Willingly researches your odd ball questions

    Writes simplified contracts that fully protect you

    And never "surprises" you with an unexpected bill ...

THEN PLEASE STOP READING HERE.

Dear Fellow Small-Business Executive,

    Running this business has given me some painful lessons on when to be demanding and when to let up a bit -- but I never got over being irritated by our lawyer's condescending manner. Not one lawyer, but several over a period of years.

    That list at the top of the page comes from my own sad experience, as well as from the complaints of most of my friends. Medium to small companies, it seems, often encounter the same difficulties with outside professional help -- lack of genuine interest.

    That's why I offered to write a short letter for the counselor we lucked into -- a supremely dedicated woman who actually uses her mind and her ears, as well as her legal background.

    All lawyers study the same books, take the same courses and pass the same bar exam before they can hang out their shingles. Professional growth from then on in is as much a matter of personal application and ability as it is of powerful contacts.

    For my money the best lawyer is the one who helps my company grow by understanding and executing our needs. Just because we're not involved in daily litigation, with consequent legal fees in the tens of thousands every year, doesn't mean our contracts and miscellaneous requirements aren't vital to our company. Chances are you're in exactly the same situation.

    So, if you'd like to find a couselor who is sensitive to your needs, why not contact ours? She won't take you on unless she feels she can do an outstanding job for you. And she won't accept more business than she can

(2)

handle by her standards -- which are very high. In fact, if I thought for
a minute that she'd permit herself to be swamped I'd never have volunteered
to write this letter! I'm not that stupid.

But if you're fortunate enough to become her client I think you, too,
will be very pleased with the results. So, fill out the coupon below and --
Good Luck.

Very truly yours,
Ingham Hall, Ltd.

A. Adams Emerson,
President

AAE:pg

- - - - - - - - - - - - - - - - - Please Clip Here - - - - - - - - - - - - - -

▬▬▬▬▬▬, Esq.
▬▬▬▬▬▬ New York, N.Y. 10017

Please call me. I would like to discuss, with absolutely no obligation,
the possibility of retaining your services as my counsel.

☐ Call my office _____   ☐ Call my home _____
                    (number)   (number)

Between _____ & _____   on _____
          (time)   (time)   (date)

Name _____
                    (please print)

Company _____

Street _____

City _____ State _____ Zip _____

Ingham Hall, Ltd.
MARKETPLACE OF THE UNCOMMON

THE NESTLÉ COMPANY "KEY" LETTER

The following letter pulled a 67% response, and was written by Milton Pierce, who said:

■ This letter had the greatest response of any direct mail letter I've ever written. Why did it do so well? Because it gave a truly sensational offer — $400 in free merchandise — to exactly the right list: 7,000 owners of new vending machines. Not only did the letter get good results, it also won a DMMA award for me.

Dear Sir:

There's a key attached to this letter — a very special key — that unlocks three valuable gifts from Nestlé for you.

It's our way of saying "congratulations" on your new vending machines. We were delighted to help in the financing of this equipment. And now we'd also like to help you get the greatest profits from this new equipment.

That's where the key enters into the picture . . .

In just a few days you'll receive a package from Nestlé. This key will unlock that package — to reveal three valuable gifts:

First, the key unlocks a personal gift for you — something you'll use and enjoy for years.

Second, the key unlocks a gift for your vending machine — a very special free offer that's worth over $200.00!

Third, the key unlocks the secret of lifetime profits from your vending machines — proven ideas that can add many dollars to your income.

So save this key — and look for your gift package from Nestlé. It will be coming in just a few days.

P.S.   Our gift package is for the man in your organization who purchases merchandise for your vending machines . . . Please forward this letter to this "Key Man." Thank you.

Dear Sir:

There's a key attached to this letter -- a very special key -- that unlocks three valuable gifts from Nestlé for you.

It's our way of saying "congratulations" on your new vending machines. We were delighted to help in the financing of this equipment. And now we'd also like to help you get the greatest profits from this new equipment.

That's where the key enters into the picture...

In just a few days you'll receive a package from Nestlé. This key will unlock that package -- to reveal three valuable gifts:

First, the key unlocks a personal gift for you -- something you'll use and enjoy for years.

Second, the key unlocks a gift for your vending machine -- a very special free offer that's worth over $200.00!

Third, the key unlocks the secret of lifetime profits from your vending machines -- proven ideas that can add many dollars to your income.

So save this key -- and look for your gift package from Nestlé. It will be coming in just a few days.

Cordially,

Albert M. Van Wagenen

Albert M. Van Wagenen
Manager- Vending Marketing

P.S. Our gift package is for the man in your organization who purchases merchandise for your vending machines... Please forward this letter to this "Key Man". Thank you.

TRANS-LUX "9 REASONS" LETTER

Long ago, smart direct mail writers learned that benefits are far more important than features in presenting a product or service. An excellent example of this "rule" put into practice is a letter created by William Steiner Associates, the New York direct marketing agency, for Trans-Lux Corporation.

It is headed:

> There are 9 Reasons . . .
>
> why you should mail the enclosed card to find out how you can replace your present telex equipment and enjoy greater speed, efficiency . . . and quiet!
>
> . . . and it won't cost you one penny more than you are now paying!

The letter, which was the first page of a letter-brochure, listed nine specific benefits, briefly amplifying each one, and closed:

> Learn about these and other benefits by mailing the enclosed card today . . . it will bring you information on how to make your telex easier to operate . . . more efficient . . . and less costly, too.

There are 9 Reasons...

why you should mail the enclosed card to find out how you can replace your present telex equipment and

enjoy greater speed, efficiency...and quiet!

...and it won't cost you one penny more than you are now paying!

Dear Telex User:

SOMETHING NEW has been introduced in telex office equipment... and scores of telex users have proven to themselves how it brings them important benefits.

To find out how you can benefit mail the enclosed card for no obligation information on the newest development in Telex Communications - The TRANS-LUX® TELEPRINTER for TELEX. It tells you about these advantages:

1. Easier to operate...its standard four-row typewriter keyboard eliminates figure and letter shifting.

2. Enjoy quiet operation...even quieter than an ordinary typewriter.

3. Faster message preparation...off-line typing capability and memory printout is twice as fast as your present telex unit.

4. More efficient...electronic memory does away with paper punch tape, mechanical perforator and reader.

5. Saves time...erasures are done simply by overtyping. You don't have to re-do entire messages.

6. Neater typing...impact paper eliminates messy ribbons.

7. Easier dialing...the keyboard itself is the "dial" and the number prints out for verification. Line busy? The memory re-dials for you.

8. Beautiful styling...The TLT is compact, modern and small as an Executive typewriter. Attractive blue with pink and white keyboard accents complement any office decor.

9. Saves money...Lease price includes service and maintenance and costs no more than your present telex.

Learn about these and other benefits by mailing the enclosed card today...it will bring you information on how to make your telex easier to operate...more efficient...and less costly, too.

Cordially,

Michael R. Mulcahy
Manager, Teleprinter Systems
TRANS-LUX CORPORATION

P.S. Your management will welcome the TRANS-LUX TELEPRINTER because it doesn't cost a cent more than your present equipment and it can cut your communications costs.

MRM:100

ACE PECAN COMPANY "DAD'S ADVICE" LETTER

Narrative letters are less common in business-to-business selling than in fund-raising or in selling consumer products. They may, however, reach business audiences when other copywriting techniques fail.

The key market for food gifts are businesses that make multiple purchases of gifts to send to customers and employees. Ace Pecan Company wanted to reach this market but was having difficulty coming up with a mailing package that would produce good results from outside lists.

When asked to create something that would get through to these prospects, Joan Greenfield decided to try the narrative approach. She gives this background:

> ■ Although they had been testing lists for over six years — lists which worked for other gourmet foods — no outside list had ever been profitable for them. And while they had a successful business from their house list, the business was not growing as fast as it should.
>
> Since I love to write emotional letters, I hoped this version would win. But experience told me that, too often, narrative letters don't work. Or at least don't work as well as direct letters.
>
> But for the first time ever, outside lists worked successfully for this client, opening up major new avenues of growth for the company.
>
> And the letter worked well with the house list, too — 88% better than the control!

Joan also had a cooperative client. All too often, copywriters are forced to turn out copy without actually having an opportunity to see and test the product they're writing about. But Joan told me:

> ■ I had a tin of their mixed nuts in front of me while I was writing, and every time I needed a little inspiration, I popped another giant nut into my mouth and delicious words streamed out of my typewriter.

Free Gift when you order! Details in letter

ACE PECAN CO.   900 MORSE AVENUE / P.O. BOX 727 / ELK GROVE VILLAGE / ILLINOIS 60007 / 312 364-3277

Dad told me,
"Joe, always give the customers a little more than they pay for."

Dear Friend:

It was tough making a dollar back in the 1930's. I was just a kid at the time, but I still remember how my dad did it.

He was in business for himself -- selling hot dogs at a nickel a piece off a pushcart to factory hands in our Italian-American "ethnic neighborhood" on Chicago's northwest side.

But in the spare time he had left over in a 12-hour workday, he started a little sideline that turned into the family business.

He shelled bag after bag of walnuts and pecans on the kitchen table, late into the night. He bought the nuts, shelled them, and then sold then back for a profit.

He started making as much money from the nuts as from the hot dogs, and soon a friend encouraged him to go into the nut business full-time.

Well, here it is more than 50 years later, and I guess you might call Dad's a "typical" American success story. Dad's little nut business has expanded from the kitchen table into three large plants -- one in Georgia -- that sell millions of dollars worth of top-quality nuts all over the United States.

I've often pondered about what made Dad successful, when so many others didn't make it. I think it was his approach to doing business.

"Joe," he used to tell me, "if you just keep giving the customers a little more than they pay for, they'll keep coming back to you."

That's what Dad did, and I really believe that's what made our business grow the way it did.

But it still took me a while to learn that lesson when I took over. Our first mail order efforts duplicated what other companies were doing -- using fancy tins and expensive packaging to sell our nuts.

One day the Controller came to me and said, "You know, we're paying as much for the tins as we are for the nuts."

I thought about it for a while, then decided to get rid of the fancy packaging. We would package the nuts in inexpensive cartons and plain tins, call them Bulk Packs, and give the customers more nuts for every dollar. That was a real turning point in the business.

That's just one of the many ways our business has changed since those early years. But our commitment to giving our customers more than they pay

(over, please)

-2-

for continues -- and it will as long as I and my kids are running the business. Here's how we live up to it in 1983:

. Our buyers travel the world over searching for the biggest, best, most perfect nuts we can find.

. We contract for the best in advance -- before they're even ready for harvest -- and before our competitors can snap them up.

. We select them, grade them, shell them, pick them over by hand, roast them carefully, and choose only the biggest, best, "Premium Grade" hand-selected nut meats for our mail order business.

(Because the supply of this top grade of nuts is so limited, we don't have enough to sell them through retail stores. So we save all the very best nuts to sell you direct-by-mail.)

. We package them for delivery to you in our unique "Shell Pack," which sucks out all the air and keeps the nuts as safe and fresh as when they leave our plant.

. We sell them to people like you -- by mail -- at prices well below what you'd expect to pay for this premium grade. We offer very fancy nuts at very "un-fancy" prices.

. We give you all the value we can, and it's always more than you pay for, in the hopes you'll buy from us again and again.

And to ensure that we live up to all this (and to our family tradition), we put ourselves on the spot with this triple guarantee:

FRESHNESS GUARANTEE. We guarantee our nuts to be the freshest you can buy. Our exclusive vacuum "Shell Pack" keeps them as fresh as if they were in their own shells.

SAFE DELIVERY GUARANTEE. We guarantee safe delivery to you. You don't have to worry about squashed packages or broken nuts. Again, the unique "Shell Pack" protects your nuts.

TOTAL SATISFACTION GUARANTEE. We guarantee your satisfaction when you buy our nuts -- no matter what. If for any reason you should ever be displeased, simply return the unused nuts to us for replacement or an immediate full cash refund.

Some Of Our Nuts Are So Big, It Takes a Couple Of Bites To Eat Them.

Have you ever watched nuts being graded? It's interesting.

Ours are graded by a screening process. Between the beginning and end of the grading line are screens with twelve different size holes for the nuts to fall through. As the nuts move along, they drop through, into the appropriate bin for their size.

-3-

As I mentioned before, the nuts we sell by mail are the largest sizes only -- they can only fall through the biggest holes. "Premium Grade" is the official term for nutmeats this big, and they just don't come any bigger.

In fact, some of our nuts are so big, you cannot politely eat them in one bite.

That's especially true of our cashews. I call them our "two-bite Cashews" because they're about twice as big as a regular cashew.

But it's also true of our luscious pecans and our crunchy Brazil nuts.

We sell most types of premium-quality nuts, your choice of either salted or unsalted, including ...

   . Brazil nuts from (of course) Brazil. We've removed the super-hard shell and bring you just the mammoth delicious kernel.

   . Cashews from Africa, India and Brazil. Did you know that a single cashew nut grows at the base of a cashew apple (which doesn't look like an apple, it looks like a pear)? You get just one nut per cashew apple because it's the seed for the next crop. (They're shelled by hand for us in India.)

   . Pecans from our own United States. Is there anything better than the fresh, sweet meat of a giant pecan? (Or any prettier nut to decorate some fresh-baked brownies?)

   . Filberts from Turkey. A little-known nut with a distinctive flavor many nut-lovers enjoy.

   . Pistachios from Turkey and California. Half the fun of a pistachio is shelling it yourself (the other half is its delicious taste).

   . Macadamia nuts from Hawaii. So rich you think you're eating candy.

And there's a lot more still. I hope you'll examine the enclosed brochure to find the hand-selected nut meats and fruit-nut blends you prefer.

No matter which products you choose, you can be absolutely sure they're fresh, because the nuts are immediately refrigerated after harvesting and rush-ed to our packing plants for sorting, shelling, grading and roasting. Some are lightly salted, others left unsalted, but all are quickly packed and sealed for guaranteed-fresh delivery to you.

Once you've decided which you want, you can either order by mail, using the enclosed order form, or by phone by calling our toll-free number. Simply call 1-800-323-9754 and order our COUNTY FAIR Premium Grade nut meats of your choice.

To make it easy for you to order direct, we're pleased to offer you a choice of major credit cards -- MasterCard, Visa, American Express, and Diner's Club -- or, if you prefer, send us a check or money order.

(over, please)

-4-

We'll rush your order to you quickly (please allow additional time for Hawaii, Alaska, Canada, APO and FPO deliveries) so you can begin enjoying the nuts right away.

Of course, for special occasions and holidays, I probably don't even have to tell you what an excellent gift these make. An especially nice present is our Deluxe Mix Nut Tin which contains the best of everything we make. It's a real bargain at only $10.95.

If you are giving our nuts as a gift, just let us know and we'll be happy to enclose a handwritten gift card with your own personal message.

But whichever you're considering -- nuts for yourself or a gift for some-one else -- I hope you've decided to see for yourself that we give our custom-ers a little more than they pay for.

However, if you're still not sure, let me make a suggestion. Order the nuts you think you'd enjoy most. Taste-test them yourself, in your own home. If you're not completely delighted, simply take advantage of our money-back guarantee and ask for a refund. There's absolutely no risk at all -- except that you're likely to become "addicted" to our nuts and keep coming back for more.

Because once you taste our nuts, I'm confident you'll agree that we are giving you the best nuts that can be found anywhere -- at very reasonable prices.

And to make our offer even more appealing, I'll throw in a free gift when you try our nuts. Send in your order and I'll send you a free Taster Box of our giant "two-bite cashews." It's another small way for us to give you a little more than you pay for.

So please order now and see for yourself. You won't be disappointed. (That's our fourth guarantee.)

Sincerely,

Joseph C. Graziano, Sr.
President

P.S. Dad's still alive and well, and down here every day making sure I do <u>my</u> job right. He told me to tell you that if you ever have any problems, to let <u>him</u> know. He'll make sure you're satisfied!

541001-L

Yeck Brothers Company "Grandfather's Watch" Letter

Bob Hutchings of IBM submitted his favorite letter, which — like so many others involved in direct mail — turned out to be written by John Yeck.

It's pretty hard to beat a letter with as much charm as this masterpiece.

Yeck Brothers Company

2222 Arbor Boulevard
P.O. Box 225
Dayton, Ohio 45401
513/294-4000

October 31, 1978

Mr. R. H. Hutchings
Marketing Development
Program Manager
Office Products Division
IBM
Parson's Pond Drive
Franklin Lakes, New Jersey 07417

Dear Bob:

I remember two things about my grandfather. One was his smile and the other was his pocket watch.

I don't know which he valued most.

"A smile," he once told me, "can bring you every important thing in the world. Love and friendship. Kindness and joy. And even forgiveness."

So he always smiled.

"And time," he'd say, pulling out his pocket watch, "is the greatest gift of all because each new minute is another chance to do something better."

So he valued time and taught me to value it, too.

That's why I'm writing.

When I was in your office, I could see you had a smile of your own ... and one that I'm sure will get you through. But I didn't see a pocket watch so I thought I'd send you one.

It might help you remember that in your effort to do things better for IBM, there's a company in Dayton that would like to help.

As much and as soon as we can.

Sincerely,

Vic Marino
Senior Vice President
Client Services

VM/ch
encl.

SECTION VII

INQUIRY AND LEAD-GETTING LETTERS

Most of the letters discussed so far have concentrated on getting a "final" action through the mails. However, there is another category of direct mail letters that is equally important — those seeking inquiries or leads for sales personnel.

Frequently, a whole series of mailings is involved. There is not only the letter to obtain the inquiry or lead, but also letters to answer the inquiry, lay additional groundwork for a sales call, and provide follow-through.

Like the business-to-business letters in the preceding section, many inquiry and lead-getting programs go to select audiences and thus are often not known to the broad direct mail community. The examples shown here, however, are representative of the letters that are designed to accomplish these important tasks.

AT&T INFORMATION SYSTEMS "MERLIN LEAD-GETTING" LETTER

The primary objective of most direct mail is to make a sale. However, reaching this objective quite often starts with a letter designed to solicit inquiries — getting the "prospects" among a list of "suspects" to raise their hands and do something to identify themselves.

The letter shown here is a typical inquiry solicitation letter — not a classic letter, but an excellent example of laying out the facts and then asking those interested to identify themselves. It starts out by identifying the audience for which it is intended — small businesses:

> Meet the MERLIN™ Communications System. The first self-programmable phone system designed and manufactured by AT&T expressly for small businesses like yours.

Then, in crisp, straightforward language, it identifies the benefits of the product:

> The MERLIN System is so simple, anyone can take calls. Put them on hold. And transfer them with just a touch. It doesn't require an operator. Or a receptionist. Or a secretary.

> The MERLIN System has built-in smarts. Like one-button dialing of your important numbers. It provides an intercom, pages, sets up conference calls and even remembers busy numbers — so you can redial them with one touch.

After laying out the benefits, it asks those interested to take a first logical step:

> To learn more about the MERLIN Communications System please read the enclosed brochure. Then call the specialists at the Small Business Connection of AT&T Information Systems. They'll answer all your questions. The number is 1-800-247-7000 Ext. 124.

AT&T
Information Systems

Dear Customer,

Meet the MERLIN™ Communications System. The first <u>self-programmable</u> phone system designed and manufactured by AT&T expressly for small businesses like yours.

> We believe it is absolutely the finest, smartest phone system available to small businesses, today.

The MERLIN System is so simple, anyone can take calls. Put them on hold. And transfer them with just a touch. It doesn't require an operator. Or a receptionist. Or a secretary.

The MERLIN System has built-in smarts. Like one-button dialing of your important numbers. It provides an intercom, pages, sets up conference calls and even remembers busy numbers--so you can redial them with one touch.

The MERLIN System has big business system features that can save time and increase productivity. And each phone can easily be custom programmed or reprogrammed to meet individual needs.

When you want to upgrade the System with additional capabilities, just insert a cartridge into the control unit. Nothing could be easier.

Phones can be moved or shifted easily anywhere within the System. And the MERLIN System can grow as your business grows because the entire System is modular. When you need an additional phone--just plug it in.

> The MERLIN System is made to exacting standards.

No other system offers you the same features, the same easy flexibility and the same simple self-programmability. And no other company builds a business phone system like AT&T.

> <u>And yet, AT&T's MERLIN System is surprisingly affordable.</u>

No other communications company has our expertise. Or our more than 100 years of experience. Or a service force as dedicated to your business as ours.

To learn more about the MERLIN Communications System please read the enclosed brochure. Then call the specialists at the Small Business Connection of AT&T Information Systems. They'll answer all your questions. The number is 1 800 247-7000 Ext. 124.

Before you make a decision on business phones, get acquainted with the MERLIN System.

AT&T Information Systems. When you've got to be right.

Yours truly,

Robert Hansen
Sales Manager

P.S. If you're planning a business move or expansion in the near future--you can reserve a MERLIN System now. And have it designed to fit your specific needs--so it's ready when you're ready. Call and ask how you can reserve the MERLIN System.

R. R. DONNELLEY & SONS COMPANY "FOUR-STEP LEAD-GETTING" LETTER

There are many times when the initial lead produced by a direct mail program needs further qualification before assigning it to a salesperson for follow-up. An outstanding "Verified Inquiry Program" developed years ago by General Electric is described in detail in Dartnell's *Direct Mail & Mail Order Handbook*. A key element in this effective program is the use of a "May we help your further?" form, which accompanies literature sent in response to initial inquiries. It is, in reality, a questionnaire that asks recipients some specific questions (the answers indicate the degree of interest in a specific product). George M. Robertson explained its role:

> ■ The idea behind the questionnaire is to determine whether the respondent's interest is casual or serious. If he is not in the market now, or if he wanted the publication for information only, the chances are pretty good he will not reply. If, on the other hand, he is serious and ready to do business, he will either call our sales office or take the time and effort to answer the questions and, presumably, we will have a lead on a bona fide prospect.

I adapted General Electric's idea several times with considerable success. The lead-getting program shown here started with a simple letter. It began:

> How long has it been since you
> took a good, hard look at the
> tools your salesmen are using?
>
> Perhaps you already have every possible sales aid . . . and your
> salesmen are using these tools efficiently to produce ever-increasing
> business for your company.
>
> But if you're like most of the business executives we've met, chances
> are you're continually looking for new ways to improve the output of
> your sales force.

The letter also offered a booklet, "Getting More Leads for Your Salesmen."

A second mailing package went to the same list a month later and offered a portfolio of "Case Studies in Profitable Printing." The letter in that package began:

> We'd like to send you a FREE portfolio
> filled with ideas on how you can increase
> the value of your promotional material.

When replies from each mailing were received, the booklet or portfolio was sent immediately, along with this additional offer:

> To give you a better idea of the type of printing we do — and a
> chance to inspect the quality of our work firsthand — we'd be most
> happy to prepare a portfolio of samples of pieces we've printed for
> companies like yours.

> If you would appreciate having such a portfolio, just fill in the enclosed reply card, checking the types of printed material in which you have special interest. We'll prepare a portfolio especially for you and see that you get it promptly. There's no obligation, of course.

As soon as a response was received, a salesperson was assigned to the account and personally delivered the requested samples. If no response was forthcoming, a carbon copy was sent 30 days later, accompanied by this note:

> Perhaps the attached letter was overlooked when you received the booklet, "Getting More Leads for Your Salesmen," which we sent you last month.
>
> We would appreciate the opportunity to prepare a special sample portfolio for you. I'm enclosing another reply card with this note. If you'd like the sample portfolio, please fill in the card and mail it to me.

The Lakeside Press
Lett **R·R·DONNELLEY & SONS COMPANY**

CORPORATE HEADQUARTERS

2223 SOUTH PARK WAY · CHICAGO, ILLINOIS 60616

TELEPHONE 431-8000 (*Area Code* 312)

How long has it been since you
took a good, hard look at the
tools your salesmen are using?

Perhaps you already have every possible sales aid . . . and your
salesmen are using these tools efficiently to produce ever increasing business for your company.

But if you're like most of the business executives we've met,
chances are you're continually looking for new ways to improve
the output of your sales force.

We'd like to offer you some helpful ideas. They're featured in
a handy booklet called "Getting More Leads for Your Salesmen."
The enclosed folder tells the background of this helpful booklet.

To receive the copy we've reserved for you, just fill out the
enclosed postage-paid reply card and drop it in the mail. We'll
see that your copy of "Getting More Leads for Your Salesmen" is
on its way to you by return mail.

We'll be looking forward to hearing from you.

Sincerely yours,

R. R. DONNELLEY & SONS COMPANY

Sales Manager

C. C. Bronson:fb

Letter #2 (Printed)

We'd like to send you a FREE portfolio filled with ideas on how you can increase the value of your promotional material.

Regardless of how you sell your products or services -- across the counter, through the mails, in the home or through sales calls to plants and offices -- modern marketing programs call for use of printed promotional material.

But to achieve the best results calls for printed pieces with built-in ability to accomplish specific objectives. This doesn't always mean spending more money for these pieces. More often it's just a matter of utilizing the skills of experienced designers, merchandising men and craftsmen.

For nearly a century, Donnelley's has been helping business executives just like yourself produce printed material with that extra value which comes through the experience of men who have specialized know-how. Sometimes the job involves improvement of existing pieces which haven't been doing as well as anticipated. Other times, the job requires planning, designing and production of completely new printed sales tools.

We've just produced an informative portfolio containing ten specific case studies telling how the unique combination of skills and experience found in the Donnelley organization has helped businesses -- large, middling and small -- achieve dramatic results. Among these interesting case studies are bound to be at least one or two which will offer ideas you can apply to your own marketing or communications needs.

The enclosed folder describes the background of this helpful portfolio, "Case Studies in Profitable Printing." We'd be happy to send you a copy. All you need do is fill out the enclosed postage-paid reply card and drop it in the mail. We'll see that your portfolio is sent promptly. There's no obligation, of course.

We'll be looking forward to hearing from you.

Sincerely yours,

R. R. DONNELLEY & SONS COMPANY

Sales Manager

C. C. Bronson:fb

Letter #3 (Autotyped)

Mr. John J. Jones, President
Jones Manufacturing Company
1234 Jones Avenue
Chicago 77, Illinois

Many thanks, Mr. Jones . . .

. . . for your interest in our booklet, "Getting More Leads for Your Salesmen."
The copy you requested is enclosed. We hope you will find several ideas in it
which will be useful in your own marketing program.

While this booklet is close at hand, we'd like to suggest you take a look at
the copy on pages 11 and 12, which tells something of the services available
to you at R. R. Donnelley & Sons Company.

Although the Donnelley plants along the lakefront have been a familiar landmark for many years, quite a few of our Chicago neighbors have never had an
opportunity to know how our organization can serve them personally.

We take pride in the fact that we have extensive facilities which are capable
of handling every type of printed material, regardless of the quantity required.
Interestingly enough, while Donnelley's serves many of the largest printing
buyers in the country, we serve even more companies with limited printing
budgets. Regardless of your printing needs, we would like to help you.

To give you a better idea of the type of printing we do -- and a chance to
inspect the quality of our work at firsthand, we'd be most happy to prepare
a portfolio of the samples of pieces we've printed for companies like yours.

If you would appreciate such a portfolio, just fill in the enclosed reply card,
checking the types of printed material in which you have special interest.
We'll prepare a portfolio especially for you and see that you get it promptly.
There's no obligation, of course.

We'll look forward to hearing from you.

                                    Sincerely yours,

                                    R. R. DONNELLEY & SONS COMPANY

                                    Sales Manager

C. C. Bronson:fb

WE'RE mighty proud of the fine printing we do for our customers and enjoy every opportunity to display it to others who appreciate quality and value. In recent months, we've turned out some especially interesting examples of printed pieces which have helped companies like yours solve specific marketing and communications problems.

We'd consider it a privilege to present you with a portfolio of samples of typical Donnelley-printed pieces. Perhaps they will suggest ideas which you can adapt to your company's needs.

All you need do is tell us (on the attached reply card) the types of printed pieces in which you're interested. Then just drop the postage-paid card in the mail and we'll see that you receive a specially prepared portfolio containing the samples you've requested. No obligation to you, of course.

- -

BY ALL MEANS . . .

send me a portfolio showing samples of the following types of quality printing you've produced for companies like ours:

Please Check One or More:

☐ Anniversary Books & Booklets

☐ Annual Reports

☐ Catalogs

☐ Direct Mail Pieces

☐ Handbooks & Instruction Manuals

☐ Company Publications

☐ Labels

☐ Magazine Inserts

☐ Product Literature

☐ Public Relations Literature

POSITION_____

NAME_____

COMPANY_____

ADDRESS_____

CITY_____ ZONE_____ STATE_____

We produce the following products (or services): _____

_____

Our annual sales volume is approximately: $_____

(This information will enable us to tailor our selection of samples to your own printing requirements.)

WESTINGHOUSE SECURITY SYSTEMS "CONSUMER LEAD-GETTING" PROGRAM

Far too many lead-generating programs developed for consumer markets show little imagination. The insurance industry, for example, has been using the same approach to get leads for so long it's not surprising mail order companies (with their highly imaginative mailings) have grabbed such a big share of the insurance business. How many times have you received this offer: "Send me your birth date and I'll give you a road atlas" (or some other common premium)?

The lead-generating direct mail program I developed for Westinghouse Security Systems was adapted from the techniques used by mail order insurance companies. The basic letter, targeted at local homeowners, began:

> I'd like to send you a valuable checklist. It's yours without obligation and will be sent by return mail.
>
> While you don't have to spend a penny to get this special Westinghouse checklist, it could prove priceless. It provides a detailed guide to things to do to protect you, your family, your home and your most valuable possessions from burglary, fire and other emergencies.

When the checklist was requested, it was sent along with a personalized letter with a further offer:

> If you'd like to know more about how a Westinghouse Home Security System can protect you, your family, your home and your valued possessions, I'd be pleased to have one of our security specialists prepare a special analysis for you.
>
> This is a free service we offer and there is no obligation on your part other than to provide the information the specialist will need to make sure the custom tailored system he or she recommends will meet your specific requirements.

A copy of this letter was sent to non-respondents with this note:

> I hope the security checklist booklet we sent recently was of special interest to you and your family.
>
> We'd still like to provide the professional security analysis of your home which I offered in my letter which accompanied the checklist booklet.
>
> I'm enclosing a copy of my letter and another postage-paid reply card you can use to request your free security analysis.
>
> This is a free service and I hope you'll take advantage of it soon.

Mr. John T. Jones
1234 Downtown Street
Anytown, State 00000

Dear Mr. Jones:

I'd like to send you a valuable checklist. It's yours without obligation and will be sent by return mail.

While you don't have to spend a penny to get this special Westinghouse checklist, it could prove priceless. It provides a detailed guide to things to do to protect you, your family, your home and your most valuable possessions from burglars, fire and other emergencies.

I won't try to disguise the fact that Westinghouse has a special interest in encouraging concerned homeowners like yourself to become more aware of the importance of home security -- that's the business of my division. But our concern is more than just selling equipment and installing security systems.

That's why we've prepared our special security checklist. It doesn't mention one word about our products or services. But we know that once many homeowners become more security conscious they're likely to consider some of the products we manufacture, install and service.

Your copy of this checklist is awaiting your request. Just return the enclosed postage-paid card and your checklist will be mailed to you promptly.

Sincerely,

Name
Title

Kilbourn Inc.

Westinghouse Security Systems

Mr. John J. Jones
1234 Downtown Street
Anytown, State 00000

Dear Mr. Jones:

Here's the Westinghouse Security Checklist you requested. It isn't big and complicated, but the information it contains can be priceless.

I'd like to urge you to not only study the suggestions it offers, but discuss them with the entire Jones family. A few minutes spent in planning today is one of the best investments you can make and, if my personal experience is typical, I'm sure you'll appreciate the peace of mind such a family conference will bring.

Even though I'm in the security business, I've found every member of my family feels a new-found confidence ever time we run down our checklist and hold our regularly scheduled fire drills.

While this Checklist doesn't mention the services offered by Westinghouse Security Systems, I hope you'll permit me the liberty of telling you a bit about what we've done to develop a total security package for concerned homeowners like yourself in the Anytown area.

We don't have any packaged security plan to offer. We feel every home and every family is unique and deserves a system tailored to its specific needs. What we have done is to utilize Westinghouse leadership in Space Age technology and wide experience in military, industrial and commercial security systems to create modules which can be linked together to provide a total security package for any home.

And we've added one other special feature -- the human element -- which is too often overlooked in less advanced home security systems.

Right now, a staff of highly trained security specialists are monitoring special Space Age control panels in a Westinghouse Communications Center not far from your home in Anytown. These panels are linked to the homes of your Philadelphia area neighbors who are already protected by a Westinghouse Home Security System.

When an emergency occurs, a coded message is instantly transmitted to the Communications Center and a skilled specialist personally summons whatever aid is required -- no tape-recorded messages or possibly confusing signals, but live _personal_ response to emergencies 24 hours every day.

And you don't have to count on just the ever-watchful automatic sensing devices of a Westinghouse Home Security System which are constantly alert whether or not anyone is at home. You can speak directly to the specialist at the Communications Center anytime, day or night, by simply pushing a special button on a control panel in your home.

All in all, we feel we have a total security system which can be custom tailored to protect any home against the threats of burglary, fire, accidents and other emergencies.

Those words, "custom tailored," are most important.
And that's a job for a security specialist.

We don't expect any homeonwer to be a security specialist. That's why we have a staff of highly trained security experts -- not just salesmen, but men and women who have received special training and are continually updated on the very latest security techniques and equipment. We make sure they have the technical knowledge to not only recommend protection devices but to fully analyze each homeowner's specific requirements and prepare a total plan which is not only complete but which combines advanced techniques to provide a maximum security system for a minimum investment.

If you'd like to know more about how a Westinghouse Home Security System can protect you, your family, your home and your valued posssessions, I'd be pleased to have one of our security specialists prepare a special analysis for you.

<u>This is a free service we offer and there is no obligation on your part</u> other than to provide the information the specialist will need to make sure the custom tailored system he or she recommends will meet your specific requirements.

I'm enclosing a postage-paid request card for your use. I'll see that it gets to a Westinghouse security specialist who is familiar with the existing protection services and any special requirements which may be unique to your area. He or she will then call to arrange an appointment at a time most convenient for you.

Once again I want to assure you there is no obligation. Meanwhile, I hope you'll study the enclosed Westinghouse Security Checklist and take the first steps to protect your family against the ever present threats of fire and burglary.

Sincerely,

Name
Title

TROY-BILT "INQUIRY ANSWERING" LETTER

One of the greatest direct marketing success stories is Garden Way Manufacturing Company. When they first started out, most people were highly skeptical they could sell a complicated piece of garden machinery — costing as much as $1,000 — without direct person-to-person contact. But thanks to a highly effective direct mail program, they not only sold their Troy-Bilt rototillers through the mail, but many other products as well.

The program starts with an offer for information about the Troy-Bilt. Garden Way uses a wide variety of promotion vehicles to make this offer including magazine ads, postcard decks, bind-ins, etc. Then, when inquiries are received, a classic direct mail inquiry answering package is sent.

The first class envelope has this message:

> Here is the Important News Report on
>
> Gardening Machines You Requested
>
> PLEASE OPEN IMMEDIATELY UPON RECEIPT

The letter inside begins:

> Thank you for your interest in our TROY-BILT Roto Tiller-Power Composters . . . and for requesting a copy of our important News Report enclosed.
>
> It should answer any questions you have about most other gardening machines as compared to all our 1978 TROY-BILT Roto Tiller models.

Very quickly, the letter gets into a special offer for immediate response:

> One reason for this great rush is, of course, our Direct-from-Factory OFF-SEASON SAVINGS Plan in effect right now through the end of March. You can save at least $60.00 or more off the current list price of all Troy-Bilt models . . .

Garden Way Manufacturing Company, Inc.
102nd Street & Ninth Avenue
Troy, New York 12180
Telephone: 518-235-6010

Dear Gardening Friend,

Thank you for your interest in our TROY-BILT Roto Tiller-Power Composters...and for requesting a copy of our important New Report enclosed.

It should answer any questions you have about most other gardening machines as compared to all our 1978 TROY-BILT Roto Tiller models.

If after reading through this material, you find you still have questions, please feel free to write or call me TOLL FREE at

1-800-833-6990.

I, or one of the folks who works with me, can advise you on most every type of gardening machine available...and, we will do our best to see that you are well-equipped for the coming gardening season.

Meanwhile...here at the Tiller Factory the big rush of Spring orders has already begun. We're not sure why, but it seems this year more than ever before, serious gardeners everywhere are deciding to own Troy-Bilts. Already we are sold out through the beginning of next month, and orders are still coming in faster than we can fill them.

One reason for this great rush is, of course, our Direct-from-Factory OFF-SEASON SAVINGS Plan in effect right now through the end of March. You can save at least $60.00 or more off the current list price of all Troy-Bilt models -- plus an additional 10% off any attachments ordered with your Tiller.

Then, starting April 1st and on through May and

June, there are no discounts.

So, in order to receive your Tiller
in time for groundbreaking and planting
this Spring...and at considerable
savings off the current list price
(for exactly how much, please see
my chart enclosed)...

You must mail or phone your order to
me no later than Midnight, March 31st.

Also starting April 1st, prices of all Troy-Bilt
"Horse" models will go up by as much as $32.00 -- about
5%.

As you know, last year was another bad one for
inflation. Though beef and a few other things went down,
overall the price of a marketbasket full of groceries
(especially fresh vegetables and fruits) continued to
climb.

And then last summer much the same thing happened
with many of the raw materials and parts that go into
making our Troy-Bilts. First, engines went up 6%...then
cast iron up 7%...sheet metal 5%...and, on it went.

So, though we have already held off far longer than
recommended by our accountants, we now have no choice but
to raise prices on all Troy-Bilt "Horse" models (which
being larger, have more cast iron, more costly engines,
etc. than our smaller "Pony") just to keep up with
inflation.

That's why it's so very important -- doubly important
(because of the price rise and the OFF-SEASON SAVINGS now
in effect) -- that if you are planning on getting a
Troy-Bilt at all during the coming gardening season, you
let me know before the March 31st deadline.

As Little As 20% Deposit Guarantees Your ''Double Savings'' [as much as $105.60]...Plus, Delivery in Time for Gardening and Planting This Spring!

You can, if you wish, send payment in full by check
or money order, or charge your Tiller to your VISA/Bank-
Americard, Chargex, or Master Charge card.

Or, if you prefer, you need enclose only 20% deposit with your order, and then pay the balance shortly before delivery (check or charge apply here, too). Whichever way you decide will be "okay" with us.

So, please do -- quickly -- look through the enclosed information and Report. You'll find a complete explanation of our unique no-time-limit promise to you...our low-cost service...and why we say you're even _more_ important to us _after_ the sale than before. You'll be able to decide soon _enough_ whether one of our much different (and, we believe, _better_) TROY-BILT gardening machines is right for you.

Over 300,000 -- better than 80% -- of all rear-end tillers owned in America are now TROY-BILTS...So, now, won't you let us build one for you?

Thank you very much...
and I hope to hear from you
soon.

Sincerely,

Dean Leith, Jr.

Dean Leith, Jr., Sales Manager for
Troy-Bilt Roto Tiller-Power Composters
102nd Street and Ninth Ave., Troy, N.Y.

P.S. Please remember —

By ordering now — before the March 31st "Double Deadline" — you'll save...

• Up to $32.00 off the new list prices that take effect on April 1st.

• At least $64.50 per machine while our 10% Off-Season Savings are still in effect.

• A total _double savings_ of as much as $105.60 (depending on which model you choose) — if you can decide and let me know before the March 31st deadline. D.L.

GENERAL TELEPHONE COMPANY OF ILLINOIS "CARBON COPY" LETTER AND MEMO

For many years, direct marketers have known carbon copy follow-ups — particularly personalized letters — can produce profitable response. The usual rule of thumb has been to expect the follow-up to pull about 80% of the response generated by the original letter. Imagine my surprise when the carbon copy follow-up of a letter I had written to secure sales leads for General Telephone Company of Illinois pulled over 500% more response than the original mailing.

The mailing package introduced a new security system that could be connected to existing telephone lines. The letter began:

> You may not realize it, but you already have half of a security system to protect your home against such hazards as fire, smoke and burglary.
>
> It's your telephone.
>
> But a telephone by itself only provides protection when there's someone handy to make a call. That's why General Telephone has devoted a lot of effort to develop total security systems for homes and businesses — systems which function whether or not there is someone to dial the phone when an emergency happens.

The role of the letter was to develop sales leads. So copy explained:

> Because we know each home is different, we don't offer any standard security "package." Instead, each Phone Alarm System is individually designed to provide the exact types of protection you require, where you require it.
>
> In fact, we have a variety of different devices to detect movement, smoke, heat, changes in temperature, etc. Some are relatively simple, others highly complicated. But each has been selected after careful study because we've found it is the best of its kind for a given situation.
>
> But we don't expect you to know which devices best fit your needs. That's a job for specialists. And we have specialists on our staff to fully analyze your needs and create the best possible security system for you.

Then came the "unique selling proposition":

> There are, of course, lots of different security devices and systems on the market. But we honestly feel we have something extra to offer — the added security you'll have in knowing your system is maintained by always-available local telephone service personnel who have been specially trained to keep your system in top working order.

The original mailing, with individually typewritten address and salutation fill-ins, pulled a 1.3% response in two test markets. Careful records were kept and all those who failed to respond to the original mailing received a carbon copy follow-up two weeks later. This follow-up pulled a 7% response. When the first letter arrived, the majority of recipients had no idea such a service was available and weren't ready to respond. But, after two weeks to think about it — and possibly relate the service to various news reports about fires and burglaries they had heard during that time — they were now ready.

In lead-producing mailings, it's important to pay attention to how many sales conversions result. This mailing was particularly successful in sales as well as responses. Previously, GTE personnel making sales calls without a direct mail-generated lead closed at approximately a 10% rate. With the leads generated by the mailing program, sales rose to 30%.

GTE
GENERAL TELEPHONE COMPANY OF ILLINOIS

February 22, 1977

Mr. Jack Hasten
615 North 10th
Monmouth, IL 61462

Dear Mr. Hasten:

You may not realize it, but you already have half of a security system to protect your home against such hazards as fire, smoke and burglary.

It's your telephone.

But a telephone by itself only provides protection when there's someone handy
to make a call. That's why General Telephone has devoted a lot of effort to
develop total security systems for homes and businesses -- systems which function whether or not there is someone to dial the phone when an emergency happens.

We call this our Phone Alarm System.

While each system is individually tailored to the specific needs of a home or
business, the heart of the Phone Alarm System is an automatic telephone alarm
dialer. This little machine, which can be attached to your existing phone
lines, automatically calls the police, fire department, a neighbor or any other
telephone numbers that fit your needs.

The Phone Alarm System can also provide many other important services to help
you protect your home -- the specific services you need. In some cases, you
may prefer that it silently dial the police or a neighbor; in others, you may
want it to trigger a loud alarm to alert everyone that some emergency has
occurred.

That's one of the unique features of a General Telephone security system -- it
is tailored to fit your specific needs. We've analyzed all of the security
devices available and identified those most efficient for each task.

Because we know each home is different, we don't offer any standard security
"package." Instead, each Phone Alarm System is individually designed to provide the exact types of protection you require, where you require it.

In fact, we have a variety of different devices to detect movement, smoke, heat,
changes in temperature, etc. Some are relatively simple, others highly com-

- 2 -

plicated. But each has been selected after careful study because we've found it is the best of its kind for a given situation.

We don't expect you to know which devices best fit your needs. That's a job for specialists. And we have specialists on our staff to fully analyze your needs and create the best possible security system for you.

There are, of course, lots of different security devices and systems on the market. But we honestly feel we have something extra to offer -- the added security you'll have in knowing your system is maintained by always-available local telephone service personnel who have been specially trained to keep your system in top working order.

If you'll call Mrs. Rashid toll-free at 800-322-3596, she'll arrange to have one of our security specialists survey your requirements at a time most con- venient for you. Or, if you prefer, you can just return the enclosed postcard and we'll call you to arrange an appointment.

There's no obligation on your part. We offer this complete analysis of your requirements and the preparation of a suggested security plan as one of our important public services.

We'll look forward to serving you.

Sincerely,

ED M. COUGHLIN
Area Sales Manager

EMC MS
Enclosures

CHAMPION "HERE IT IS A SECOND TIME" LETTER

I have no idea who wrote it, but one of the most unusual and effective follow-up letters ever to come across my desk arrived some years ago from Champion Printing Company in Ross, Ohio.

The envelope copy read:

> You asked for it.
>
> Here it is a second time.

Enclosed was a second copy of Champion's catalog with this lead:

> DID YOU MISS IT THE FIRST TIME BY?
>
> It's just possible that you may have missed Champion's printing/pricer/handbook. You requested it. We sent one. We're enclosing another. Just in case the original somehow went astray.

Most often, a follow-up catalog is mailed without any accompanying message at all. That's what makes this great mailing so special. Here's an idea I recommend to anyone sending a follow-up to an inquiry.

box 148 / ross, ohio 45061 / ac 513 – 863-2114

DID YOU MISS IT THE FIRST TIME BY?

It's just possible that you may have missed Champion's printing/pricer/handbook.
You requested it. We sent one. We're enclosing another.
Just in case the original somehow went astray.

Speaking of that — you may be interested in knowing that low prices and
solid, commercial quality is not the whole story at Champion.
Orders rarely go astray. Jobs are processed and shipped promptly without a hitch.
It's one thing to be low-priced. We are.
It's one thing to do quality work. We do.
It's another to run an efficient operation where promptness counts.
That's us, too.

We invite you to peruse our pricer and try us out. We are now dealing with
hundreds of top companies throughout the U.S.A. If we're not
already serving you, we'd like to.

Cordially,

John Hrebenyar
President

JH:sm

SECTION VIII

RETAIL AND SERVICE LETTERS

All across America, retailers and service organizations regularly use direct mail to build store traffic, cement customer relations, and perform a host of other functions. Often, when compared to the work done for direct marketers, the letters used for local retail and service organizations are somewhat amateurish. But that's not always bad. Since direct mail is "the personal medium," the down home quality of such letters has special appeal.

Locating representative examples of retail and service letters is a difficult task. Fortunately, I've been saving examples over the years and have drawn from this file in addition to turning to a number of friends who have written such letters to supplement what I had collected. I've also included some outstanding letters used on a national basis to promote various types of services.

COMMUNITY FEDERAL SAVINGS "WHAM" LETTER

Along with his many great consumer mail order letters, Herschell Gordon Lewis has written a classic for an entirely different type of client: a chain of local savings and loan associations. It's a letter with a "wham" — a handwritten word at the start of the letter. And, according to the client, that "wham" woke up some of their sleepiest depositors.

The subject was increasing mortgage loan payments to cover the ever-increasing cost of taxes — the lighthearted opening helped soften the blow.

The call-to-action makes it easy to respond:

> You needn't fill out a million papers to get this going. You can drop off the bottom portion of this letter next time you're in any of our offices; or you can mail it in the envelope I've enclosed; or you can phone us in Palm Beach County at 845-3200 and in Martin County at 283-5200. I do suggest you not wait too long, because much as we all dislike tax bills, they have to be paid, and delays cause penalties making the tax bite even greater.

COMMUNITY
FEDERAL
SAVINGS
and LOAN ASSOCIATION
OF THE PALM BEACHES

POST OFFICE DRAWER 10673 RIVIERA BEACH, FLORIDA 33404-1673

We can't make your property taxes go away...
but we can help you avoid the nasty October surprise.

Dear Homeowner:

Wham !!

That's the sound of a taxpayer being hit between the eyes with the annual property tax bill.

This is the time of year when we dig deep into our pockets to pay the tax. Even as we pay it, we know we'll get another one next year --- probably even higher. Wham!

But this year's blow can be cushioned, and next year's won't even be felt, if you put us to work for you. We'll lend you the money for this year's taxes and set up a monthly escrow program for next year's. No problem, because your mortgage loan is with us.

Here's how it works:

1.   You call us or drop in. If you already have your tax bill, tell us the amount; if you don't have it yet, we'll prearrange a loan so the money will be there when the bill comes in.

2.   For this year's tax, there'll be a small increase in your payments, to cover the new loan.

3.   For next year's tax, you won't have to worry about suddenly having to come up with a big lump sum, because you'll already have provided for the tax with our easy monthly escrow program. When you get your tax bill, it already will have been paid.

You needn't fill out a million papers to get this going. You can drop off the bottom portion of this letter next time you're in any of our offices; or you can mail it in the envelope I've enclosed; or you can phone us in Palm Beach County at 845-3200 and in Martin County at 283-5200. I do suggest you not wait too long, because much as we all dislike tax bills, they have to be paid, and delays cause penalties making the tax bite even greater.

I'm delighted to be able to offer you this service. I hope you'll take advantage of it and end forever the annual "Wham!" of your property tax bill.

Sincerely,

Pat J. Snow, Jr.
Senior Vice President

P.S.   Once Community Federal is handling your tax bill, you'll be able to cover most annual increases by simply adjusting <u>next</u> year's amount. We're <u>your</u> savings and loan and we intend to prove it every day!

THE ALLEY DELI "FREE LUNCH" LETTER

Murray Raphel is not a prophet without honor in his own country. His classic copy works just as well in Atlantic City as it does in Melbourne. For example, a letter he created for a newly-opened restaurant was sent to 120 VIPs in the area near the new restaurant. More than 100 of the recipients accepted the free lunch offered, and more than half of them ordered additional lunches at the same time. Within a week, about 75 of the recipients came to the restaurant and most of them are now steady customers.

The restaurant owner, Norman Gordon, comments: "It would have taken me six months to bring in the kind of business direct mail brought me in six days. And I couldn't afford to wait six months."

the alley deli

Gordon's Alley. Atlantic City, N.J.
Established 1984. Proprietor: Norman Gordon
Take out & delivery service: 345-1060

August 15, 1984

Richard Squires
County Executive
1125 Atlantic Avenue
Atlantic City, NJ 08401

WHOEVER SAID THERE'S NO SUCH THING

AS A FREE LUNCH DIDN'T KNOW ABOUT THIS LETTER.

Good morning...

Let me introduce myself.

My name in Norman Gordon. I own the just-opened Alley Deli
in Gordon's Alley.

And if you're wondering whatever happened to the good old-fashioned
(and delicious) deli sandwich...it's back. Right here!

I've enclosed a copy of our menu. And I'm so proud of the excellent
quality and superb taste of everything we have, I would like
you to be a charter member of our TASTER'S CLUB.

It's a great organization. No dues. No meetings. All you have
to do is eat and enjoy.

Your only requirement is to accept one free lunch from me.

Whoever said there's no such thing as a free lunch?

There is.

For you.

I'll call you in a few days. Pick and choose what you want from
the enclosed menu. And I'll have it delivered to you a stort time
after you call.

Enjoy!

Norman Gordon

NORMAN GORDON

DICK'S SUPERMARKETS "CONGRATULATIONS" LETTERS

Murray Raphel shared this story about one of the most effective direct mail letter programs in American retailing:

■ In southwestern Wisconsin, Dick's Supermarkets are a dominant force in the food retail business. The president, William Brodbeck, says that a good deal of their growth and success is due to an effective, ongoing, results-oriented direct marketing program. New residents moving into any of the five communities with a Dick's Supermarket receive a personal letter from the manager of the store nearest them. The residents may have arrived from another part of the state or country, or they may be newly married.

The letters are identical except for the opening paragraph: "Congratulations on your recent marriage" for one and "Congratulations on your new home" for the other. Each letter explains the different services and departments in Dick's Supermarket. Each also contains six coupons for the recipient to use: two a week for the next 3 consecutive weeks. Each coupon has one item of food the customer receives free: a half gallon of ice cream, 5 pounds of potatoes, a pound of ground beef, a pound of butter. Rare is the individual who will throw away a coupon for free food. Nearly 95 percent of all the coupons Dick's mails are used.

At the middle of the third week, the president, Bill Brodbeck, writes his own letter. He thanks the people for shopping in their local Dick's store (he knows this from the coupons). He welcomes them to the Dick's family, and then he asks them for some help. He encloses a three-page questionnaire on the various departments in Dick's. For taking the time to fill out the questionnaire, Dick's includes six more coupons.

A new baby is born to the family. Again a letter is received from Bill Brodbeck addressed to the child, beginning, "I trust this is the first business letter you will receive." The letter welcomes the child to the world and to the community and encloses a $2 gift certificate that must be used for baby merchandise only: milk, formula, diapers, baby accessories. One year later, a card goes out to wish the child a happy birthday and offer a discount on his or her first birthday cake from the bakery department.

One year after the customers fill in the initial questionnaire, they receive another questionnaire from Brodbeck, saying, "A year has passed, and we want to know what you think about our store now." There is another coupon attached for them to use in exchange for taking the time to fill out the questionnaire.

BRODBECK ENTERPRISES, INC. • 255 McGREGOR PLAZA • PLATTEVILLE, WISCONSIN 53818 • (608) 348-2345

October 9, 1984

Mr. & Mrs. John Jones
220 West Pine Street
Platteville, WI 53818

Dear Mr. & Mrs. Jones:

We are delighted to hear the good news of your recent marriage!
All the friendly personnel at DICK'S would like to add their
congratulations to your many others.

To help you begin this new phase of your life, we'd like to extend
a special invitation to visit our home owned super market. To
briefly acquaint you with DICK'S:

1. Our meat department features meats with "T.V.T." --
   Top Value Trim, trimmed at our market, not your table. . .
   for proven better meat value. Choose between Dick's and
   Lean and Tender and U.S. Choice Beef.

2. If you like salads, and who doesn't, our produce department
   boasts the largest selection of fresh fruits and vegetables
   around.

3. The best of "what comes naturally in Wisconsin," plus
   a complete frozen food, fowl, and fish selection is
   available in our dairy-frozen food department.

4. Our grocery department features the BEST in fine foods
   at DICK'S everyday low prices. Please compare; you'll
   find them lowest.

5. Our bakery contains home baked goodness of unexcelled
   quality and variety at reasonable prices.

We would enjoy serving you and showing you that it pays to shop
DICK'S where reasonable prices are always in effect. Enclosed you
will find six coupons which we hope you will use during the next
three weeks. Please bring them with you to our store and ask for
me, for I would appreciate the opportunity of meeting you.

Sincerely,

Store Manager

Dick's SUPER MARKETS

United States Marine Corps "Yes-No" Letter

One of my early assignments as an officer in the Marine Corps was to write recruiting letters. I quickly learned how difficult that kind of direct mail selling can be. By the time I was assigned to recruiting duty, the Marine Corps had hired J. Walter Thompson agency to create its direct mail — and they've been doing an effective job of it for the past 35 years.

One of their most effective letters utilizes several tried-and-proved commercial mailing techniques. First of all, there's a screening lead:

> It's the tough choice — the Marine Corps. We're a small, elite branch
> of the Service. We aren't for everyone.

The letter offered a premium:

> We have a poster we'd like to send you. If the Marine spirit grabs
> your imagination, you won't want to miss getting a copy.

And it had an action device:

> Affix the yes stamp to the enclosed postage-paid reply card. Find out
> if you qualify to be one of the few, the proud, the Marines . . . today.

HEADQUARTERS • UNITED STATES MARINE CORPS • WASHINGTON, D.C. 20380

Dear Sir:

It's the tough choice -- the Marine Corps. We're a small, elite branch of the Service. We aren't for everyone.

Saying yes to the Marines means choosing hard training and challenge. It also means saying yes to some great benefits. These stamps are your way to say yes to the Marines. You just affix the stamp of your choice to the enclosed reply card. Because we're the tough choice, we'll understand if you say no.

But ... before you make the decision, take a good look at the Marine Corps. What makes it the elite Corps? What can you gain on the tough team?

The Marines offer you the same great benefits as the other military services: skill training for a better job -- in or out of the Marines; good salary; promotions; free housing and food; medical and dental care; a chance to go on to higher education. But there's something extra for you as a Marine.

That <u>extra</u> is a pride and spirit unique to the Corps. Our training is rugged. Our recruiting is selective. We want the best; we train you to be the best. We don't make a lot of promises. What we do promise is challenge and hard work ... plus the prestige and recognition that come with the uniform.

We have a poster we'd like to send you. If the Marine spirit grabs your imagination, you won't want to miss getting your copy.

We're getting a lot of requests for it. To make sure you receive your copy, let us hear from you soon. When we send you your booklet on

(over, please)

Marine Corps programs, we'll send your poster along. There's no obligation.
Affix the yes stamp to the enclosed postage-paid reply card. Find out
if you qualify to be one of the few, the proud, the Marines ... today.

Sincerely,

Jerry Hudak

Jerry Hudak
Major, U.S. Marine Corps

JH/wfp

P.S. Occasionally the lists we use contain names that are inappropriate
for our recruiting message. If this is so in your case, we
apologize, and ask for your understanding. Perhaps you would pass
this along to a friend who might be interested in what we offer.

The Few. The Proud. The Marines.

AIRCRAFT OWNERS AND PILOTS ASSOCIATION "FLYING START" LETTER

Recruiting new members is a never-ending challenge for associations, and direct mail is the method most often used. Usually there's lots to tell and a strong letter is often the best way to present the necessary information.

A good example of a new member recruitment letter is one written by Washington copywriter Ginny Daly for the Aircraft Owners and Pilots Association (AOPA). It starts off with this salutation:

> Since you're off to a flying start,
>
> . . . why not start off flying smart?

The letter introduces AOPA to the new pilot and quickly gets into the benefits of membership:

> As an AOPA member, you're entitled to Big Benefits that help you get the most out of your flying experience. We offer publications to keep you informed about the world of flying, new developments, trends, etc. We offer informational services covering personal assistance on everything from flight routings, both domestic and international, to questions about FARs and your general flight operatior. Plus, we offer insurance and many discount opportunities. Add it all up, and that's "flying smart" . . . being informed and well covered!

The letter continues for four pages and expands the benefits that come with membership and ends with a strong close:

> AOPA . . . 30 MAXI-BENEFITS
>
> As you can tell by now, AOPA is a well-rounded association . . . run by and for pilots! AOPA was designed with you, the pilot, in mind . . . and has the experience and proven ability to put you in touch with all facets of general aviation. It's simple: AOPA works for you!
>
> . . . FOR 29 MINI-BUCKS!
>
> All this for a low $29 a year now. $29 is minimal compared to the investment you've made in effort and expense to get into flying . . . and yet $29 is a big investment in your future flying pleasure!

AIRCRAFT
OWNERS
AND
PILOTS
ASSOCIATION

Since you're off to a flying start,
... why not start off flying smart?

Dear Pilot:

Welcome to the world of flying! As a pilot, I know what a heady feeling it is when you first solo — there's nothing like it!

And now that you've experienced some flying time ... I'm able and most pleased to invite you to enjoy another great flying experience: membership in AOPA — the world's largest and most influential organization for pilots.

You may have already heard about us — for AOPA is made up of more than 255,000 pilots all over the country as concerned and conscientious about flying as you are. But you may not have heard about all we have to offer you as a pilot.

<u>With AOPA, You're
Flying Smart!</u>

As an AOPA member, you're entitled to <u>Big Benefits</u> that help you get the <u>most</u> out of your flying experience. We offer <u>publications</u> to keep you informed about the world of flying, new developments, trends, etc. We offer <u>informational services</u> covering personal assistance on everything from flight routings, both domestic and international, to questions about FARs and your general flight operation. Plus, we offer <u>insurance</u> and many <u>discount opportunities</u>. Add it all up, and that's "flying smart" ... being informed and well covered!

To show you what I mean, here's what you'll find coming your way when you join:

- <u>AOPA PILOT</u>— The colorful monthly magazine exclusively for AOPA members ... with fascinating articles ... practical flying know—how ... facts on new developments ... aircraft ... equipment ... FAA rules and regs ... tips on pilot proficiency ... safety skills ... less expensive and more enjoyable flying ... pages more!

- <u>AOPA NEWSLETTER</u> — Crammed with "behind-the-headlines" aviation news ... facts and figures on trends, industry happenings, airport procedures, safety innovations, more.

- <u>AUTOMATIC ACCIDENT INSURANCE</u> —a $700 Flying-only Group Personal Accident Insurance policy ... increases $100 for each year of continuous AOPA membership ... and additional coverage is available at advantageous rates.

7315 Wisconsin Avenue (Air Rights Building) / Bethesda, MD 20814   Telephone (301) 654-0500 · Telex 89-8468   Cable Address AOPA Washington
When writing ALWAYS use your AOPA number
Member: International Council of Aircraft Owner and Pilot Associations

Most importantly, with increasing government regulation of airspace and airports, AOPA acts as your "Washington Watchdog" — giving you active representation to protect your flying interests. The AOPA policy team provides testimony on "the Hill" at Congressional, FAA and FCC hearings ... whatever it takes in Washington to protect your rights as a general aviation pilot, we're there! While it may seem intangible, this service is vital to your future as a pilot!

FREE GIFT WHEN YOU JOIN!

By now you can tell that AOPA is specifically designed with your flying needs in mind — and here's another example: When you join we'll send you one of these valuable gifts — free. Each is uniquely useful for pilots...and your choice comes to you with our compliments to say, "Welcome to AOPA.!"

Choose either ...

The Aviator's Catalog — Great to have at this stage of your flying - the perfect choice to introduce you to everything in aviation. This valuable sourcebook will help clear up questions that are buzzing around your head right now — questions every student pilot needs answers to. Do you have questions about pilot certificates? Medicals? Ballooning? Buying an airplane? Weather? All you need to do is flip the pages of The Aviator's Catalog to find the answers. A $16.95 value ... yours FREE when you join.

or ...

Aero Flex-Lite — a lightweight, compact flashlight that clips securely to your pocket, sun visor or a panel — leaves both hands free for cockpit duties. The flexible neck lets you focus a pinpoint beam of light wherever you need it. Great for night flying. A $10 value — yours free when you join.

Find out more in the enclosed brochure ... then make your selection on the application. Besides your free gift, when you become a member you'll receive your golden AOPA WINGS ... an eye-catching pin to wear with pride. You'll also receive WINGS decals for your plane and car ... and AOPA's Air-Aid — our unique navigational tool that fits in your shirt pocket.

AOPA WORKS FOR YOU!

Most of us on the AOPA staff are pilots, too. So we know what your needs are as a pilot for information and services. When it comes right down to it, AOPA is a group of pilots working for other pilots ... it's that simple. That's why you'll find useful services such as ...

Personal Pilot Inquiry Service — fast, expert help on your specific flying questions or problems. From medical certification to FAA regulations to aircraft use and maintenance, all you have to do is ask!

<u>Free Domestic Flight Routing</u> — Just tell us where you're going, stopovers, restrictions and special requirements, and we'll send you a routing in an easy-to-follow format you can use enroute as your flight log.

<u>Legal Assistance</u> — We hope you won't need this, but if you do, we'll provide legal guidance about aviation law for your own attorney ... or give you names of AOPA member attorneys near you who handle aviation law matters.

When you become a member, you'll also receive your choice of one of these exclusive AOPA publications — as part of your regular member benefits:

<u>AOPA'S AIRPORTS U.S.A.</u>: Lists, locates and describes more than 13,500 airports, heliports and seaplane bases in the U.S ... elevations ... runways ... repair facilities ... lighting ... phone numbers ... NDB frequencies ... instrument approaches ... identifiers ... fuels. Plus: more than 2,100 airport diagrams!

<u>AOPA HANDBOOK FOR PILOTS</u>: 400 pages filled with useful information on federal regs ... performance and conversion tables ... emergency procedures ... Enroute Flight Advisory Service ... Flight Service phone numbers ... survival techniques ... loads more!

<u>AOPA'S 1982 PILOT APPOINTMENT CALENDAR</u> (1982 Optional Selection): for the pilot on the go! Twelve of the best photos from the AOPA PILOT bound into a sturdy calendar/notebook. Easy-to-carry format lets you take the Calendar wherever you go. Writing space on each date. Beautiful full color reproduction on high quality paper makes the photos suitable for framing. 7"x8".

Extra selections are available to you at special member-only savings. And each year when you renew your membership in AOPA, you'll again have the oportunity to make your free book selection.

AOPA SAVES YOU MONEY TOO!

In these days of rising inflation, it's hard to hang on to a dollar! That's why we try to help you save by arranging for <u>discounts</u> wherever possible ... for armchair or actual travel. For instance, here are some of the discounts you're eligible for as an AOPA member ...

*** <u>Aviation Trading Post and Av Books</u> — Special offerings of aviation related products and publications, at member-only prices.

*** <u>Car Rental Discounts</u> — At HERTZ, AVIS and NATIONAL that can save you your membership dues with your very next rental.

*** <u>Low-Cost Tours</u> — Low-cost group travel vacations to virtually any country in the world!

<u>AOPA . . . 30 MAXI-BENEFITS</u> . . .

As you can tell by now, AOPA is a well-rounded association . . . run by and for pilots! AOPA was designed with you, the pilot, in mind . . . and has the experience and proven ability to put you in touch with all facets of general aviation. It's simple: AOPA works for you!

. . . <u>FOR 29 MINI-BUCKS</u>!

All this for a low $29* a year now.
$29 is minimal compared to the
investment you've made in effort and
expense to get into flying . . . and yet
$29 is a big investment in your
future flying pleasure!

So act now! All you need to do is complete the enclosed application form and mail it back today. We've even paid the postage . . . so you won't lose any time before you can take advantage of all the benefits of being an AOPA member. I'll be waiting to welcome you to AOPA!

Sincerely,

Harmon O. Pritchard, Jr.

Harmon O. Pritchard, Jr.
Senior Vice President

P.S.   Don't forget to check the FREE gift you prefer: the Aviator's Catalog or the Flex-Lite! You'll also receive your golden WINGS pin, a complete membership kit and the next issues of the AOPA PILOT and Newsletter.

* Note: 50¢ is optional contribution to the AOPA Air Safety Foundation.

Robert Bartlett Realty Co. "Just Suppose" Letter

Classic letters don't come from just the big companies. Often small, local mailers turn out copy gems. Unfortunately, most of these are seen only by their intended audiences and fail to get recognition from the direct marketing world. Fortunately, Jim Kobs keeps files of his old work, and he sent along the classic letter shown on the facing page.

Jim comments:

■ My first year as a direct mail copywriter, I did over a dozen letters for Robert Bartlett Realty. This is one of my favorites.

You often hear people say they wish they had bought a house or bought some land years ago when they had a good opportunity to do so. For some reason, this is a message that realtors and homebuilders seldom seem to get across in their advertising.

This letter tries to do that by turning the clock back five years and talking about how different somebody's life would be.

ROBERT BARTLETT REALTY CO. (NOT INC.)
111 W. Washington St. • Chicago
PHONE: ANdover 3-4141

Suppose,

Just suppose...that five years ago you had bought some well-located land.
Think how different your life could be today...!

Perhaps buying that land would have been the first step toward owning a
new home of your own. Right now you and your family could be enjoying
comfortable, convenient suburban living...far away from the noise and
cares of the city, but within minutes of new shopping centers, schools,
and churches.

Even if you hadn't built on that land in the last five years, today it
might be worth twice what you paid for it. It's a fact--property I sold
in the Fifties is now selling for double the purchase price. No wonder
there isn't any better investment than well-located land. It doesn't
depreciate like an automobile, its value doesn't fluctuate up and down
like stocks and bonds.

But notice that I'm talking about well-located land. If land is going to
make a good homesite or be a good investment, there are a lot of things
the buyer must consider. That's why I think you'll find the folder I'm
enclosing so interesting. It gives specific questions you should ask
yourself about buying land. The folder also points out the advantages of
choosing a homesite now...even if you don't plan on building until later.

When you're interested in land, you can always trust Bartlett -- the oldest
and largest creator of choice communities in Chicagoland. I have a wide
selection of desirable property available, at a wide variety of prices.
With as little as $170 down, you can afford a Bartlett homesite now!

Isn't it time you start thinking seriously about becoming a property owner?
Simply check the kind of property you're interested in on the enclosed
postage-free Reply Card -- and mail it today. We'll phone you with complete
information. Naturally, there is no obligation, and no salesmen will visit
you without your invitation.

Better mail that card now -- it can mean a happy and secure future for you
and your family!

Cordially yours,

Robert Bartlett

ROBERT BARTLETT

RB:jfk

FAIRVIEW MEDICAL RESEARCH SURVEY ON A CHECK

One of the many interesting techniques developed by Clark-O'Neill, the New Jersey medical mailing house, is conducting a survey on the backs of checks. It's a great way to get maximum response to a survey. The letter and two sides of the enclosed check shown opposite are typical of many such surveys that have been conducted in the health care field.

Clark-O'Neill has also used the check technique for an intriguing research project of its own. They keep hearing skeptics claim that doctors throw all their direct mail away unopened. So Clark-O'Neill inserts checks in test mailings of various types. On the back where the doctor will endorse the check is a brief questionnaire asking whether the doctor found the check himself . . . or if it was brought to his attention by someone else. And, if it had been called to his attention, does he normally read the type of mail in which it was enclosed. Interestingly, a high percentage of those doctors who may claim they throw away all advertising mail unopened cash the checks and answer the brief questionnaire. Most of them, it turns out, find the checks without anyone else's aid.

Fairview Medical Research

ONE BROAD AVENUE, FAIRVIEW, N.J. 07022

April 28, 1983

Dear Doctor:

Last week I was in to see my personal physician. Emergency surgery detained him at the hospital and his waiting room looked as if it were six chairs short.

Doctor, we understand how busy you are. Our goal is to provide you with educational information and products that relate to your patients' needs. In order to do a better job, we are asking for a moment of your time.

Will you please answer the two questions on the reverse side of the enclosed check? This will help us get important information in the hands of physicians who need it .... but not burden physicians who have no need for it. The dollar check is not meant as payment for your time, Doctor .... we know your time is more valuable than that. The real pay back will come in professional services that this survey will enable us to offer to you.

The response thus far has been excellent, but we need your response if this type of information is important to you and your patients. Won't you take a moment to provide us with this information?

Thank you very much for your help.

Sincerely,

J.B. Martin
Director
Fairview Medical Research

FAIRVIEW MEDICAL RESEARCH   1
1 BROAD AVE.
FAIRVIEW, N. J. 07022

0760 55-33/270

MARCH, 1986

Pay TWO DOLLARS and NO/100_____$2.00

TO
THE
ORDER
OF

1617
DICK HODGSON, MD
P.O. BOX 1049   31082
WESTTOWN, PA.   19395

OR BEARER

JB Martin

NOT VALID UNLESS CASHED
WITHIN 90 DAYS OF DATE OF CHECK

THE FIRST JERSEY NATIONAL BANK
One Exchange Place, Jersey City, N.J.

⑆027000339⑈ 05 07 849071⑈

1. Which reps have you seen in the last 6-8
    weeks?
    ☐ Du Pont
    ☐ McNeil
    ☐ Smith Kline & French
    ☐ Sandoz

2. Which products do you remember being
    detailed on?
    ☐ Haldol®
    ☐ Moban®
    ☐ Stelazine®
    ☐ Mellaril®

3. Have you started using any of these pro-
    ducts because of their recent presentation?
    ☐ Stelazine®
    ☐ Mellaril®
    ☐ Moban®
    ☐ Haldol®

4. Does any one of these product presentations
    stand out in your mind?
    ☐ Moban®
    ☐ Haldol®
    ☐ Mellaril®
    ☐ Stelazine®

Endorse _____

Specialty _____

THANK YOU

THE SMITHY COMPANIES "BACKWARDS" LETTER

In the nation's capitol, where thousands of government clerks turn out some of the most unimaginative letters ever created, there lived a man who wrote some of the most imaginative letters ever seen in direct mail. He told about many of them in the 10 books he published, most recently in *Letter Perfect — How to Write Business Letters That Work.**

That man is the late Ferd Nauheim, and a letter he wrote for a local real estate firm, The Smithy Companies, is a classic. It begins at the end:

> Like to locate your offices where you will enjoy:
>
> • geographic convenience
>
> • splendid features and services
>
> • within-the-building parking
>
> • banking and dining
>
> Phone me at 775-9255. Let's talk about what you need and want . . . and 2000 M Street.
>
> Cordially,
>
> Steve Corey
>
> P.S. Just in case you are even busier than usual, I have given you the final summarizing paragraph first. When you have the time, here's the rest:

. . . and then the letter starts.

---

*Letter Perfect, *Ferd Nauheim, Van Norstrand Reinhold Co. Inc., New York, 1982.*

THE SMITHY COMPANIES
SINCE · 1930

H.G. SMITHY COMPANY

1110 Vermont Ave., N.W.
Washington, D.C. 20005
(202) 775-9255

Real Estate Finance ·
Management · Insurance ·
Leasing · Sales · Consulting

Like to locate your offices where you will enjoy:

- geographic convenience

- splendid features and services

- within-the-building parking

- banking and dining

Phone me at 775-9255. Let's talk about what you need and want ... and 2000 M Street.

Cordially,

Steve Corey

Steve Corey

P.S. Just in case you are even busier than usual, I have given you the final summarizing paragraph first. When you have the time, here's the rest:

Dear Sir,

If you need more space, less space, better space, a more desirable location, better services and facilities or additional parking, I probably have some gratifying answers for you.

At 2000 M Street, N.W., there is a handsome, modern, eight story office building. The Federal Government has been the sole tenant. They are going to move and that creates some attractive opportunities in this tight market for choice office space. This is one case where the government could be doing something <u>for</u> you.

There are 155,105 square feet of office space available ... 28,083 square feet per floor. At this time you may have all, or any part. On the lower level another 10,493 square feet can be used for computers, other office machines or for files.

And the in-house parking is good news. There are 300 spaces – and what a great fringe benefit parking is these days ... the sooner we can know your desires, the more we can do for you

Your full service lease includes cleaning, security and

-2-

utilities. Budgeting can be precise. You will control your own air-conditioning and heat. Six high-speed electronically controlled elevators keep traffic moving swiftly and efficiently.

The street floor houses a branch of Security National Bank, two restaurants and shops. Study the vicinity map in the folder I'm enclosing. You'll see that Connecticut Avenue, with its restaurants, hotels and shopping, is just two blocks away. M Street fairly bristles with interesting eating places. Turn in the other direction and you are on the threshold of Georgetown. A five minute walk (three minutes if it is raining or snowing) takes you to Metro's Red, Blue and Orange subway lines.

2000 M Street is a prestigious location. By January, 1982 the government will be out and you can be in.

So, if you would like to locate your offices where you'll enjoy geographic conveniences, splendid features and services, within-the-building parking, banking and dining, phone me at 775-9255. Let's talk about what you need and want ... and 2000 M Street.

Cordially,

Steve Corey

Steve Corey

A different P.S. H.G. Smithy Company has been managing some of Washington's finest office buildings for more than 50 years. Smithy management is something else you can look forward to. It is an important extra.

THE PRESIDENTIAL CARD "DID I LOSE A LETTER FROM YOU" LETTER

As you travel throughout the world, one thing is certain: Murray Raphel has been there before you and left his mark on direct mail being turned out in every country. He's an Atlantic City retailer who believes direct mail is the ideal medium for promoting retail sales. He's written a column on the subject for *Direct Marketing* magazine every month for over 20 years* and travels the world over presenting spellbinding seminars. He's also coauthor of one of the most interesting books on idea generation ever written — *The Great Brain Robbery.***

He's also an excellent letter writer. A good example of the Raphel mark on the direct mail of the world is a series of letters he wrote for The Presidential Card of Australia. My favorite is one that starts out:

> DID I LOSE A LETTER FROM YOU?
>
> Every day the mailman delivers hundreds of letters to our Melbourne office.
>
> Once in a while a letter is lost. Falls off the desk. Tucked into the wrong pile. Or . . . simply, not delivered.
>
> And then someone will call us and ask, "Why didn't my Presidential Card arrive in the mail?" Or, "I wrote to you three weeks ago and I'm still waiting for my Presidential Card to come."
>
> Frustration.
>
> We can understand how that can happen with new members. (We can understand, but constantly upgrade our system to minimize errors.)
>
> But we are positively, absolutely, uncontrollably perplexed when it happens to a valued member of the past.
>
> That's you.
>
> THE REASON FOR OUR CONCERN: YOUR PRESIDENTIAL CARD EXPIRED AT THE END OF LAST MONTH AND WE DID NOT RECEIVE YOUR RENEWAL MEMBERSHIP FEE.

Did such a clever approach work? Retention rate doubled.

A selection of Murray Raphel's direct marketing columns have been reprinted in But Would Saks Fifth Avenue Do It? *published in 1981 by Murray Raphel/Advertising, Gordon's Alley, Atlantic City, NJ.*

**The Great Brain Robbery, *Ray Consodine and Murray Raphel, Rosebud Books, Los Angeles, 1980.*

Melbourne Office: 13th Floor, State Bank Building,
270 Flinders Street, Melbourne 3000
Telephone 63 8180 63 5523
Commercial Sales 63 8587

Adelaide Office: 12th Floor, Royal Insurance Building,
13 Grenfell Street, Adelaide 5000
Telephone (08) 212 5899 212 5651

Tony Ingleton
President

DID I LOSE A LETTER FROM YOU?

Every day the mailman delivers hundreds of letters to our Melbourne office.

Once in a while a letter is lost. Falls off the desk. Tucked into the wrong pile. Or . . . simply, not delivered.

And then someone will call us and ask, "Why didn't my Presidential Card arrive in the mail?" Or, "I wrote to you three weeks ago and I'm still waiting for my Presidential Card to come."

Frustration.

We can understand how that can happen with new members. (We can understand, but constantly upgrade our systems to minimise errors.)

But we are positively, absolutely, uncontrollably perplexed when it happens to a valued member of the past.

That's you.

THE REASON FOR OUR CONCERN: YOUR PRESIDENTIAL CARD EXPIRED AT THE END OF LAST MONTH AND WE DID NOT RECEIVE YOUR RENEWAL MEMBERSHIP FEE.

That happens, of course. There are vacations. There is the first-things-first approach where you deal with emergencies and must-do decisions at once. Everything else waits. Our concern is that sometime within the next few days you will go to the movies. Or dine at a favourite restaurant. Or be called away suddenly on a trip. And find yourself paying too much money for your entertainment, meal or hotel room.

The many reasons you joined The Presidential Card club in the beginning are still there. Only more so. Today there are more than 500 establishments that honour the Presidential Card throughout Australia. Your membership renewal lets you continue to save up to 50% off the regular price of hotel and motel rooms, restaurant meals, movie tickets, amusement centres, rental cars . . . and more.

You know from past experience your annual membership fee comes back to you the first few times you use your Presidential Card – (the ONLY travel and entertainment card that saves you money every time you use it).

As valuable as your Presidential Card was for you in the past, it becomes even more so in the future – with more places to go, visit, stay and dine.

Return the enclosed invoice with your cheque, thus enabling you to get full use of your renewal Presidential Card, which was forwarded to you at the beginning of last month.

Sincerely,

TONY INGLETON
Club President

PS.   If someone told you the new membership rate increased to $40.00, they are correct. But as a re-subscriber, you may re-enroll for your last membership rate of only $35.00

PPS.   We've enclosed an order form and postage reply paid envelope, just to make sure your answer comes directly to us.

L 1

BACHE FINANCIAL PLANNING "RATING A GENERAL" LETTER

Writers addressing sophisticated audiences about sophisticated products all too often feel a need to exhibit their own sophistication through the use of big, academic-sounding words and long, involved paragraphs. Sig Rosenblum, who has written classic letters for a host of direct marketers, knows better. In this letter for The Bache Financial Planning Program, he sticks to short, action-packed words and easy-to-follow sentences and paragraphs.

The letter begins:

> How would you rate a general . . .
>
> . . . who rushed into a battle without a plan? A general who squandered blood, sweat and tears without a blueprint?
>
> And yet you fight the toughest battle in history. Every day. And it's not just your skin that's at risk. But your nest egg. Your home. And those you love.
>
> You fight a battle against inflation that erodes your purchasing power . . . against recession — or worse — squinting ominously over the horizon . . . against volatile markets, rearing and plunging this way and that.

When it comes to describing the product, the action continues:

> Your plan covers every aspect of your financial life. It gives you specific answers to key questions such as:
>
> Can I cut my taxes? How?
>
> Can I improve my cash flow?
>
> What's right — and wrong — with my investments?
>
> Do I have enough insurance? Too much? The right kind?
>
> How do I plan a comfortable retirement now?
>
> What's the best way to protect those I love?
>
> And there's much more. All of it in straight talk, not the jargon of specialists. With all the facts and figures you need to make it work. And remember, it's your plan. As individual as your fingerprint.

The language of the letter amplifies the "straight talk" of the plan. And the same straight talk continued when it came to the price:

> It's not cheap. But it will be the best $1,200 you ever invested. Yes, twelve hundred dollars. But just measure that against the hundreds of thousands of dollars such a plan can protect. Not to say multiply.

How would you
rate a general...

...who rushed into battle without a plan? A general who squandered
blood, sweat and tears without a blueprint?

And yet, you fight the toughest battle in history. Every day. And it's
not just your skin that's at risk. But your nest egg. Your home. And
those you love.

You fight a battle against inflation that erodes your purchasing power...
against recession--or worse--squinting ominously over the horizon...against
volatile markets, rearing and plunging this way and that.

There isn't a general who fights a tougher battle. And through it all,
you have to do your job, build your estate, be parent, mate, lover,
citizen--all at once.

If you're feeling stress, pressure, tension--is it any wonder?

But let me ask you a question, general. For you are the general of your
life and those who look to you for support and love...let me ask you a
brutally frank question:

Are you "winging it"? Improvising? Hoping that hard work and luck will
do the trick? No general, however two-fisted, would fight without a
plan. So why fight without a financial plan?

You can have such a plan in short order. Not some mass-market paperback. Not some computer-generated, one-size-fits-all scheme. But a _personal_ plan designed for you. With every number, every goal, every dream your very own.

When you mail the card enclosed, you'll see just why a financial plan transforms the battle. Makes life less confusing. Less pressured. Less uncertain. You'll follow this plan. However the economy twists and turns. Whatever lies ahead. Mail the card right now for a _free_ _introduction_ to:—

THE BACHE FINANCIAL PLANNING PROGRAM

There's a lot to tell about this _personal_ planning technique. And a letter is not the best place to do that. But, briefly:

Your plan covers _every aspect_ of your financial life. It gives you _specific_ answers to key questions such as:—

    Can I cut my taxes? How?
    Can I improve my cash flow?
    What's right—and wrong—with my investments?
    Do I have enough insurance? Too much? The right kind?
    How do I plan a comfortable retirement now?
    What's the best way to protect those I love?

And there's much more. All of it in straight talk, not the jargon of specialists. With all the facts and figures you need to make it work. And remember, it's _your_ plan. As individual as your fingerprint.

It's no lightweight plan: You end up with a 60 to 80-page <u>detailed</u> blueprint of where you are headed and how to get there.

It's not cheap. But it will be the best $1,200 you ever invested. Yes, twelve hundred dollars. But just measure that against the hundreds of thousands of dollars such a plan can protect. Not to say <u>multiply</u>.

This plan is not for everyone, certainly. Not for lieutenants, sergeants or privates. But I believe this plan is for you.

You'll be the ultimate judge, of course. And when you mail the card to get all the facts, it will be without the slightest obligation or commitment. That's understood.

If you think the battle is tough today, tomorrow's battles will be rougher still. They <u>will</u> be, that is--without a <u>plan</u>. Perhaps it's time <u>you</u> had one, general. Please complete and mail the card in the enclosed envelope today. It's already addressed. And the postage is paid.

        Sincerely,

SECTION IX

PERSONALIZED LETTERS

Some of the most effective direct mail letters are those that include elements of personalization in the body of the letter. Tests have shown such personalization can substantially increase response; however, there are additional costs involved. Thus, to be truly effective, personalization must draw enough additional response to offset the added expense.

Unfortunately, about all some direct mail letter writers know how to do is to add a recipient's name within the body of the copy. While this can be somewhat effective, it seldom produces the lift in response that occurs when other elements of personalization are added.

There are many elements of personalization which are relatively easy to capture from existing data bases. For example:

- *Using available programs, the Zip Code will enable you to personalize a letter with the recipient's city, county, area and state. And by overlaying Zip Codes with readily available computer programs, you can include such elements of personalization as the distance between your offices and the homes or offices of customers, your recipient's nearest airport, locations of close-by dealers, etc.*

- *The U.S. Weather Bureau provides rainfall and temperature information for each Zip Code area.*

- *From the Disease Control Center in Atlanta, you can obtain local, area and state disease statistics.*

- *License bureaus offer information on makes of automobiles owned.*

- *Registration bureaus can provide types of airplanes or boats licensed.*

- *Overlaying magazine subscription lists or organization membership lists will indicate recipients' specific hobbies and interests.*

It's important to constantly keep in mind a possible invasion of privacy when using personalization in direct mail letters. However, careful use of the types of available non-threatening information such as the personalization elements listed above seldom raises an invasion of privacy concern.

Even though there are lists that will give you ages, birthdays, names and number of family members, and other highly personal information, use of such elements of personalization may not only hurt response, but could easily stir up privacy concerns.

On the other hand, customers are usually flattered when you "play back" information they have given you. Such personalization can help build a stronger bond between a buyer and seller. Your internal files should be able to provide you with such easy personalization opportunities as:

- *A thank you for a first purchase.*

- *The first anniversary as a customer.*

- *The number of years a recipient has been a customer.*

- *An opportunity to make a repeat offer of a specific product previously purchased.*

- *Recommending related products to purchase.*

- *The number of purchases made in the past.*

- *The date of a recipient's first or last order.*

- *References to previous mailings.*

- *Geographical references.*

- *Date of a telephone contact.*

- *The name of the telephone operator with whom the customer talked.*

- *Amount of a previous donation to a charity.*

I've personally used every form of personalization for prospects and customers mentioned above, often in head-to-head tests against non-personalized versions. And, in every single test, the personalized letter produced greater response than the non-personalized version.

Although the recipient may be aware that personalization has been added by a computer, there is still a bit of magic about such letters for they say, in effect, "you have been specially selected to receive this message."

Not all copywriters — even some of the top names in the direct mail letter writing field — understand the intricacies of computer personalization. Writing successful personalized letters requires a unique set of skills, but if you haven't already tested this results-enhancing technique, you owe it to yourself to at least give it a try.

READER'S DIGEST LETTERS

No one uses customer personalization more effectively and more consistently than *The Reader's Digest*. A typical letter begins *[comments in italics are mine]*:

> Imagine the thrill of walking into a bank near the Hodgson *[my name]* home — and surprising the teller if you deposited a check for $250,000 into your account.
>
> And think of the look on the faces of your West Chester *[my town]* neighbors if you drove down Johnny's Way *[my street]* in a brand new car — a car you completely paid for in cash.
>
> Or how would you like to start out from Philadelphia Intl. Airport *[my closest airport]* on an around-the-world vacation — your pockets bulging with spending money?

Later this paragraph:

> A mailman from your West Chester Post Office may soon be knocking at your door with a check for $250,000!

And a reference to a previous purchase:

> As an owner of "That Old Time Religion" *[a product I had previously purchased from them]*, you obviously enjoy *Digest* music. You'll find the same kind of enjoyment in "Jim Nabors Sings."

Sweepstakes Letter of Intent

DEAR MR. & MRS. HODGSON:

IMAGINE THE THRILL OF WALKING INTO A BANK NEAR THE HODGSON HOME--AND SURPRISING THE TELLER IF YOU DEPOSITED A CHECK FOR $250,000.00 INTO YOUR ACCOUNT.

AND THINK OF THE LOOK ON THE FACES OF YOUR WEST CHESTER NEIGHBORS IF YOU DROVE DOWN JOHNNYS WAY IN A BRAND NEW CAR--A CAR YOU COMPLETELY PAID FOR IN CASH.

OR HOW WOULD YOU LIKE TO START OUT FROM PHILADELPHIA INTL. AIRPORT ON AN AROUND-THE-WORLD VACATION--YOUR POCKETS BULGING WITH SPENDING MONEY?

THESE DREAMS COULD COME TRUE BECAUSE YOUR SWEEPSTAKES DEPOSIT SLIP ABOVE GIVES YOU A CHANCE TO WIN THE GRAND PRIZE OF $250,000.00 CASH (OR $125,000.00 NOW PLUS $1,000.00 A MONTH FOR LIFE--<u>YOUR CHOICE</u>) IN READER'S DIGEST $1,000,000.00 SWEEPSTAKES.

A MAILMAN FROM YOUR WEST CHESTER POST OFFICE MAY SOON BE KNOCKING AT YOUR DOOR WITH A CHECK FOR $250,000.00!

BUT YOU CAN'T WIN UNLESS YOU ENTER. AND ALL YOU HAVE TO DO IS RETURN YOUR SWEEPSTAKES DEPOSIT SLIP IN EITHER OF THE ENCLOSED ENVELOPES BY FEBRUARY 28! (RETURN IT BY MARCH 2 AND YOU COULD WIN ANY OF 40,710 OTHER CASH PRIZES BUT <u>NOT</u> THE GRAND PRIZE.) THAT'S ALL THERE IS TO IT. THERE'S NO OTHER OBLIGATION; NOTHING TO BUY. AND THE <u>SOONER</u> YOU REPLY, THE <u>MORE</u> MONEY YOU COULD WIN.

WHY WERE YOU SENT THIS OPPORTUNITY TO ENTER OUR SWEEPSTAKES? TO CALL YOUR ATTENTION TO READER'S DIGEST PRODUCTS...AND IN PARTICULAR TO THE BRAND-NEW ALBUM WE'RE OFFERING FEATURING A REMARKABLE PERFORMER..."JIM NABORS SINGS."

AS AN OWNER OF THAT OLD TIME RELIGION, YOU OBVIOUSLY ENJOY DIGEST MUSIC. YOU'LL FIND THE SAME KIND OF ENJOYMENT IN "JIM NABORS SINGS."

(OVER, PLEASE)

FROM AMAZING GRACE TO TENNESSEE WALTZ, YOU'LL HEAR 82 MEMORABLE PERFORMANCES ...INSPIRATIONAL HYMNS, LOVE SONGS, POPULAR HITS, BROADWAY CLASSICS, COUNTRY TUNES, MOVIE THEMES...THE LARGEST COLLECTION OF JIM NABORS' SONGS EVER!

WHY NOT HEAR THEM ALL FOR 7 DAYS HOME TRIAL ON YOUR CHOICE OF 7 RECORDS, 3 8-TRACK TAPES OR 3 CASSETTES. AFTER 7 DAYS, IF YOU'RE NOT SATISFIED WITH "JIM NABORS SINGS," SIMPLY RETURN THE ALBUM. YOU'LL OWE NOTHING AND WE'LL EVEN REIMBURSE YOU FOR THE RETURN POSTAGE.

IF YOU AGREE, THOUGH, THAT "JIM NABORS SINGS" BELONGS IN YOUR MUSIC LIBRARY, THEN KEEP IT AND PAY THE LOW PRICE OF ONLY $39.96, PAYABLE IN 4 MONTHLY INSTALLMENTS OF JUST $9.99 EACH, PLUS $1.55 POSTAGE FOR RECORDS, 86¢ POSTAGE FOR 8-TRACK TAPES OR 63¢ POSTAGE FOR CASSETTES. THERE'S NO FINANCE CHARGE, NO ANNUAL PERCENTAGE RATE OF INTEREST, NO CHARGE FOR HANDLING. THE POSTAGE WILL BE ADDED TO YOUR FIRST INSTALLMENT.

TO AUDITION "JIM NABORS SINGS" FOR 7 DAYS HOME TRIAL AND ENTER THE SWEEP- STAKES AT THE SAME TIME...RETURN YOUR DEPOSIT SLIP IN THE ENCLOSED YES ENVELOPE. (PLEASE INDICATE IF YOU WANT RECORDS, 8-TRACK TAPES OR CASSETTES BY PUNCHING OUT ONE OF THE CIRCLES ON THE ENVELOPE FLAP.)

IF YOU DON'T WANT TO AUDITION "JIM NABORS SINGS" FOR 7 DAYS HOME TRIAL BUT YOU DO WANT TO ENTER THE SWEEPSTAKES...RETURN YOUR DEPOSIT SLIP IN THE ENCLOSED NO ENVELOPE. WHATEVER YOU DECIDE, RETURN IT BY FEBRUARY 28 TO BE ELIGIBLE TO WIN THE $250,000.00 GRAND PRIZE OR BY MARCH 2 FOR ANY OF THE 40,710 OTHER CASH PRIZES. ALL PRIZES WILL BE AWARDED! THE SOONER YOU RETURN YOUR DEPOSIT SLIP, THE MORE MONEY YOU COULD WIN!

Carolyn Davis

READER'S DIGEST
$1,000,000.00
SWEEPSTAKES

Sweepstakes Deposit Slip

RETURN THIS DEPOSIT SLIP BY FEB. 28

TO READER'S DIGEST:

R-906C-C

Please deposit my name:

MR. & MRS. RICHARD S. HODGSON

MR. & MRS. RICHARD S. HODGSON
1431 JOHNNYS WAY R 3
WEST CHESTER, PA 19380

in your new $1,000,000.00 Sweepstakes and tell me if I am a winner. I understand that if I return this Deposit Slip by Feb. 28, I'll be eligible to win the $250,000.00 Grand Prize...or by March 2 for any of the 40,710 other cash prizes you are giving away. I understand all prizes will be awarded. I also understand that I do not have to buy anything in order to have a chance to win.

04706 73070   40162   0   78

- - - - - - - - - - - - - - - - DETACH HERE AND RETURN DEPOSIT SLIP ABOVE - - - - - - - - - - - - - - - -

Deposit your name in the Reader's Digest $1,000,000.00 Sweepstakes by February 28...and you could soon be depositing $250,000.00 in your own personal bank account! (See below)

READER'S DIGEST
$1,000,000.00
SWEEPSTAKES

Sweepstakes Statement

THIS IS TO ADVISE THAT IF YOU, MR. & MRS. RICHARD S. HODGSON, ARE THE GRAND PRIZE WINNER IN OUR NEW $1,000,000.00 SWEEPSTAKES, A CHECK IN THE AMOUNT OF $250,000.00 COULD BE DEPOSITED IN A BANK IN OR NEAR WEST CHESTER AND YOU COULD BE WRITING PERSONAL CHECKS SUCH AS THESE:

Deposit in Personal Account ▶ **$250,000.00**   Balance as of ▶ | 4/3/84 | $250,000.00

Transactions

Date	Checks	Amount	Daily Balance
		$19,900.00	$230,100.00
5/29/84	DOWN PAYMENT TO HOME BUILDERS	10,000.00	220,100.00
6/18/84	PAID TO PENNSYLVANIA CAR DEALER	7,000.00	213,100.00
6/22/84	DEPOSIT IN CHILDREN'S COLLEGE FUND	3,215.55	209,884.45
7/9/84	PAID TO PENNSYLVANIA TRAVEL AGENT	1,500.28	$208,384.17
7/25/84	PAID TO PENNSYLVANIA APPLIANCE DEALER--TV, REFRIG., STOVE		

MR. & MRS. R. HODGSON---IF YOU WIN THE GRAND PRIZE, YOU COULD HAVE ALL THIS CASH LEFT OVER EVEN AFTER YOU MAKE YOUR DREAMS COME TRUE.

TIME-LIFE BOOKS NON-COMPUTER PERSONALIZATION

You don't have to utilize the computer to create personalized mailings, however. This was demonstrated in a classic letter used by Time-Life Books to sell its *Encyclopedia of Gardening.*

One of the initial problems in selling this series was that readers weren't convinced the books would necessarily cover the types of gardening problems they experienced where they lived. So Time-Life created separate versions for each state and sales increased substantially.

The letter I received in Pennsylvania, for example, started off:

> Dear Pennsylvania Gardener:

There were just two other paragraphs in the six-page letter with specific references to Pennsylvania, plus a lift memo with a special message for Pennsylvania gardeners. But those extra touches converted a loser into a winner.

The second paragraph of the letter made reference to a famous Pennsylvania garden:

> The perennial border in your backyard is supposed to be a vision of beauty, a miniature copy of the one you may have seen at Longwood Gardens in Kennett Square . . .

And there was a whole paragraph with Pennsylvania references:

> Where does your garden grow? Along the wooded byways of Bryn Mawr, Haverford, Chadds Ford and Paoli? In beautiful Fox Chapel, Sewickley or burgeoning Coraopolis and Camp Hill? Along the wide, tree-lined streets of Stroudsburg, or Carlisle, with its row-upon-row of stately colonial homes? Near York, when May brings apple-blossom time? In picturesque Bucks County, with its rolling hills, early stone houses and handsome barns? In the rich soil of Lancaster County, with its abundance of limestone, or around historic Valley Forge?

Every part of the state got its reference, quietly suggesting there would be helpful advice in the series no matter where you lived.

Dear Pennsylvania Gardener:

Gardening is such a rewarding pastime and can add so much beauty to your home; but, despite all your efforts, sometimes your great expectations turn into dismal disappointments...

The perennial border in your backyard is supposed to be a vision of beauty, a miniature copy of the one you may have seen at Longwood Gardens in Kennett Square. Instead, it's untidy and overgrown. The delphiniums are growing too closely together and the color selections of your phloxes are just not harmonious. How much better it would be if you had solid, step-by-step advice on how to plan and control that border.

Now you can learn how to develop a foolproof gardening plan — working out size, shape, location and combination of plants — and how to put that plan into action in THE TIME-LIFE ENCYCLOPEDIA OF GARDENING volume on <u>Perennials</u>.

That beautiful African violet your daughter gave you for your birthday — look at it now: wilted, straggly, limp, flowerless. But this will never again happen to your cherished house plants, once you know their special needs.

Now you can discover what those needs are — and much more — in THE TIME-LIFE ENCYCLOPEDIA OF GARDENING volume on <u>Flowering House Plants</u>.

You love tomatoes, but hate the hard, tasteless little ones sold in boxes in the supermarkets. So last year you planted your own tomatoes — but you were disappointed. Your plants didn't seem to bear nearly as many tomatoes as your neighbor got with his.

You'll learn all about growing tomatoes — including a new way to get more blossoms to form fruit, and how an ordinary paper cup can help prevent cutworm injury — in THE TIME-LIFE ENCYCLOPEDIA OF GARDENING volume on <u>Vegetables and Fruits</u>.

You love that gracious old maple near the driveway. But you're heartsick over the ugly barren spot beneath it where grass refuses to grow, no matter what you do. But there are attractive, inexpensive <u>ground covers</u> ideal for planting under shallow-rooted trees like maples, if only you know what to choose...

Now you can discover what these ground covers are — and all about solutions to other lawn problems — in THE TIME-LIFE ENCYCLOPEDIA OF GARDENING volume on <u>Lawns and Ground Covers</u>.

The Editors of TIME-LIFE BOOKS invite you to see for yourself how practical, how complete, how easy to follow, how breathtakingly beautiful this widely acclaimed gardening library really is. Here's all you do:

<u>Return the postpaid order card and we will send you Perennials for 10 days' free reading as your introduction to THE TIME-LIFE ENCYCLOPEDIA OF GARDENING without any obligation to buy.</u>

-2-

THE TIME-LIFE ENCYCLOPEDIA OF GARDENING Is an Invaluable Source of Practical Gardening Methods and Techniques

Where does your garden grow? Along the wooded byways of Bryn Mawr, Haverford, Chadds Ford and Paoli? In beautiful Fox Chapel, Sewickley or burgeoning Coraopolis and Camp Hill? Along the wide, tree-lined streets of Stroudsburg, or Carlisle, with its row-upon-row of stately colonial homes? Near York, when May brings apple-blossom time? In picturesque Bucks County, with its rolling hills, early stone houses and handsome barns? In the rich soil of Lancaster County, with its abundance of limestone, or around historic Valley Forge?

No matter where you live, you can turn to any volume in THE TIME-LIFE ENCYCLOPEDIA OF GARDENING — regardless of its subject — and find instructions geared to your section of the country...to your soil, climate, rainfall and temperature patterns, your particular growing season.

You'll discover which varieties of a particular shrub or tree do well where you live and which are best avoided... how to compensate for the acidity or alkalinity of the soil in your region...when to begin planting in your locale.

Are you a new homeowner confronted for the first time with the challenge of creating a lawn? choosing shade trees? planning a garden? Or are you a veteran gardener seeking fresh ideas and new inspirations to suit your inevitably changing tastes and widening interests?

No matter how experienced a gardener you are, or how familiar with gardening techniques and terminology you may be, you can depend on every volume in THE TIME-LIFE ENCYCLOPEDIA OF GARDENING — whatever its subject — to give you detailed yet easy-to-grasp explanations...ingenious shortcuts used by gardening authorities.

Whether your problems are as "elementary" as how to sow the tiny seeds of the snapdragon...or as "complex" as how to propagate budding rose plants by grafting...you will never go wrong if you follow the step-by-step series of drawings that appear literally by the hundreds in THE TIME-LIFE ENCYCLOPEDIA OF GARDENING.

Are you eager for a yard brimful with a variety of blossoms from spring through fall? Do you yearn for the lushness of tropical flowers to brighten your home or city apartment through the cheerlessness of winter? Do you simply take pride in watching things grow and being surrounded by beauty?

No matter what your gardening tastes or preferences; no matter what your budget...whether you have a great deal or very little time and energy to spend...whether your garden is in a window-size greenhouse or on a spacious back lawn...you will find that every volume of THE TIME-LIFE ENCYCLOPEDIA OF GARDENING, regardless of its subject, is organized so that you can locate the exact information you want in the shortest possible time.

-3-

You'll Find Hundreds of Tried-and-true Tips and Simple Tricks Like These in THE TIME-LIFE ENCYCLOPEDIA OF GARDENING:

- How to Get More Vegetables and Fruits out of a Small Garden - You can get maximum yields by growing successive crops on the same patch of soil, using midget varieties, growing tomatoes, beans, cucumbers and squashes vertically, and using planters on terrace or patio for vegetables and dwarf fruit trees.

- Healthy Perennials - The pH of your soil can spell the difference between success or failure. Perennials do best when the pH is around 6.5 (slightly acid) to 7.0 (neutral).

- Lawn Work Saver - The simplest, surest way for you to get fertilizer onto a lawn in the right amount is to use an adjustable fertilizer spreader that can also perform double duty as a distributor for seeds, lime, sulphur, etc.

- Herbs— to Look at, as Well as Use in Cooking - To most people, herbs mean seasoning. But they can also be used to add accent to your flower beds, or as a complete decorative garden all by themselves.

- Bonsai— the Art of Dwarfing - The kind of tree to select (among the narrow-leaved evergreens, mugo pine, Sargent Juniper and Norway spruce lend themselves particularly well to bonsai training), and how to prune, pot, wire and groom.

- When Grass Isn't the Answer - Most ground-cover plants are better suited to steep slopes than grass which is difficult to mow in such locations; under certain circumstances they also control erosion better than grass because their leaves break the force of rain and their roots dig deeper to hold the soil.

- African Violets - These popular indoor plants do best in bright, indirect or curtain-filtered sunlight, with night temperatures of 65° - 70° and day temperatures of 70° or higher. Soil should be barely moist at all times.

- A Way to Keep Your Tulips Blooming "Like New" for Years - If you plant your tulips deeply (ten inches deep instead of usual five or six inches) they will produce beautiful large and uniform flowers for up to eight years.

- How to Increase Your Number of Rose Blooms - Foliar feeding (a mixture of inorganic plant foods dissolved in water and sprayed on the leaves) is an easy and quick way to supplement midspring and midsummer fertilizer feedings, particularly if blossom production seems to lag.

- You Want a Nut Tree—but Don't Know Which One - The Chinese chestnut and the black walnut are fast growing, bear nuts as early as two years after planting, cast useful shade within five or six years, and are relatively free of pests and diseases.

- Feeding Foliage House Plants - They should be fed fertilizer infrequently—no more than once every three to six months, and this schedule should begin no sooner than six months after the plant is purchased.

-4-

Scores of "How-to" Illustrations that Instruct, Inspire and Illuminate

When it comes to acquiring a skill or mastering a new technique, one picture is often worth more than a thousand words. Here, for the first time, is an inexpensive,-professionally illustrated gardening reference library that abounds with visual aids — photographs, diagrams, paintings, drawings — that will help you achieve the easy-to-care-for, beautiful garden you've always wanted. In addition, each volume contains specially commissioned maps and charts that break down the United States and Canada into zones that tell you what seeds, plants, trees and shrubs you can grow in your area, and when they should be planted. Here is a glimpse of what you will see in THE TIME-LIFE ENCYCLOPEDIA OF GARDENING:

It will show you how to get your landscape plan on paper, progressing from lot map to rough analysis and final plan.

You will find out how to start a lawn from scratch: grading, loosening soil, conditioning the soil, adding nutrients, preparing the bed, when to plant grass, what seed to use, sowing the seed, watering and mowing a new lawn.

It will show you four ways to dig holes for planting bulbs.

You will discover when and how to pot a plant — the type of pot to use, drainage, improving the soil, easy potting techniques.

It will help you plan a food garden — how much to plant, when to plant, distances apart for rows and seed, frost-resistance, days to germination, days to eating, when to harvest, nutrients in each.

You will learn how to properly prune roses — with special techniques for teas, bush types, as well as climbing and tree roses.

You will discover how easy it is to make your own soil analysis.

You will see that there are two superior ways to water annuals and find out why early morning is the best time of day for watering them.

It will show you how to convert your leaves and other organic debris into clean, odorless, rich fertilizer with less effort and cost than it takes to stuff them into plastic bags for trash collection.

You will learn how to plant, prune, graft and train fruit trees.

You will find out how to identify and correct 12 simple lawn problems from fertilizer burn to slime mold; how to spot the 12 common pests that infect lawns and how to control them; how to diagnose 14 types of lawn diseases and how to remedy them.

You will discover a technique called "disbudding" that will permit you to produce giant-sized chrysanthemums.

You will learn all about roses, including, where necessary, how to provide beds — built-in watering for hot, dry locations and built-in drainage for wet locations.

It will show you some fascinating ways to use foliage house plants in decorating schemes and explain how you can grow plants using only artificial light.

-5-

<u>Add to All This, the Generous Use of Full-color
Photographs and Plain-talking, No-nonsense Prose</u>.

If you love flowers, plants and other growing things, you'll find the photographs in THE TIME-LIFE ENCYCLOPEDIA OF GARDENING an endless source of pleasure and inspiration.

Picture these volumes: Each one is a big 8 1/2 by 11 inches. There are dozens of photographs in lustrous natural color in every volume. Many occupy a full page. Some take up two facing pages: flowers, shrubs, gardens, landscapes — in glorious. close-ups and breathtaking long shots; lush lawns and stunning indoor arrangements.

But the hundreds of color photographs in THE TIME-LIFE ENCYCLOPEDIA OF GARDENING are not there merely to provide beauty. They also serve as living examples of what you, too, can achieve if you follow the authoritative advice which each of the photographs illustrates. In every volume you get 40,000 words of straightforward guidance and reliable factual knowledge.

<u>Plus a Unique Encyclopedic Inventory of Everything
You Need to Know about Hundreds of Plants</u>.

Whatever its subject, <u>every</u> single volume of THE TIME-LIFE ENCYCLOPEDIA OF GARDENING includes a special encyclopedic section of recommended species and varieties, created by the Editors and author James Underwood Crockett...

Here you'll find — at a glance, alphabetically catalogued — literally hundreds of bulbs, ground covers, annuals, perennials, flowering house plants, shrubs, trees; their growing habits and special needs, their colors, fragrance and other botanical data.

Alongside this information, you'll see dozens upon dozens of full-color paintings of many of the varieties described: scientifically accurate, visually lovely paintings rendered expressly for the encyclopedic section by outstanding botanical artists.

<u>Perennials, Your Introductory Volume, Reflects the Utility, Breadth and Beauty
of the Entire TIME-LIFE ENCYCLOPEDIA OF GARDENING</u>.

In every way, <u>Perennials</u>, your introductory volume, exemplifies the comprehensiveness, practicality, simplicity of presentation and colorful beauty of the complete TIME-LIFE ENCYCLOPEDIA OF GARDENING. Here is a preview of the kind of valuable information you will find in this volume:

The different species and varieties of perennials; their origins, genealogy and lore; how to prepare for planting them, and where and when; how to care for perennials, including feeding, watering and mulching; how to protect plants against diseases and pests; various methods of propagation; how to cut, arrange and exhibit them; all the regional variations and exceptions; the simple tools you will require and how to use them... plus, of course, the encyclopedic section, in this case, over 265 species and varieties of perennials.

-6-

Accept our invitation to examine <u>Perennials</u> without obligation to buy for 10 days. Then, and only then, need you decide whether you wish to keep the book and become a subscriber to THE TIME-LIFE ENCYCLOPEDIA OF GARDENING.

If you do, we'll bill you $5.95 plus shipping and handling for the introductory volume. Future books in the series will then come to you one at a time approximately every other month. You need never accept any book without first examining it for 10 days, without cost or obligation. No matter how many or how few you ultimately decide to keep, you pay only $5.95 plus shipping and handling for each volume. There is no minimum number you must buy, and you may cancel your subscription at any time simply by notifying us.

For now, though, take a leisurely 10-day look through <u>Perennials</u>. It costs you nothing to do so, and it is the best way of seeing for yourself how practical THE TIME-LIFE ENCYCLOPEDIA OF GARDENING is to anyone who loves to garden...or wants to learn how. Use the postage-paid order card today!

Sincerely,

Joan D. Manley
Publisher

JDM/EG

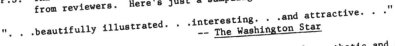

P.S. THE TIME-LIFE ENCYCLOPEDIA OF GARDENING has been receiving "bouquets" from reviewers. Here's just a sampling:

". . .beautifully illustrated. . .interesting. . .and attractive. . ."
           -- <u>The Washington Star</u>

". . .don't miss these books. . .They are worthwhile for esthetic and artistic reasons as well as horticultural ones."
           -- <u>Winston-Salem Journal</u>

"Always welcome are the new editions of the Time-Life 'Encyclopedia of Gardening'. . ."
           -- <u>The New York Times</u>

"As a gift or for reference, this beautiful and highly informative book (<u>Annuals</u>) will delight beginner or pro. . .à visual gem. From cover to cover, the eye-catching photography alone is worth the price of the book."
           -- <u>House Beautiful's Gardening and Outdoor Living</u>

<u>Lawns and Ground Covers</u> ". . .a must for anybody who tends a lawn."
           -- <u>Times Union and Journal</u> (Jacksonville, Fla.)

<u>Annuals</u>. . ."is colorful, attractive, easy to read and a boon to the newer gardener in particular. Profusely endowed with colored illustrations, it caters to all parts of the country."
           -- <u>Horticulture</u> Magazine

HELENE CURTIS "BEAUTY SALON" LETTER

Personalization is just as effective in business-to-business letters as it is for consumer mailings. An outstanding example is a letter written by Shelia Stogol and Barbara Anrod for the Professional Division of Helene Curtis Industries.

The letter, introducing a new permanent wave formula to beauty salons, used area personalization to make it special. It began:

> We are pleased to offer Mary's Beauty Salon a unique opportunity to try a unique product. For a limited time, you can get 3 free Quantum perms to use on your own clients in your Chicago area salon — with absolutely no obligation.

Later, the letter repeats the name of the salon and references to the area in which it is located:

> Most importantly, Quantum can actually save Mary's Beauty Salon from stocking dozens of specialty perms for different hair types. And that can save money and shelf space.
>
> Professionals in Chicago, all over Illinois, and coast to coast are having great results with Quantum. They are saying that Quantum is even better than they expected and are coming back for more.

Helene Curtis Industries, Inc.
4401 W. North Avenue
Chicago, Illinois
60639

Professional
Division

Office of the President

Mary's Beauty Salon
1234 Main Street
Anytown, Il 60006

Dear Salon Professional:

We are pleased to offer Mary's Beauty Salon a unique opportunity to try a unique product. For a limited time, you can get 3 free Quantum perms to use on your own clients in your Chicago area salon -- with absolutely no obligation.

Last September our Professional Division introduced Quantum one of the most revolutionary examples of Helene Curtis wave-of-the-future technology. Already this remarkable perm is one of the most successful products to come out of our laboratories. Now we are inviting salon professionals, like you, to use Quantum yourself.

What makes Quantum so unique is that this one salon perm formula works wonders on these three hair types -- normal, tinted and frosted hair. And Quantum delivers the waves and styleability you want with one short 20-minute processing time -- without a dryer.

Most importantly, Quantum can actually save Mary's Beauty Salon from stocking dozens of specialty perms for different hair types. And that can save money and shelf space.

Professionals in Chicago, all over Illinois, and coast to coast are having great results with Quantum. They are saying that Quantum is even better than they expected and are coming back for more.

We're making this offer so you, too, can have the opportunity to try Quantum on these three hair types. Then, we're sure you will be back for more, because your clients will certainly be.

All you do to get the 3 Free Quantum perms reserved for Mary's Beauty Salon is return the enclosed, personalized Free Perm Certificate in the postage paid reply envelope.

(over, please)

Or better yet, call toll free today. There is a minimal $2.00 postage and handling charge (considerably less than our cost!) which you can enclose or charge to your VISA or MasterCard.

Please be sure to indicate your Helene Curtis distributor if you're already familiar with one. If not, select one that's convenient for you from the list of our authorized dealers on the back of the Certificate. We can't process your request unless you indicate a distributor.

We're enclosing a product brochure that gives you the full story on Quantum®. This brochure gives you the product specifications you need to know, a Quantum "Permfection" Chart and answers to the most-asked questions about Quantum. Then, you'll know all about Quantum and you can start using your FREE perms the day you get them.

And, to bring you up-to-date on what our Helene Curtis Professional Division is doing to help you ring up bigger profits, we're also enclosing an informative "Partners in Professionalism" booklet. It includes all the facts about how our exclusive "Hot Line" for salon professionals works -- and how you can get the most out of this Helene Curtis service.

We urge you to read and keep this valuable educational material. And, don't forget to act before the deadline date shown on your Certificate and get the 3 free Quantum waves (an $8.95 normal value!) reserved for you -- before we are forced to release your perms to another salon.

Join the thousands of professionals who are making waves -- and profits -- with Quantum. Mail your Free Perm Certificate today. Or call toll-free 1+800-323-9429 (in Illinois call toll-free 1+800-942-1885). You have nothing to lose. The 3 free perms are yours for the asking -- absolutely free!

Your Partner in Professionalism,

Michael Goldman

Michael Goldman, President
Helene Curtis Professional Division

P.S. When you act now, we'll rush you your 3 free perms by mail. But that's not all! You'll get a "Partners in Professionalism" I.D. card featuring our toll-free "Hot Line" phone number. Plus, you'll also get a coupon for 4 more free Quantum waves!

QUILL CATALOG "WRAP" LETTERS

Two catalog wrap letters I created for a Quill Corporation prospect mailing illustrate how elements from a company's own file and outside databases can be combined effectively. A letter on the front of the wrap began:

> Last year, 18,202 money-wise organizations in **New Jersey** enjoyed big savings on their office supplies and equipment. And they received super-fast service as well!
>
> In the **Newark area** alone, there are 5,508 buyers who take advantage of the savings and superior service we offer here at Quill Corporation of Lincolnshire, IL.
>
> "But that's **800 miles away**," you may be saying.
>
> We're well aware of your concern. That's why we're making a special offer to encourage you to discover how Quill's unique service wipes out the problems distance might seem to create . . .

Then, another letter on the back of the wrap picked up on the mileage personalization and began:

> I would cordially like to invite **Simonetti & Sull** to become a Preferred Customer.
>
> Though we are **800 miles** away from **Bayonne**, we are as near as your phone or mailbox.
>
> We're proud of the fact that more than **18,202** other organizations throughout **New Jersey** turn to Quill to take advantage of the money-saving offers we provide on quality office supplies and equipment. Yes, our low prices are important, but so is our super-fast service . . .

OFFICIAL MEETING FACILITIES GUIDE LETTER

There are times when name personalization can be the ultimate in creativity. Such was the case with a classic letter written by the late Linda Wells to help Ziff-Davis Publishing Company sell its Official Meeting Facilities Guide.

The outer envelope has this personalized message:

> MEET WITH SUCCESS,
>
> MR. JOHNSON
>
> Plan meetings the fast, easy, professional way that wins you new respect from everyone in the company: your secretary to your CEO!

Picking up on that theme, the inside letter began with a personalized Johnson Box:

> "Keep your eyes on Johnson, gentlemen. When a man can plan a meeting as time-and cost-efficient as that, he's sure to move up in the company — fast."
>
> "How does that Johnson guy do it? His job's tougher than mine, yet he stages such smooth conventions, you'd think he was some big-shot Broadway producer."
>
> "Johnson's running it? Certainly, I'd be delighted to speak. My wife will want to come, too. He's making a name for himself with everyone these days."
>
> "Working for Mr. Johnson is something else, Debby. With most bosses, setting up a seminar is a hassle. With him and that book of his, it's easy — and fun!"

Then the first paragraph continued the theme:

> They'll be doing it in the boardroom, the backroom, the mailroom, around the water cooler. After the next big meeting you plan, they'll be talking about you, Mr. Johnson.

Linda Wells commented: "This was the first business letter I'd ever done that injected a little humor into a serious subject. It was a shot at writing about a business publication in the same way you'd write to the buyer at home about a leisure book — and it worked."

Linda Wells (212) 753-3069

Ziff Davis
OMFG
Letter -- page 1
August 14, 1981

"Keep your eyes on Johnson, gentlemen.
When a man can plan a meeting as time-
and cost-efficient as that, he's sure
to move up in the company -- fast."

"How does that Johnson guy do it? His
job's tougher than mine, yet he stages
such smooth conventions, you'd think
he was some big-shot Broadway producer."

"Johnson's running it? Certainly, I'd
be delighted to speak. My wife will
want to come, too. He's making a name
for himself with everyone these days."

"Working for Mr. Johnson is something
else, Debby. With most bosses, setting
up a seminar is a hassle. With him and
that book of his, it's easy -- and fun!"

Dear Mr. Johnson:

    They'll be doing it in the boardroom, the backroom, the mail-
room, around the water cooler. After the next big meeting you
plan, they'll be talking about you, Mr. Johnson.

    Planning a successful seminar, meeting or convention can give
you important new visibility in your company. It can gain you recognition throughout your organization and industry as an executive
who knows how to get things done -- how to do things right.

    A successful meeting can give you a real leg up the ladder.
And when you do it the professional way -- with the OFFICIAL
MEETING FACILITIES GUIDE -- you'll be amazed at the time, money,

Linda Wells (212) 753-3069

effort, energy, work and worry you'll save for yourself, your secretary and your whole staff.

What do I mean when I say "the professional way?" Well, the OFFICIAL MEETING FACILITIES GUIDE comes to you twice a year from Ziff-Davis, publishers of the definitive Meetings & Conventions magazine for full-time professional meeting planners and the Official Hotel & Resort Guide, which has become the "bible" of top-flight travel professionals.

The OFFICIAL MEETING FACILITIES GUIDE gives you the same kind of information in the same way they demand. Accurate information. Authoritative information. Up-to-the-minute information. Instantly accessible and usable information.

The latest information on 1025 top meeting sites

In this lavishly illustrated 1034-page guide, you get complete descriptions of premier sites worldwide. To save you time, they're arranged geographically: The United States including Hawaii, followed by Canada, the Atlantic and Caribbean Islands, Mexico, Central America, South America, Europe, Africa, the Middle East and the Far East.

To make comparing properties easier, each half-page site listing has a consistent format. You get...

...The Basics. Name, number of rooms, address, telephone numbers, key personnel. Toll-free numbers. Sales office numbers and addresses. Telex and cable addresses. Chain affiliations.

...Type and location. Each property is categorized: Conference center, convention/exhibit center, midtown resort, suburban club, cruiseship. Then its exact location is pinpointed with reference to transportation availability and transfer costs.

...Accommodations. A general description of the property's architecture and decorative style is followed by a listing of the equipment and special features like balconies in individual rooms.

...Services, shops, dining, entertainment, recreational and amusement facilities. The highlights of on-site facilities are described in terms of ambience, cuisine, entree price ranges, types of en-

Linda Wells (212) 753-3069

tertainment and hours of operation.

...Principal Meeting Facilities. The number of meeting rooms available, their location and access, their structural features and conveniences. A chart includes data on specific rooms -- their dimensions, locations, floor surfaces, flexibility and capacities in varying usages and configurations.

...Meeting Equipment and Support Services. Details exactly and completely what equipment and services are provided by the hotel, free or at a charge -- and what you can obtain from local vendors. For instance:

PA systems. Podiums. Chairs. Blackboards. Easels. Tables. Corkboards. Lobby bulletin boards. Microphones. Portable stages. Lighted lecterns. Flannel boards. Reel and cassette recorders. Players.

Phonographs. Multilingual simultaneous translation equipment. CCTV equipment. Projectors. Screens. Typewriters. Duplicating machines. Trucks and vans. Pads, pens and pencils. Direction signs. Namecards.

Musicians. Entertainers. Electricians. AV operators. Photographers. Carpenters. Display builders. Sign painters. Painters. Plumbers. Decorators. Translators. Tour leaders. Registrars. The works!

...Rates. Group rates, seasonal rates, European and American Plan rates. Taxes. Check-out times. Credit cards. Direct billing arrangements. With the OFFICIAL MEETING FACILITIES GUIDE, you get everything you need to know about prices to make sound cost comparisons and cut down on-site inspections.

The easy way out that's also the best way out

The OFFICIAL MEETING FACILITIES GUIDE is more, much more, than a listing of sites and their amenities.

It gives you destination reports -- mini guidebooks that describe 80 appealing and popular meeting destination areas! It gives you convention center listings -- pagelong, detailed descriptions of convention and exhibit centers in major cities. It gives you a directory of transportation executives and companies -- specialists who can speed your people to the meeting with the greatest com-

Linda Wells (212) 753-3069

fort and convenience -- at the lowest possible cost.

With the OFFICIAL MEETING FACILITIES GUIDE, you have -- in one, big, handy, cross-referenced and indexed volume -- all the facts, figures and objective information you need to plan your next meeting the time-saving, money-saving, work-saving, worry-saving professional way!

Your secretary will thank you for ordering the OFFIC-IAL MEETING FACILITIES GUIDE. So will your staff and all the other meeting workers and speakers. So will all the attendees -- all the way up in your own organ-ization and throughout your entire industry.

With the OFFICIAL MEETING FACILITIES GUIDE, you'll make even more of a name for yourself, Mr. Johnson!

And if you join us today, we'll be glad to give you savings of 50 per cent on your first year's subscription.

That's right! Mail the enclosed card in the postpaid envelope today and get two issues (one year) -- of OF-FICIAL MEETING FACILITIES GUIDE for just $15. That's half the regular price -- like getting an extra thou-sand-plus pages of need-to-know information -- free!

And there's no need to send money now. We'll be glad to bill your company later. But please place your order today. The soon-er we hear from you, the sooner we can start helping you build a reputation as an executive who knows how to get things done -- and how to do things right!

Thank you.

                                        Sincerely,

                                        Name
                                        Title

Canadian Office Of Tourism Letters

Personalization in direct mail isn't used just to add one-by-one personal elements to a letter. Many times, it can also be used to create messages designed to appeal to whole segments of a list. The Canadian Government Office of Tourism, for example, utilized the computer to tailor messages to specific travel interests of their neighbors south of their border.

A long-running promotion campaign first sought to identify specific travel interests through an inquiry program. Then, once an American's name was on their list, they mailed a series of travel-stimulating letters to each segment. Each of the letters not only pinpointed recreational interests, but was tailored to the particular section of the United States where a recipient lived.

If you are a skier and live in Chicago, for example, an October letter would say:

> This year when you "THINK SNOW," think Skifari Country in Alberta's fabled Canadian Rockies.
>
> It doesn't matter if you're a hotshot or a novice, there's a fantastic experience waiting for you. All-Inclusive Skifari packages put it all together — and they're packed with value.
>
> A full week's skiing in magnificent Banff/Lake Louise with three great ski areas is yours from $117 (up to $174 in high season). If you're a cross-country skier, it's even more economical . . .
>
> A long way to go for a week's skiing? Not a bit! Skifari Country is an easy Air Canada flight away from Chicago.

If you live in the East and like spur-of-the-moment travel, a letter might say:

> We specialize in helping people with those spur-of-the-moment holidays that are often the most enjoyable of all. Even if you've practically completed your holiday thinking, give Canada another thought. This year, more than ever, your next-door neighbor offers the affordable vacation.
>
> We're different, but nearby and friendly. Not an overseas air fare away. Easy to get to . . . and easy on the budget . . .
>
> Come to Atlantic Canada and enjoy some of the most beautiful scenery on the continent, with the salty tang of the ocean everywhere.

If a Canadian convention or conference is scheduled, special letters go to potential registrants:

> We are pleased that Dr. W.K. Lindsay and his colleagues at the Hospital for Sick Children will host the 3rd International Congress on Cleft Palate and Related Craniofacial Anomalies in Toronto, June 5–10.

Toronto is a vibrant and entertaining city. But to make your visit even more memorable, take this opportunity to see other parts of Canada as well.

Business executives might receive a letter that begins:

It is almost a tradition for business executives to take a spring vacation. We would like to make a suggestion.

Next spring, come to Southern Ontario for a change-of-place, change-of-pace vacation that offers a unique blend of relaxation and excitement for every member of your family.

And there are follow-up letters to continue to stimulate interest in Canadian travel:

Last year, we were pleased to answer your request for information about vacationing in Canada.

I hope you're including our country in your vacation planning again this year.

127/6206

 Canadian Government   Office de tourisme
Office of Tourism   du Canada

Ottawa, Canada
K1A 0H6

October 21, 1976

Mr. R. Hodgson
Box 46
Westtown
PA 19395

Dear Mr. Hodgson,

This year when you "THINK SNOW", think Skifari
Country in Alberta's fabled Canadian Rockies.

It doesn't matter if you're a hotshot or a novice,
there's a fantastic experience waiting for you.
All-inclusive Skifari packages put it all together
- and they're packed with value.

A full week's skiing in magnificent Banff/Lake Louise
with three great ski areas is yours from $117 (up to
$174 in high season). If you're a cross-country
skier, it's even more economical -- from $74 to $122.
At spectacular Jasper, prices start at $131 (all
prices per person, 2 to a room, airfare extra).

A long way to go for a week's skiing? Not a bit!
Skifari Country is an easy Air Canada flight away
from Chicago. Then a comfortable coach or your own
skierized rental car to the slopes.

For the ultimate skiing thrill, the guided helicopter
skiing option takes you up to deep, dry virgin powder
high on the glaciers. Breathtaking!

A great thing about a Skifari holiday is the CHOICE:
you choose when (there's dependable snow right into
May)...and where (there's a wide choice of ski areas
and accommodation)...how long and how much.

Get the complete story on Air Canada's Skifari
Country. It's free, and it's yours if you simply
drop the enclosed card in the mail. Do it today.

Ski your heart out!

George Tawse-Smith,
Director of Marketing.

Canadian Government   Office de tourisme
Office of Tourism   du Canada

Ottawa, Canada
K1A 0H6

May 5, 1975

Mr. R. Hodgson
Box 46
Westtown
PA 19395

Dear Mr. Hodgson,

If you're one of those people who puts off vacation planning to the last minute...welcome to the club!

We specialize in helping people with those spur-of-the-moment holidays that are often the most enjoyable of all. Even if you've practically completed your holiday thinking, give Canada another thought. This year, more than ever, your next-door neighbour offers the affordable vacation.

We're different, but nearby and friendly. Not an overseas air fare away. Easy to get to...and easy on the budget.

You have a fine choice of complete Canadian vacation tours. Your local travel agent, airline office, bus or rail company or auto club can give you details.

Come to Atlantic Canada and enjoy some of the most beautiful scenery on the continent, with the salty tang of the ocean everywhere. Long, uncrowded beaches...Highland gatherings and Acadian French soirées reflecting our diverse heritage...lobster get-togethers in weathered old fishing villages...theatre festivals...superb fishing in sea or stream...gorgeously situated parks and campgrounds...and traditional Atlantic hospitality at moderate prices.

Let me send you our free 32-page booklet "Canada This Summer". Just mail the reply card. But please remember, the calendar tells you to act soon!

Cordially,

Canadian Government   Office de tourisme
Office of Tourism   du Canada

Ottawa, Canada
K1A 0H6

June 4, 1976

Mr. R. Hodgson
Box 46
westtown
PA 19395

Dear Mr. Hodgson,

We are pleased that Dr. W.K. Lindsay and his
colleagues at the Hospital for Sick Children
will host the 3rd International Congress on
Cleft Palate and Related Craniofacial Anomalies
in Toronto, June 5 - 10, 1977.

Toronto is a vibrant and entertaining city. But
to make your visit even more memorable, take this
opportunity to see other parts of Canada as well.

Contact your Travel Agent for information on
Canada's variety of attractions. The magnificent
outdoors offers unparalleled opportunities for
golfing, fishing and boating that complement
equally delightful indoor pursuits, theatre, dining,
top entertainment and fine shopping.

Canada is an unspoiled natural playground big
enough to provide you and your family with a lifetime of varied vacations. Return the enclosed
reply card for free literature and contact the
official Air Carriers of the Congress who will be
pleased to give you detailed information and
assistance. We hope your attendance in Toronto will
be just the beginning of many delightful visits to
our beautiful country.

Cordially yours,

G. Tawse-Smith,   112/6503
Director of Marketing.

Canada ☀

Canadian Government   Office de tourisme
Office of Tourism   du Canada

Ottawa, Canada
K1A 0H6

October 17, 1974

Mr. R. Hodgson
Franklin Mint Corporation
Rfd 1
Franklin Center
PA 19063

Dear Mr. Hodgson,

It is almost a tradition for business executives to take a spring vacation. We would like to make a suggestion.

Next spring, come to Southern Ontario for a change-of-place, change-of-pace vacation that offers a unique blend of relaxation and excitement for every member of your family.

Spring blooms early in Southern Ontario for much of the Province lies south of the Northern California border. As the fields and orchards spring to life again, it's great motoring weather for the air is fresh, the roads uncrowded and the accommodation is readily available.

City attractions of theatre, dining and shopping are more fun when crowds are thinner, the temperature milder. Many of the more popular hotels offer special rates for springtime groups.

So why not come to Southern Ontario for that spring break next year?

Cordially,

Dan Wallace,   241/0409
Director of Marketing.

P.S. We have just published a new guide book called "Touring Canada". Its 60 pages are crammed with 150 colour photographs and over 50 maps. If you would like to receive your free copy, simply mail back the enclosed pre-paid reply card.
We'll do the rest. D.W.

148/2071

Canadian Government   Office de tourisme
Office of Tourism   du Canada

Ottawa, Canada
K1A 0H6

February 23, 1977

Mr. R. Hodgson
P. O. Box 46
Westtown
PA 19395

Dear Mr. Hodgson,

Last year, we were pleased to answer your request
for information about vacationing in Canada.

I hope you're including our country in your vacation
planning again this year. There's so much to go for.
Our unspoiled forests, lakelands and magnificent
coastlines. Sophisticated, lively cities. Summer
theatres and festivals. Fine accommodation and
cosmopolitan dining. Great golf, the finest fishing
in the world — in fact activities for everyone!

          And this year, Canada adds EXTRA VALUE to
          our traditional welcome for U.S. visitors.

One of the best ways to enjoy the many pleasures of
this big land is to take one of the many tours and
vacation "packages" available from your area.
Wilderness adventures...fly-and-drive vacations...
summer festival and city packages...boat cruises..
tours by bus and train. The choice is wide.

This way you get additional benefits--including
all-inclusive rates and itineraries planned by
experts, plus the convenience of having a local
travel agent make all arrangements for you.

We've put together a new, informative and colour-
ful vacation planning kit for 1977. It's FREE.
All you have to do is mail the reply card today.
We'll include a highway map in case you like to
plan your own route. You'll see how easy it is to
get to Canada by road, rail or air.

Cordially,

George Tawse-Smith,
Director of Marketing.

Canadian Government   Office de tourisme
Office of Tourism   du Canada

Ottawa, Canada
K1A 0H6

August 19, 1975

Mr. R. Hodgson
P. O. Box 46
Westtown
PW 19395

Dear Mr. Hodgson,

Americans who know Canada well say that late summer
and fall is the ideal time of year to visit us. In
view of your earlier interest in Canadian vacations
we would like to send you our autumn vacation guide.

From late August through October, most days are warm
and sunny. Our fine resort hotels, our beautiful
parks, our golf courses, scenic spots and historic
sites are uncrowded. And our cosmopolitan cities
are alive with fall-season activity.

It's a great time of year. And this is a good year
for you to come. Here's why. It's easy to get to
Canada...and when you don't have to travel far, your
vacation dollar goes farther in these days of high
travel costs. Incidentally, your travel agent can
tell you about the variety of complete vacation
tours available. We have so much to show you...

Your free vacation kit will help you plan your visit
to any part of Canada, from the Atlantic fishing
village of Heart's Content, Newfoundland to the wave-
washed beaches of the Pacific Rim National Park;
from the majestic Rockies through the rolling foot-
hills to the lake-filled mid-west; from big-city
excitement to the solitude of our great northern
lakes and forests.

There is far more than I can describe in a letter,
so please let me send you our free fall vacation
planning kit. Mail the reply card for it today.

Cordially,

                                    3521u363

Dan Wallace,
Director of Marketing.

SECTION X

THE LIGHT TOUCH

Direct mail isn't all work; sometimes it can be fun, too — for both recipients and writers.

One caution: writing letters with a touch of humor is extremely difficult. What may seem funny to you can easily draw yawns from an audience. It takes very special writing talent to make such letters entertaining and result-producing.

Here are two series of letters with a lighter touch which, if space had permitted, would have been included in Section III as "classics."

S. ROSE, INC. "S. MOUSE" LETTERS

No collection of classic direct mail letters would be complete without some of the "s. mouse" letters created 30 years ago by Robert Silverman, Cleveland's highly creative direct marketing service, for S. Rose, Inc., a local office equipment dealer.

The first letter read:

> i am s. mouse of s. rose, inc. and im the boss. when bob rose and dick rose leave at night im in charge.
>
> if i want i can put my feet up on dick roses desk and squeak my head off. but im in trouble now for answering the phone.
>
> last night a man called up and said send me out 10,000 filing cabinets, 23 used comptometers and 341 new and used desks and chairs.
>
> well, i said, o.k and he said, to whom am i speaking. and i said, this is s. mouse of s. rose, thats whom. and he said, oh, well be sure and tell dick or bob what i want, and then he hung up. so i feel like a rat.
>
> if i tell dick rose somebody wanted 10,000 filing cabinets he would just laugh at me, because i didnt get the guys name or address.
>
> so im writing you on this electric typewriter they left plugged in and i hope youre the guy who talked to me last night.
>
> but even if you arent, why not order something from dick rose or bob rose. theyll give you a good deal. and theyve got everything in office fixtures, furniture and machines. just call them up at ch 1-1060 and tell em i sent you.

The letter was signed with a mouse paw print . . . and a postscript added:

> p. s. the roses will treat you right. if you dont want to buy it theyll rent it to you. and if you dont want to buy or rent you can sell your stuff to them.

There was a smattering of response. But when letter number two came from s. mouse two weeks later, the phone really began to ring. Orders began to flow in (many addressed directly to s. mouse and some even included checks made out to "s. mouse" — the company framed one, but cashed the rest).

Letter No. 2:

i am s. mouse of s. rose, inc., and the reason i dont use capital letters is because im tired.

a man asked me about that this evening. he called up and said whos this squeaking and i said s. mouse, night manager, and he said, why dont you write capital letters, it looks terrible.

buddy, i said, you should try standing on the shift key and step on another letter at the same time. every time i try it, i said, this electric typewriter bucks and i am dam tired of getting thrown in the wastebasket.

all right, said the man, i am picking on you because you moused up my order. you mean loused up, dont you, i said, and he said, no, you moused it up. i wanted 12,500 filing cabinets not 10,000. you tell dick or bob rose to straighten it out pronto.

but you told me 10,000, i said and he said see here, are you trying to mouse me up again. i said no sir.

so now im waiting for his conscience to start hurting him about hanging up on me. in the excitement i forgot to get his name and address again.

sometimes i think i will never learn this business as well as dick or bob. they know everything about office furniture and machines and equipment. and theyll give you a good deal. theyll sell you what you need or rent it to you or even buy what youve got.

so will you call bob or dick rose and buy something and tell them i tried. call cherry 1-1060 and tell them not to bring that cat back in here.

p.s. the roses never mouse up anybody.

Letter No. 3:

i am s. mouse of s. rose, inc. and i am the night manager.

maybe you would like to know what the s. stands for. people call up at 3 a.m. and ask about the s. and when i tell them they just say, oh, and hang up without buying anything.

this makes me look bad. i have been the night manager for three months now and i have not sold a paper weight even. if dick rose or bob rose knew about it theyd fire me sure, or bring a cat in here.

so i am going to be a rat. i will resort to low tactics.

i won't tell you what the s. in my name stands for until you buy something from s. rose.

the s. in s. rose stands for satisfaction. and service. and for superb office machines, office furniture and fixtures. but youll never know about my s. unless you play ball.

you call dick rose or bob rose tomorrow and order something and i will divulge the secret. call cherry 1-1060.

but please dont tell the roses im using this just to get your business because they will think its dirty pool.

the roses are very ethical and they would not be so sneaky as to use a mouses first name to get you to come to their store at 1213 prospect ave. free parking across the street.

Letter No. 4:

i am s. mouse of s. rose, inc. and im sorry about that last letter. the one about the s. in s. mouse.

it has caused a lot of trouble with the roses.

people come in and buy desks and office machines and fixtures and chairs and shelves and things and then they look at dick rose or bob rose and say, all right, what does the s. stand for.

oh, the roses say, ha, ha, not our s. well, good.

its your mouses s. we want to know about, the people say. whos s., the roses say, and the people say, your night manager s., thats whose s. now, what does the s. stand for. and then both of the roses start sweating and you can see the whites of their eyes.

so ive got to admit something. i havent told the roses that ive taken over the store at night.

i thought id run things and surprise them. make it a good going proposition before i made my salary demands.

thats why i said i wouldnt tell what the s. stands for unless you buy something. but i will tell you anyhow.

the s. stands for sinnamon. because im a sinnamon color.

so you call dick or bob and order anything you want. just call cherry 1-1060 and theyll give you the best deal youve ever had in office furniture and fixtures and machines. they rent stuff and they buy stuff too. and tell them that s. mouse sent you.

Letter No. 5:

i am s. mouse of s. rose, inc. and the s. stands for sinnamon. you can spell sinnamon any way you want. my mother spells it with an s.

that man whose account ive been handling for the roses just laughed and laughed at me over the telephone. you cant even spell sinnamon, he said.

i told him he was lucky to get a mouse that could spell at all. i said, most mice couldnt even answer the phone.

and he said, i meant to ask you about that, how do you answer the phone. and i said, well you watch the little buttons and the one that lights up, thats the one you press and say, hello.

why you little rat, he said, dont get smart with me. im tired of waiting on those filing cabinets, anyhow. all 15,000 of them.

you mean, 12,500, i said, you told me 10,000 and then changed your mind. and he said, youve moused me up for the last time. turn in your night managers suit, mouse, he said. im canceling my order.

wait, i said, i am trying to learn the business.

im giving you the business, he said. from now on i will deal with bob rose and dick rose direct. thats cherry 1-1060, isnt it.

yes, sir, i said. i only know the underside of this business. bob and dick know everything about office furniture and fixtures and machines. theyll sell you what you want or theyll rent it to you or theyll even buy your equipment. just call cherry 1-1060.

i know that, he said, so why should i deal with a stupid mouse.

gee, i wish that man would leave me alone. the worst part of it is i dont even know his name. sometimes i wonder if i will ever be a hard-hitting go-getter in the business world.

Letter No. 6:

i am s. mouse of s. rose, inc., and that noise outside dick rose's door is the cat.

i see now that i should have told bob and dick that i've taken over as night manager. but i hate being laughed at.

this man called up up and said, hey, you should see the mouse i got working for me. i said, you, sir, are a copy cat.

no kidding, said the man, this mouse is 39, 22, 37. well, i said, if you don't know for sure how old he is why don't you ask

this has nothing to do with her age, you dope, he said. she's young and she's got everything.

does she have white whiskers and an extra long tail, i asked, just to be polite.

and he said, of course not, and i said, is she your night manager, and he just laughed and laughed and said, you kill me, mouse, and i said, i only wish i could, but he didn't hear me.

Letter No. 7:

i am s. mouse, the night manager of s. rose, inc. and if they wanted to fire me they could have given me two weeks notice.

i certainly wouldnt rip up the floor and tear out partitions to get rid of a night manager, would you. and then lie about it to customers.

when people ask about the pounding, dick rose smiles and says, oh were remodeling. and bob rose laughs and says, it will make the store look a lot nicer when people come in to buy desks and office machines and things. who do they think theyre kidding.

that remodeling talk may fool some people but i know why they put those carpenters in here. hah. they think they can succeed where the cat has failed. i will show them.

this is my closing out sale as i am moving upstairs in a rolltop desk. two can play at this remodeling game. the confidential price list is one i got out of dick roses drawer and ive done exactly what you are supposed to do with a confidential price list. you mark up the prices before you show it to a customer, so i have marked it up good.

p.s. you may order by phone if you like. just call ch 1-1060 and ask for dick or bob. and mention my name. they dont act jealous of me in front of customers.

Letter No. 8:

a free gift for you from s. mouse . . .

now that im the boss here at s. rose, inc., im going to think big.

i will start out by giving you something just to get you to come down here and buy filing cabinets, and desks and chairs or new and used office machines and equipment.

so i will give you the second story of this building.

i don't think anybody ever gave away so much just to drum up trade. but thats the way a big executive operates.

actually i got the idea from dick rose. bob was talking to him the other day and he said, hey, dick, what will be do if whatsisname comes in and wants to buy all that stuff on the second floor. and dick said, give him the whole story.

so thats what i will do. you come in and ask for the story and dick or bob will give it to you, i am sure. they will give you one story or another. and i bet theyll give you one of those coin purses too . . .

theyve got a box of rose colored coin purses that they were going to give away to people who come in to see the new store so youll get something all right. you come in and see.

while they were tearing up everything, looking for me and not finding me, tra la, they got things in such a mess they had to remodel everything.

so come in and look and ask for your free gift from me. thats 1213 prospect ave. free parking. the place to get the best values in new and used office furniture, machines and equipment.

This, the final letter, was signed "s. mouse, executive."

A wonderful thing about the s. mouse letters was they not only reached the 4,000 business executives to whom they were sent, they were passed along to thousands of others. Secretaries made sure the boss got them (but first ran and made copies for all their friends). The most wonderful thing of all was that they did the job for which they were intended — regaining old accounts and bringing in new ones. After all, that's what makes great direct mail letters great!

PLAZA HOTEL "LETTERS FROM A CHAMBERMAID"

Perhaps the all-time greatest series of novelty letters was a 1962–63 campaign created by The Lavenson Bureau of Advertising for New York's Plaza Hotel. The problem: how do you "unstuff" a sometimes stuffy reputation and increase room occupancy? The solution: create a "must be read" series of letters directed at one of the toughest-to-reach business audiences — presidents, board chairmen and executive vice presidents of companies doing more than a million dollars annually.

The method: five personalized letters sent to an audience of 40,000, with copy so charming executive secretaries not only passed the letters along to their bosses, but shared them with dozens of others within each organization.

The letters appeared on regular Plaza Hotel stationery with a special, added touch — a little line on the appropriate letters reading "Office of the Chambermaid."

Letter No. 1

The first letter was mailed August 1, 1962 on "Office of the Chambermaid" stationery:

Dear Mr. Jones:

I'm the Chambermaid.

I have my own stationery.

I take care of the rooms at The Plaza.

The rooms at The Plaza are The Plaza's heart and soul, the real reason The Plaza is such a lovely memory in the minds of our guests who visit us so often.

I like the rooms (and suites) better than anything else at The Plaza. The reasonable room rates are our most important asset (that's what our management says, so why there are special summer rates I'll never know.) Anyway, the rooms have all sorts of advantages over the other attractions at The Plaza.

You can eat magnificent food this summer in the Persian Room (they're keeping it open . . . with entertainment), the Oak Room or the Edwardian Room — but you can't lie down there. You can sip tea or cocktails at five in the Palm Court — but you can't sleep there. You can admire the beautiful new carpeting in the spacious halls and lobbies of The Plaza — but not in your bare feet.

In your room at The Plaza you can dine, drink a toast, and be entertained (FM or television). A room at The Plaza is home — or an office if you want to be busy. Businessmen seem to love it.

You know how I know the rooms are the most important part of The Plaza? Because The Plaza just spent over four million dollars redecorating and air-conditioning them.

To top it all off they had this stationery engraved for me (that was in addition to the four million).

Isn't it elegant? So is The Plaza.

Won't you come see for yourself?

Yours truly,

Mary O'Sullivan

Letter No. 2

The second letter sent on October 25, 1962 was on the stationery of "Office of the Vice President and Managing Director":

Dear Mr. Jones:

I have a problem.

It's like this. Recently, one of our chambermaids, Mary O'Sullivan, wrote a sales letter which you may have received. (A privilege that I usually reserve for myself, as I am rather good at it.) But, after all, it made her happy, and I'm a big one for employee morale . . . we have company picnics, bowling leagues, elevator races and all that kind of stuff. Well, the point is, Mary O'Sullivan got 387 replies to her letter including over 100 orders. (We have a quaint custom of calling them reservations instead of orders.)

But her letter talked only of our bedrooms. She didn't say a thing about the function rooms. (As perfect for Boards of Directors meetings as wedding receptions.) And the fact that we spent $175,000 to restore the unsurpassed beauty of our Ballroom escaped mention altogether. She probably thought you never planned a lunch, speech or special event in your life. It's not that I have anything against boudoirs, but Mary O'Sullivan simply ignored everything else.

Now tell me . . . as one businessman to another . . . what should I do?

Fire Mary O'Sullivan? Sentence her to 3 months in the laundry? Bar her from the Persian Room?

I would appreciate your valued advice. By the way, if you have any thorny problems bedeviling you, let me know. I'll be glad to return the favor and do whatever I can . . . particularly if your problems involve one of the many services at The Plaza.

Very sincerely yours,

Paul Sonnabend

Vice President and Managing Director

P.S. I hope Mary O'Sullivan cleans better than she writes. I think I'd better check on that . . .

Letter No. 3

On January 3, 1963 another letter from "Office of the Chambermaid" arrived. By this time, Mary's fans included not only the bosses, but the bosses' secretaries. They made sure her letter was on top of the "to be read today" mail:

> Dear Mr. Jones:
>
> It's me again. The Chambermaid. Remember?
>
> How are you? I'm fine, but a lot has happened here recently. For one thing, Mr. Sonnabend, our Managing Director, found out that I wrote you and almost fired me for going over his head in the sales letter department. Luckily he asked everybody what they thought. That's what saved me. We got a lot of new guest reservations. One man even said Mr. Sonnabend and I should trade jobs. Isn't that funny? Mr. Sonnabend didn't think so.
>
> Anyway, maybe it was you who asked if we think The Plaza is the only hotel in New York. Of course it isn't. There are some bigger and a lot of them newer. Sometimes people ask why we don't tear it down and build a shining new Plaza. We did, back in 1907. And now we've redecorated it, and it couldn't be nicer and more comfy. And the rooms are still the big, luxury, leg-stretching size that gives a man space to relax in (men do love to spread out).
>
> You like to laugh?
>
> Come see Julius Monk's show "Dime a Dozen" at the new PLaza 9-. It's in the same place where the Rendezvous Room used to be. It's very funny, but to me it's even funnier to see all our guests trying to crowd in to see it. Or to see the star in The Persian Room. I still say the bedrooms are the best part of The Plaza!
>
> Try The Plaza yourself and try everything — we're very good for group meetings, too.
>
> You can write either to me or Mr. Sonnabend for a reservation. We show our letters to each other now.
>
> Yours truly,
>
> Mary O'Sullivan

Letter No. 4

On May 9, 1963, still another letter arrived from the "Office of the Chambermaid":

Dear Mr. Jones:

Don't tell me about labor problems!

Just as Mr. Sonnabend and I were developing a nice working relationship (he was just beginning to see things my way), he ups and gets promoted to President of The Plaza. Then he took on a new Vice President and General Manager to run the hotel for him. And here I am trying to train the new man . . . right in the middle of the busy season. Now I ask you!

It could be worse. He isn't really new. He used to be Resident Manager of The Plaza some years back . . . and has all kinds of experience in hotels. His name is Alphonse Salomone. (He says it rhymes with alimony. Isn't that clever? That's Mr. Salomone for you!)

Which reminds me. Just the other day he came up with a lovely and clever idea. He's started a new service for men who make so many trips to New York they practically live at The Plaza. He says you can leave a change of clothes at The Plaza between trips and we'll see that they're laundered and dry cleaned and waiting for you on your next trip back. That means you can make trips with nothing but a brief case. I have to admit it's a good idea even if I didn't think of it, although of course I could have thought of it if I weren't so busy keeping the rooms the way you like them!

Anyway, come see us soon. Me, Mr. Sonnabend and Mr. Salomone are looking forward to seeing you. But see me first . . . the other two don't make up your bed.

Yours truly,

Mary O'Sullivan

P. S.   The other night they gave a party to welcome Mr. Salomone to The Plaza and a photographer took a picture of me with Mr. Sonnabend and Mr. Salomone. I wanted to enclose a copy of the picture with this letter but Mr. Sonnabend said, "Who cares what a chambermaid looks like?" You care, don't you? Drop me a note and I'll send you the picture.

Talk about response! Hundreds of busy business executives took time to write Mary and ask for the picture. What they got was a glossy photo with Mr. Sonnabend and Mr. Salomone sitting side-by-side with Mary, showing her a letter. And, as you might guess, the letter covered Mary's face!

Letter No. 5

The final letter in the series was mailed on July 8, 1963, on the "Office of the Vice President & General Manager" letterhead:

Dear Mr. Jones:

It's not true!

Mary O'Sullivan will not sing in the Persian Room this summer. She must have started this rumor herself . . . out of a suppressed desire to see her name in lights. Recently she started calling her uniform a bunny costume and singing Irish lullabies while making up the beds. She even asked Julius Monk for a walk-on part in "Dime a Dozen" at the PLaza 9-!

We appreciate her zeal, but her talents as a chambermaid are more valuable in the bedroom than the Persian Room. And anyway, she'll be very busy this summer. Why?

Because it's summer. People are flocking to New York just for the fun of it. And why not? It's the one time of year when the city has every-thing working in its favor. Beautiful weather. Special events as part of the Summer Festival. No poison ivy. Nor mosquitoes.

Naturally The Plaza is going three better: special summer rates ($17 single, $22 double), air conditioning and no charge for children under fourteen who stay in the same room with their parents. Mary, who is more famous for her limericks, is now brushing up her Mother Goose. We're always appropriate at The Plaza.

But we're not stopping there. The Persian Room will remain open. (Without Mary O'Sullivan's assistance!) It promises to be the bigg-est attraction at New York's Summer Festival. Now all we need is your attendance to make this summer at The Plaza the jolliest one in history.

See you soon?

Very sincerely,

Alphonse W. Salomone, Jr.

Vice President and General Manager

P.S.   I hope you'll use the enclosed card for a personal and spe-cial introduction when you visit The Plaza this summer!

The result? The Plaza's occupancy rate rose sharply, even in the face of extra competition from new hotels.

SECTION XI

HOW TO START A LETTER

One of the most difficult jobs a letter writer faces is simply getting started. There are many different possibilities, but the most common are the "you" approach, asking a question, telling a story, or extending an invitation. Examples of each of these methods are discussed throughout this book. Shown in this section are several examples of each of these letter-opening approaches to provide you with a quick reference idea source. Common salutations and Johnson Box approaches are also included.

THE "YOU" APPROACH

First choice among most of the leading copywriters for a letter lead is the "you" approach. In some cases, it involves actual use of the word, "you," while in other cases it's an implied "you." Consider these examples for idea starters:

We're so sure you'll agree Kroy lettering can give your work the professional appearance it deserves, we want to give you a closer look.

We'll send you a free copy of our brochure along with a sample of Kroy lettering. You'll see how Kroy lettering can make a remarkable difference in the appearance and effectiveness of your printed communications.

Roy Beauchamp for Kroy, Inc.

You owe it to yourself to find out what the Armed Forces can offer you. It could make a very big difference in your life.

Roy Beauchamp for Department of Defense

You don't have to be a sitting duck for burglars, Mr. John J. Jones. With the increasing rate of crime and burglary in our nation, it is time you consider the protection you need for your home and your valuables. We would like to help.

Saul Mills for Montgomery-Ward

If you are worried about the future . . . about increasing inflation . . . and the factors that make for such a nervous economy, I have some ideas you should seriously consider . . .

Bill Steiner for Numismatic Funding Corp.

I'm in an interesting position. In this letter I'm going to ask you to pay for something that I give your boss for nothing.

Bill Steiner for *Folio* Magazine

Management executives like you are a special breed. They couldn't care less about free gifts just because they're free. But if they see one that can help them be more effective, put more black ink in the company's books, and put more money in their own banks and investment portfolios, their minds are wide open. That attitude is one reason they hold the jobs they do.

I think in a moment you'll agree with me that an Executive Portfolio I have reserved in your name is such a gift.

Dick Neff for *Business Week*

You have a true friend who cares about your safety and convenience. As a loyal and satisfied Member of the AAA-Chicago Motor Club, your friend has asked us to send you this special invitation to join the Club for year-round peace of mind and protection.

Dick Trenbeth for The Chicago Motor Club

These days, like most women, you play a very important role in helping your family make ends meet. Maybe more important than you realize!

The fact is, if you're in that majority of American mothers that work outside the home, your family depends on your income now and in the future. They also depend on you for all the child-raising, cooking, cleaning and household tasks that you perform every day.

Ask yourself: Where would my family turn if they had to make it without me?

Sheila Stogol for Bankers Life

According to the U.S. Department of Commerce, millions of people end up with a retirement income of only a few hundred dollars a month. And that includes their Social Security benefits!

That simply wouldn't be enough money for you to enjoy all the things you've promised yourself after your working days are over, would it, Mr. Jones? In fact, it's barely enough to survive on!

A monthly check made out to Mr. John J. Jones for A THOUSAND DOLLARS — or more — would be a lot more to your liking, I'm sure.

Tom Brady for Bankers Life

Thousands of small businesses will pay very good money for one essential business service. A service you can provide easily — without ever moving from your desk!

Yes, you can make $150 to $250 a week, just by working part-time whenever you please. Or, if you want to dig in your heels and roll up your sleeves, you can make much more — while enjoying every minute of it!

Sig Rosenblum for Jayhill's

If you're like thousands of other G.I.'s and Vets, memories, stories, drama and dreams are going to flood back to you when you hold the new G.I. Jerrican Lighter in your hand.

The faces of friends . . . the scents and sounds of far-off places . . . the good times and tough times will cross your mind's eye. But the Jerrican will do much more than spark your imagination . . .

Sig Rosenblum for Pembroke-Court Co.

If you, like me, are one of those particular people who don't like to compromise on the quality of anything they put in their mouths. If you already know the gourmet's secret — that just a little extra flavor can make all the difference in the extra enjoyment you can get from anything you put on your table — then I believe you will benefit greatly from accepting my invitation to join a club which I suspect fits your particular tastes to a "tee."

John Lyle Shimek for Hale Indian River Groves

Good customers deserve the best. That's why keeping you informed about everything new at the Clearing House is Top Priority business with us.

Marvin Barckley for Publishers Clearing House

If I came into your home or office, I bet I'd find magazines within easy reach of where you read your mail. I know so because they're a normal complement of people who are making their mark in this world.

But now I'll go a step further and also bet you pay more for your magazines than you have to. I say so because I see you're not one of our regular customers . . .

Marvin Barckley, Publishers Clearing House

In these days of hustle and bustle, home is an important place to each of us . . . a place to relax with family and entertain friends. And, if you're like me, you like to surround yourself with interesting works of art that reflect your unique taste and style . . .

Herschell Gordon Lewis for Calhoun's Collectors Society

Hurry ! ! !

It may be a slight shock to get mail beginning with "Hurry" from me. "Hurry" is not exactly my middle name. It usually hurts me even to think about rushing someone else. But this time it's a favor . . . to you.

Bob Stone for the Direct Marketing Association

I suppose it is a bit presumptuous of us to ask you for a favor when you are already one of our valued customers. But, quite frankly, we need your help rather urgently. And, believe me, I would not intrude on your time if there were anyone else who could help us.

Southern Living Magazine

If my letter has reached the right hands, Channel 13 is on your television set perhaps as much as any of the other six stations. Maybe even as much as the other six combined. And chances are you have seen our appeals for new members and said to yourself: Yes, I really should send them some money. Well, no one knows better than I that when one is relaxing it's pretty hard to find the resolve to stand up, write a note and a check, find an envelope and a stamp. I understand the problem fully, believe me.

This is the reason I'm writing you today . . .

John P. Walsh for WNET

If you could trade places with the Man in the Moon . . . you might well become the best informed person who ever lived!

For then, you could look down — as he does — at this whirling earth, to view the kaleidoscope pattern of events in the proper perspective.

But unfortunately, you cannot take a trip to the moon . . .

Maxwell Ross for *Look* Magazine

I'm writing because I have reason to believe you are a person who appreciates exceptional food. If I'm right, you will be interested in this offer . . .

Omaha Steaks International

There's a special treat awaiting you this Christmas. No matter how hard the winds howl in Chicago, you can enjoy the beauty of springtime in Holland right in The Jones Home.

This is a particularly advantageous time to discover for yourself the very special way Dutch gardeners bring a touch of beauty to their yards and gardens year after year with only a minimum of gardening effort . . . and without spending a lot of money.

Dick Hodgson for Breck's

I'd like to share with you a Holiday gift idea which has long been a tradition here in Holland. I think you'll find it the answer to many gift problems which may have been troublesome for you in the past.

Dick Hodgson for Breck's

Your place has been reserved!

As a First Card accountholder, you are automatically eligible for an exclusive offer.

Continental Casualty Company

In today's fast moving business world, you spend as much time out of the office as you do in it . . . and that means being out of touch with your staff and business associates.

Bell Atlantic Mobile Systems

I would like to share with you a few words about the newest Card from American Express.

This Card is beyond the aspirations and reach of all but a few of our Card members. Appropriately called The Platinum Card, it is reserved solely for those whose long association with American Express and annual volume of travel and entertainment charges indicate that they require and deserve to command the best.

Receipt of the Invitation certifies that you are among them.

American Express

Since I consider you a friend of Learning Dynamics, I would appreciate your evaluation of a new program we are about to introduce.

Learning Dynamics Inc.

If you'd just as soon see the Plaza torn down and never pay any attention to Wall Street and already know everything about the men who will challenge John Lindsay for mayor and couldn't care less about crime and pollution and slums and narcotics and traffic and don't give a hoot what happens to Welfare Island and find street trees a bore and have no interest in whether they build a new jetport or put up a bridge between Long Island and Connecticut or finish Interstate 80 West and don't mind if the World Trade Center does kill TV reception and hate Central Park and feel that any celebrity who gives interviews is an out-and-out exhibitionist and never go to the theatre or galleries or ballgames or movies or concerts or read books or do crosswords and never go shopping and never eat out and don't wear clothes, YOU DON'T NEED *NEW YORK* ANYMORE, AND YOU'RE RIGHT TO LET YOUR SUBSCRIPTION EXPIRE, which it has.

Bill Jayme for *New York* Magazine

Imagine for a moment that you are one of them — a slave.

You are forbidden to leave your master's property without written permission. Your house is searched twice a month.

You may see only two of your friends at a time — never more. Your children can be shipped hundreds of miles away without notice. Learning to read? Earning money? Freedom in worship — or marriage? Trial by jury? All denied.

Escape, and you will be publicly whipped the first time, branded the second, lose an ear the third, and be castrated or endure flagellation the fourth.

Are you in barbaric Baylonia? In ancient Egypt? Not at all. You are in the United States of America before the Civil War.

> Bill Jayme for the University of Michigan Press

It is my pleasure to inform you that the editors of *WHO'S WHO IN AMERICA* have selected your name for inclusion in the new, Thirty-Ninth Edition, now in compilation.

I have enclosed a data form and ask that you complete it and return it to the editors. A manuscript of the biography prepared for your data will be sent to you for checking prior to publication.

> Marquis Who's Who, Inc.

This is your chance to catch up with your life insurance needs, $10,000.00 worth of term protection for as little as $2.92 a month at age 34, even if you already have G.I. or any other kind of life insurance.

> Walter Weintz For National Liberty Marketing, Inc.

Many people, when they grow up — when they become worldy, educated, sophisticated, absorbed in their own personal success — set aside their sense of wonder in the same way they set aside the toys of childhood.

Forever.

Many people. But we hope, not you.

In you, we believe we have found a person still open to life's magic. Still exhilarated by meeting new people. Still eager to discover new places, assess new ideas, probe new interests. A person who loves to look at what others find "ordinary" in fresh new ways.

If this description fits you, then we have a magazine that fits you.

Emily Soell for Knapp Communications Corp.

You did it. You promised. You offered. You invited. Now what?

Do you panic? Do you worry? Do you roll your eyes and wonder why you ever started this? Do you fleetingly consider canceling? Claiming a sudden trip, a searing headache, a sick child, an unexpected visit from an aging, anti-social aunt?

Not any more, you don't!

Now, you turn calmly to *The Bon Appetit Dinner Party Cookbook* . . .

Emily Soell for Knapp Communications Corp.

Here's a free First Edition invitation you deserve so much, it would just be criminal to deny yourself the pleasure.

You work so hard all day. You cope with the nonsense and noise, the rip-offs and rudeness, the vulgarity and violence, of modern society. You owe it to yourself to find respite in a gentler time, a gentler place, where the two loudest sounds you'll ever hear are those of Hercule Poirot twirling his well-waxed moustaches . . . and Miss Marple clicking her knitting needles over something fluffy.

Linda Wells for the Agatha Christie Collection

If you love and appreciate fine American furniture as I do, then what I'm about to tell you is truly exciting news . . .

The Franklin Mint

If you are fascinated, as I am, by works of art in miniature, and if you have the collector's instinct for exquisite craftsmanship, you will be especially interested in the opportunity open to you now.

The Franklin Mint

As one who appreciates objects of rare beauty and fine craftsman-ship, I think you will be most interested to learn of an unusual oppor-tunity that is open to you now. For you are one of a select group of collectors who are being invited to commission a spectacular work of exceptional distinction.

The Franklin Mint

You can do yourself — and certainly your company — a favor. It all has to do with an information gap your company may be suffering from . . . without even knowing it!

You see, one of the things that makes computer professionals so effective — so important to their company's efficiency and growth — is the fact that they read *Computerworld*, every week. The computer field's leading weekly is a management tool no responsible decision maker can afford to be without.

But what about you? Do you read *Computerworld*? . . .

Steven R. Tharler for *Computerworld*

Imagine this cozy scene taking place in your home just a short time from now . . .

. . . It's a chilly winter evening. Rather ordinary, until this moment. Your dinner guests are gathered around the glowing hearthside. They chat quietly.

Suddenly you appear . . . with a platter of thick, luxurious Omaha Steaks . . .

Omaha Steaks International

You know Omaha Steaks are delicious, and that's why I'm writing. To encourage you to try more of these exceptional steaks. Here are just 10 of the many good reasons why you may want to order them again . . .

Omaha Steaks International

If you are worried about the future . . . about increasing inflation . . .

. . . and the factors that make for such a nervous economy, I have some ideas you should consider. Almost every newspaper, magazine and economic report we read these days bring additional "bad news" . . .

Bill Steiner for Numismatic Funding Corp.

I'd like to share with you some special new rug designs which are this year's favorites of our many customers in Europe . . .

Dick Hodgson for Wool Design, Inc.

As one of our valued fund contributors, I feel you will be interested in this year's annual drive celebrating our 125th Anniversary.

Bill Steiner for Polytechnic Institute of New York

You don't have to be a sitting duck for burglars, John J. Jones.

With the increasing rate of crime and burglary in our nation, it is time you consider the protection you need for your home and your valuables. We would like to help.

Montgomery-Ward Enterprises, Inc.

Luck is about to ring the bell for more than 75 specially selected customers who act on our Sweepstakes Registry Invitation.

And you can be one of them . . . one of those triumphant new winners who reached for the brass ring one more time . . . and got it!

Just picture it — YOU celebrating success in a $125,000.00 vacation hideaway . . . spinning around town in a brand-new Chrysler Imperial . . . being pampered and living royally on a luxurious 15-day vacation in the Far East. YOU winning once — maybe twice — in our Giant Double Sweeps. And if Lady Luck stays with you all the way . . .

. . . YOU could win the superprize that tops them all . . .

Marvin Barckley for Publishers Clearing House

To a man who likes the sound of "Merry Christmas!"

YOU are that person! Why, of course, you are! You like to hear a cheery word of greeting on Christmas Morning, and so do the folks who have done business with you in the past!

So plan now to send your customers a warm and friendly greeting at Christmas. Let them know you are thinking of them . . .

Martin Baier for M. P. Brown, Inc.

Surely you must see the logic in our belief that sometime soon, you and *Horizon* must cross paths.

If you have not as yet held a copy of this totally different magazine in your hands, or heard of its remarkable beauties from a friend (possibly one of its 160,000 plus subscribers) . . . certainly, you shall experience either, or both, very shortly.

There. We've said it. At first blush, what would appear to be a totally out-of-character, high-pressured claim for a "low pressure" publication. But not so, since we know something of you, and where your tastes lie.

To be addressing this letter to you now, you can readily see that we have had to carefully cull your name from a great many sources. . .

Horizon Magazine

You are richer — infinitely richer — than you think, if you love the beautiful, the unusual, the mysterious and the enchanting. And I am inviting you today to discover a wonderful way to enjoy the boundless wealth that is already yours without ever leaving home unless you choose to do so.

John Lyle Shimek for *Arizona Highways*

This letter is your announcement of an open enrollment that starts now and closes October 15. It's for our group hospital insurance plan.

As a Keyholder in good standing, you are eligible to participate.

This not only gives you the obvious security provided by the insurance . . .

. . . it gives you the advantage of buying at low, group rates!

Hal Laurence for Playboy Preferred, Inc.

Your keen sense of keeping costs down while enjoying a life of safety and convenience is a matter of record. About a year ago your interest in giving yourself worry-free driving with substantial savings was made known to us, either by a recommendation from a friend of yours or by your own act of filling out a card for the AAA-Chicago Motor Club.

For reasons best known to yourself, you postponed joining the world's most distinguished motor club, with services no other club can match . . .

Dick Trenbeth for Chicago Motor Club

If you're like every other parent I know, you worry about the effect television is having on your children.

Harry Walsh for Grolier Enterprises Corp.

I want to thank you, with all my heart, for your help in electing me President of the United States.

Without your generous financial support, we could not have won such a major and important victory.

As you and I both know, this was an election we Republicans had to win in order to lead America through this extremely critical period in our history.

I will always be grateful for the faith you have placed in me and for your steadfast loyalty in our Party during this important national campaign.

Republican National Committee

The reason I'm writing you this morning is very simple: I need your help now to defeat Jimmy Carter in 1980.

And the single most important thing you can do to help is accept the special Republican Party Membership Card I have enclosed for you.

Let me explain why your personal support is so crucial.

Republican National Committee

ASKING A QUESTION

The second most popular letter lead technique — and one fraught with problems — is to start by asking a question. The problem: Readers may answer your question in the opposite way from what you want.

On the other hand, a "negative" answer may prove an effective screening technique. You may be seeking only those who answer in a positive way and immediately screen out those who have no interest in the proposition.

Here are typical uses of letter-opening questions:

Have you ever felt lonely — even with other people around? Or like your whole world seemed to be coming apart? Or asked yourself, "Is this all there is for me?"

Robert C. Westenberg for Foundation for Christian Living

Did you ever see a mother give her baby warm beer in his bottle?

> Robert W. Westenberg for David C. Cook Foundation

Did you know that you are smarter than any computer we have around today?

> Linda Wells for American Museum of Natural History

Have you ever had a project turn out far better than you could possibly have imagined?

> The Franklin Mint

How many people, do you suppose, are wishing, hoping — even dreaming — that Mr. John J. Jones will send them a delicious gift of Omaha Steaks this Holiday Season?

> Omaha Steaks International

What's the fastest way to get the news?

It's on the radio. That's why *Newsweek* wants you to have — as an introductory gift for new subscribers — this superb AM/FM radio.

But what's the best way to get the news?

It's with *Newsweek*.

> Milton Pierce for *Newsweek*

First, three brief questions, if we may:

1. Did everyone who should have reported in to work today — report in?

2. And those who did — did they bring their minds to the job, as well as their bodies?

3. Is everybody happy? Working well? Building the company?

> Bill Steiner for Elliott Service Company, Inc.

Wouldn't it be wonderful if you could feel that you have COMPLET-ED all your Christmas shopping . . . with gifts that are sure to please everyone on your list . . . and you could DO IT IN THE NEXT 10 MINUTES?

Bill Steiner for Arthur T. White

Would you like to take total listening enjoyment with you . . . wherever you go? Would you like to have access to up-to-the-minute news and weather information? Listen in on police and fire communications? CB road reports . . . and even hear cassette tapes?

Montgomery-Ward Enterprises, Inc.

How long has it been since you've read something ornery? That's right, ornery. Cussed. Contrary. It's a great old tradition in American journalism but today it's more often honored in the breach.

The New Republic Magazine

How can you say "no" to 30 days' accident coverage for one thin dime?

Eugene Waddell for Old American Insurance Company

Have you heard about today's miracles? I mean the miracles that are happening to ordinary American people like you and me and Debbie Parvin?

Let me tell you the story of Debbie's miracle as it appeared in *Guideposts* recently.

Patrick Lee for *Guideposts*

Have you ever wondered if God really hears your prayer? Have you ever doubted His power in today's world? Have you ever questioned the depth of your faith?

Alan McQuiston for *Guideposts*

Have you ever dreamed of learning to draw or paint? Or play a guitar or banjo? Or simply to view art or listen to music among congenial people?

Today you have an exciting opportunity to do all of these things and more in a charming landmark setting, just minutes from your home. It's ideal for children and families or singles of all ages.

Dick Trenbeth for The David Adler Cultural Center

How many times have you admired a friend's apparent "knack" for growing lush, thriving houseplants . . . or your neighbors' "luck" at keeping their yard a showplace of beautifully vigorous foliage?

Patricia Kelly for Grolier Enterprises

How would you like to beautifully paint a 9'x12' room — walls and ceiling — in less than one hour? Including clean-up time!

Sounds a little hard to believe? We thought so, too. But then we discovered an invention that outpaints any brush, any roller, any compressor-powered spray gun ever made for the homeowner.

Montgomery-Ward Enterprises

How would you rate a general who rushed into battle without a plan? A general who squandered blood, sweat and tears without a blueprint?

And yet, you fight the toughest battle in history. Every day. And it's not just your skin that's at risk. But your nest egg. Your home. And those you love.

You fight a battle against inflation . . .

Sig Rosenblum for Bache

If somebody finds or steals your credit cards and runs up a bill in your name . . . who has to pay?

Unfortunately, the answer may be John J. Jones.

Montgomery-Ward Enterprises

Let me ask you — what if . . .?

What if you weren't able to work? In fact, it has happened to millions, suddenly and unexpectedly.

Security Pacific National Bank

If you wouldn't give two cents to make your business run more efficiently, would you give 1.5¢?

Because that's all your supplies will cost for each individual copy you make in your own office on the Xerox 550 copier.

Xerox Corporation Direct Marketing

Who do you call . . .

. . . when you need to give a gift, but don't have time to go shopping?

Or you don't want to waste time shopping, because you haven't the slightest idea of what to buy?

. . . If flowers or candy just won't do? You don't have the time to look through mail order catalogues? Or if you're uncomfortable about always asking your secretary to buy gifts for you?

Diners Club Gifts

Do you know why no books are used at the Harvard Business School?

. . . Simply because only a portion of the information contained in most books is of direct interest to the reader. And quite often that information becomes obsolete before the reader has a chance to use it!

Do you know where to obtain information on the latest money-saving business techniques? If, like most of us, you are involved in a demanding business operation, you probably have little time left for research and study. Thus you rely on professional advice.

United Media International, Inc.

You're accustomed to challenges. You meet them successfully every day of the week.

But what do you do when you need a critical piece of correspondence and it can't be located?

Or what happens when you've called a staff meeting and discover a key staff member isn't there to meet with you?

And how do you react when you learn your customer collection notices aren't getting much reaction?

IBM Canada Ltd.

Can you recall the best steak you ever tasted in your life? One that was tender, juicy and just full of flavor? I'll bet you can. Most likely, it was served at an exclusive restaurant or supper club.

You may have wondered why the steaks fine restaurants serve taste so good. It's simple, really. The chefs in these places know that all their skill in food preparation is absolutely useless — unless they begin with first quality cuts of meat.

Omaha Steaks International

Stop and think, for just a moment. When was the last time you were able to buy a cigar for around 12¢ that didn't drive everybody out of the room — yourself included? Probably not since the Big Three meeting at Yalta.

John Lyle Shimek for Thompson Cigar Co.

TELLING A STORY

All of us have a certain amount of the storyteller in our veins, and we often call on this ability when we can't think of any other way to start a letter.

Some years ago this was much more common in direct mail letter writing than it is today. Hershell Lewis suggests we've entered "The Age of Skepticism."

"Even as we buy," he says, "we expect a catch somewhere. We're looking for trouble." I suspect that skeptics in our audience may be suspicious of writers who try to "hook" them into reading with a bit of storytelling. They want to know right up front what the mailing is all about. If the subject has to be sugar-coated with a story, their skepticism puts them on guard, possibly creating an impression the proposition may lack merit if it has to be "hidden" behind a story.

But there are still many out there who enjoy being entertained or, perhaps, brought closer to the subject by an intriguing story. The following are examples of how direct mail letter writers have utilized this technique.

Most people never expect to get sick enough to be laid up in a hospital bed.

A hospital confinement? That's something that happens to other people.

Never in her 63 years had Catherine Vollers been anything but strong and healthy. She was a woman who never believed she'd have to make a health insurance claim herself.

But one day her luck changed. And she become "the other person."

There she was . . . flat on her back in the hospital.

It was a coronary occlusion with complications (not indigestion from the Lobster Newburg served at her birthday dinner).

Joe Marreone for National Home Health Plan

I got the message around 7 p.m., and I got going at once!

I knew I had to drive all night in an ancient jeep through a steaming jungle that would scare a tenderfoot like me out of three years' growth, even in the daytime. I also knew that if I could get to where I was going in time it was worth a few prickles up and down my spine during the tight spots.

In this business, those that don't get the word don't get the good tobacco. It's so competitive down there in Honduras that even when you do get the word you may not get it in time.

The jungle grapevine was working overtime that day in San Pedro Sula, but I had set up a private vine a long time ago so that if this kind of message had to get through I'd be the first to know.

John Lyle Shimek for Thompson Cigar Co.

By way of welcoming you to that select group for whom gold holds a special charm, let me tell you a favorite story.

In February 1886, two hired hands named George Harrison and George Walker set out to build a shed on a farm near Johannesburg. One of the stones they selected for the foundation was quartz streaked with fine yellow bands.

Could it be . . .?

Harrison had worked in the gold fields of Australia, and the fever still raged in him. He quickly pulverized the quartz with a sledge, threw the granules into a frying pan — the first container he could find — and filled it with water. The yellow particles went straight to the bottom.

Both men staked claims the next morning, and their affidavit identified what became known as Witwatersrand Reef, the richest vein of gold the world has ever known. Harrison was pressed for money at the time, however, and sold his claim for ten pounds sterling —about $50!

Malcolm Decker for The Gold Collection Limited

Just two days ago I was chatting with a friend on St. James Street about investments, and he astonished me by saying: "Do you know, Brian, I have a couple of thousand dollars spare cash myself at the moment, and even with all I know about the market — I'm not really sure where to put it!"

Bill Steiner for *Financial Times of Canada*

I have been a hunter and fisherman since I was knee high to a mallard, and I have given enough blood to the mosquitoes to stock a good-sized blood bank!

Man and boy, I have been battling outdoor insects all my life and up until I discovered the remedy I'm going to tell you about, I had lost every battle.

I have fished with one hand and fought black flies with the other. I have gotten gnats in my eyes and welts on my pelt, mosquitoes have crawled in my hair and down my back, I've itched and scratched, I've had bites fester and become infected. I wasted one whole week on one trip; couldn't get out of the tent because of the bugs. I've used gallons of goo and yards of mosquito netting. I have smeared myself with lotions and potions like a savage and the bugs only seemed to grow more numerous and aggressive.

The bugs always won. I was always outnumbered.

John Lyle Shimek for Cole Outdoor Products of America, Inc.

It all began just 5 short years ago on a business trip for Wayside Gardens, America's most magnificent nursery. My original mission was to buy some rare bulbs at the flower auction in Aalsmeer, Holland.

While on the trip, I visited some friends I had known during my childhood (not having seen them since my family left Holland over 35 years ago). They lived near Alkmaar, the age-old cheese marketplace.

The whole family greeted me, gathering round to ask millions of questions about America. And at the same time, they stuffed me with all kinds of native foods — especially cheese.

NEVER in all my years had I ever tasted such delicious cheese! As I sampled it, I vaguely remember hearing them attribute the characteristic flavor to the special herbs and grasses on which their cows feed.

But there was more to it than that . . . their cheese was made from a special Dutch recipe handed down from generation to generation for almost 800 years.

The Gouda cheese was mild, and left a full, rich aftertase. The Edam was tangier than Gouda with more body. All the while I was tasting the cheese, I had one thought in the back of my mind . . . "If only they would agree to export their special cheeses to Wayside, my problems would be solved."

Lee Racanelli for Wayside Gardens

One of my happiest childhood memories . . . and perhaps one of yours . . . is gathering around the piano in the parlor for a good old sing-along songfest. There's just something warm and wonderful about a home that's filled with good music!

Jim Kobs for American Peoples Press

To my surprise the other day I found that one of my friends was not a member of the Art Institute. Knowing his tastes, I asked him why he hadn't ever joined. His answer was equally surprising: "No one ever asked me to."

Dick Trenbeth for The Art Institute of Chicago

I myself am middle-aged. I really enjoy life. But when I heard that Dr. Hrachovec could help me live past 100, my first reaction was, "Who wants to?"

I was thinking of some old people I've seen. Senile. Incontinent. So weak they can hardly walk. If that's what old age is, I don't want it.

Bob Matheo for Personal Improvement Corp.

When I was a boy, there were three furnishings a genteel family would display with pride — a grand piano, a grandfather clock, and a globe.

Times have changed. Today, a family's proudest possessions are likely to be — a swimming pool, a video tape recorder, and a globe.

The reason a globe is still on the list is that times have changed. And, in the 1980's, a globe has become essential to understand and follow what is going on.

Bob Matheo for Time, Inc.

It is late at night. I'm tired and my burning eyes are telling me it is time to quit.

The last of my staff packed up and headed home around 8 p.m. The light over my desk is the only one still burning. But before going home, I wanted to write to you and ask for your help.

American Civil Liberties Union

Norma is a frustrated mother.

With her husband gone, her children are more than a handful. Her small, fixed income and the little she gets from occasional work seems to shrink in buying power every day. To make things worse, Christmas is coming.

John Yeck for The Salvation Army

Jim got the coffee. I went for the Danish. Mrs. Edwards held our place in line for King Tut tickets that wintery day. Three perfect strangers had been drawn together by a shared desire to see the treasures of ancient Egypt and find out more about the world of long ago.

Linda Wells for *Portfolio* Magazine

Andre Meyer was a dominating figure in both New York and international high finance, the senior partner of Lazard Freres and its head for 33 years. His Wall Street colleagues said he loved only three things in life: complex deals, beautiful women and great art.

But even this financial wizard and art authority could not have known what he was doing as he acquired his private collection of modern and post-impressionist paintings. Not even he could have imagined that six of his favorites would sell for more than a million dollars each and establish a new auction high last fall.

The chic crowd at Sotheby Parke Bernet that night was stunned as record after record was toppled. But art world insiders weren't taken by surprise at all . . .

Linda Wells for *Connoisseur* Magazine

Secretary of Agriculture, Bob Bergland, recently participated in a face-to-face press conference sponsored by the Agriculture Council of America. He met with reporters and community leaders in San Francisco, Atlanta and Chicago. Of course, that in itself is not unusual for a Cabinet member.

The remarkable thing is that Secretary Bergland never left Washington, D.C. Mr. Bergland, along with a panel of experts to help field questions, visited the three cities in just over 4 hours for less than $500.00 — approximately the cost of one coast-to-coast plane ticket.

Travel time and money were saved as was our nation's dwindling energy supply. This productive meeting took place with the Bell System's new video conferencing network.

Sheila Stogol for C & P Telephone Co.

America's newest folk hero is a plain-spoken, no-nonsense common man who finally got to be our President.

And now, almost 25 years after leaving office, everyone is suddenly wild about Harry. Books about him have been on the best-seller list for months. A one-man play is drawing standing-room-only crowds. Movies and TV shows are in the works. Historians are beginning to consider him as one of our great Presidents. Young people have adopted him with Truman T-shirts and bumper stickers. There's even a hit song that proclaims "America needs you, Harry Truman."

Jim Kobs for the Harry S. Truman Library Institute

On December 31, 1974, the government of the United States will lift its 41-year ban on ownership of modern gold coins by Americans.

Just seconds after that ban is lifted, The Franklin Mint will begin striking the first gold coin minted in the United States since April 1933 which can be owned by American citizens — the 1975 One Hundred Balboa gold coin of the Republic of Panama.

The Franklin Mint

I can well remember the special fragrance which always greeted me when I got my spring vacation from grammar school and went to visit my grandparents. Right outside the room where I slept was a very special tree.

At least in my small eyes it seemed like a tree and was covered with the sweetest smelling flowers in all the world. To me, grandma's Lilac was the most wonderful thing alive.

Dick Hodgson for Spring Hill Nurseries

I wish you could have been with me this spring as I made my tour of leading Tulip growers here in Holland. That record cold weather we were having in January must have given the Tulips extra incentive to reach out for the sun. I've never before seen the fields as colorful and bright with absolutely gorgeous Tulips.

Dick Hodgson for Breck's

Hasn't it happened to you and your child? It used to happen to me:

You wanted to help your preschooler begin to understand some important concepts . . . develop basic skills that would give your little one a valuable head start in school.

So you sat down with your youngster one afternoon and decided to teach him or her the letters of the alphabet . . . or shapes . . . or color recognition . . . or opposites.

And you found that your child was so curious and enthused that you soon wished you had more ideas.

Sesame Street Magazine

When we checked into the hotel in Copenhagen, we didn't know a single soul. By nine o'clock that night, we were sitting in a circle of brand-new friends under the twinkling stars in the Tivoli Gardens.

They "skoaled" America! We "skoaled" Denmark! We all "skoaled" the light, clean and aromatic cheese we were enjoying with our drinks.

Whenever I taste Cream Havarti, I think of smiling faces, generous spirits and the world's warmest hospitality. That's why I'd like to be your host the first time you try it . . .

Linda Wells for Figi's

1955. Eisenhower was in the White House. A first-class letter mailed for 3¢. The Brooklyn Dodgers beat the Yankees 4–3 to win their first World Series. Jimmy Stewart, John Wayne and Grace Kelly were leading box office attractions. The economy was up, hemlines were down.

Folks followed the "$64,000 Question" on television. The AFL and CIO merged under Meany. "Pajama Game" and "My Fair Lady" were hit musicals. "Marty" was the movie to see and "Yellow Rose of Texas" the song to sing.

Virginia Daly for The Direct Marketing Club of Washington

Back when I was growing up, we used to put pennies in parking meters. I paid a nickel for a candy bar and three cents for a postage stamp.

Today, that same parking meter gobbles quarters. A candy bar that looks a heck of a lot smaller costs 30 cents. And I'm sure I don't have to tell you the sad story about postage stamps — 18¢ and going up soon.

That's why the message I'm about to give you is so remarkable.

Now you can buy something that wasn't even available when I was growing up — for less than two cents!

Joan Greenfield for Xerox

When you and I were growing up, financial security planning was probably the last thing a woman thought of for herself. If your childhood was like mine, when the subject of life insurance came up, Mother usually stayed in the kitchen and let Dad handle everything.

But our lifestyles are different now! Not only are women concerned with running the household and raising the children, many mothers are also holding a job to make ends meet.

Sheila Stogol for Bankers Life

Since the beginning of time, all mankind has shared a dream: the dream of flight.

Only in this century has the dream come true. Man soars with the birds, speeds through the heavens like a hawk in his powerful, sleek, silvery machines.

Yet the dream of flight continues. It's part of us, forever. Who among us hasn't watched the giant jets taking off and landing, with a secret wishfulness in our hearts?

Herschell Lewis for The Ghent Collection

Remember the fantastic pitching of Satchel Paige?

Ted Williams, one of history's greatest hitters, with a lifetime batting average of .344, got one hit in forty-one tries off Old Satch.

That's an average of .024!

Joe DiMaggio, the pride of the Yankees, outfielder magnificent, clutch hitter extraordinary, did a bit better.

Two for sixty-five . . . a sparkling .030!

Satch did let some of the weaker batters hit once in a while, and when Bill Veeck asked him why, Ol' Rockin' Chair replied: "I just like to help keep those po' boys in the league."

John Yeck for The Miami University Fund

Down went the dusty, dark-red portieres!

Off came the dreary damask wallcoverings!

Out flew the crowded Victorian clutter!

She invented decorating as we know it today. She painted walls white. She let in the light. She tweaked antiques with the freshness of chintz. She loved comfort, she loved style, she loved life. Her joy in living showed in joyful decorating — and it is to Elsie de Wolfe, Lady Mendl, that we dedicate our new *House & Garden*.

Linda Wells for *House & Garden* Magazine

Five hundred years before the birth of Christ, the ancient Romans used ingots of precious silver as a medium of exchange. This year, more than 20 centuries later, a prominent Roman bank — Banco di Roma — will issue its first sterling silver ingot.

The Franklin Mint

The weight of Tutankhamun's coffin puzzled the diggers who discovered the boy-king's tomb in 1922. Was it fashioned from some strange leaden substance not known to modern man?

The coffin, carved of wood in the shape of a mummy, then guilded, was opened — only to reveal a second similar coffin. It was decorated with gold leaf and inlaid with a mosaic of multicolored glass. But neither of these coffins, if emptied, could weigh more than a hundred pounds.

The secret had to lie inside the second coffin. It was opened and within it was a third coffin, much different from the other two: it was solid gold! It weighed 2,448 pounds and two ounces — a metal value of almost $18,000,000 based on $600 per ounce!

Within this gold coffin lay the mummy of Tutankhamun — masked in solid gold!

Nearby were four more solid gold coffins, nearly exact replicas of the third coffin — in miniature! They held the king's viscera.

No, the archaeologists reflected, the material that added such weight to the wooden coffin was not strange. It was, in fact, familiar. Gold was man's first metal, older than Egypt itself. The puzzlement was the extravagant use of gold — unknown and unimaginable, even to learned men!

Malcolm Decker for The Gold Collection Limited

The entire United States, including Alaska, could fit within the vast Sahara Desert with room to spare. But it was not always an arid waste. Some 3,000 years ago, large lakes and open grasslands supported vast herds of cattle. Important trade routes crisscrossed the Sahara, and it was extensively cultivated. Overcultivated. And overcultivation and overgrazing led to erosion. Periodic droughts hastened the process consuming more and more of the savannahs which stood between the desert and the fertile woodlands until the Sahara grew to four million square miles of desert.

Six years ago, with the advent of another drought cycle, the relentless Sahara resumed its southward march. Mile by mile, it overwhelmed the marginally fertile grasslands which had been so dearly won from the desert's grasp. Cattle by the millions died on the edges of dust-choked water holes. Thousands of Sahelians perished from starvation, disease and malnutrition. Children, pregnant women and the elderly were the chief victims. The hardier survivors fled southward to cities already overcrowded with drought refugees . . . only to encounter new miseries.

Malcolm Decker for Tribal Arts Society

The beaches here in Normandy are quiet, but you and I know this scene looked drastically different 40 years ago today.

I was here on that day, along with thousands of other American and allied soldiers, who were dropped from the air over Normandy, and who stormed ashore from ships, to liberate the people of Europe from the terrible reign of Adolph Hitler and the German Army of the Third Reich.

The date was June 6, 1944. Beginning with the invasion of Nazi occupied Normandy, and ending with the liberation of Paris and Western Europe, "Operation Overlord," D-Day as it is called, will be remembered as one of the greatest military achievements in history.

Republican Presidential Task Force

She hoisted herself up noiselessly so as not to disturb the rattlesnakes snoozing there in the sun.

To her left, the high desert of New Mexico. Once Indian country. Now abandoned. To her right, the rock carvings she had photographed the day before. Stick people. Primitive animals.

Up ahead, three sandstone slabs stood stacked against the face of the cliff. In their shadow, another carving. A spiral consisting of rings. Curious, the young archeologist drew closer. Instinctively, she glanced at her watch. It was almost noon. Then just at that moment, a most unusual thing happened.

Suddenly, as if out of nowhere, an eerie dagger of light appeared to stab at the topmost ring of the spiral. It next began to plunge downwards — shimmering, laser-like.

It pierced the eighth ring. The seventh. The sixth. It punctured the innermost and last. Then just as suddenly as it had appeared, the dagger of light was gone. The young scientist glanced at her watch again. Exactly twelve minutes had elapsed.

Coincidence? Accident? Fluke? No. What she had stumbled across that midsummer morning three years ago is an ancient solar calendar. And in scientific circles, it's being hailed as one of the most intriguing archeological discoveries of recent years.

It changes forever history's perceptions of America's early Indian colonists. And as an astronomical and geometrical marvel, it rivals Stonehenge.

Bill Jayme for *Science 82*

Once upon a time, there was a big, big word. It was spelled "s-e-r-e-n-d-i-p-i-t-y," pronounced "ser'en dip' a te," and it came to us all the way from Persia.

Everyone agreed it was a very fine word, but nobody ever used it.

"Serendipity," you see, meant "an aptitude for making fortunate discoveries accidentally," — and people had a lot of trouble working it into their conversation.

Then, one day, somebody EXPERIENCED serendipity. Quite by accident, someone found the super-perfect place to use that very big, very fine word: as the name of a set of books — the most delightful, most beautiful books ever produced for little children!

Patricia Kelly for Serendipity Books

It is 12:45 p.m. The entrance to New York's "21" Club is crowded with men, most of them expensively dressed. The door opens, the crowd parts as the Red Sea did for Moses, heads turn, women lick their lips and toss their hair, the owner and maitre d' smile. David J. Mahoney has arrived for lunch.

There are richer men in the room, more famous men, even better-looking men. But Mahoney, CEO of the Norton Simon Corporation, has that certain something that sets a man apart and smooths his road to success. He has class.

Class shows. Class counts. And class can be learned.

Linda Wells for Playboy Fashion

EXTENDING AN INVITATION

Also popular as a letter opening is to extend an invitation. Sometimes the invitation is set off in a separate panel, while at other times it is simply the way the letter begins. Here are a few examples:

> This letter is a personal invitation for you to see a new Bell System communications service in action.
>
> C & P Telephone Company

> Here's a special invitation to use the world-famous Thomas Register free for 10 days.
>
> Thomas Register

> I invite you to become a Charter Member of the Citizens Advisory Board of the Florida Crime Prevention Commission.
>
> Florida Crime Prevention Commission

> To a limited number of friends I am sending this invitation to look at what I believe is a once-in-a-lifetime opportunity . . . an opportunity to enrich the children of the entire world with music while getting your money back five or tenfold.
>
> Dick Neff

> I'd like to offer you a special privilege which is being extended to a select group of Spring Hill customers this fall.
>
> Spring Hill Nurseries

> I'd like to invite you to bring a cherished Dutch tradition to America this spring. It will add an interesting touch of Holland to your home at Eastertime and bring special joy to your friends and loved ones.
>
> Breck's

You're invited, Mrs. Jones . . .

. . . to be one of the first gardeners in Illinois to plant and enjoy an amazing new rose which has just been released from field tests and which will be available in limited quantity for planting this spring.

American Beauty Roses

As a valued Foley's charge customer, we invite you to come to an extraordinary sale of carpeting. A private sale so big we are holding it during special hours on Wednesday, November 12, 6:00 to 9:00 p.m. in our carpet departments Downtown, Sharpstown, Almeda, Northwest, and Memorial City. It will not be advertised to the general public.

Foley's of Houston

Because of your fine standing, we've opened a Spiegel Charge account in your name. It is pre-approved and ready for you to use right now.

To accept this special invitation to become a Spiegel Charge customer, simply charge an order to your new account . . .

Spiegel

You are cordially invited to join America's most successful restaurateurs and food-service executives as a Member in Good Standing of The National Restaurant Association, receiving the sixteen valuable members-only benefits described herein.

National Restaurant Association

Congratulations, Pilot . . .

. . . on your recent accomplishment of earning your certificate . . . or upgrading your rating. At the same time, you've made membership in AOPA an even more worthwhile investment . . . and we're pleased to invite you to take your place with other involved pilots in the world's largest and most influential pilot organization.

Aircraft Owners and Pilots Association

A Charter Subscription Invitation to a woman who wants to look better, feel better, understand yourself better — and like yourself a whole lot better!

An invitation to get in on the beginning of the prettiest, peppiest, most provocative "how to" magazine for women that's ever been published!

An invitation to preview the Premier Issue of *SELF* at no risk or obligation . . . then, if you like, to join as a Charter Subscriber at savings of $7.03!

Self Magazine

I know you receive many "personal" (i.e., computer-printed) invitations but this is special.

By accepting this particular invitation you will join a special group of Americans whose importance to our national culture I'll explain later.

Smithsonian Institution

THE SALUTATION

Even before the first paragraph of a letter is written, there's the question of what to use as a salutation, or whether a salutation is really necessary. Most personal letters do, of course, have a salutation. And since the best direct mail letters are those with a person-to-person approach, a salutation can be one of the ways to add a personal touch to a letter.

Even in my personal business correspondence, I prefer a so-called "dearless" salutation (i.e., Many thanks, Mr. Jones . . .). And such conversational approaches are becoming more common in direct mail letters — even those with personalization.

Although I'm sure there have been tests of one salutation versus another, I've yet to hear anyone report that a particular salutation played a measurable role in increasing or decreasing response. My general rule of thumb is to utilize a salutation to pinpoint the audience for whom the message is intended (plain common sense is probably your best guide).

Of the 800 letters collected for this book, here's what I found:

- *137 were personalized "Dear (name)"*

- *115 used "Dear Friend"*

- *106 had no salutation*

- *81 used "Dear Customer"*

- *59 used "Dear Reader"*

- *58 used "Dear (name of company) Customer"*

- *31 used "Dear Collector"*

- *31 used "Dear (adjective) Friend"*

- *31 used "Dear Friend of (name of organization)"*

- *24 used "Dear Member"*

- *17 used "Dear Subscriber"*

- *16 used "Dear Sir"*

- *13 used "Dear Executive"*

- *13 used "Dear Fellow (title)"*

Sixty-two of the letters used some other "Dear" salutation, including Doctor, Investor, Homeowner, Steak Lover, Colleague, Gourmet, Boss, Connoisseur, Taxpayer, Cheese Lover, Music Lover, Concerned Citizen. The remaining 31 used a "dearless" salutation. Some of the more interesting included:

> This certificate is made out to you, (name) . . .

> Can you see yourself . . .

> Just mail the card enclosed . . .

> Yes, dear friend, we want to astonish you . . .

> We're making an offer you can't refuse . . .

> Thank you for your interest . . .

> We've just worked out a plan . . .

THE JOHNSON BOX

In looking over the hundreds of direct mail letters collected for research, somewhere around 20% of them featured a Johnson Box at the top of page one. The following is a selection of various styles.

> WE WANT TO SEND YOU ONE OF THE MOST REVOLUTIONARY *PAINTING INVENTIONS TO DATE.* YOU'LL BE PAINTING UP TO 400% FASTER WITH VERY LITTLE MASKING EVER NEEDED *FREE FOR 15 DAYS.* WE'LL EVEN SEND YOU TWO QUARTS OF PAINT — *FREE!*

Make sure that *YOU* are taking advantage of all the benefits for which you are eligible!

Join the American Veterans Group Insurance Trust and enjoy big-dollar cash benefits *at low group rates* from National Home Life Assurance Company.

But you must reply by midnight of the date stamped on the Enrollment Form enclosed.

Now, a chance for a no-risk trial on
America's only no-nonsense newsmagazine:
Try 2 issues at no cost to you —
no commitment whatsoever — *then* decide
if *U.S. NEWS & WORLD REPORT* is for you.

You are one of only a handful of art lovers in the entire United States who is being given this opportunity to see and touch the exquisite LIMITED EDITION Portfolio of *ANTIQUE CHINESE PORTRAITS.*

This Portfolio, bound in satin and containing a set of ten fine art reproductions in the subtley rich colors of the Antique Originals, is *the first in the First Series of four Whitney McDermut RICORDI Art Portfolios.*

Each Portfolio will present the work of different artists. Others in this series:

MICHELANGELO — PICASSO — DRAWINGS OF THE MASTERS

BRAND NEW $250,000 SUPER PRIZE

Everybody liked our first SuperPrize so much that we're doing it again — WE'RE GIVING AWAY *ANOTHER* BRAND-NEW $250,000 SUPER PRIZE TO ONE SUPER LUCKY PERSON! That's on top of one win (maybe two!) in our regular Giveaways. What's really exciting is the next 500 winners will come from people who act on this limited invitation. So use your 10 fresh, new chances to win. GO FOR IT . . . ALL!

BEAT APRIL 22, 1981 DEADLINE

Thousands of Africans in the Sahelian zone are suffering the ravages of a six-year drought. Now they and other Africans are offering you their art. When you purchase even the simplest piece, you help hundreds to survive including, perhaps, the artist himself. You may also be making a very interesting investment.

- If I am willing — without question or quibble — to send you an *introductory shipment* of the world's most wanted oranges, grapefruit or a mixture of the two at my expense

- If I am willing to guarantee they must be better than any other citrus fruit you have ever tasted or you may return the unused portion and owe nothing

- If I am willing to continue sending you fabulous Indian River Citrus every month for seven more months — or until you say, "Enough!" *and let you pay me later*

Are you willing, then to do me
this one small favor?

Take just a moment right now to read this letter and see for yourself how easy, inexpensive, and downright enjoyable it is to pamper yourself like a potentate as a member of my

SEASON SUPPLY CLUB

You'll sell more wine —
Your wine profits will increase —
You'll tie up less capital —
You'll have more loyal customers.

If you insist on the best in books, music, theatre, entertainment, cultural events, conversation, food, wine, travel, and the other amenities of civilized living . . .

If you love the finest houses, furniture, paintings, sculpture, silver, china, crystal, jewelry, objets d'art, and collector's items from Aston Martins to Victoriana . . .

If you thrill to the excitement of finding things of lasting beauty . . . of buying them . . . of creating valuable collections for yourself and future generations of your family . . .

You are a connoisseur. And you are ready for the aristocrat of international art and art investment magazines. *CONNOISSEUR*, now yours at savings of fifty per cent.

Come home to Agatha Christie, and leave your worries behind. Breathe in the spirit of sanity, kindliness and humor that have endeared her to millions. Enter a world where the butler is summoned by the call of a bell, voices are seldom raised, manners are more important than money, and a really good herbaceous border counts much, much more than a coronet.

Come home to Agatha Christie, the mistress of mayhem and master of the classic English whodunit, in the First Edition of the first complete, matching library of her work in hardcover. It's the Agatha Christie Mystery Collection and Volume I, *Murder on the Orient Express*, is yours for 21 days free . . . with *The Agatha Christie Mystery Companion*, a $10.00 value . . .

ABSOLUTELY FREE!

Imagine enriching your home with a great private library like no other . . .

each book carefully chosen for you by Oxford University dons . . .

each book masterfully quarterbound in fine leather, the leather inlaid with 22 karat gold . . .

The *Oxford* Library of the World's Great Books. Magnificent. Definitive. And it can be yours for just $24.50 per volume.

If I am willing — even eager — to send you
A FREE $17.50 Piezo Electronic Lighter,
50 FREE CIGARS after I've sent you five shipments —
Up to $29.50 in FREE BONUSES altogether

If I am willing to guarantee you'll *always* get a better cigar at a better price direct from me here in Tampa,

If I am willing to offer you more options and priviledges than the potentate of an emirate to make sure you always get what you want in a smoke,

Are *you* willing to read this letter right now and see for yourself how much you can increase your cigar-smoking pleasure as a member of my

BONUS BOX CLUB?

"All development is struggle. Only force rules. Force is the first law . . . If one should ask whether this struggle is gruesome, then the answer could be: For the weak, yes; for humanity as a whole, no."

— Adolf Hitler

Learn how you can view two video cassette chapters in this epic struggle for 10 days absolutely free . . . and keep one as a gift!

Your gift video tape is called *Walter Cronkite Remembers & The Battle of the Bulge.* It is an explosive introduction to all the sweep and drama of a historic new video library produced by CBS News . . .

World War II With Walter Cronkite

An invitation to an adult with a ten-billion-dollar brain. From a magazine created by a brain trust of the world's leading scientists, explorers, artists and nature photographers.

An invitation to enjoy a serious, thoughtful, beautiful, intellectually challenging magazine that serves as a forum where the brightest minds in the natural sciences can meet and share ideas.

An invitation to enjoy *Natural History* Magazine and become an Associate Member of the American Museum of Natural History, entitled to the five valuable extra benefits described herein.

CATCH THE SPIRIT OF SUMMER

It's easy — and fun — when you treat
family and friends
to an Omaha Steaks cookout.
Save up to $13.00 if you order now!

If You Want More Knowledge . . . More Satisfaction . . . More Profit From Stamp Collecting, Start a Subscription to *LINN'S STAMP NEWS* . . . The First 4 Issues Are Free!

Happy Plants Cards — the plant
care system that puts an end to the hit or miss
approach to gardening! We'll give you FREE Gifts
just to try it!

DO NOT READ THIS LETTER ! ! !
. . . if you feel YOU DON'T NEED A CONTINUING FLOW
OF SOUND AND TESTED PUBLIC RELATIONS IDEAS

What: A Deluxe, Compact Mini Desktop Calculator with eight-digit capacity, LCD display and four-key memory which operates on batteries that are good for a year . . . *yours absolutely free!*

Why: Because we owe you more than a sincere and grateful thank-you for letting us help kids to learn the most important thing they'll ever learn — to be able to *read*.

How: By ordering *anything at all* in the enclosed catalog in time! Along with your books, we'll send you a $24.95 calculator that has countless professional uses at no charge whatsoever.

Kroy^R

lettering can give all your written communications the look of success.*

In fact, to prove it we'll send you our brochure and a sample of Kroy lettering — FREE. Plus, details on Kroy's unusual FREE trial offer.

You work for *yourself*.
And your family.

Until today, that honest fact meant you may not have been able to enjoy all the benefits of low-cost *group* hospital protection that are now available to people who work for big companies.

Now you win at last!

A touch of class. Cary Grant has it. So do Dan Rather, Gay Talese, Robert Redford, Art Buchwald, Andy Warhol, William F. Buckley, Jr., and most men who make it to the top in their professional and personal lives.

A touch of class. You can get it, too. Four issues of the new PLAYBOY FASHION GUIDE FOR MEN can be yours for only $6.50 — 35% less than the single-copy price on the newsstands. You save $3.50.

A $175,000 touch of class! Whether you join us or not, you may already have won one of 2,069 classy prizes in THE $175,000 PLAYBOY LIFESTYLE SWEEPSTAKES! Mail your numbered card now and find out!

How can we offer this critically acclaimed 21-volume encyclopedia for 1/3 of its original price?

You have been selected to receive a free issue of *GUIDEPOSTS* — the magazine that publishes the true stories of today's miracles —like the story of Virginia Lively . . .

She Can See Jesus In Your Eyes

SECTION XII

HOW TO CLOSE A LETTER

Just as in any sales presentation, the most critical moment is "the close." Here's where the action takes place. There is no standard method for concluding a letter. In some cases, the entire statement of the offer is delayed until the last two or three paragraphs. More often, however, the basics of the offer have already been woven into the body copy of the letter, and the letter concludes with a reminder of the next step to be taken or a restatement of the primary benefit to be gained if action is taken.

But, since so many readers move down to the signature on a letter before starting to read a letter, it is important to have an interest-arousing conclusion. It often catches the eye as the reader is checking to see who the letter is from. Equally important is a postscript, since it will be the first thing read after the recipient has viewed the signature.

As a handy reference file, I've included a number of typical concluding paragraphs of direct mail letters and a selected group of effective postscripts.

CONCLUDING PARAGRAPHS

The following letter closes have been selected at random and show a variety of typical concluding paragraphs.

> Go ahead. Put us on the line. Send the enclosed card today. And we'll send you the Kroy brochure, complete with sample, absolutely free. Or if you prefer, call us today Toll-Free — 1-800-328-1306 — and we'll be glad to answer any questions you might have.
>
> Either way, we're ready for you. With the best machine in the business.
>
> Roy Beauchamp for Kroy Inc.

> Do mail the Form today, please. You won't regret it. That's also guaranteed.
>
> Thank you for reading my letter and I do hope to hear from you in just a day or two.
>
> John P. Walsh for *Enter* Magazine

I'll look for your Preferred Reservation Card on my desk. It's a pleasure and a privilege for me to bring you a series of collector's plates as worthy of your attention as these are!

Hershell Lewis for American Collector Club

It's a simple invitation with no strings attached. Why not accept it now? Please sign the enclosed card and mail it back to me today. This offer expires December 31, 1982. Thank you.

Ed McLean for Industrial Automation Reporter

So take a few minutes to relax and browse through the colorful brochure. Decide which luscious foods you want — and phone or mail your order today.

Omaha Steaks International

As you can see, you have nothing to lose by finding out if Wards Wide World of Travel is for you — and you have a whole, wide, wonderful world to gain.

Mail your Official Entry Certificate today . . . and have the opportunity to become a winner!

Montgomery-Ward Enterprises

So please enroll now, while you're thinking of it. It'll take but a few moments for you to join the finest Auto Club in the country. I know you'll enjoy being with us.

Montgomery-Ward Enterprises

The sooner you act, the sooner protection begins. So get your WCCSS Enrollment Certificate in the mail today.

Montgomery-Ward Enterprises

Don't miss this very unusual opportunity to receive the finest skin care system money can buy. Send us your Gift Certificate/Analysis right now.

Don't go on wondering how much better your skin could be. Find out by giving it the benefits of EUROPA.

Act now and get ready for beautiful results!

The Europa System

Give yourself a chance to see what it's like to feel really great — healthier, more energetic (more alive!). Sign the Certificate and mail it in the postpaid envelope, so we can rush our gift of good health to you.

Montgomery-Ward Enterprises

This unusual offer may be withdrawn at any time, so we suggest you return the order certificate in the enclosed postpaid envelope today.

Richard Silverman for The Hirsch Organization Inc.

FREE extra bonus! Would you like a free reprint of one of the outstanding Esquire features published in recent years? Return the reply card subscribing to *Esquire* promptly, and it's yours.

A list of these features is enclosed. Simply check the one you want on the reply card, return it in the postpaid envelope, and get started on this delightfully habit-forming magazine. Do it now while the supply of reprints lasts. We can't wait to make you an *Esquire* friend.

Dick Neff for *Esquire* Magazine

But act now — mail in the enclosed postage-free card today. It is a fact that each year Thomas Register is sold out. Because TR is the most complete directory, it is always the most wanted directory, so mail the card today for your 7 volume set for 10 day Free Examination — with no obligation to buy it! — and be sure.

Bill Steiner for Thomas Publishing Company

This offer is available for a limited time only. To take advantage of this saving just initial and return your New Subscriber Invitation card enclosed. You need send no money now — we will bill you later.

Bill Steiner for *American Journal of Clinical Nutrition*

Why not send in your renewal today? Take advantage of the money-saving prices for 2 and 3 year subscriptions, too. You'll be glad you did!

Bill Steiner for *Autobody* Magazine

But you must act right away to get your free copy of "Investors' Questions Answered" along with your subscription to *The Financial Times*, because copies of the booklet are limited. Simply initial the enclosed certificate and mail it to me today. We will gladly bill you later.

Bill Steiner for *The Financial Times of Canada*

Remember, you needn't send one cent now. (You can pay later, after your magazines start.) So pick the magazine or magazines you want. There are nearly half a hundred best-sellers on your coupons. Many are only $2.98 or even less. All are far below rates offered to the general public.

The only thing is, there may not be another chance to save like this, because Clearing House bargains are available only by mail. Moreover, publishers limit the number of new subscriptions we may accept at these reduced rates, and some offers will surely be withdrawn soon.

So please don't delay. Take your pick now and mail your order at once, while all these money-saving bargain prices are still in effect.

Marvin Barckley for Publishers Clearing House

As president of the "world's largest bookstore" and the largest retailer of bargain books in America, I assure you that this is the best bargain we have ever offered. Please hurry — our supplies are limited, and going fast.

Barnes & Noble Bookstores, Inc.

So why not send for your free gifts today! They're yours to keep no matter what you decide about future sets. And remember, by trying Happy Plants Cards you have nothing to lose, and a green thumb to gain.

Patricia Kelly for Grolier Enterprises, Inc.

Remember, you get every book on approval. You can cancel at any time. You can buy as many or as few as you wish — even none at all. That is your privilege.

Harry Walsh for Grolier Enterprises, Inc.

Mail your Enrollment Form today. The open enrollment period ends October 15, 1982. The sooner you enroll, the sooner you can start enjoying the fine, reassuring protection of Playboy Hospital Plus.

Hal Laurence for Playboy Preferred, Inc.

There's no need to send money now. Just return the card by itself or in the postage-paid envelope. We'll bill you later.

Virginia Daly for *U.S. News & World Report*

So act now! Try a membership for one year and see for yourself how much you get in return. Simply complete the enclosed application form and mail it today. Don't let any time fly before you cash in on all the benefits of membership in AOPA.

Virginia Daly for Aircraft Owners and Pilots Assn.

In view of the desirability of this offering, you may wish to place your order now for one or more stamps by calling toll-free 800-243-9438 and charging your credit card. Please call us during office hours, 9:00 A.M. to 5:00 P.M. Eastern time.

Or, if you prefer, use the order form below. All orders will be shipped within sixty days of receipt. Early orders will earn first priority.

I look forward to your early response.

Malcolm Decker for The Gold Collection Ltd.

Send your membership check today and come soon and often to your three museums. You'll be reminded again and again that belonging to your Museum Society is an open door to the best things life has to offer.

Dick Trenbeth for The Art Institute of Chicago

It's easy to give yourserf all of this peace of mind and driving pleasure. Just complete the enclosed membership application and rush it to us with your check or credit card authorization today — before your next flat tire, winter stall, or radiator boil over causes costly delays and frayed tempers. You'll be glad you have your own AAA-Chicago Motor Club membership all year long, and you'll thank your friend for recommending you.

Dick Trenbeth for The Chicago Motor Club

So if you're thinking, "Maybe I should — what can I lose" — please do! You can't lose anything. You can change your mind later. And you may make your life richer than you ever thought possible!

Guideposts Magazine

Just sign the "Request Form" and mail it back in the postage-paid envelope. Then, when you "Sign & Fly," you can forget about airplane flight insurance. We'll do the remembering and handle all the details for you. Sign and return your request form TODAY.

Tom Brady for American Express

To discover the enjoyment the Concerto 800 Electric Home Organ can bring your family, mail the postpaid card today for your no-obligation 15-day Free Trial!

Jim Kobs for American Peoples Press, Inc.

We hope you will accept this invitation. It will mean a great deal to us if you do so, and we are certain it will mean a great deal to you.

But whether you wish to accept this invitation to become an Honorary Fellow or not, please let us know within 14 days. We have contracted for a special clerical task force which will be available for processing new memberships, and your prompt reply will help them complete their tasks within the time allotted. Thank you for the courtesy of your reply.

Jim Kobs for Harry S. Truman Library Institute

What if you don't agree? What if the lighter is not for you — for any reason at all? Perfectly OK. Just return the Jerrican. And back will come your refund. Every penny. And no foot-dragging, either. No need to explain anything. Just return the lighter. And that will be that. You'll still have my thanks for giving the G.I. Jerrican Lighter the once-over.

So complete and mail the Free Examination Form enclosed. The moment I get it, I'll rush your lighter out to you. But please don't wait. Because they are going fast. Send for your G.I. Jerrican Lighter, today. You don't risk a cent when you do!

Sig Rosenblum for Pembroke-Court Company

So please check the enclosed Super-Life brochure. Here's the plan made for the inflation squeeze. A plan of pure-protection. Low cost, high-benefit protection. An "impossible plan" they said, when we first proposed it. And yet, here it is — Super-Life. For you — and those you love. Please complete and mail the conditional enrollment form, today!

Sig Rosenblum for APA Insurance Services

The pamphlet is free. Please send for it today, won't you? Just complete and mail the card, and I'll do the rest.

Sig Rosenblum for Prodynamics, Inc.

Thank you for taking time from your busy schedule to read my letter. I hope to hear from you soon — and to be able to pamper you in the months ahead with Indian River's finest citrus.

John Lyle Shimek for Hale Indian River Groves

If your coffee hasn't done much for you lately, do something special for yourself right now. Treat yourself to the wonderful experience of savoring the extra richness and aroma of Coffee House coffee — then go back to Dick and Jane coffee, if you can!

John Lyle Shimek for The Coffee House

I don't see how any man who really likes good cigars could lose too much sleep over how he's going to come out on this one. Why lose any more time either? Why not simply look over the enclosed folder, check your choice of wrapper and shape on the enclosed card and mail it to me right now? You don't even have to send money. We'll bill you.

John Lyle Shimek for Thompson Cigar Co.

Look it over. Discuss it with your boss. See why P.S. is exactly "your cup of tea" — a sophisticated, intelligent service for secretaries of like kind!

And the cost? Negligible — when you consider the benefits to be derived. The enclosed order card will give you the full story. Why not mail it today?

Julie Spector for The Bureau of Business Practice

It won't cost you a penny more to mail the enclosed postpaid card TODAY. Tomorrow, something else may divert your attention — and your foremen, who are responsible for much of the effectiveness of your organization, are worthy of all the consideration you can give them now — and in the future.

Julie Spector for The National Foremen's Institute

Please make haste, if you will, since this proposal will last only so long as extra copies of our current issue are available. Once they're gone, this offer goes with them. A good proposition you're not likely to see again for the next nine or ten months, if then. And thank you for having come this far.

Julie Spector for *Horizon* Magazine

To take advantage of our "dynamite" offer, simply return the postpaid Reservation Card I've enclosed with this letter. You'll receive your first issue, posthaste, with a trial subscription you may cancel immediately (or anytime in the future). No matter what you decide, the sample copies are yours to keep. Could anything be fairer?

Shell Alpert for Clemprint Inc.

So please don't delay. Return the enclosed reply card now, while you're thinking about it, and I'll take care of everything for you.

Shell Alpert for The Center for Small Business Advancement

But right now, all I ask you to do is look — and that doesn't cost anything! Why delay? Such fun and festivity await you. Return the order card and let The Dinner Party Cookbook plan your next party.

I will eagerly wait to hear from you.

Emily Soell for Knapp Press

To repeat — your first issue of *GEO* is free. Your subscription is not a condition of this special offer. So send back your reply card in the postage-paid envelope provided. And prepare to share the pleasures of *GEO*, a most remarkable magazine with a fresh point of view of the human adventure.

Emily Soell for Knapp Communications

With interest in the Civil War at its current fever pitch, First Edition copies of *Antislavery* are certain to be grabbed up quickly. Orders from libraries and educational institutions alone will put copies at a premium; so will demands from collectors and bibliophiles who recognize the value of obtaining an initial printing.

In order to avoid disappointment, may we therefore suggest that you return the advance reservation form (enclosed) at your earliest convenience?

Bill Jayme for The University of Michigan Press

And you can try *Science 82* at our risk. Just return the enclosed card, and we'll send you the next issue to examine free at no cost, obligation or commitment. We'll also send you a bill of $12 — an immediate savings of $3.00 off the regular subscription price for one year. If you decide *Science 82* doesn't live up to your expectations, all you have to do is write "cancel" on the bill and return it to us.

May we look for your subscription reservation by return mail — so you won't have a lengthy wait before your first issue arrives? Thank you — and welcome to mysteries! enigmas! whodunnits! To answers! explanations! solutions! Welcome to *Science 82*.

Bill Jayme for *Science 82* Magazine

For extra-fast service, call us Toll Free with your credit card order at (800) 228-9055.

And keep this promise in mind:

You must be pleased with everything you order from us — or we'll replace your order or refund your money, whichever you prefer. You have my word on it.

So, truly you have no risk at all. That's why I hope you'll take advantage of my special sale to order plenty of Omaha Steaks. They'll help make the most of the last full month of summer.

Omaha Steaks International

So order — while you're thinking about it. You'll bask in the compliments of your friends and family members. From now on, they'll think of you with a little more admiration. After all, you showed them the time of their lives!

Omaha Steaks International

Find out how. Call us at the toll-free number that appears on the front of this letter. You'll speak directly with a Bell Business Consultant who is prepared to answer your questions and recommend ways your company can utilize the Selling Existing Customers application, along with Outward WATS, to increase sales and boost profitability.

We look forward to hearing from you.

Bell System

To enter your subscription, you need only mail the accompanying application. No payment is required at this time. But please note that your reply is requested by July 31, 1982.

The Franklin Mint

But please note that the enclosed authorization is solely for your personal use as a registered Franklin Mint collector. It may not be transferred to anyone else. And, to be considered valid, your private commission authorization must be mailed no later than March 31, 1982.

The Franklin Mint

Do drop the form in today's mail, please. It's really the only way you can be sure that it does get done and that there will be a copy of Volume I, Number I left for your home.

I wish there were more parents like you.

John P. Walsh for Children's Television Workshop

To subscribe, fill in the reservation card and return it in the postage-paid reply envelope. If you prefer, you may charge your subscription to your BankAmericard or Master Charge card, or if you'd rather, we can bill you later.

I sincerely hope you'll join us today. For more than 50 years, *Architectural Digest* has been serving people with your kind of taste, your kind of style, your kind of imaginative approach to life. All of us here would be proud and happy to be of service to you and your family, too.

Linda Wells for Knapp Communications

So turn on that mighty mind of yours. Fill out the enclosed reservation card and mail it in the postage-paid envelope today. No need to send money now; we'll bill you later at the low rate of just $12 for a year-long membership, including a one-year subscription to *Natural History*, a monthly magazine.

Twelve dollars a year for a magazine that really respects your intelligence. Plus valuable cultural benefits. Plus the knowledge you are furthering scientific research and discovery!

It all adds up to something bigger and better than any computer could figure out. I sincerely hope you'll accept our invitation today.

Linda Wells for American Museum of Natural History

Please do not send money now. Because *Portfolio* is so very different from other, older art magazines, we'd like you to try it before you buy. And then? Well, seeing is believing, as they say — so welcome to *Portfolio* as a friend and Charter Subscriber!

Linda Wells for *Portfolio* Magazine

So come! Come home to Agatha Christie now! Shut the door on the workaday world and sip sherry by the colonel's fire. Let the maid lay out your evening clothes. Then dress, eat a hearty dinner and play the Murder Game into the night.

Linda Wells for Agatha Christie Collection

Send no money now! We want you to see the Premier Issue first. Read it! Enjoy it! Use it to achieve new physical and emotional fitness! If *Self* doesn't help you look better, feel better, understand yourself better and like yourself better, don't pay us a single cent!

You've nothing to lose! A new self to gain! So jog off to the mailbox with your card this minute!

Linda Wells for *Self* Magazine

Ordering is easy. Just fill in the enclosed order form and send it to Breck's U.S. Reservation Center at 6523 North Galena Road, Peoria, Illinois 61656. We'll take over from there. Our Dutch Bulb experts will select the very finest sprouted bulbs, carefully plant them in a pot with our special growing medium and pack them for safe shipment. We'll ship them to each of the addresses you've given us and then bill you the way you request.

Dick Hodgson for Breck's

But I must mention one caution. We have only a limited quantity of these exceptional Lilacs and when they are shipped we won't have any more for at least another year. Orders will be filled on a first come, first served basis. So I would urge you to send your reservation now.

Dick Hodgson for Spring Hill Nurseries

Order Without Risk. Even then there's no risk for you since every Breck's bulb is fully guaranteed to grow and bloom. If, for any reason, you are not fully pleased with your Crown Royal Daffodils upon receipt, after planting or once they grow and bloom, all you have to do is write Breck's anytime before July 1, 1987. We'll refund every cent you paid or send you a replacement without charge, whichever you prefer. We won't ask any questions. You, and you alone, will be the judge.

But let me urge you to place your order promptly. The quantity of these superior Daffodils we've been able to reserve is very limited and all orders must be filled on a first come, first served basis. I'll look forward to serving you.

Dick Hodgson for Breck's

I sincerely hope you will want to take advantage of this special opportunity to obtain a collection of these truly exceptional Lifetime Peonies. There's no risk involved since you'll have the opportunity to inspect and approve every root before you pay a cent and then will be fully covered by Breck's Guarantee of Complete Satisfaction.

Dick Hodgson for Breck's

THE POSTSCRIPT

Just as important as the closing paragraphs of a letter is the postscript. Since it is generally the first part of a letter read thoroughly, it can entice a reader to want to find out more about your proposition. Here are some representative postscripts used by top direct mail copywriters.

P.S. In today's tighter money market you must run your business more efficiently than ever. To recoup every $100 you waste on expenses, your company may have to generate up to $1,000 or more in sales. That's why the $3 per month you'll spend subscribing to *Business Monthly* becomes so valuable. Our coming article on inventory control, for example, may save you up to $1,000 per year on one inventory item alone.

United Media International, Inc.

P.S. If you have a friend or relative that you feel would like to know about our unique "tools," just let us know (feel free to use the enclosed postage-paid envelope) and we'll mail them color brochures on our products.

DRI Industries

P.S. The enclosed leaflet tells about another, different kind of good value from Publishers Clearing House. I thought you might like to take a few moments to look at it.

Publishers Clearing House

P.S. Even if you don't wish to enroll or call us now, I value your opinions as a Cardmember. I would appreciate your spending a few moments to complete and return the enclosed survey so we can better serve you and your fellow Diners Club Cardmembers.

Diners Club Gifts

P.S. With Alex service you get choice. See the enclosed brochure for details on all our rental packages starting from just $49.95 a month. There's one just right for you. Simply call toll-free 1-800-255-BELL.

Bell Atlantic Mobile Systems

P.S. Perhaps some of your friends or relatives have an interest in rug making. We'd be pleased to send them a free copy of our 1986 Rug Book with your compliments. I'm enclosing a special friendship card which you can use to send us their names and addresses. We'll make sure they get their free Rug Book promptly.

Wool Design, Inc.

P.S. Be sure to return your special Bonus Certificate before its expiration date to save $5.00 on your first Wool Design rug kit.

Wool Design, Inc.

P.S. I'd like to send you a very special gift to thank you for reserving Breck's Spring Garden Collection for shipment this fall. With every Collection, I'll include six gorgeous Blue Moon Tulips absolutely free. This is one of the most distinctive Tulip varieties ever grown in Holland and I know you'll enjoy the big, dramatic orchid-lavender blooms in your spring garden and bouquets.

Breck's

P.S. Let me urge you to place your order promptly. Only a limited number of these special Dutch bulbs have been prepared for 1985 Holiday blooming and they will be shipped on a first come, first served basis.

Breck's

P.S. I would like to urge you to place your rose reservation as soon as possible. While we will do our best to fill every order we receive, we can only guarantee Spring 1985 delivery for those reservations we receive by November 30, 1984.

Spring Hill Nurseries

P.S. To claim your introductory discount, please enclose the "discount check" with your order, or mention it when you telephone. This check will entitle you to a discount of $10 if you order 6 filets, or $20 if you order 12 filets. Note that the check expires on October 31, so please order promptly.

Omaha Steaks International

P.S. Please note that the prices on your order form have already been changed to reflect the extra 20¢ per pair discount we're offering in this sale. We've done the work, you get the savings!

P.P.S. You'll notice that our deadline for ordering is August 31. Please observe that deadline. I hate to say no to an order, but rules are rules.

L'eggs

P.S. Our gift package is for the man in your organization who purchases merchandise for your vending machines. Please forward this letter to this "Key Man." Thank you.

The Nestlé Company

P.S. If you are experiencing roof maintenance problems on some of your buildings, you'll want to learn about our re-roofing solution, too. Just let us know on the reply card, and we'll send our re-roofing brochure.

Armco Building Systems

P.S. For faster service, please call Susan Smith toll-free. Her number is 1-800-327-2782.

Cushman Fruit Co., Inc.

P.S. You needn't send money now. When you receive your Certificate of Insurance, look it over thoroughly. Take up to 10 days to make up your mind. If you decide you don't want it, send it back and you'll owe nothing.

Playboy Preferred, Inc.

P.S. Having your continued support is so important to me that I'm enclosing your renewal card now, even though there's still a month or two before it's due. Don't worry — if you'd prefer to wait, we'll be sure to jog your memory. But if you renew today, you'll not only save the Association some money, you'll allow us to devote our full attention to the pressing issues that face aviation.

Aircraft Owners and Pilots Assn.

P.S.   Want to save even more? Take a two-year subscription for just $22.00, and save $21.00. You'll get 11 more regular issues and another Buying Guide Issue as well!

Consumer Reports

P.S.   Some special programs fill up fast. So don't delay. Return your information request right now.

P.P.S. Remember — by requesting information, you are not under any obligation whatsoever. So please be sure to fill out your reply card clearly and completely. This will enable us to send you the information you want as quickly as possible.

U.S. Marine Corps

P.S.   Women all over the world are benefiting from the new science of age controlling skin care. Now you can experience the same benefits in your own complexion FREE just by returning the Gift Certificate. We'll bill your account $1.00 to help cover postage and handling.

The Europa System

P.S.   While you're at it, why not get an early jump on the Christmas list. There are a lot of goodies in this mailing that make excellent gifts.

Haband of Patterson

P.S.   I'm also going to send you an extra free gift: the electronic "Everything Card" (a $49.95 value) described in the enclosed folder. I know you'll like it!

Electronic Office

P.S.   Of necessity, only a limited number of photography booklets and current issues of *GEO* can be set aside for this generous introductory offer. Therefore, to avoid disappointment, you are urged to post your reply within 15 days of receipt of this announcement.

Knapp Communications

P.S.   If you're half the independent-minded "tough customer" I believe you are, you're probably still looking for one last persuasive reason to take advantage of this offer.

You'll find it on the enclosed reply card. (It starts with the word, "Finally".)

U.S. News & World Report

P.S.   I've also got a surprise Mystery Gift for you. Like surprises? I have a special one for you. Order within 10 days, and with your shoes and your Free Billfold, I'll also enclose a FREE Mystery Gift. Can't tell you what it is. But it's yours to keep — even if you decide to send back the shoes.

The Stuart McGuire Co., Inc.

P.S.   The enclosed note explains why you are being invited to become a National Associate. Please take a moment to read it now.

Smithsonian Institution

P.S.   If you already have a copier that you're pleased with, the Xerox 550 is still a great bargain for you. It's the ideal "second" copier on heavy volume days. And it's great as a back-up unit when your other copier is down. Don't forget you can charge it conveniently to your MasterCard, Visa, or American Express card.

Xerox Corp.

P.S.   These days, it's more important than ever to make your business as cost-efficient as possible. Our new rate structure could help a business like yours do just that. Call us or mail the enclosed postage-paid card today.

Southern Bell

P.S. I'd also like to mention the Double Cash Benefit feature. When you and your wife are both under age 65 and insured in the plan and are both hospitalized by any covered accident at the same time, you EACH collect $100.00 a day, $3,000.00 a month, for as long as you both remain hospitalized. That's a total of $200.00 a day, $6,000.00 a month!

American Independent Businessman's Group Insurance Trust

P.S. Don't forget: there will be a wealth of useful information for you in your free handbook, *The Home Tool Kit.*

Time-Life Books

P.S. Ever wondered what a "Management Grid" is? Or a "Linking Pin"? Or a "Mix Model"? With your trial subscription, we'll include a complimentary copy of *Behavioral Science Terminology.*

Behavioral Sciences Newsletter

P.S. Be sure to check the enclosed Extra Free Bonus flyer and claim the extra free gift it describes — an added reward to you for replying promptly. And also see the back of your Membership Application for a special Gift Membership offer that saves you a full 50%!

Cheeselovers International

COMPLIMENTARY CLOSES

While I was analyzing my file of letters for this book, I checked to see what types of complimentary closes were most common. Here's what I found when I took a look at 853 letters:

- *443 used "Sincerely"*

- *131 used "Cordially"*

- *78 used "Sincerely yours"*

- *64 used "Very truly yours"*

- *24 used "Best regards"*

- *21 signed with a name and title*

- *17 used "Cordially yours"*

- *14 used their name only*

- *11 used "Good luck"*

- *9 didn't have a signature*

- *6 used "Best wishes"*

- *6 used "Very sincerely"*

- *5 used "Respectfully yours"*

- *5 used "Faithfully yours"*

- *4 used "Best of luck"*

- *4 used "Peace"*

- *4 used "Yours sincerely"*

- *3 used "Thank you"*

- *2 used "Yours very truly"*

- *2 used "Yours truly"*

The remainder used a variety of less common expressions, including "Happy Days," "Yours for a lower price," "Yours for happy feet," "Have a good day," "Why take a chance," "We look forward to serving you," and "Good eating."

SECTION XIII

100 TIPS FOR BETTER DIRECT MAIL SALES LETTERS

1. STRESS BENEFITS, NOT FEATURES

Customers are more interested in what your products or services will do for them than in their features. Nearly every guide to effective sales letter writing suggests leading off with your most important benefit, then expanding on it.

A good guide for planning a letter is to first make a list of all the features your product or service offers. Then, following each feature on your list, add the words "which means." Now, add the benefit. If a feature doesn't offer a benefit for the buyer, chances are it is relatively unimportant.

2. YOU, NOT WE

All letters should be "you" oriented. Concentrate on what readers want to know; not on what you want to tell them. One of the surest ways to get your letter discarded quickly is to start out by trying to convince readers how important you are, rather than how you can be of service to *them*.

Many writers make the mistake of thinking you-oriented simply means inserting the word "you" into the copy as frequently as possible. It's not that simple, however. It's more a matter of attitude and approach — constantly remembering your readers are more important than yourself, and keeping their interests in mind with every word you write.

3. KNOW YOUR AUDIENCE

This may sound elementary, but it's surprising how often letter writers just assume everyone to whom they're writing is like themselves — or like their close friends, business colleagues, or some other group they know intimately.

This is seldom the case. It pays to take time to study the specific nature of your audience before you write a word: where do they live, what do they do, what have they bought from you before, what else do they buy, how old are they, are they male or female, do the majority speak a common language (i.e., familiarity with computer terminology, medical terms, legal language, etc.)?

4. STRESS YOUR USP

Rosser Reeves, who originally coined the term "Unique Selling Proposition," suggested that every product has some special feature, or benefit, that represents its primary appeal to the majority of customers and prospects.

It's important to note that "proposition" is singular, not plural. Your product or service may have lots of unique features and/or offer lots of benefits. But for letter writing, it's important to isolate the *most* important *single* thing around which you can build your presentation. Having lots of unique features or benefits may, indeed, be your USP, but only if you offer more than anyone else. In this case, the individual features and/or benefits become of less importance in themselves; but, in common, become your USP.

As a general rule, concentrate on promoting your Unique Selling Proposition, and then try to connect supplementary selling propositions to the featured USP.

5. MAKE YOUR OFFER INTERESTING

Of every element in a direct mail sales letter, the most important of all is your offer. How you present an offer can often make or break a mailing. Yet, many writers just take the offer for granted and do little to make it interesting for their readers.

Before you start writing, sit down and make a list of a dozen or more ways in which you can present the offer. Just the process of creating such a list often leads to a better, more interesting way to present your proposition to the reader.

There are so many different ways to present the same offer, but only one of them will be best. The important thing is to take time to make your offer as interesting as possible.

6. WRITE TO INDIVIDUALS, NOT AUDIENCES

The main difference between direct mail and general advertising is that the best direct mail letters convey the sense of being a message from one individual to another. Most advertising is addressed to groups of people, but direct mail letters, even though they are being sent to many people, will — if well written — convey the feeling of a one-to-one communication. As direct mail seminar leader, Bob Hemmings, says, "The best direct mail is a letter to Mom — multiplied."

7. COIK

Don't ever lose sight of this acronym meaning "Clear Only If Known." What you say about a subject may be perfectly clear to you, your boss, and your business colleagues. But that doesn't mean it will be clear to your readers, who most likely aren't as knowledgeable about the subject. If they have to pause for even a moment to decide "what you meant by that," chances are you'll lose your readers before you can convince them to take the action you want them to take.

8. DON'T OVERESTIMATE THE KNOWLEDGE OF YOUR AUDIENCE . . .

. . . or underestimate their *intelligence*. In other words, don't "write down" to your readers, but assume they don't know your product or service as well as you do. Treat them as intelligent, but recognize they will appreciate having things explained in some detail.

9. BEWARE OF GRAMMARIANS

When writing direct mail sales letters, you're not writing to get an "A" in an English class. There are times when following the pure rules of English grammar actually get in the way of communicating. You shouldn't purposely violate the rules of good grammar, but they shouldn't be allowed to get in the way of easy communication.

In my seminars, I note that a few English teachers may complain about what you've written. But don't worry about them. I believe disciples of the fine points of grammar often ruin excellent letter copy by trying to edit "correctness" into it.

10. WATCH OUT FOR PET WORDS

We all have them — favorite words we tend to overuse. It's important to be aware of them and try to reduce their use in our letter copy. I find myself, for example, overusing "basically," "actually," and "which" in writing or speaking. So, when I edit what I've written, I keep an eye out for these three overused words. Most often when I delete them or find a substitute, I end up with stronger copy. Also be careful of the word "that." Most Americans tend to overuse this word. In 90% of cases where it is used, the copy would communicate more quickly just by eliminating it. Finally, be particularly careful about using words that may not be quickly understood by all. For example, many of today's writers like to use the word "paradigm." I suspect, however, that a high percentage of their readers can't describe "paradigm" without getting out a dictionary, and I often wonder how many of those writers really understand the word.

11. APPLY THE CROSS OUT/WRITE IN TEST

After copy is written, go through it and cross out every mention of your company and your product. Then substitute the name of your competitor and its product. If the copy still fits, fire the copywriter! A good direct mail writer should find ways to present what you have to offer in a unique way that will make your company the *preferred* source, and your product the *preferred* product.

12. EDIT FIRST PARAGRAPHS

An experienced editor once told me he always deleted the first one or two paragraphs of copy he was editing. This is because too often, the first paragraph or two do not get the reader started; they do, however, get the writer started. And the writer does not start talking to the reader until subsequent paragraphs.

The toughest thing for a writer is getting started. And once written, writers seldom want to edit out these copy "gems." But a good editor should keep an eye open for these "starters" that may lose readers before they get into the important part of the selling message.

13. MAKE SURE COPY FLOWS

One thing distinguishing good copy of all kinds is the ease with which one sentence flows into the next; each paragraph into the next. The flow should be natural, just as a good conversationalist doesn't jump from one thought to another. Good connecting words help, but more important is keeping the reader constantly in mind. What's a logical way to take your readers from what they've just read into a new thought? Get the readers started, and they can't resist staying with you — paragraph after paragraph — until you've been able to tell your full sales story.

14. REWRITE AFTER THE COMMITTEE HAS DONE ITS DAMAGE

It's been said that a camel is a horse created by a committee. And copy that's been edited and reworked by a committee is often about as sleek as a camel.

That's not to say you can ignore the "must-musts" and "no-nos" of the review committee. But it's best to let the final rewrite be done by a good copywriter who can build smooth flow back into copy that has been heavily edited.

15. RETAIN WORKING COPY

David Ogilvy, the founder of the Ogilvy & Mather advertising agency, once said, "One of the greatest wastes in advertising is to do away with copy that's still working."

There's an advertising axiom which says that when you and your colleagues get sick and tired of something you've been using is about when your audience starts to notice and pay attention to it. Some of the greatest direct mail sales letters have been used successfully for 10, 20, or even 30 years — almost without change. Although it's important to continue testing to make sure your old favorite is still working, don't be afraid to stick with it until you find something better.

And that doesn't apply only to complete letters. It often helps to develop a file of sentences and paragraphs that you can utilize repeatedly, even though the basic structure of a letter may change.

16. MAKE SURE ALL ELEMENTS FIT

As just one of the ingredients of a direct mail package, it is important to make sure the letter is carefully coordinated with every other element. Do the words describing your product match the illustrations in the brochure? Does your presentation of the offer match the language on the response device? Is there consistency in the typography and design of all elements?

17. BACK UP YOUR CLAIMS

Why should the reader believe you? Provide proof to back up every claim you make.

18. TELL THEM WHAT TO DO, AND HOW TO DO IT

Don't assume every recipient of your direct mail will understand the action you are asking them to take — and how to take it. Do you prefer phone or mail offers? Give your reader a good reason to take the preferred action, and explain how to do it.

19. KEEP LANGUAGE CONSISTENT

In direct mail, you're dealing with an unseen audience. They have to visualize who you are. If the way you express yourself isn't consistent throughout the entire direct mail package, the reader is likely to be confused about your identity. And confused people don't order.

20. KEEP COPY SIMPLE

There are a host of mathematical formulae for developing effective copy. The late Max Ross, for example, suggested a letter should have between 70 and 80 words of one syllable for every 100 words you write. Rudolf Flesch's formula calls for sentences that contain no more than 150 syllables. Paul Bringe suggested limiting sentences to 20 words. Drayton Bird claims the easiest length of sentence to read is eight words long; the average length for easy reading is 16 words; and any sentence longer than 32 words tends to be hard to read.

While such formulae may be useful in editing copy, I've yet to encounter a top-notch copywriter who actually uses them while writing a letter. By all means use short words, particularly action words. Avoid words that may not be fully understood by the majority of your readers. And don't try to show off your vocabulary by tossing in an "elegant" multisyllable word now and then.

You'll always be best off when you follow the "KISS" principle — Keep It Simple, Stupid!

21. Make Letters Inviting

Be vigilant in constructing the format of your letters. Maintain ample margins. Keep the majority of paragraphs to five lines or less. Type should be as large as possible; consistent with type a secretary would use when preparing an individual business letter. Avoid dark colored papers and those with an obvious background design.

22. Use Direct Marketing's "44 Magic Words & Phrases"

• *Free*	• *The truth about . . .*	• *New*
• *Bargain*	• *You*	• *Amazing*
• *Now*	• *Miracle*	• *Win*
• *Improved*	• *Easy*	• *Last Chance*
• *Introducing*	• *Hurry*	• *Announcing*
• *Just Arrived*	• *Today*	• *Revolutionary*
• *Save*	• *How to . . .*	• *Guaranteed*
• *Break Through*	• *At Last*	• *Discount*
• *Send No Money*	• *Limited*	• *First Time Ever*
• *Bonus*	• *Opportunity*	• *Special*
• *Gift*	• *Yes*	• *Instantly*
• *Valuable*	• *Charter*	• *Discover*
• *Priority*	• *Secrets*	• *Forever*
• *Unique*	• *Never Before*	• *Premium*
• *Rush*	• *It's Here*	

23. Get to Your Main Point Quickly

There was a time when many direct mail letters started off with an "attention-getting" story, which might or might not be directly related to the offer. Today, the majority of successful letters lose no time establishing what the letter is all about. Often, you'll find the offer summarized in a Johnson Box, appearing at the top of page 1, before the salutation and body copy. Some writers can use storytelling to capture attention and create a thirst to continue reading. However, most will be more successful if they get right to the point.

24. Don't Be Afraid of Long Copy

Once you've captured readers' attention, explained your offer, and outlined the benefits, the role of additional copy is to answer questions readers need answered before they are willing to take the action you want them to take. If it requires 20 pages to provide the answers, so be it.

25. Don't Overwrite

If you can keep the letter to just a single page, and still answer the majority of questions, stop right there. Redundancy seldom helps to emphasize a point (except perhaps in a Johnson Box, the lead paragraph, or a postscript). Instead, it can be a stop-action device. When readers recognize they're reading something for a second time, they've got a good excuse to stop reading.

26. Most Important Sentences — First and Last

Most often, your first and last sentences will be the most important in a direct mail letter. If the first sentence doesn't immediately capture interest, many readers will stop right there. And the last sentence that is read — wherever it might appear in a letter — should sound the trumpet call to respond.

27. Work with a Copywriter's Rough

It helps to have a road map when writing direct mail letters. Many leading copywriters create a rough dummy of how they envision the entire package. For the brochure, they sketch in areas for illustrations, headlines, testimonials, and special details. They sketch out both the front and back of the envelope. And they prefer to work with a fully developed order device. The dummy is not intended as the final design.

28. Use Active Sentences and Phrases

Wherever possible, build action into your letter. Make it come alive for the reader. When you find your letter getting too detailed, inject "Here's what this means to you." Or tell how it has proved important to others. This often "wakes up" lazy copy.

29. Duplicate Secretary-Prepared Letters

Direct mail has been described as the personal medium. And the letter is the most personal element in a direct mail package. So make the letter look as personal as possible — like a letter from one individual to another.

This doesn't mean using a lot of computer personalization or simulated handwriting. A good rule of thumb is to give the direct mail letter the appearance of a secretary-prepared letter. This means it should have a salutation and a complementary close, be signed by an individual, and have margins traditionally used for business correspondence. The one exception to the secretary-prepared rule is that response is not lost when your letter appears on both sides of a piece of paper — something a secretary seldom does.

30. Stick with Common Letter Typefaces

For your direct mail letters, use whatever typefaces secretaries in your organization use for individually prepared business letters. Although it doesn't have to be a traditional mono-spaced typewriter type (as we always recommended before most secretaries began using word processors), you'll more likely create the feel of a personal letter if you continue to use typewriter type. By all means, don't get carried away with the many fancy typefaces built into most of today's word processors and computer printers. They may be "fun" to use, but they can quickly destroy any feeling of a one-to-one letter. Keep your letter *looking* like a letter — not a printed advertisement.

31. Take Advantage of Postscripts

Eye camera studies have shown there's a common reading pattern for letters. The reader first looks at the letterhead to see from whom the letter has been sent. Next, the eye looks to see to whom the letter is addressed. Then, the eye searches out the signature. Then, if there is a postscript, it will be read before the reader heads back to the beginning of the letter. Thus, the postscript is the first thing read by the majority of letter readers.

Take advantage of this pattern to capture the readers' interest and encourage them to read the rest of the copy. I like to create a bit of mystery (*"Don't forget the special gift you'll receive if you respond within the next ten days!"*)

Do not repeat your opening paragraph as a postscript because readers will notice the redundancy, and may decide that reading the letter isn't worth their time.

32. Tell Them What They Will Miss

All too often, copywriters are so busy extolling the virtues of their product, they fail to add what the readers will be missing if they don't take advantage of an opportunity.

33. Make Your Copy a Dialogue

As you write your letter, keep in mind the questions most likely to enter the reader's mind. Some portions of letters can even be in question-and-answer format. But more likely it will simply be a matter of envisioning yourself in a dialogue with the reader and framing your thoughts as though you are answering logical questions the reader may raise.

34. Put Emphasis on Your Guarantee

Since you are dealing "sight unseen" with your audience, the guarantee of satisfaction becomes a vital part of your message. Don't try to hedge your guarantee for fear people will take advantage of you. Experience has shown that the more wide open a guarantee can be, the greater confidence it gives customers in feeling "safe" in dealing with someone they don't know personally. And the greater the confidence you can establish, the greater the response to your offer. For example, your company attorneys insist on legal language, use your letter to interpret the guarantee in friendly, non-threatening terms.

And don't be afraid to repeat the guarantee in your letter even though it may be included in your brochure, order device, or somewhere else in the mailing package. It's so important, it deserves to be stressed. And then, as motivation speaker Ray Considine says, "D.W.Y.P.Y.W.D. — Do What You Promised You Would Do."

35. KEEP YOUR COPY FRIENDLY

Guarantees aren't the only copy that should be friendly and non-threatening. Make every effort to write as though you are writing to a good friend.

36. ACCENTUATE THE POSITIVE

Remember the old song, "Accentuate The Positive, Eliminate The Negative"? Good advice for direct mail letter writers.

37. AVOID STOPPING POINTS

Don't give your readers a chance to break the momentum they've built up as they read a letter. Make sure ideas flow easily from one thought to another. For example, don't suggest the reader look at the brochure or anything else until they've finished the letter. And don't end a page with a period or a complete thought. Encourage them to turn the page and keep reading. A good device is to hyphenate the last word on a page so the reader has to turn the next page to complete the word.

38. THE LESS THE COMMITMENT, THE MORE LIKELY THE ORDER

Watch out for complicated offers. Try to keep the commitment as simple as possible. If at all possible, keep everything to a basic yes-or-no decision.

39. MAKE IT EASY TO ORDER

Keep the entire ordering process as simple as possible. Use the letter to explain at least the first step (*"Pick up the phone now and call us toll-free at 1-800-999-9999 . . ."* Or perhaps *"Just use the enclosed order form and indicate the quantity you wish to have us ship to you . . ."*)

40. DON'T STOP WITH YOUR FIRST LEAD

The lead to your letter is the most important paragraph of all. If it doesn't capture the readers' attention, they're not likely to continue to read. So don't quit after you've written just one lead. Try at least five approaches. Chances are one of the alternate leads will prove to be stronger than the first.

41. KNOW YOUR COMPETITION

Make it a point to study every possible competitor — not just those who are trying to sell the same or similar products, but also those whose mail will be joining yours in recipients' mailboxes, competing for attention. And don't forget: The biggest competition may be from local or area merchants or someone who uses other forms of media to sell sight unseen.

42. REVIEW PAST COPY

Take time to review letters that have been successful in the past — particularly those that went to audiences similar to the ones you'll be addressing. Don't be afraid to copy things that have worked well before. Very few in your audience (probably only your business colleagues and possibly your competitors) will remember what you said previously.

43. DON'T BE A COPYCAT

Just because something works well for someone else doesn't mean it will work equally well for you. Your letter copy should reflect the personality of *your* business. If you discover someone using a phrase you like, look for opportunities to adapt it for your use rather than simply copying it verbatim.

44. UTILIZE TESTIMONIALS

One of the greatest selling devices in a direct mail letter is quoting what others have to say about you, your product, and your service. It helps build credibility into the copy. Testimonials don't have to come from customers. Sometimes even more important can be what publishers or broadcasters have said about you, your products, and your services.

45. MAKE YOUR BEST OFFER

It pays to constantly test to determine if some variation of your offer might improve response. Often an "add on" to a basic offer can dramatically boost results. Some options to consider:

- *Discounts*

- *Rebates*

- *Free trial*

- *Easy terms*

- *Multiple payments*

- *Free gift*

- *Adding a bonus for early or larger orders*

- *Offering a bonus "upon payment"*

- *Free shipping and handling*

- *Expedited shipment*

- *Delayed billing*

- *Limited quantity available*

- *Deadline date for ordering*

- *"Two-fer" — a discount price for quantity orders*

- *Improved guarantee (i.e., "Double Money Back")*

- *Introductory or charter offer*

- *"Beat probable price increase"*

- *Yes/No Offer (or the current version: "Yes/No/Maybe")*

- *Send No Money (i.e., pay later)*

46. SAY SOMETHING OF EXCEPTIONAL INTEREST

Drayton Bird suggests these examples:

- *Newly improved product.*

- *News item related to your product.*

- *Prices are about to rise. Buy now.*

- *We don't know how long we can hold this offer open . . . prices may rise.*

- *Lots of powerful testimonials.*

- *"We're repeating this offer because is was such a smash hit last time."*

- *Limited opportunity for a certain number of people.*

- *Specially imported from somewhere else where it was a great success.*

47. WHY THIS PRODUCT RATHER THAN SIMILAR PRODUCTS

Comparisons help selling points get across. Make sure your reader understands the features and benefits your product offers as compared with what is offered by others.

48. MAKE SURE YOUR AUDIENCE KNOWS WHAT YOU'RE SELLING

This may sound so obvious, but you might be surprised how often this is taken for granted and the reader just assumes you're offering something quite different from what you're really selling. Take time to put yourself in your readers' shoes and make sure your offer is perfectly clear.

49. MAKE THE COPY SPARKLE

Use short, picture-creating words. As H. Phelps Gates put it:

> ■ "There is strength and force in short words, words that blast and boom, throb and thump, clank and chime, hiss and buzz and zoom. There is grace and charm in short words, too, in words like lull and hush and purr. There are short lush words like dank, muck and drench; and short dry ones like crisp, parch and husk. There are words that work hard at their job, that pry and push, that slash and hack, that cut and clip, that chip and saw. Words that tease the taste, make glad the eye, whet the nose, and please the ear. There's nip, twang, bite and tang in short words. They're sweet,

sour, tart, or dry, as the need be. There are words you can hear like the swish of silk, soft words with a feel of swan's-down, words with a smell like musk, smoke, cheese, mint and rose — all of them good sales tools."

50. WHAT IS YOUR AUTHORITY?

Why should anyone believe what you're writing? It's a matter of perceived authority. Understand your accepted level of authority, and you'll be able to better communicate with your audience. And if you lack authority, consider quoting someone with authority — and that may often be your satisfied customers.

51. WHY DO IT NOW?

Have you built immediacy into your letter — a reason to take action *now* rather than setting the letter aside until a more convenient time? Give your readers a good reason for responding promptly, and you'll be able to capture some of the procrastinators.

52. HAVE YOU INCLUDED EVERY REASON FOR RESPONDING?

Don't be afraid to present multiple reasons for responding to your offer. Everybody doesn't necessarily have the same motivations.

53. HAVE YOU TAKEN ANYTHING FOR GRANTED?

We sometimes get so familiar with our subject, we just assume others are equally familiar. That's one of the biggest dangers a copywriter faces.

Read, reread, and read once again what you've written. Try to put yourself in your readers' shoes. Have you taken something for granted that is best explained? And by all means have someone unfamiliar with your company and its product read what you've written — and listen carefully to the questions they ask.

54. STICK TO YOUR SUBJECT

A direct mail sales letter should have just one objective: to get the recipients to take the *single* action you're asking them to take. All too often, extraneous information is added (i.e., "Don't forget to tell them we've got a new plant in Paducah" or "Let them know we're going to be celebrating our 25th anniversary next year").

55. IS YOUR COPY LOGICAL AND BELIEVABLE?

Sometimes we get so busy trying to make our product sound like the greatest thing that we lose sight of how the reader will view what we have to say. While everything may be perfectly true, overuse of superlatives can put the reader on guard. Read and reread your copy to make sure it comes through as logical and believable.

56. Dazzle Them with a String of Pearls

Seminar leader Ray Jutkins says:

> ■ "Your headline is the place to hook the reader with one dominant benefit. But once they are reading, pile on all the secondary benefits to increase the reader's appetite for your product.

"Take the reader from one strong benefit to another, all the way through your clincher copy. Put the strongest benefits at the beginning, but keep one big one for last. Especially if it's unexpected or unusual."

57. Does the Recipient Know Who You Are?

Even if you're writing to a good customer, don't assume they really know you. And when writing to a prospect, assume they *don't* know you. It may take just a phrase or two, but somewhere in your letter make sure every reader knows who you are.

58. Keep Thoughts in Logical Order

An effective aid to writing is to take a stack of index cards and write a brief paragraph about each subject you'll want to include in your letter — one paragraph per card. Then arrange the cards in a logical sequence before you start writing the letter.

59. Write the Order Form First

There are very few *absolute* rules for creating direct mail packages. Here's one: Always write the order form before you write anything else. The order form is where you must put all the terms. And it's where your reader is headed. Thus, the order form becomes your target. And everything you write in the letter should aim your reader toward that target.

60. Watch Out for Internal Language

Every organization develops an "internal language." You quickly understand what's being said. However, the conversation often sounds like a foreign language to an outsider.

61. Read "White Mail"

A good way to understand your customers' language is to take time to read some "white mail" (i.e., any correspondence other than an order or payment received from customers). You'll often be surprised to find that customers use words quite different from your internal language to describe your company's products and/or services. (I've often been surprised to find that customers frequently use different adjectives than I would normally use in writing letters. Such discoveries can build a working vocabulary that helps reduce redundancy.)

62. Call Your Customers

If you don't get a chance to look at the white mail, use the telephone. When you get ready to write, call a few customers. Describe the product or service you will be writing about and encourage them to ask questions about it. You'll not only learn the language they use, but their questions will often open your eyes to important subject matters you may not have planned to include in your letter.

63. Don't State the Obvious

Beware of loading your letter with the obvious. You don't have to tell them noon is twelve o'clock, or that a foot is twelve inches. It is reported that Sears once instituted a catalog copy review and found they could eliminate 25% of copy just by eliminating things that didn't need saying — the obvious.

64. Why Buy from You

Perhaps the most frequently overlooked — and often most important — subject that should be included in every direct mail sales letter is *why* the customer should buy this product from *you*. Even if the product or service is an "exclusive" available only from you, make sure the reader knows this.

65. Keep Copy Timely

Although it's a crime to do away with copy that's still producing results (at least until you've tested to find something that works even better), beware of copy that has become dated.

66. Avoid Superlatives

Perhaps it would be more appropriate to say "keep superlatives to a minimum." And be careful not to exaggerate. Remember, when people order your product or service and discover it doesn't live up to the glowing copy that led them to order, they won't trust you in the future. And people who don't trust you won't order from you. As Vrest Orton of the Vermont Country Store says, "Make sure the story isn't better than the store."

67. Don't Be Redundant

No need to keep repeating yourself. Make your point and then move on. If you repeat something, readers will believe you have nothing else worthwhile to say and will stop reading.

68. Be Believable

Check each claim you make and ask yourself if what you've said is believable. Once readers decide you're not being completely truthful (even if you're telling the truth, but what you've said somehow doesn't sound believable), they will be skeptical of everything else you write.

69. Be Complete

Have you left anything unsaid that readers need to know before they can take the action you're asking them to take?

70. Be Specific

Ask for a single, specific action. Don't say you can order by mail or go to a store. That's a good reason to delay taking immediate action. Readers who otherwise may have sent in their order may decide to "stop by your store the next time they're in the vicinity." But that "next time" may be delayed so long, they don't remember they want what you're selling.

71. APPLY THE "HAT TRICK"

The general tendency of writers is to take their just-completed copy and read it to someone in the office. That's probably the worst thing you can do. Instead, apply the "hat trick" — get out of the office, hand the copy to someone who isn't close to the subject, and have them read the copy to you. Listen carefully to where they put the emphasis and pauses. And be particularly alert when they ask, "What do you mean by that?"

72. DON'T TRY TO BE SHAKESPEARE

You're not writing prose or poetry; you're writing to communicate action-compelling thoughts for the here and now. Don't let your ego get in the way of communicating as you try to impress your audience with your writing style.

73. WATCH YOUR HUMOR

Beware of trying to be funny. Too often, what may be humorous to you will not necessarily be humorous to the majority of the recipients of your direct mail letters.

Humor, when done well, can be highly effective; however, the majority of writers don't have the skill to do it well. You may think you are just as funny as Garrison Keillor, but don't believe it . . . even if your friends laugh at all your jokes. If you believe you are a skilled humorist, test your humor copy against a straight copy, and observe the response carefully. Chances are your attempt at humor will be the loser.

74. GET TO THE POINT

Direct mail letters should not be like a mystery novel, where you have to wait until the very end to find out "whodunit." As Vic Schwab said in his poem, "Tell me quick, and tell me true (or else, my love, to hell with you)!"

75. ELIMINATE "STOP ACTION"

Once you capture the readers' attention and get them reading your letter, don't introduce thoughts that stop the reading action. Words they don't immediately understand will do that. If they have to pause to figure out what you're trying to say, you've probably interrupted their train of thought which, hopefully, is headed toward the action you want them to take. Suggesting readers take time to refer to an enclosure or to look up something can also work to your disadvantage.

76. KEEP COPY CONVERSATIONAL

Beware of the suggestion that you should "write like you talk." What's really meant is to write with *the ease* with which you talk. Avoid stiff language and words you wouldn't use if you were talking with someone like your readers.

77. ELIMINATE USELESS WORDS

Check your copy to delete unnecessary words that may only fill space without helping you communicate. In the majority of cases, for example, the words "that" and "which" only slow down readership. Many adjectives may be useless: A *full* quart is just a quart. A *long* mile is just a mile.

78. BEWARE OF QUESTIONS

Be careful in asking questions of your readers, particularly those which call for either a "yes" or "no" answer. When the answer is "no," it may easily provide a reason *not* to read your letter.

79. USE "LETTER" PAPER

Print your letter on a sheet of paper that *looks* and *feels* like a letter. Stick to colors that are traditionally used for business correspondence. Avoid coated papers that make your letter look too much like an advertisement.

80. AVOID COLORED BODY TYPE

Research has indicated there is less comprehension of what is read when type is in any color other than black.

81. KEEP THE LETTER SEPARATE

A letter should be a letter — not a part of something else. Combination letter-brochures are seldom as effective as using a separate letter and a separate brochure.

82. DON'T WORRY ABOUT HOW THE LETTER IS FOLDED

Tests have indicated it doesn't matter whether you fold your letter in or out as long as it looks like a letter.

83. ELIMINATE DUPLICATED WORDS

Edit for multiple use of the same words in a single sentence or paragraph and, wherever possible, in preceding and following paragraphs. Speed readers may quickly jump from a word first seen to the same word that quickly catches the eye, missing the copy in between.

84. CONNECT YOUR PARAGRAPHS

Max Ross suggested using "a bucket brigade" through copy — the joining together of paragraphs through the use of connecting links. Some of these connecting links, he said, are little sentences like, "But that is not all" . . . "So that is why" . . . "Now here is the next step" . . . "But there is one thing more."

85. DON'T BE POMPOUS

Remember it's the reader who is important. Bury your own ego and flatter the reader.

86. Don't Use Three Words When One Will Do

Keep on the alert for places where just a single word will communicate as quickly as three, four, or a whole sentence.

87. Don't Keep Shouting

There's an old saying that when everyone is shouting, you don't hear anyone. That's also true when writing letters. Mute your tone and save your shouting for cases where you need extra emphasis. Be a friend having a casual conversation with another friend.

88. Make It Sound Easy

Make ordering sound effortless (i.e., "Just check the 'Yes' box on the enclosed order card and mail it today. We'll pay the postage.")

89. Tell 'Em What You Told 'Em

There's the philosophy of the old southern preacher who said, "I tells 'em what I'm going to tell 'em; I tell 'em; and then I tells 'em what I told 'em." It's a good philosophy for writing effective direct mail letters. A good summary will often capture positive action from readers who may have missed a key point in the body of the letter.

90. Prove Your Claims

Back your claims with customer testimonials or case histories.

91. Personalize

Whenever possible, personalize letters for each recipient. Most readers today know that a computer has added elements of personalization to a direct mail letter. But the simple fact that personalization has been added suggests that, for one reason or another, the recipient was *specially* selected to receive the message. If done well, personalization — particularly when it utilizes more than just the recipient's name — can produce a substantial increase in response.

92. Who Will Sign the Letter?

As a general rule, it is advisable to have the most highly placed individual in a company sign a letter — if that individual would logically write the things said in the letter.

93. Is the Letter Language the Language of the Signer?

Decide in advance who will sign the letter and then write the letter in the language of the signer.

94. Is There Assurance of Satisfaction?

Don't just count on including a guarantee in your copy. Ask yourself what else a customer needs to know to order with complete confidence.

95. Incite Action

Is there anything more you can do to incite action now? Would it help to have an action device such as a stamp or a token? Should you suggest customers pick up their phones and call a 24-hour, toll-free order line? Should you offer a special incentive for immediate response? Do whatever it takes to generate maximum response. Readership is fine, but it pays off only in orders.

96. Give Your Letter News Value

Every journalism student is taught to be sure to include the five "Ws" up front in every news story and, when necessary, add an "H" . . . and that's good advice for direct mail letter writers:

Who: Tell them who you are.

What: Tell them what you are going to do for them.

Where: Tell them where to send their response.

When: Tell them when to respond — NOW!

Why: Tell them why they will benefit from accepting your offer.

How: Tell them how to respond.

Use facts. Be specific. And make every effort to build "news" into your letter.

97. Are You Just Trying to Be Clever?

Take another look at your letter. Is everything really oriented toward the reader, or were you just trying to be clever?

98. Is It Honest?

Another reason to reread your letter: Have you been dishonest in anything you've written?

99. Is There a Strong Reason for Immediate Response?

Still another final point to check: have you given the strongest reason possible for taking action *now*?

100. Don't Be Proud!

And finally, don't be proud! Don't be afraid to utilize results-proven copy written by someone else. Subject your letter to as many editors as possible, and listen to their every comment.

SECTION XIV

TIPS FROM THE EXPERTS

As you might suspect, letter writers are also prolific producers of articles, books, and speeches on their favorite subject — writing letters. My files are filled with examples of what leading direct mail copywriters have written on the subject of creating effective letters.

At the end of this section, I've included a bibliography of selected books you may want to read for additional guidance in creating your own great direct mail letters. From these and other sources, I've selected some tips to help you write effective direct mail letters..

THOUGHTS FROM ED MAYER

Anyone involved in direct mail for more than 20 years started with an advantage not available to those who entered the field more recently. They most likely learned from "The Dean of Direct Mail" — Edward N. Mayer, Jr.

Ed was a prolific author who established the first regular seminars for the Direct Marketing Association, Inc. Literally thousands of "students" throughout the world learned the basics of effective direct mail from the teachings of this pioneer.

His book, *How to Make More Money with Your Direct Mail* (first published by Printers' Ink Books in 1950) has long been out of print; however, many of the more recent direct mail writers have used it as their basic reference. In this book, Mayer offers four key suggestions when applying the theory of "writing the way you talk" to direct mail copy:

1. **Eliminate objectionable words and phrases.** The average man or woman, educated or uneducated, usually has the horrible habit of filling his or her conversation with objectionable and useless words or phrases. If you're going to eliminate them in your copy, it isn't altogether necessary to get rid of them orally, but be darn sure you recognize them for what they are: interlopers that disprove the theory you should "write the way you talk."

2. **Eliminate improper arrangements of words and phrases that depend on accenting and tonal quality for real meaning.** Good conversationalists often capitalize on the improper arrangement of a sequence of words. Accenting, change of tone, and other vocal tricks make the arrangement sound better and in many cases convey a clearer meaning. But carry that habit (and lots of people do) over into your writing and you're facing a real problem. Be sure you don't carry over into your writing tricks of improper arrangement of words and phrases whose real meaning is achieved only by clever accenting and marked tonal quality.

3. **Eliminate long and unintelligible words.** Most of us include in everyday conversation a lot of words we think we and our listeners understand and can define. More often than not, we're wrong in our use of the words or expressions. We like the sound of a word or phrase and use it at every opportunity. It matters little that it does not express our true

meaning as long as we think it does, and it may be even completely objectionable or unintelligible to our listeners. Yet these same words and expressions are apt to creep into our copywriting. Fine shades of meaning that are of little import in social or even business conversations have a nasty habit of confusing readers when they appear in advertising copy. Similarly, all of us have fine "five-dollar" words that we like to use.

4. **Eliminate extra and useless words.** Our conversations, probably because most of us really do like the sound of our own voices, are usually filled with extra and useless words that don't add a single thing to the final effect or value of our remarks. Nevertheless, we do use too many words when we talk, and the temptation to carry these word "parasites" into our writing is often apparent. Brevity is certainly one of the important rules of copywriting, even if it has no place in conversation. Don't cultivate brevity for its own sake, but remember extra and useless words add nothing but increased boredom to even the best piece of copy.

BEWARE THE BEDBUG LETTER

Whenever I had the opportunity to discuss letter writing with Mayer, the conversation often got around to the subject of using form letters for certain customer service situations. One of his favorite stories on the subject was included in his book:

■ Many years ago, a gentleman whom we will call Smith made an overnight trip on one of the name trains of a famous railroad. Along with the other inconveniences of train travel in those days, Mr. Smith made the horrifying discovery that there were other occupants of his berth, namely, several nauseating bedbugs. When he finally arrived home, he set himself down and wrote a letter to the railroad telling them in no uncertain terms what he, his family, and his friends thought of a famous railroad that allowed such things to happen to paying passengers.

By return mail, Smith received a masterpiece of apology, beautifully typed on engraved stationery and hand-signed by the president of the road. Poor Smith was so impressed with the letter that he was turning over in his mind the proper wording of an acknowledgment that would apologize for his own strong language, and that would compliment the president on the speedy and satisfactory handling of the complaint.

And just then he happened to notice that the railroad's stenographer had inadvertently attached Smith's original "beef" to the president's answer. He looked it over . . . and you can imagine his feelings when he found written in the upper corner of his own letter the succinct notation: "Joe, send this nut the bedbug letter."

SOME TIPS FROM BOB STONE

There are three books on direct marketing I recommend to those who ask for a starting point in investigating this growing field. The first, of course, is *Direct Mail and Mail Order Handbook* I wrote for Dartnell. Another is Bob Stone's *Successful Direct Marketing Methods*. Stone is not only a great letter writer, but his book does a great job of making the whole subject understandable. Included in the book are these special tips on letters:

- *Form letters using indented paragraphs will usually outpull those in which paragraphs are not indented.*

- *Underlining important phrases and sentences usually increases results slightly.*

- *A separate letter with a separate circular will generally do better than a combination letter and circular.*

- *A form letter with an effective running headline will ordinarily do as well as a filled-in letter.*

- *Authentic testimonials in a sales letter ordinarily increase the pull.*

- *A two-page letter ordinarily outpulls a one-page letter.*

In his book, Bob also provides this set of guidelines for good, professional copy developed by Don Kanter:

1. Does the writer know his product? Has he or she dug out every selling point and benefit?

2. Does the writer know his market? Is he or she aiming the copy at the most likely prospects rather than at the world in general?

3. Is the writer talking to the prospect in language that he will understand?

4. Does the writer make a promise to the prospect, then prove that he or she can deliver what was promised?

5. Does the writer get to the point at once? Does he or she make that all-important promise right away?

6. Is the copy, especially the headlines and lead paragraphs, germane and specific to the selling proposition?

7. Is the copy concise? There is a great temptation to overwrite, especially in direct mail.

8. Is the copy logical and clear? Does it "flow" from point to point?

9. Is the copy enthusiastic? Does the writer obviously believe in what he or she is selling?

10. Is the copy complete? Are all questions answered, especially obvious ones like size and color?

11. Is the copy designed to sell? Or is it designed to impress the reader with the writer's ability? If somebody says, "That's a great mailing," you've got the wrong reaction. What you want to hear is, "That's a great product (or service). I'd love to have it."

DRAYTON BIRD'S CHECKLISTS

The other book I recommend to everyone comes from England. *Commonsense Direct Marketing* by Drayton Bird — one of Europe's brightest direct marketing professionals — is filled with interesting case histories and a host of valuable checklists. Among those are:

Seven Questions to Ask before You Write a Word

1. Who are you selling to?

2. What need in your prospect does your product or service fill?

3. What makes your product or service special?

4. What benefits are you offering?

5. What do you consider the most important benefit to be?

6. Can you make a good offer?

7. If you cannot make a good offer, can you say something of exceptional interest?

21 Simple Ways to Ensure People Read and Act Upon Your Copy

1. Use a rifle, not a shotgun. Address people personally, giving thought to their particular likes and dislikes. Try to get them agreeing early on. Imagine you are sitting across the table from them, and explaining things.

2. Start your copy either by expanding on the benefit in the heading, or by asking your prospect a personal question.

3. Look down your copy to the second, third, and fourth paragraphs. See if you couldn't start there.

4. Try beginning your copy with the word "You." To your prospect it's the most important word in the world, after his own name.

5. Don't ignore other words that people like to see. Free. New. Now. At last. Introducing. Announcing. First time ever. Never. Before. Save. Discount. Gift. Premium. Opportunity. Offer. Instantly. Forever. Rush. Priority. Love. Darling. Mummy. All words like this have heavy emotional power.

6. Use a P.S. in your letters. And a P.P.S. if you wish. Research shows startling jumps in response when an offer is mentioned in the P.S.

7. Be helpful. Give people news and information about things they don't know.

8. Use short sentences. They are easier to read and understand.

9. Use short paragraphs. Make sure each paragraph contains just one thought, if possible.

10. Count the number of times the word "you" is used in your copy. Talk about your prospect, not yourself.

11. Use guile to keep people reading. End a page half-way through a sentence so people have to keep going.

12. Use "carrier" words and phrases at the ends and beginning of sentences and paragraphs. Like ending your paragraph with a question. Or saying, "And there is more . . ."

Start sentences with Also . . . Moreover . . . For instance . . . What is more . . . And . . . anything to keep them moving. Anything to signal that some added, interesting information is coming up.

13. Don't use pompous latinizations. Use short, Anglo–Saxon–based words, like folks use themselves.

14. Don't use three words where one will do.

15. In tone, be credible. Talking in a loud voice does not make people listen. It just annoys them.

16. Be specific. It reassures people that you know what you are talking about and that they will get exactly what you have promised.

17. If the product is at all technical, give the specifications.

18. If it is a compilation, like a record album or anthology, give every title. Thus you convince people they are getting a lot for their money.

19. Write in the present tense as far as possible, as though the reader already owned the product. Imagine you are trying to give people the feeling of having a "test drive" of your product or service.

20. Make it sound easy. Don't talk about the buyer having to do anything . . . talk about the product doing it for them.

21. Restate your benefits before closing.

Have You Forgotten Anything?

1. Have you included every convincing reason for responding?

2. Is there anything you've taken for granted?

3. Have you built in maximum credibility?

4. Have you started instilling urgency right from the beginning?

5. Do your words say what your pictures show?

6. Are you going all out for telephone orders?

7. Have you given sufficient weight to the ordering mechanism?

8. Are you getting what you paid for? Perhaps you can include some extra element without going over the postal limit.

9. Have you gone all out for action?

10. Don't be proud. Show what you have created to others. You are not a genius. Others may not comprehend what is obvious to you. All the most professional creative people I know accept criticisms and welcome comment. It all helps.

Copywriting Tips From Herschell Gordon Lewis

When it comes to direct mail copywriting, some of the most helpful advice today is coming from the prolific pen of Hersh Lewis. He writes magazine columns and books on the subject and is a sought-after speaker at direct marketing meetings throughout the world. Much of his advice centers around what he calls "Lewis's Laws of Mail Order Advertising" and his 12 copywriting "rules."

Lewis' Laws of Mail Order Advertising

1. Effective advertising is that which reaches, at the lowest possible cost, the most people who can and will buy what you have to sell.

2. In this Age of Skepticism, cleverness for the sake of cleverness may well be a liability, not an asset.

3. E^2 equals 0. This simplest of equations means simply that when you emphasize everything, you emphasize nothing.

4. Tell the reader what to do. Subtlety doesn't work. You have to induce action from a single exposure. Don't just describe. Get the order.

12 Rules for Copywriters

1. If you make a claim, prove it.

2. Don't lie.

3. Tie your claims to credible testimonials.

4. Don't clown. Don't make jokes. Don't have the reader say, "What a clever fellow that writer is. By the way, what was he selling?"

5. Imply bulk or community acceptance.

6. Personalize.

7. Be positive and specific.

8. Cut down the puffery.

9. Don't assume your "in" terminology is familiar to the public.

10. Showing innocence or artlessness can prove your sincerity.

11. Tie newness to an established base. Whatever you're selling isn't new. It's newer than something.

12. Don't make something big out of something little.

Victor O. Schwab's 22 Ways to Hold Interest

One of the pioneer mail order copywriters was Victor O. Schwab. Among the many helpful suggestions he offered other writers was a list of 22 ways to hold interest longer:

1. Start copy with a pertinent question to help get people into it. Throughout the copy, work in questions that stimulate interest in answers to follow.

2. Or begin with your strongest consumer benefit.

3. Give copy news value.

4. Avoid vague generalities.

5. Speedily identify copy with the needs and desires of the reader.

6. Stick to buying points, concerning the reader, not selling points, concerning the advertiser. Sell people advantages, not things.

7. Select sales angles with greatest general appeal. Don't clutter up copy with minor claims.

8. Get in plenty of emotional appeal.

9. Touch people on points of common human contact. Make them say, "Yes, that is just like me."

10. Avoid flat claims. Use vivid portrayal of dramatic situations, humanized facts, word pictures to inspire the reader to want, as soon as possible, what the product will do for, and get, for him.

11. Put as much personality, human interest, showmanship into it as you can with naturalness.

12. Try to make it entertaining to read.

13. Make copy relevant to product, not filled with distractive influences.

14. Use subheads having news . . . or make them tell a quick, sequential sales story of their own — for the glancer.

15. Use vigorous, non-static style to help copy suggest action and march toward action.

16. Use short, simple sentence construction, crystal-clear in meaning.

17. Use vivid present tense, singular instead of plural.

18. Use active verbs, pictorial nouns.

19. Avoid too many adjectives, adverbs, pronouns, demonstrative articles, dependent clauses and phrases, subjunctive mood.

20. Use the vocabulary of the least erudite of your prospects, then everyone will follow you.

21. Grammatically, lead carefully from one point of interest to the next; link them clearly.

22. Longer copy does not mean looser copy, mere verbiage. Keep it compact, well integrated.

ELMER WHEELER'S FIVE POINTS

Elmer Wheeler's much-publicized five points for successful salesmanship were originally directed toward personal contact selling. However, they are often applied equally well to direct mail copy:

1. Don't sell the steak — sell the sizzle.

2. Don't write — *telegraph* (Find the sizzle in what you're trying to get across and then express the sizzle in a telegraphic statement).

3. "Say It With Flowers" (After you've found your sizzle and expressed it telegraphically, fortify your words).

4. Don't ask if — ask *which!* (Always frame your words so that you give the other person a choice between something and something else — never between something and nothing).

5. *Watch your bark!* (The way you say a thing may be as important as what you say.)

CLYDE BEDELL'S GUIDEPOSTS

Long considered one of the nation's top advertising copy experts, Clyde Bedell suggested seven guideposts for sales letters:

1. Always say quickly the *best* thing you can say.

2. Follow a route. Have a planned road map of your work to guide you.

3. Be lucid, be clear. Readers must get the story quickly.

4. Be believed. Do not raise doubts.

5. Be complete. Do not dangle customers.

6. Sell — sell — *SELL* every word of the way.

7. Print it as clearly as you think it.

BUS REED'S THREE BS

A handy formula was created by the late Orville ("Bus") Reed, whose direct mail copy spelled success for dozens of leading advertisers for many years:

Benefits — tell the reader right off how your service or product will benefit him.

Believability — back up your statement of benefits with believable evidence.

Bounce — Webster defines it as "enthusiasm, vivacity, spirit, verve." Keep your copy moving. Keep the prospect interested. Transfer your enthusiasm for the benefit to the prospect.

HOWARD DANA SHAW'S 14 POINTS

A longer, but also valuable checklist, was created some years ago by Howard Dana Shaw:

1. *The goal* — What is the aim of your letter?

2. *Who* — Define your market or audience.

3. *Characteristics* — What kind of people and what's on their minds?

4. *Benefits* — What will your product do for the buyer?

5. *Objections* — Why the reader won't do what you want him to.

6. *Build Confidence* — What can you say to gain the reader's confidence?

7. *Opening* — Some copywriters claim it's 90% of the letter.

8. *Hurry-up* — Offer premiums, set deadlines, mention price increases, limited quantities, and so forth.

9. *Tone and Attitude* — Decide on the general slant and tone of voice.

10. *Dramatization* — Comparisons, graphic ways, gadgets, and illustrations.

11. *Sales Points* — Things to stress.

12. *Phrases* — Colorful terms, good sentences from previous letters.

13. *What was wrong with other letters on the same subject?*

14. *How to make the price seem low* — Contrast with competing prices, break down into weekly or daily figures, and so forth.

As you will quickly note, this is a checklist of things to do to prepare yourself to write copy rather than a guide to follow when you get into the writing itself or in analyzing written copy. Your copy pre-planning may be the most opportune time to utilize formulas and checklists.

PAUL BRINGE'S ADVICE FOR WRITERS

One of the all-time great letter experts was Paul Bringe of Milwaukee. Unfortunately, he never wrote a book to share his knowledge. But, many learned from the advice he gave during one of his frequent speeches at direct mail meetings. In one of his presentations, he offered this advice on what it takes to be a good direct mail letter writer:

> ■ Good writing requires a knowledge of the abilities and limitations of your reader. We cannot talk with people successfully until we know a lot about them. You won't be able to get into the mind of another with little black marks on a piece of paper until you know which door to his mind is open and how wide open it is. Or, if the door is closed, you must know how to unlatch it. There is a door waiting for you in the mind of every reader and if you know your reader, it will swing open for you.

Test It.

I suggest testing everything you write for readability. This is not difficult nor time-consuming. After you do it a dozen or two dozen times, you will estimate reading level without testing. There are many different formulas for measuring readability, but the most popular, and certainly easiest to use, is the Rudy Flesch formula.

The Flesch formula, and most other formulas, are based on two facts that have been demonstrated over and over.

1. The longer the sentence, the less the reader will get out of it.

2. The more short words, the more the reader will get out of it.

Now this sounds very simple, and if we follow it to its logical conclusion we would write nothing but one-syllable words and three or four-word sentences. Surely, then, everyone would understand so they would, but few would read.

The Flesch formula is based on the *average* length of sentences and the *average* length of words. Some sentences must be long and some words must be long, but if they are varied with short sentences and short words, the overall readability will be good. Writing at the correct level of readability for your audience will not in itself ensure a successful piece of copy — but at least you will know you are not throwing roadblocks in your reader's path.

Verb-Adjective Ratio.

The next thing to watch for is the verb-adjective ratio. Verbs are the motion words of communication — they carry the reader along, they paint pictures of action in which the reader can see himself as an actor. Verbs bring movement, excitement, and flow, and lead the reader quickly to the conclusion you want him to reach.

Writing you cannot put aside until you have finished has a high verb-adjective ratio, about three verbs to each adjective. This ratio follows reading difficulty. Too many adjectives force the reader to stop and reconstruct his mental picture — each additional adjective adds more qualification to your statement, adds another fact the reader must carry in his mind to arrive at complete understanding. Comic-book copy uses almost no adjectives; theses written for college degrees run as high as two qualifying adjectives for every verb.

Try to keep all action words in the present. Try to keep your story happening today, not yesterday or tomorrow. No one ever lived yesterday or will live tomorrow. All human beings have always lived today — the future and the past are artificial concepts we build in our minds — that takes effort and imagination. Anything you do to lessen the effort required of your reader will make your copy more successful. It takes far less effort to think about what is happening now than to reconstruct what happened yesterday or will happen tomorrow. Do not give your reader any unnecessary mental tasks — do as much thinking for him as possible and he will reward you with closer attention.

Stick to Anglo-Saxon.

Have you ever had to use the word "belch" in a letter? Some people think it is an inelegant word. Suppose you were told not to use it but still had to express the action. What could you use? There is only one word and that is "eruct." Did you know there is such a word as "eruct"? And can the word ever mean "belch" to you — or could it mean "belch" to anyone else if you use the word? This is an unusual example to point up the importance of using Anglo-Saxon words whenever possible in your writing.

More Americans know more Anglo-Saxon words and use them in their normal speech than will ever know Latin root words. Anglo-Saxon words are generally short — and given a choice, we will choose a short word before a long one. They are forceful, they are direct, they are action words. They express your thoughts fast and without confusion.

Here are some common Anglo-Saxon expressions: "Stop, thief!" "Ready, aim, fire!" "Who goes there?" "Get ready, get set, go!" "I love you." "You are fired!" "Be still!" Try expressing any of these with Latin root words and you will throw away the power. When we want words of command, words to start or stop action, we use Anglo-Saxon words. And when we want to release energy, we swear, also in Anglo-Saxon.

You won't have to look up all the words you use to determine their origins. If you have a choice of words, the shorter word will usually be Anglo-Saxon, the shorter word will be more concrete, and the shorter word will be easier to understand.

Don't Be Trapped.

Some of us try to avoid repeating a word too often for fear of boring the reader. So we hunt for synonyms to give variety and change of pace. But we are likely to fall into a trap in our search for synonyms. There is no word in English that has the same meaning as another word. If it ever happens, one of the words will die quickly. Each word in the language has its own special meaning or it would not exist.

When you use a synonym instead of your original word, you move away from the first meaning you planted in your reader's mind. You are asking your reader to change his thought, the thought you have just given him. That is mental work for the reader. He doesn't like it and it won't do you any good. I would rather take the risk of boring the reader by repeating words and thoughts, than of losing him by quick change of mental direction. Putting it in a few words — be careful when you use synonyms.

The best way to become a good direct mail copywriter is to practice writing about other people's products or service when you don't have to do it. When you get a poor letter, try rewriting it your way. It can be a lot of fun. Sometimes you will have difficulty improving the original. But every bit of rewriting you do will strengthen your ability to write clearly, concisely, and with a readable style.

THE TEN COMMANDMENTS — TAKE YOUR PICK

You might think some of the world's greatest copywriters would create terribly clever titles for the checklists they developed to help others make their direct mail letters more effective. But it's amazing how many simply produce what they title the "Ten Commandments." Over the years, I've seen dozens of "Ten Commandments for Better Letters," but here are four I believe are most helpful:

Bus Reed's Ten Commandments

1. Be clear.

2. Be convincing.

3. Be interesting.

4. Convert features into customer benefits.

5. Answer the prospect's subconscious question: "What's in this for me?"

6. Use adjectives sparingly.

7. Use active verbs.

8. Never make a claim without offering proof you can deliver.

9. Give your copy rhythm.

10. In place of hard sell or soft sell, use sensible sell.

Paul Bringe's Ten Commandments

1. Select the right list for your product or service. Without it, you have nothing.

2. In all your writing, talk to one person only. Never address a letter "To our Customers," or "To our Suppliers." Direct mail is always from one person to another.

3. Offer your most important benefit immediately. Recognize that your reader is as selfish even as you and I.

4. Resist the temptation to display your learning. Discard all "elegant" English. Use the plain word whenever possible and it is possible most of the time.

5. Your writing friends are verbs and nouns — your enemies, adjectives. Every unnecessary adjective eliminated increases your chance for success.

6. Don't overestimate the knowledge of your reader, but never underestimate his intelligence. He will act if you give him all the facts.

7. Don't talk about yourself and your product. Do talk about your reader and his problems — a letter is interesting to him if it is about him.

8. Give your reader a reason to believe what you say. Even the truth is unbelievable if you don't make it logical.

9. If you don't believe what you are writing — stop writing. There are no wealthy confidence men.

10. Ask for the order — again, and again.

FERD NAUHEIM'S TEN COMMANDMENTS

1. What is the precise thing I want the mailing to do?

2. What kind of people am I writing to?

3. Now that I can visualize them, what is there in my proposition that will be most appealing to them?

4. Have I discarded the thought of what is most important to me in favor of what is most important to them?

5. Taking all of my first four thoughts together, can I create an opening sentence that will make the reader want to read more?

6. Am I able to explain my proposition with unquestionable clarity?

7. Can I make it compelling without resorting to exaggeration, or even true statements that sound unbelievable?

8. What can I say to support my claims?

9. What is the easiest way for my prospects to take the action I want to take?

10. Can I give any honest reasons why they will benefit by taking immediate action?

LYNN SUMNER'S TEN COMMANDMENTS

1. Learn all about your proposition before you write anything about it.

2. Organize your material. Get it down in order, from the viewpoint of the buyer's interest — not yours.

3. Decide to whom you are writing. Remember, it is a person, not a circulation or a list. You are writing a letter, not a speech.

4. When you are ready to write, keep it simple. That does not mean writing down to anybody. Avoid high-flown phrases.

5. Use meaningful words and phrases — words that stir the emotions, make the mouth water, make the heart beat faster.

6. Don't try to be funny. To try and fail is tragic. Few people can write humorous copy, few products lend themselves to it. Remember, the most serious of all operations is separating a man from his money.

7. Make your copy specific — names, places, what happens to whom.

8. Write to inspire confidence. Prove your points.

9. Make your copy long enough to tell your story — and quit. No copy is too long if it holds the reader's interest. One sentence can be too long if it doesn't.

10. Give your reader something to do and make it easy for him to do it. Tell him where to get what you have to sell, how much it costs, and why he should do it now. You've written the copy — cash in on it !

THE SEVEN DEADLY SINS

Almost as numerous as "The Ten Commandments" are the multitude of "Seven Deadly Sins" checklists. One of my favorites is the best guide for evaluating business-to-business advertising I've yet seen. It was prepared by the late Howard G. "Scotty" Sawyer. While written to guide industrial advertisers, this checklist applies equally well to other types of advertising.

1. *The sin of being a braggart.* A lot of industrial advertising is like the blow-hard — the man who interminably insists that he's better than the next guy. Claiming superiority, in itself, is not necessarily wrong unless little or nothing is done to substantiate the claim in a friendly, persuasive, and convincing manner.

2. *The sin of talking to yourself instead* of thinking of the other fellow. The most creative industrial advertising is that which directs its remarks to the interests of the readers — not the company doing the talking.

3. *The sin of preaching.* Faced with white paper to fill, some advertisers get a compulsion to lecture. Looking down upon the reader from the high altitude of their superiority, they tell the reader — rather than invite him — to do what they want him to do.

4. *The sin of being noisy.* Everybody hates the bugler, but a good many advertisers believe they have to make a big noise in order to get readers to stand at attention. If you have something interesting to say about a subject of interest to readers, there's no need to set your hair on fire in order to catch their eye.

5. *The sin of being messy.* Nobody likes the man who is messy, dirty, or inconsiderate. A lot of advertising, unfortunately, can be so described.

6. *The sin of trying to be cute.* Don't be a smart-aleck in industrial advertising. Deliver your story in as straightforward a manner as possible — you'll get more applause from your audience than if you put on an act.

7. *The sin of being dull.* Of all the deadly sins of industrial advertising, the worst by far is being dull. About all an advertising man is expected to do is enliven the sales message with a crisp presentation of visual elements and some fast-moving copy.

PAUL BRINGE'S ADVICE FOR COPYWRITERS

Many years ago, Paul Bringe offered this valuable advice, which is just as true today and it was when he wrote it:

> ■ A good copywriter isn't in love with words, he is in love with people. All kinds of people, everywhere and anywhere. He is intensely interested in people, watches them closely, listens when they talk, lives their bad moments with them and rejoices in their victories. He is so interested in other people he forgets all about himself, his own needs and wants, and after a time he knows why they think as they do. And he recognizes himself in them and knows what they do he is capable of doing whether it is good or bad. The way to write believable copy is to love people. Know what every living person fears, hates, loves and rejoices just as you do. Let everything you write say to your reader, "I understand you. I have been in your shoes, I can help you, please let me try."

BOB SILVERMAN'S "PEOPLEISMS"

Bob Silverman, whose Cleveland direct marketing service organization was one of the most creative "lettershops" in the country, once suggested that writers must recognize — and overcome — a number of common "peopleisms":

- *People are procrastinators.* **Be sure to give them at least one reason to act promptly.**

- *People are skeptical.* **Make sure your message is believable.**

- *People are lazy.* **Make it easy for them to respond.**

- *People avoid risk.* **Include iron-clad guarantees to help them feel comfortable.**

- *People pay little or no attention to things which don't interest them.* **Mail to targeted audiences.**

- *People move. **From home to home, and from job to job. Make sure mailing lists and databases are updated frequently.***

- *People want to know "what's in it for me?" **Be sure to tell them clearly and appealingly.***

- *People are easily confused. **Make sure your message is crystal clear.***

- *People want to know when they'll receive your response to their response. **Tell them how long fulfillment, delivery or other action will take. And be sure to meet that commitment.***

- *People are fearful of disappointment. **Overcome their fears by reassuring them with guarantees of satisfaction.***

THE BOB SILVERMAN TEST

Bob also suggested applying this test before mailing a direct mail package:

Is your headline or lead sentence a grabber?	❏ Yes	❏ No
Does it relate to the rest of the copy?	❏ Yes	❏ No
Does copy emphasize benefits rather than features?	❏ Yes	❏ No
Does it urge action?	❏ Yes	❏ No
Do copy and graphics tie together? And do they command attention and interest?	❏ Yes	❏ No
Is copy written from the reader's viewpoint, not yours?	❏ Yes	❏ No
Does the copy talk with, and to, prospects, instead of at or down to them?	❏ Yes	❏ No
Does the copy tell readers where you want them to do? And is it easy for them to do it?	❏ Yes	❏ No
Have you included a meaningful offer?	❏ Yes	❏ No
Have you specified a realistic response deadline?	❏ Yes	❏ No
Have you included an iron-clad guarantee of satisfaction?	❏ Yes	❏ No
Does the package contain high impact graphics which show the product — or the offer — or both?	❏ Yes	❏ No
Is the response device written in friendly, non-threatening language?	❏ Yes	❏ No
Does the response device allow room for prospects to fill in the information you have asked for?	❏ Yes	❏ No

Does the total package get the reader involved — through action devices, compelling copy or some other technique?   ❑ Yes   ❑ No

Is copy easy to read n visually as well as grammatically?   ❑ Yes   ❑ No

Does the letter have a P.S. that emphasizes a major point already noted in the body copy?   ❑ Yes   ❑ No

Have you asked for the order — or for whatever action you want the reader to take?   ❑ Yes   ❑ No

What's Your Score?

16–18 yes answers should be a winner. Go with it!

13–15 yes answers is "iffy." Think about revisions to strengthen it.

12 or fewer yes answers — back to the drawing board!

Sig Rosenblum's 10 Secrets of Better Sales Letters

Sig Rosenblum has not only created hundreds of successful direct mail sales letter for a wide variety of clients, but he also creates some brilliant self-promotion direct mail. Included in one of his self-promotions is a valuable checklist of "Secrets of Better Sales Letters," which is digested here:

Secret 1: Select Selling Ideas. Good writing, as such, has little to do with the successful sales letter — one that jolts the reader out of his indifference. You may fashion the fancy phrase but people may still turn from you with a yawn. Without selling ideas, your letter will not work. It may impress. It may even entertain. But it will not sell.

Secret 2: Hop the Fence. Use a you-oriented approach. But don't just stuff the word "you" into your letter. Using "you" won't do it. Your letter should be built around the needs, fears, desires, profit, and happiness of the reader. It should proceed from his side of the fence. And that's where you should be when you write it.

Secret 3: Don't Waste Words. This doesn't mean terse, clipped, stingy writing without the transitions that give grace and style. But use your blue pencil on sentences filled with fat and bloated with bombast.

Secret 4: Be Specific. If your new screwdriver works faster, tell the fellow at the other end of the mail route *how much* faster. Tell him the number of additional screws he can drive. What will he save in dollars and cents? Or time? If you use flabby, fuzzy claims such as "very fast" and "improved performance," a snicker of skepticism will cross the reader's mind. Don't shirk the essential drudgery. Get the facts. And get them to the reader. Be specific.

Secret 5: Be Believable. It is not enough for your sales story to be true. It must sound true, too. What do you do when there is an embarrassment of riches — when the plain facts seem exaggerated? Use testimonials that ring true. Develop solid facts and figures that build your case point by point. Be believable.

Secret 6: Watch Your Windups. Most sales letters are improved by deleting the first sentence. We call this sentence a windup because it lets the writer "get into" his subject. But if you don't immediately arrest the reader's interest, *he* will not get into the subject, and into the wastebasket go you and your message. That is why your very first word — your "opening" — must be compelling. Powerful openings grab the reader in an iron grip.

Secret 7: Write in Three Phases. It's a common misconception that "real" writers do it all effortlessly, without fumbling. Writing is tentative — a little here, a little there, rather than a master stroke, complete in an instant. More like sculpting than taking a snapshot. Your first attempts will never be more than an approximation of what you want. They must be incomplete and clumsy to *some* degree. It isn't easy to accept that. But try.

Those who have studied the creative process seem to agree that it is broken into three distinct phases. In the first phase, you round up facts, absorb ideas, explore approaches. This is a period of *taking in.* In the second phase, you put down ideas, make notes, outlines, doodles. *You try to get things out.* But there is a third phase: the editorial, critical phase. Here you kill inappropriate words and ideas. Just as the first two phases were marked by openness, this phase is highly discriminating and selective. Here you filter, prohibit, weigh and balance subtleties.

When the writer tries to be *open to new ideas* and at the same time exercise his critical judgment and *filter* ideas, he gets into trouble. You cannot do both at the same time.

Secret 8: Put in People. You'd never guess from most sales letters — indeed most business writing — that there are *people* on this planet. Is anybody living and breathing out there? Or hoping, fearing, planning? You'd never think so from a peek at the files. But they are. So the vigorous writer brings people — himself and the reader — into the action.

When you introduce people into your writing, you help create a word picture of someone doing something. And a *word picture* is a lot easier to grasp than an *abstract concept*, which then must be translated into specifics in the reader's mind. Put in people.

Secret 9: Mimic the Movies. Good filmmakers keep their cameras moving. If we are watching a cowboy ride across the prairie, the camera might start with a long shot, zoom in slowly, circle the man, shoot from ground level, with the sun silhouetting the lonely rider, then rise and shoot down from a boom or helicopter. Just a man and his horse plodding across an open plain. But the agile camera works its alchemy — and light, shadow, angles, and accents cast their spell.

There's a lesson here for the writer: If you vary the pace, tempo, shading, and beat of your prose, the reader will find it more interesting.

Secret 10: Keep It Active. Perhaps you've noticed a certain overlapping: If you select selling ideas, you are inclined to be specific. Something specific is likely to be from the reader's side of the fence, hence believable. And so it goes: One rule helps another. And if you cast your ideas in *active* rather than passive form, your sentences tend to be shorter. They tend to move.

RAY W. JUTKINS' EIGHT GOLDEN GUIDELINES

One of the most entertaining speakers on the subject of direct mail is "Rocket" Ray Jutkins. His presentations are filled with a lot of down-to-earth ideas, including his "Eight Golden Guidelines" for writing the perfect sales letter.

1. The best way is the simple way. Write it like you say it. Don't worry about grammar. Don't concern yourself with punctuation (we overuse it anyway). Don't wordsmith every sentence. Make it human.

2. The best mail is personal mail multiplied. Write to your Aunt Minnie (or if you don't like Auntie M., then your favorite somebody). And do it over and over and over to others. It works.

3. If your audience is octogenarians in Oshkosh, then you become an octogenarian in Oshkosh. Pretend you are the recipient and write to yourself.

4. Never, but NEVER talk down to your audience. Look them straight in the eye, aim at them directly. Or even better yet, look up to them.

5. Do not tell a lie. Be honest, straightforward, up front, true. Tell a funny story, be entertaining, weave a theme to make your point, play games any way that will help your cause, but do not tell a lie. Ever.

6. Have something to say. This may seem funny to have to say, but many letters don't say anything. Have something specific to say, a message, and then say it. Don't beat around the bush — come out with it.

7. Make an offer. The offer says if you do this now these good things will happen to you now. The offer is the reason a certain percentage of your audience will respond — and it many times is the difference between success or failure. Move those "considering" you to your side with a good offer.

8. Ask for the order! Be specific — ask your audience to do something. Don't just hint. Spell it out in spades.

15 THINGS YOU NEED TO KNOW ABOUT YOUR READERS

Ray Jutkins found a good set of things you need to know about your readers as people in the *Mail Order Connection* newsletter. He revised them this way:

1. *People are procrastinators.* Give them a reason to respond now. Try a limited time offer.

2. *People are skeptical.* Overcome that attitude with a believable message.

3. *People are lazy.* Make it easy to reply to your offer.

4. *People worry about making a wrong decision.* Use case histories to give them assurance.

5. *People avoid risk.* Give them a guarantee.

6. *People say: "I can't read all this."* Give them all they need to make a decision and not a word more.

7. *People say: "I didn't ask for this."* Send your message to a qualified audience — one interested in what you have to offer.

8. *People say: "I'm feeling crummy."* It may be a bad day. At least make your mailing cheerful!

9. *People ask: "What is the offer?"* Make it perfectly clear.

10. *People ask: "How will I benefit?"* Emphasize what they will earn, save, make, enjoy, learn. Talk benefits, not features.

11. *People say: "Should I order?"* Provide facts and stats to back up your benefit claims. Hide nothing.

12. *People say: "Can I believe and trust you?"* Write believable copy, use testimonials, provide references.

13. *People say: "What's next?"* Tell them what they need to do not to take advantage of your offer.

14. *People say: "When do I get it?"* Tell them how long delivery, fulfillment, or installation will take.

15. *People say: "What if I'm dissatisfied?"* Reassure them with your guarantee.

KEEP YOUR COPY MOVING!

"Writing good copy," Max Ross once explained, "is like running a 440-yard dash in a track meet. If you don't start fast enough, you are left behind. If you don't keep up the pace on the back stretch, you will fall back with the pack. And if you don't have a finishing spurt left, you will surely lose the race." He then offered 20 concrete suggestions for direct mail copywriting:

1. Show your prospect how what you have to sell will bring him pleasure, or save him money, or increase his knowledge, or better his living standard — or any dozens of things he wants.

2. It will help you in making notes to study your own company's past literature — the direct mail pieces, the trade paper clippings, pamphlets, advertisements. Also study competitors' material that may have been accumulated by your company.

Sift out the unnecessary items. Arrange the points in order of their importance. Then — and only then — are you ready to chart the most direct, efficient route to your prospect's pocketbook. This enables you to concentrate your full energies on one idea, then the next, in proper sequence.

Copy is likely to gallop off into 40 different directions at once unless the writer follows a route. The best way to devise a satisfactory route is to get your selling points down on paper.

3. If you think that setting down your work plan is too difficult, simply try writing the close of your letter first — before you write anything else. That will help determine exactly the purpose of the letter.

4. Don't begin writing unless you are in the right frame of mind for it! Don't start writing copy at 10:00 if you are to attend a meeting at 10:30. Don't face a stream of office traffic. Don't sit by a window that will attract your gaze. In other words, eliminate as many distracting factors as you possibly can.

5. Not only is it necessary to start writing copy with an uncluttered mind, it is also important to start with an uncluttered desk. Clear your desk before you begin to write — except for all notes, papers, and other material that you will refer to as you are doing the job. But don't clean up your desk again until the job is done — even if it means leaving your desk cluttered overnight.

6. If your thinking mechanism stalls when you first sit down to the typewriter, go ahead and start writing part of the letter. Begin in the middle if you have to — but begin!

7. Try phrasing your lead at least six different ways on the first sheet of paper. Then detach yourself from the project for a moment. Pick out the lead that you think will best attract and hold attention. Keep in mind a principle from advertising consultant Richard Manville: "Advertisements that attempt to give people what they want outpull advertisements which present those things which people do not want as much — or do not want at all."

8. When you have trouble getting a lead that satisfies you, look two or three paragraphs down from the top of your letter. The lead you want may be there.

    You will find many instances where your copy can be improved by cutting away the top paragraphs. But it works the other way too! There will also be instances where the addition of a paragraph above the copy you have already written will make a better letter.

9. It will pay you to keep thinking of leads all the time while you are reading the newspaper, when you are listening to the radio, while you are studying magazines or books. Dramatize your lead in copy if you can.

10. Many direct mail leaders keep a "starter" file. Clip out or jot down sentences or phrases that catch your eye, that may apply to your product. Either keep them in a file folder or paste them on looseleaf sheets that can be filed in a notebook.

11. Tell your prospect exactly what your proposition is — and what you want him to do — right at the very beginning of your letter! But be sure to conduct your own tests to see if this idea works for you.

12. Once your lead is written, and you progress to the body of the letter, please remember to *keep your copy moving!* One way to do this is to say what you have to say in an interesting way.

Writing in an interesting manner is one of the most difficult of all copywriting tricks to learn. I say learn because I don't think it can be taught. You have to want to learn — and you have to do this job yourself.

13. Read good books by authors who have a definite style. If fiction, study the style, not the plot. If non-fiction, read only the paragraphs that attract you. Then go back to observe how what you missed could have been said in a more interesting way.

14. Subscribe to magazines that seem to have a style of their own — magazines like *Newsweek, Reader's Digest, Time. Time* is a particularly good one to study. Read good columnists whose stock in trade is telling things in an interesting way.

15. Make a conscious effort to make your daily conversation more stimulating. It will help your copywriting.

16. Another way to keep your copy moving through the body of the letter is the use of "connectors." Connectors are transitional sentences or phrases that either end one paragraph or begin the next. They are simply little devices that give copy swing-movement. Here are a few examples:

- *But that's not all.*

- *Now — here is the most important part.*

- *And in addition . . .*

- *Better yet . . .*

- *You will see for yourself why . . .*

- *So that is why . . .*

- *More important than that . . .*

- *What is more . . .*

- *But there is just one thing.*

- *Make up your mind now to . . .*

- *Take advantage of this opportunity to . . .*

- *Now — for a limited time only —*

- *Here is your chance to . . .*

- *So mail your order today — while the special offer is still in effect.*

17. Don't leave it up to the reader to decide what you want him to do. If you want him to put his name on the order form and mail it in the reply envelope that you are providing, tell him so. Make it so plain, so easy, that he cannot possibly misunderstand! Also, tell your reader what he will lose if he doesn't act at once. If your price is going up, if there are only a few articles left, if he must mail his order by a certain date, tell him. Be specific! If you can offer him something extra for acting promptly, do so. Everyone likes to get something for nothing. That's only human nature working on your side. *But in any event, don't hesitate to ask for the order!*

18. Never run your paragraphs too long, or too solid. Use punctuation to break up the copy. Use underlining and indentations wisely. Make your copy inviting!

19. Write your letter on a typewriter if it is at all possible. Then rewrite it and rewrite it and rewrite it. They say de Maupassant recopied everything he wrote 100 times. That's out of the question, of course. But do as Robert Stone suggests — recopy your work at least three times. This will help you achieve that goal of *keeping your copy moving!*

By writing and rewriting, you will develop a better style. You will find that you unconsciously begin to

a. use the present tense when possible

b. use the active voice instead of the passive

c. use periodic sentences instead of loose, except occasionally in the case of writing leads

d. use short, simple sentence construction

e. use connectors that keep your copy moving.

20. Use these suggestions as a guide, as a working manual. Follow this step-by-step outline as much as you can. Take your time. Don't hurry. See if some of these suggestions don't make your copywriting job a little bit easier.

COPYWRITING CHECKLIST

Max Ross suggested the following steps to use when writing direct mail copy:

BEFORE YOU START TO WRITE

- *List on paper the points that will interest your prospect most.*
- *Decide which ones are most important.*
- *Sift out the unnecessary items.*
- *Prepare yourself mentally.*

LEAD WITH YOUR BEST FOOT FORWARD

- *Phrase your first words several different ways and pick out the one best suited to the task.*
- *Keep trying to improve your lead.*

AS YOUR STORY UNFOLDS

- *Keep your copy moving.*
- *Say it in an interesting way.*
- *Use connectors.*
- *Study to improve your style.*

DON'T HESITATE TO ASK FOR THE ORDER

MAKE YOUR LETTERS LOOK ATTRACTIVE

d. splitting infinitives

e. repeating your company name too many times?

20. Does your letter look the way you want it to?

a. placement of page

b. no paragraphs over six lines

c. indentation and numbered paragraphs

d. underscoring and capitalization used sparingly

e. punctuation for reading ease.

TOM COLLINS' CREATIVE CHECKLIST

Some time ago, Tom Collins devised a simple point-by-point checklist that many direct marketers use regularly as their guide to evaluate the effectiveness of their direct mail packages.

1. Do you have a good proposition?

2. Do you have a good offer?

3. Does your outside envelope select the prospect?

4. Does your outside envelope put your best foot forward?

5. Does your outside envelope provide reading motivation?

6. Does your copy provide instant orientation?

7. Does your mailing visually reinforce the message?

8. Does it employ readable typography?

9. Is it written in readable, concrete language?

10. Is it personal?

11. Does it strike a responsive chord?

12. Is it dramatic?

13. Does it talk in the language of life, not "advertising"?

14. Is it credible?

15. Is it structured?

16. Does it leave no stone unturned?

17. Does it present an ultimate benefit?

18. Are details presented as advantages?

19. Does it use, if possible, the power of disinterestedness?

20. Does it use, if possible, the power of negative selling?

21. Does it touch on the reader's deepest relevant daydreams?

22. Does it use subtle flattery?

23. Does it prove and dramatize the value?

24. Does it provide strong assurance of satisfaction?

25. Does it repeat key points?

26. Is it backed by authority?

27. Does it give a reason for immediate response?

28. Do you make it easy to order?

ANDY ANDREWS' READABILITY CHECKLIST

In analyzing copy for fund-raising mailings, Francis S. Andrews uses this checklist:

1. Is the basic premise stated in simple, understandable terms?

2. Is the basic premise followed immediately by believable proof?

3. Have complex ideas been simplified by understandable examples?

4. Have material needs been translated into human terms?

5. Have jolting ideas or problems been followed immediately by logical solutions?

6. Is the action requested of the reader a logical solution to the problem?

7. Is the request of the reader logical in terms of the scope of the problem?

8. Has the basic premise been restated in different ways?

9. Does the letter have a beginning, a middle, and an end?

10. Have most of the words been simple, monosyllabic words?

11. Have action words been used in place of passive words?

12. Have warm personal words been used in place of stiff and pompous words?

13. Have unknown, unusual, or foreign words been eliminated?

14. Has the word "you" been substituted for the word "I" in every place possible?

15. Are most sentences limited to 10 words or less, and have simple sentences been used in preference to compound or complex sentences?

16. Are most paragraphs limited to three or fewer sentences?

17. Have personalizing inserts been used in a natural, easy manner?

18. Is each paragraph clearly devoted to its structural purpose — problem, proof, action, and summary?

19. Has the proper suggested gift been evaluated over and over again?

MAXWELL ROSS' SELF-EVIDENT TRUTHS

In copywriting courses taught by Maxwell Ross and in a monograph for the Direct Marketing Association, "How To Write Successful Direct Mail Letter Copy," he suggests some key things you need to know before you start to write:

Self-Evident Truths

To write good copy, you must understand human nature thoroughly. You will need to make a continuing study of people because people change just as times change. Consider these self-evident truths:

1. People are slow to accept the new and untried until it has become firmly established.

2. People are reluctant to break established habits.

3. People dread to make decisions.

4. People need to be disciplined when it comes to reading copy.

5. People prefer to ride with a winner.

MAILING LISTS

Rose Harper, president of The Kleid Company, asked several of the nation's top direct mail copywriters about the importance of knowing the list to which a mailing will go. Here are some of their comments:

Chris Stagg.

■ Writing in a vacuum cries for air. No professional in the direct response business can create a winning package when he doesn't know everything there is to know about the human he's writing to. When a writer creates in a marketing vacuum, he creates a loser.

Hank Burnett.

■ I think I always start with a pretty clear notion of who I'm writing to. But there's only one way I know of to verify it, and that is by finding out which lists have — and just as important, haven't — worked. I can recall no instance in which my original notion wasn't reshaped by its collision with the facts.

Stu Maltin.

■ You mail to millions. I write to one person. The person I'm convinced is the best prospect, the most likely respondent to your offer. Of the hundreds, even thousands, of direct mail packages that I've done, I can't think of one that I wrote without having an actual person in mind.

I know his name. His income. His interests. His desires. If I'm writing to the right person and he's on your mailing lists, we've got a winner. But the time to find out, to review the lists, is right at the start.

Dick Archer.

■ To bang out a mail order offer without knowing your lists is like the Blind Man of Banares sizing up an elephant by feeling its leg! Tell me more about your list — its demographics, buying habits, and history — and you give me an extra edge, a better handle on structuring my offer, and positioning my product for sale.

A Final Tip

Probably the most often quoted advice on advertising copywriting is in the form of a poem written many years ago by Victor Schwab:

> I see that you've spent quite a big wad of dough
> To tell me the things you think I should know.
> How your plant is so big, so fine and strong;
> And your founder has whiskers so handsomely long.
>
> So he started the business in old '92?
> How tremendously int'resting that is — to you.
> He built up the thing with the blood of his life?
> (I'll run home like mad, tell that to my wife!)
>
> Your machinery's modern and, oh, so complete!
> Your "rep" is so flawless; your workers so neat.
> Your motto is "Quality" — capital "Q".
> No wonder I'm tired of "your" and "you"!
>
> So tell me quick and tell me true
> (Or else, my love, to hell with you!)
> Less — "how this product came to be";
> More — what the damn thing does for me!

BIBLIOGRAPHY

Andrews, Francis S. *Billions by Mail — Fund Raising in the Computer Age.* Tabor Oaks, 1985.

Bird, Drayton. *Commonsense Direct Marketing.* The Printed Shop (England), 1982.

Brann, Christian. *Cost-Effective Direct Marketing.* Collectors' Books (England), 1984.

Caples, John. *Tested Advertising Methods.* Harper & Brothers, 1961, *Making Ads Pay.* Harper & Brothers, 1957.

French, Elburn Rochford. *The Copywriter's Guide.* Harper & Brothers, 1959.

Fruehling, Rosemary T. and Bouchard, Sharon. *The Art of Writing Effective Letters.* McGraw-Hill, 1972.

Gosden, Freeman F., Jr. *Direct Marketing Success.* John Wiley & Sons, 1985.

Hatch, Dennison. *Million Dollar Mailings.* Libbey Publishing, 1992.

Hodgson, Richard S. *Direct Mail and Mail Order Handbook* (Third Edition). Chicago. Dartnell, 1980.

Huntsinger, Jerry. *Fund Raising Letters.* Emerson Publishers, 1982.

Jutkins, "Rocket" Ray. *Direct Marketing: How You Can Really Do It Right.* HDL Publishing, 1989.

Kobs, Jim. *Profitable Direct Marketing.* Crain Books, 1979.

Lewis, Herschell Gordon. *Copywriting Secrets & Tactics.* Chicago. Dartnell, 1992.

Meyer, Harold E. *Lifetime Encyclopedia of Letters.* Prentice-Hall, 1983.

Nauheim, Ferd. *Letter Perfect.* Van Nostrand Reinhold, 1982, *Business Letters That Turn Inquiries Into Sales.* Prentice-Hall, 1957.

Norins, Hanley. *The Compleat Copywriter.* McGraw-Hill, 1966.

Raphel, Murray and Erdman, Ken. *The Do-It-Yourself Direct Mail Handbook.* The Marketers Bookshelf, 1986.

Sawyer, Howard G. "Scotty." *Business-to-Business Advertising.* Crain Books, 1978.

Stone, Bob. *Successful Direct Marketing Methods* (Third Edition). Crain Books, 1984.

Trenbeth, Richard P. *The Membership Mystique.* Fund-Raising Institute, 1986.

INDEX

S

S. Rose, Inc., 411–418
Sales records, 22
Salutation, 3, 5, 425, 457–458. See also Letters, direct mail, starting
Salvation Army, 447
Samstag, Nick, 6
Sawyer, Howard G. ("Scotty"), 514
Schultz, Frank, 188
Schwab, Victor O., 15, 498, 507, 529
Science 82, 454, 474
Security Pacific National Bank, 441
Self, 457, 476
Serendipity Books, 454
Sesame Street (magazine), 449
Seven Deadly Sins (Sawyer), 514–515
Seven Guidelines for Editing Direct Mail Copy (Yolton), 19, 20
Shaw, Howard Dana, 509
Shimek, John Lyle, 97, 161, 427, 436, 442, 443, 445, 472
Signatures, 5
Sig Rosenblum's 10 Secrets of Better Sales Letters, 517–518
Silverman, Bob, 515, 516
Silverman, Robert, 411
Simulated handwriting, 490
Smithsonian Institute, 457, 482
Smithy Companies, 372–374
Soell, Emily, 432, 473
Southern Bell, 482
Southern Living, 428
Southern Poverty Law Center, 281–285
Specification sheet, 21, 22
Spector, Julie, 472, 473
Spiegel, 456
Spring Hill Nurseries, 449, 455, 477, 479
Squiggling, 3
Stagg, Christopher 37, 179, 528
StarGram, 306
Star-Chain-Hook approach, 16
Steiner, Bill, 425, 426, 434, 438, 439, 444, 467, 468
Stogol, Sheila, 166, 394, 426, 448, 450
Stone, Bob, 16, 122, 123, 428, 503
Stone & Adler, 105, 124–128
Stuart McGuire Co., Inc., 482
Successful Direct Marketing Methods, Third Edition (Stone), 45, 503
Sumner, Lynn, 514
Sweepstakes, 119

T

Telling a story, 442–457. See also Letters, direct mail, starting
Testimonials, 493
Tharlet, Steven R., 433
Thomas Publishing Company, 467
Thomas Register 455
Thompson Cigar Co., 97–100, 442, 443, 472
Tighe, John Francis, 238
Time, 6
Time, Inc., 6, 446
Time-Life Books, 246–250, 387–393, 483
Times-Mirror Publishing Company 281
Tokens, 34, 101, 119, 206
Tom Collins' Creative Checklist, 525–526
Trans-Lux Corporation, 320–321
Trautman, Ed, 90
Trembath, William J., 116
Trembeth, Dick, 255, 426, 436, 440, 446, 470
Tribal Arts Society, 453
Troy-Bilt Roto Tillers, 342–345
Typefaces, 3, 199, 491
Typography, 488

U

Unique Selling Proposition, 485, 486
United Media International, Inc., 441, 478
United Republican Fund of Illinois, 270
United States Marine Corps, 359–361, 481
University of Michigan Press, 431, 474
U.S. News & World Report, 469, 482

PUT THESE DIRECT MARKETING EXPERTS AT YOUR FINGERTIPS

SALES PROMOTION HANDBOOK, 8TH EDITION

by Tamara Brezen Block and William A. Robinson

The management of sales promotion has become increasingly sophisticated and complicated. The need for a handbook on the topic is perhaps greater than ever before for anyone involved in the planning, implementation, and analysis of sales promotion programs. Every chapter is written by an expert in the field of sales promotion. Hundreds of real examples and case histories are included throughout, often accompanied by pictures and exhibits to bring each promotion to life.

900 Pages; Hardcover; $69.95

MARKETING MANAGER'S HANDBOOK, 3RD EDITION

by Sidney Levy, Howard Gordon, and George Frerichs

Newly revised and updated, this exhaustive compendium places the wisdom of the marketing experts from all over the world at your fingertips. Each chapter is written by an authority in a particular field of marketing, working hand in hand with a marketing executive team to offer insights and ideas on such topics as: organizing the marketing function; establishing your objectives; developing plans for consumer products and services and industrial products; industrial marketing; and more.

1200 Pages; Hardcover; $69.95

WINNING WITH PROMOTION POWER

by Fran Caci and Donna Howard

Jump-start your creative team and boost sales on upcoming promotions. Put this compendium to work for you as a sourcebook of invaluable "how to" ideas. Fine-tune the most successful and compelling promotions of the past 10 years to create your own off-the-charts promotion program. The Reggie (short for "cash register") award-winning promotion campaigns presented in this book have been honored by the Promotion Marketing Association of America, Inc. (PMAA) based on their originality, execution, and results. With the lessons you learn from the winners in this book, you could be accepting a Reggie award next year.

248 Pages; Hardcover; $59.95

POWER COPYWRITING

by Herschell Gordon Lewis
Words make a colossal difference — especially when those words are supposed to get somebody to buy something. *Power Copywriting* will arm both beginner and veteran wordsmith alike with powerful, sales-building techniques — more than 60 easy-to-use Power Communication Rules. The book is chock-full of examples and more than 50 illustrations — all tricks of the trade — to make a sales message come to life and stand out among the clutter.
335 Pages; Paperback; $29.95

HOW TO WRITE POWERFUL CATALOG COPY

by Herschell Gordon Lewis
Herschell Gordon Lewis, columnist and feature writer for *Catalog Age* and *Direct Marketing Magazine*, lays out solid principles for making catalog copy pull.
You'll learn how to write copy to establish the image of your catalog, clarify your product descriptions — while increasing sales purchases — and provide details the reader needs to buy your product. Plus, Lewis provides a list of 20 questions you should ask yourself before sending copy out the door and 20 rules to writing successful catalog copy that will turn any novice into a superstar and any journeyman into a hero. **331 Pages; Hardcover; $49.95**

TO ORDER IN U.S. OR CANADA CALL: (800) 621-5463
OR FAX US YOUR ORDER: (800) 327-8635

Yes! Send me the books I have checked. (Shipping and handling charges will be added to each order.) IL residents add 8.75% tax, IN add 5%. I understand if I am not completely satisfied, I may return my purchase within 30 days for a full refund.

❐ **Power Copywriting** $29.95
❐ **Marketing Manager's Handbook, 3rd Edition** $69.95
❐ **Sales Promotion Handbook, 8th Edition** $69.95
❐ **Winning With Promotion Power** $59.95
❐ **How to Write Powerful Catalog Copy** $49.95

Save 10% when you use your credit card to order.
Bill my: ❐ Company ❐ Credit card ❐ Visa ❐ MasterCard ❐ American Express ❐ Optima

Acct. # _____ Exp. Date _____

Name _____ Title _____

Company _____

Address _____

City/State/Zip _____ Phone ( ) _____

Signature _____ E-mail # _____

(Signature and phone number required to process order.)

DARTNELL
4660 N RAVENSWOOD AVE, CHICAGO, IL 60640-4595

PURCHASE ADDITIONAL COPIES FOR YOUR EMPLOYEES!

Whether you write copy yourself, or hire others to do it for you, the information covered in *The Greatest Direct Sales Mail Letters of All Time* will ensure that you and your people will possess the best knowledge available today about the art and science of direct mail sales letters. Use this information, and you will boost your response rates every time.

ALSO AVAILABLE ON COMPUTER DISK! With the purchase of *The Greatest Direct Sales Mail Letters of All Time*, you'll receive all the letters on a computer diskette. With this user-friendly version, you can print any letter or copy any letter onto your hard drive, so you can easily adapt it to your own needs.

YES, I want to create direct mail letters that sell big! Send me the following:

_____ copy(ies) of *The Greatest Direct Sales Mail Letters of All Time*, Revised Edition and computer disk for $69.95*.

_____ copy(ies) of *The Greatest Direct Sales Mail Letters of All Time* ON COMPUTER DISK for $25.00*.

*Shipping and handling charges will be added to your invoice. (IL residents add 8.75% tax, IN residents add 5% tax)

☐ Bill my company   ☐ Check enclosed

Save 10%. Order your copies using your credit card and we'll take 10% off your purchase price.

Charge my: ☐ VISA   ☐ MasterCard   ☐ American Express   ☐ Optima Card

Account #_____Expiration Date _____

Name_____

Title _____

Company _____

Address_____

City/State/Zip _____

Signature _____

Phone (   )_____

(Signature and phone number necessary to process order.)

FOR FASTEST SERVICE, PHONE YOUR ORDER TO US AT: (800) 621-5463 OR FAX YOUR ORDER TO: (800) 327-8635

D A R T N E L L

4660 N RAVENSWOOD AVE, CHICAGO, IL 60640-4595 PHONE: (800) 621-5463 or FAX: (800) 327-8635

Letter Directory for Diskette

GREATEST DIRECT MAIL LETTERS OF ALL TIME

Classic Direct Mail Letters — Section II

1. Newsweek "If the list upon which...name"
2. Psychology Today Bathroom Door
3. Reader's Digest "Two Pennies"
4. Admiral Richard E. Byrd Polar Center...Expedition
5. Kiplinger Washington "Boom & Inflation"
6. Barron's "Windows & Orphans"
7. Highlights for Children "Happy Faces"
8. Mercedes Benz of NA - "Americans Won't Buy it."
9. Old American Insurance Co. "Empty Shoes"
10. Games Magazine "Connect The Dots"
11. Nature Conservancy "Devil"
12. Ambassador Letter-Brochure Combination
13. First Baptist Church "Organ"
14. Franklin Mint "100 Greatest Books"
15. Breck's Personalized Catalog Wraps
16. Thompson Cigar Company "15 Rivers to Cross"
17. American Bible Society "Your Faith Can Move Mountains"
18. Hewlett-Packard Pocket Calculator
19. Hewlett-Packard Pocket Computer
20. Wall Street Journal "Two Young Men"
21. American Express "Quite Frankly"
22. Greystone Press "Frankly I'm Puzzled"
23. DMEF - Personalized Letter from Bob Stone
24. DMEF - Bob Dale Letter by John Yeck
25. Tom Collins' George McGovern
26. Nat. Rep. Sen. Com - Repub Pres. Task Force
27. Humor In Direct Mail: Haband Letters
28. John Yeck's Let's Have Better Mottoes Assoc.

Consumer Mail Order Letters — Section III

29. Franklin Mint Norman Rockwell Plate
30. Franklin Mint Gallery of American/Western Art
31. Natl. Wholesale Co. "Sarah Smith"
32. Banker's Life "One Woman to Another"
33. Personal Improvement Corp "Lover of Life"
34. Calhoun's Collectors Society "My Stock Broker Husband"
35. National Liberty Cancer Insurance
36. Omaha Steaks Prospecting
37. Frankl Lewis Miracle Grapefruit

Circulation and Book Promotion — Section IV

38. Organic Gardening "Five Mistakes"
39. Business Week Invitation Letter I
40. Business Week Invitation Letter II
41. Business Week Invitation Letter III
42. Bon Appetit "Sangria"
43. Quest/78 Charter Subscription
44. Psychology Today "Hitler"
45. Prevention Magazine "Memories of Grandmother"
46. Publishers Clearing House "Transparent"
47. Publishers Clearing House "Advance Notice"
48. Fly Fisherman Magazine "Trout Spoken Here"
49. Popular Mechanics Encyclopedia Dirty Hands
50. Time Life Books "Cowboy"
51. Good Housekeeping "33 Ways"